Perspectives on Element Theory

Studies in Generative Grammar

Editors
Norbert Corver
Harry van der Hulst

Founding editors
Jan Koster
Henk van Riemsdijk

Volume 143

Perspectives on Element Theory

Edited by
Sabrina Bendjaballah
Ali Tifrit
Laurence Voeltzel

DE GRUYTER
MOUTON

ISBN 978-3-11-126201-7
e-ISBN (PDF) 978-3-11-069194-8
e-ISBN (EPUB) 978-3-11-069197-9
ISSN 0167-4331

Library of Congress Control Number: 2021938029

Bibliographic information published by the Deutsche Nationalbibliothek
The Deutsche Nationalbibliothek lists this publication in the Deutsche Nationalbibliografie;
detailed bibliographic data are available on the Internet at http://dnb.dnb.de.

© 2023 Walter de Gruyter GmbH, Berlin/Boston
This volume is text- and page-identical with the hardback published in 2021.
Typesetting: Integra Software Services Pvt. Ltd.
Printing and binding: CPI books GmbH, Leck

www.degruyter.com

Contents

Introduction —— 1

Phillip Backley
Elements and structural head-dependency —— 9

B. Elan Dresher
Contrastive hierarchies and phonological primes —— 33

Eric Raimy
Privativity and ternary phonological behavior —— 65

Harry van der Hulst
A guide to Radical CV Phonology, with special reference to tongue root and tongue body harmony —— 111

Markus A. Pöchtrager
English vowel structure and stress in GP 2.0 —— 157

Kuniya Nasukawa & Nancy C. Kula
Reanalysing 'epenthetic' consonants in nasal-consonant sequences: A lexical specification approach —— 185

Connor Youngberg
The role of the elements in diphthong formation and hiatus resolution: Evidence from Tokyo and Owari Japanese —— 207

Henk van Riemsdijk
Elements of syntax. Repulsion and attraction —— 251

General Index —— 275

Language Index —— 279

Introduction

This volume aims at providing an overview and an extension of the Element Theory program by exploring new lines of research, mainly in phonology but also at its interface with phonetics and syntax. The main goal is to reassess theoretical and empirical questions that have been implicitly taken for granted until now. The present collection of papers reflects on issues that are central to this line of research.

The collection is organized around the general definition of the privative framework and the nature, the use and the number of primes; the interactions between the primes and the structural relationships between the elements (head-dependent, C/V segregation); the interfaces: the phonetic interpretation and the grounding of the elements, on the one hand, the interactions with the syntax (i.e., the possible analogy between the operations in privative frameworks and the syntactic component) on the other hand. The articles in this volume offer a wide variety of new data, which leads to a reassessment of the classical analyses in Element Theory, opening new empirical and theoretical perspectives.

Element Theory (ET), as proposed in Kaye et al. (1988, 1990), gave rise to a rich literature devoted to the characterization of elements, their use in the syllabic structure, and their possible interactions (Angoujard 1997; Charette 1988, 1990, 1991; Harris 1990, 1994; Harris and Lindsey 1995; Scheer 1996). In parallel to Government Phonology, some other frameworks – starting with the seminal work of Anderson & Jones (1974), Particles Phonology (Schane 1984), Dependency Phonology (Anderson and Ewen 1987), and its variant Radical CV Phonology (Hulst 1999, 2005, 2020; Hulst and Weijer 2018) – developed the same idea of smaller privative phonological units whose interaction is constrained by specific operations. The contributors to this volume explore the possibilities of applying elements to the analysis of specific languages and phonological phenomena.

Elements became a central topic in phonology, starting with Kaye et al. (1988, 1990). Prior to that, the units used in phonology, binary features, were based either on articulatory (Chomsky and Halle 1968; Clements 1985; Clements & Hume 1995; Halle *et al.* 2000) or on acoustic properties (Jakobson et al. 1952; Jakobson and Halle 1956; Jakobson and Lotz 1949). Although elements inherited this property,

---

Acknowledgements: We would like to thank the contributors to this volume for their kindness and patience while editing the manuscript. We are also thankful for the scientific rigor of the comments they provided in reviewing the papers in this volume. We are especially grateful to all the participants of the conference *Elements: State of the Art and Perspectives* held in Nantes in June 2018 and to the Laboratoire de Linguistique de Nantes (UMR6310) and the Université de Nantes for their fundings and support in this event.

as they have been defined as acoustic or articulatory, one of their salient characteristics is the fact that, unlike the *traditional* features, they are directly mapped to phonetics. This idea dates back to Anderson and Jones (1974), in which the three primes |A|, |I| and |U| are mapped to the three vowels [a, i, u]. Since then, it was adopted and further extended by Government Phonology (GP): "[. . .] the ultimate constituents of phonological segments are themselves autonomous, independently pronounceable units." (Kaye et al. 1988: 306). Therefore, "each and every subsegmental prime, not just those involved in the representation of vocalic contrasts, is independently interpretable." (Harris and Lindsey 1995: 2).

The relationship between the 'mental representation' of speech sound and its phonetic exponent leads to two conflicting views on the phonetic module in the modular approach of grammar. The *one to one* mapping (Backley 2011; Harris 1990; Harris and Lindsey 1995) gets rid of this conflict since elements are phonetically interpretable at all stages of the derivation. This type of mapping implies a strict match between a phonological representation and its phonetic exponent (to adopt Scheer's (2014) terminology, no 'slack' is allowed). However, a wide range of phonology-phonetics mismatches (i.e., the same phonetic form but different phonological representation or vice versa) suggests that the physical aspects of speech sound are not correlated to the phonological objects. The phonological objects, being completely independent of the acoustic signal and defined with respect to their behavior in phonological processes (i.e., the 'Phonological Epistemological Principle' (Kaye 2005), see also, on a more general perspective on phonology, the debate on substance especially Reiss (2017), Hall (2014) and contributions in this volume), are not obviously designed to fit into the phonetic exponent. This work is carried out by the phonetic module. Whether only phonological patterns or 'linguistically relevant acoustic patterns' – the so-called phonetic signature of elements – count is the core question to be asked for the definition of elementary representations: on which base should elements be established?

The present volume revolves around the general definition of the privative framework and discusses the nature, the use, and the number of phonological primes. While Backley's (2011) handbook to *Element Theory* aims at providing a general overview of elements and a description of their use, the set and the number of primes that are used to characterize the segments still varies according to the authors. New elements have been introduced to account for specific phenomena (e.g., |B| for labiality and roundness in contrast with |U| for velarity in Scheer (1999), other authors have underlined the fact that certain elements are redundant (e.g., given the close relation between voice |L| and nasality |N|, Nasukawa (1997) proposes to use the same element |N| to express both properties) and recent proposals claim that some of them should be eliminated (this is the case of Government Phonology 2.0, which discusses the need for specific primes for the representation of consonants and proposes to encode the laryngeal properties, aspiration, and occlusion, in structural terms). ET is initially motivated by the desire to restrict the number of phonological units and their possible interactions to avoid overgeneration. This restrictive perspective has (re)opened the door to the question of the structural complexity (and the question of recursion in phonology, see Nasukawa (2020), which was already present in Kaye et al. (1985, 1990): headedness was/is a way to mark the prominence of one element in the combination of several primes and to allow for more contrast between the segments containing the same primes (see also Charette & Göskel (1996)).

Recently, various frameworks propose to inject more structure within the segments either in an X-bar fashion, like GP 2.0 (Pöchtrager 2006; Živanović & Pöchtrager 2010; Pöchtrager & Kaye 2013, see also den Dikken & Hulst 2020) or using dependency trees, as it is the case for Precedence-free Phonology (Nasukawa 2011, 2014, 2015, 2016; Onuma 2015) or Radical CV Phonology (Hulst 1999, 2005). This leads to a reevaluation of the internal organization of segments where heads are still present but serve more a functional role in that they host the melodic elements and support the entire segmental projection.

The articles in this volume discuss these questions and provide a unique overview and update of the research carried out in the ET program by leading scholars in the field.

Abstracts

Phillip Backley

Elements and structural head-dependency

Backley discusses the integration of melody (elements) and prosody (syllables, feet) within Precedence-free Phonology (PfP), a recent development of the Element Theory model. In PfP, the three resonance elements |I|, |A| and |U| act as structural heads which provide the foundation for a recursive, hierarchical structure consisting of chains of head-dependent relations between elements. The elements themselves have a dual function: at lower levels of the hierarchy they have a melodic (*interpretive*) function while at higher levels their function is prosodic (*organisational*). This approach removes the need to refer to traditional prosodic categories, and also resolves the 'translation' problem between melody and prosody. In addition, it addresses the question of phonetic implementation by allowing the hierarchical structure to determine precedence relations between segments.

Elan B. Dresher
Contrastive hierarchies and phonological primes

In this paper, **Dresher** presents an overview of the tools and principles underlying the building of contrastive feature hierarchies (the SDA, the importance of phonological activity, the Contrastivist Hypothesis and its corollary) and a way to compute the optimal number of features needed to build a hierarchy. By discussing the place of the *Contrastivist Hypothesis* in the debate opposing substance-free and substance-based theories, Dresher gives arguments in favor of *markedness* as a way to compute complexity and as a way to link both binarism and unarism. The main claim is that contrast is not incompatible with ET and that it has already been implemented in this framework. The paper argues that feature hierarchies are variable (e.g. in apparently equivalent vowel systems) and offers new insights concerning the delineation between phonetics and phonology and, ultimately, UG.

Eric Raimy
Privativity and ternary phonological behavior

Raimy's contribution is at the heart of the discussion on privativity. It provides an overview of *Featural Realism*, as a theory of *substance impoverishment*, that goes beyond the mere use of Feature or Elements as primes. The paper focuses on laryngeal states and develops a privative feature system encoding ternary phonological behavior. It also shows how hyper-modularity may explain how underspecified phonological representations are phonetically interpreted. The proposals are applied to the case of voicing assimilation in Polish varieties (Cracow and Warsaw) as a way to show the congruencies, and discrepancies, with models using elements.

Harry van der Hulst
A Guide to Radical CV Phonology, with special reference to tongue root and tongue body harmony

In this paper **van der Hulst** outlines the model of segmental and syllabic structure developed in van der Hulst (2020). Key properties of this model are the use of dependency relations, and a reduction of the set of phonological elements to just two elements: |C| and |V|. Each of those two elements correlates with different although related phonetic interpretations, depending on their positions in the segmental and syllabic structure and on their status as heads or dependents. The paper shows how the Contrastivist Hypothesis can be applied to elements to predict a learning path into the phonetic space, albeit by postulating a universal ranking of elements. The paper briefly discusses the differences and similarities with Dependency Phonology and Government Phonology. It then shows how certain aspects of the RCVP model can be reconsidered to better represent ATR and RTR harmonies.

Markus Pöchtrager

English vowel structure and stress in GP 2.0

Pöchtrager's contribution looks at the phonological representation of vowel quality, length, and tenseness/laxness in English from the point of view of Government Phonology 2.0 where **A** is replaced by structure and where segments themselves are structured in an X-bar fashion. In this model, *openness* is seen as a function of structural size. Length contrasts are expressed by relations contracted between heads and non-heads (*melodic command*) within the space provided by the recursive structure of these constituents. Concerning the tenseness/laxness contrast, the paper proposes that *p-licensing*, as an extension of the *Empty Category Principle*, explains (amongst other things) the laxness of a vowel before a "coda": In this case, the following onset position *p-licenses* an unclaimed complement of a nuclear head. The proposed bipartite structure of vowels (containing up to two nuclear heads) not only allows for the expression of openness, length and tenseness/laxness, but also offers a way to treat *strength* and to account for the affinity of certain vowel qualities with particular prosodic positions.

Kuniya Nasukawa & Nancy C. Kula

Reanalysing 'epenthetic' consonants in nasal-consonant sequences: A lexical specification approach

Nasukawa and Kula explore Nasal-Consonant sequences in Bemba and Lungu which result from the appearance of an intrusive consonant between an underspecified nasal prefix and a vowel-initial verb root. When preceding a consonant-initial stem, the nasal and the consonant are homorganic and no epenthesis takes place. Stems beginning with a vowel show two types of epenthetic consonant: $\widehat{dʒ}$ before front vowels and glides, and *g* preceding back vowels, glides and *a*. They discuss the element content of the prefix and propose a treatment where post-nasal consonants are seen not as epenthetic but as part of a morpho-phonological operation, *(a)symmetric overlap concatenation*, which forces agreement by overwriting conflicting elements. Nasukawa and Kula then discuss the outcome of this process (homorganicity of the nasal as a phonetic effect, voicing) and those cases in which the process is blocked (e.g. between prefixes, *symmetric overlap concatenation*).

Connor Youngberg
The role of the elements in diphthong formation and hiatus resolution: Evidence from Tokyo and Owari Japanese

Youngberg's contribution discusses the status of diphthongs and hiatus in Tokyo and Owari Japanese. The paper illustrates how Element Theory and conditions on licensing can explain the patterning of vowel sequences in these varieties of Japanese. To do so, Youngberg uses the formal tools of Government Phonology to which he adds a new kind of government: InterVocalic Government. This new type of government relies on the elementary makeup of segments and blocks the expression of an intervocalic consonant. He explores the consequences of this innovation, taking advantage of structural proposals for the element |A| and raising questions for future work.

Henk van Riemsdijk
Elements of syntax. Repulsion and attraction

The core idea in this paper from **van Riemsdijk** is to introduce a phonological perspective into syntactic analysis. Moreover, it underlines that, as the syntactical and phonological domains share formal similarities, it is difficult to deny that some principles would be present and active in a domain but not in another. The proposal though reassesses a kind of isomorphism between syntax and phonology but relying on principles like the OCP and the hypothesis of the monovalency of features. In this perspective, the paper aims at developing a theory of categorial representations (*Unlike Feature Constraint, Categorial Identity Thesis, Law of Categorial Feature Magnetism*) defined and explained using phonological tools (*privative features, autosegmental tiers, OCP*). The paper discusses a research program providing the guidelines for a theory of syntactic categories and representations that is of great interest for both phonologists and syntacticians.

References

Anderson, John M. & Colin J. Ewen. 1987. *Principles of Dependency Phonology*. Cambridge: Cambridge University Press.
Anderson, John M. & Charles Jones. 1974. Three theses concerning phonological representations. *Journal of Linguistics* 10. 1–26.
Angoujard, Jean-Pierre. 1997. *Théorie de la syllabe: rythme et qualité*. Paris: CNRS éditions.
Backley, Phillip. 2011. *An introduction to Element Theory*. Edinburgh: Edinburgh University Press.
Backley, Phillip & Kuniya Nasukawa. 2009. Headship as melodic strength. In *Strength relations in phonology*, 47–77. Berlin/New York: Mouton de Gruyter.
Charette, Monik. 1990. Licence to Govern. *Phonology* 7.2. 233–253.
Charette, Monik. 1991. *Conditions on phonological government*. Cambridge: Cambridge University Press.
Charette, Monik & Asli Göksel. 1996. Licensing constraints and vowel harmony in Turkic languages. *SOAS Working Papers in Linguistics and Phonetics* 6. 1–25.
Chomsky, Noam & Morris Halle. 1968. *The Sound Pattern of English*. Cambridge/London: The MIT press.
Clements, George Nick. 1985. The Geometry of Phonological Features. *Phonology Yearbook* 2. 225–252.
Clements, George Nick & Elizabeth Hume. 1995. The Internal Organization of Speech Sounds. In John Goldsmith, (ed.), *Handbook of Phonological Theory*, 245–306. Oxford: Blackwell.
Den Dikken, Marcel & Harry van der Hulst. 2020. On some deep analogies between syntax and phonology. In Kuniya Nasukawa (ed.), *Morpheme-internal recursion in phonology*, 57–116. Berlin/New York: Mouton de Gruyter.
Hall, Daniel Currie. 2014. On substance in phonology. *Actes du congrès annuel de l'Association canadienne de linguistique 2014 / Proceedings of the 2014 annual conference of the Canadian Linguistic Association*.
Halle, Morris, Bert Vaux & Andrew Wolfe. 2000. On feature spreading and the representation of place of articulation. *Linguistic Inquiry* 31.3. 387–444.
Harris, John. 1990. Segmental Complexity and Phonological Government. *Phonology* 7.2. 255–300.
Harris, John. 1994. *English sound structure*. Cambridge: Blackwell.
Harris, John & Geoff Lindsey. 1995. The elements of phonological representation. In Jacques Durand & Francis Katamba (eds.), *Frontiers of phonology: Atoms, structures*, derivations, 34–79. Harlow: Longman.
Hulst, Harry van der. 1999. Features, segments and syllables in radical CV phonology. In John Rennison and Klaus Kühnhammer (eds.), *Phonologica 1996. Syllables?!*, 89–111. The Hague: Holland Academic Graphic.
Hulst, Harry van der. 2005. The molecular structure of phonological segments. In Phillip Carr, Jacques Durand & Colin J. Ewen (eds.), *Headhood, elements, specification and contrastivity*, 193–234. Amsterdam and Philadelphia: John Benjamins.
Hulst, Harry van der. 2020. *Principles of Radical CV Phonology – A theory of segmental and syllabic structure*. Edinburgh: Edinburgh University Press.
Hulst, Harry van der & Jeroen van de Weijer. 2018. Degrees of complexity in phonological segments. In Roger Böhm & Harry van der Hulst, *Substance-based Grammar–The (Ongoing) Work of John Anderson*, 385–430. Amsterdam/Philadelphia: John Benjamins.

Jakobson, Roman, Gunnar M. Fant & Morris Halle. 1952. *Preliminaries to speech analysis. The distinctive features and their correlates*. MIT Press, Cambridge MA.

Jakobson, Roman & Morris Halle. 1956. *Fundamentals of Language*. Berlin: Walter de Gruyter.

Jakobson, Roman & John Lotz. 1949. Notes on the French phonemic pattern. *Word, Journal of the international linguistic association* 5.2. 151–158.

Jensen, Sean. 1994. Is? an Element? Towards a Non-segmental Phonology. *SOAS Working Papers in Linguistics and Phonetics* 4. 71–78.

Kaye, Jonathan. 2001. Working with licensing constraints. *Trends in Linguistics Studies and Monographs* 134. 251–268.

Kaye, Jonathan D., Jean Lowenstamm & Jean-Roger Vergnaud. 1985. The internal structure of phonological elements: A theory of charm and government. *Phonology Yearbook* 2. 305–328.

Kaye, Jonathan D., Jean Lowenstamm & Jean-Roger Vergnaud. 1990. Constituent structure and government in phonology. *Phonology* 7. 193–231.

Kaye, Jonathan & Markus A. Pöchtrager. 2013. GP 2.0. *SOAS Working Papers in Linguistics & Phonetics* 16. 51–64.

Reiss, Charles. 2017. Substance Free Phonology. In Stephen J. Hannahs & Anna R. K. Bosch (eds), *Handbook of Phonological Theory*, 425–452. London & New-york: Routledge.

Nasukawa, Kuniya. 1997. Melodic structure in a nasal-voice paradox. *UCL Working Papers in Linguistics* 9.

Nasukawa, Kuniya. 2011. Representing phonology without precedence relations. *English Linguistics* 28.2. 278–300.

Nasukawa, Kuniya. 2014. Features and recursive structure. *Nordlyd* 41.1. 1–19.

Nasukawa, Kuniya. 2015. Recursion in the lexical structure of morphemes. In *Representing Structure in Phonology and Syntax*. 211–238. Berlin/New York: Mouton de Gruyter.

Nasukawa, Kuniya. 2016. A precedence-free approach to (de-)palatalisation in Japanese. In Martin Krämer & Olga Urek (eds.), *Glossa: a journal of general linguistics* 1 (1).

Nasukawa, Kuniya. 2020. *Morpheme-internal recursion in phonology*. Berlin/New York: Mouton de Gruyter.

Onuma, Hitomi. 2015. *On the Status of Empty Nuclei in Phonology*. Doctoral Dissertation. University Tohoku Gakuin.

Pöchtrager, Markus A. 2006. *The structure of length*. Doctoral Dissertation. University of Vienna.

Pöchtrager, Markus A. 2010. Does Turkish diss harmony? *Acta Linguistica Hungarica* 57.4. 458–473.

Živanovic, Sašo & Markus A. Pöchtrager. 2010. GP2, and Putonghua too. *Acta linguistica Hungarica* 57.4. 357–380.

Phillip Backley
Elements and structural head-dependency

Abstract: When elements combine in an expression, they do so asymmetrically: traditionally, one element is the head while all others are dependents. The difference between head and dependent status is significant because it affects how an element contributes to a resulting segment. This paper reconsiders the nature of asymmetry between elements, and argues that head-dependency is even more central to element representations than previously thought. This forms the basis of Precedence-free Phonology (PfP: Nasukawa 2015, Nasukawa & Backley 2017), in which *all* elements in an expression enter into asymmetric relations. PfP expresses these relations as a hierarchical structure in which segments are represented as chains of local head-dependency relations between elements, an element's position in the chain determining its relative prominence. Unlike in standard Element Theory, elements in PfP have a prosodic (organising) function as well as a melodic (interpretive) function, allowing melody and prosody to be integrated into a single unified structure. In the upper part of this structure, elements are organisational – they define prosodic domains and thus remove the need for conventional prosodic labels such as nucleus, rhyme, syllable and foot. This leaves just a single set of units (elements) to represent phonological structure in its entirety.

Keywords: Precedence-free Phonology; elements; melody-prosody integration; head-dependency; baseline resonance

1 Introduction

Elements offer an alternative to distinctive features as a means of representing melodic (segmental) properties in phonology. But what, if anything, is gained by using elements in representations? The literature describes numerous cases of

---

Acknowledgements: This paper was first presented at the meeting 'Elements: State of the Art and Perspectives' held at the University of Nantes in June 2018. I am most grateful to the meeting organisers for their assistance throughout and to the participants for their constructive comments. I am also indebted to two anonymous reviewers for their insightful comments on an earlier draft of this paper. I am of course responsible for any remaining errors, anomalies or inconsistencies. This work was supported by a MEXT/JSPS KAKENHI grant: Grant-in-Aid for Scientific Research on Innovative Areas #4903 (Evolinguistics), grant number JP20H05007.

Phillip Backley, Tohoku Gakuin University

https://doi.org/10.1515/9783110691948-002

how an element-based analysis can 'make sense' of a phonological pattern in a way that feature-based analyses cannot. One of Element Theory's contributions to phonology, then, has been to question the validity of using standard features to represent language sounds. But can elements achieve anything more? This paper describes how elements are used in a different way, not as units of melody but as units of prosodic structure. This idea forms the basis of the research program known as Precedence-free Phonology or PfP (Nasukawa 2014, 2015, 2017a,b; Nasukawa and Backley 2015, 2017; Backley and Nasukawa 2020), in which elements serve a dual role: they function in the usual way as units of melodic contrast, but in addition, they project to higher levels of structure where they also function as prosodic units. The aim here is to describe and motivate the PfP approach, and in doing so, to demonstrate how elements have the potential to provide insights into the nature of phonological knowledge.

It should be noted that the term 'element' is meant here as a general label which includes not only the elements used in element-based phonology (Kaye et al. 1985; Harris and Lindsey 1995; Cyran 2010; Backley 2011; Breit 2017) but also the components of Dependency Phonology (Anderson and Jones 1974; Anderson and Ewen 1987; van der Hulst 1995) and the particles of Particle Phonology (Schane 1984, 1995). Elements, components and particles all differ from standard distinctive features in that they function as monovalent (cf. bivalent, or two-valued) units. The discussion is organised as follows. Section 2 presents the case for integrating melody and prosody into a unified representation in which elements are the only kind of structural unit employed. Section 3 further motivates the use of elements as prosodic units and describes how vowels are represented in the PfP approach. From this description of vowels, it emerges that heads and dependents in PfP have more in common with heads and dependents in syntactic structure than with those in mainstream phonology. This point is explored in section 4. Consonant structure is the focus of section 5, and the representation of whole syllables is dealt with in section 6. Finally, section 7 summarises the main points.

2 Melody and prosody

2.1 The melody-prosody split

Elements are normally associated with melodic structure, not prosodic structure. In the PfP model, however, elements are present in both melody *and* prosody. This is a notable departure from the standard view of phonological representations, where the melodic and prosodic domains are clearly separated and are described using different structural units: features or elements in melody, prosodic units such as 'syllable' and 'foot' in prosody. The first question, then, is whether we should follow convention by keeping melody and prosody distinct, or whether we should consider ways of combining them into a unified melodic-prosodic structure.

Our instincts tell us that melody and prosody should be kept apart, because the two domains contain different kinds of phonological information: melody describes the structure of individual sounds, while prosody is all about how those sounds are organised in relation to one another, e.g. how they are grouped into constituents. So, given that melody and prosody have distinct roles, it seems natural that they ought to be separated in representations. This is the standard view presented to most students of phonology. And to reflect the inherent difference between melody and prosody, each one has its own unique set of descriptive terms: melody uses features ([±back], [±son] . . .) or elements (|A|, |H| . . .) to express segmental categories, while prosody uses constituent labels (onset, nucleus, syllable, foot . . .) to describe the domains within which segments are distributed.

Another reason for maintaining a division between melodic and prosodic structure is that each domain can be targeted by phonological processes independently of the other – which suggests that they belong in different parts of a representation. Segmental processes can bring about a change in melodic structure without affecting prosodic structure. For instance, in Early Modern English the long monophthong [uː] diphthongised to [aʊ] (e.g. [huː] > [haʊ] 'how'); meanwhile, the short vowel [ʊ] lowered to [ʌ] (e.g. [jʊŋg] > [jʌŋ] 'young'). In both cases a melodic (quality) change took place but prosodic structure (quantity) remained stable, i.e. long stayed long and short stayed short. The reverse situation is also found, where a phonological effect can bring about a change in prosodic structure but leave melody unaffected. This is seen in vowel-glide alternations such as [i]~[j] and [u]~[w] (Rosenthall 1994), where the members of a vowel-glide pair are phonetically the same, except in terms of their duration, but differ in prosodic status: the (moraic) vowel occupies a syllable nucleus whereas the (non-moraic) glide is in an onset.

2.2 Unifying melody and prosody

So, the practice of separating melody and prosody in representations is a well-motivated one. But at the same time, there is also evidence to support an alternative view of phonological structure in which melodic and prosodic information is integrated into a single structure. This approach, which forms the basis of the PfP model, is described here. The basic questions are as follows. What are the advantages of rejecting the traditional split between prosody and melody? And how can melodic and prosodic information be incorporated into a single representation?

There are two points which support the idea of a unified melodic-prosodic structure. One refers to a general observation about phonological behaviour across languages, while the other is concerned with a specific characteristic of the Government Phonology approach to representations (Kaye at al. 1985, 1990; Harris 1990; Kaye 2000). The general observation is that melody and prosody regularly interact. Of course, interaction is possible between autonomous parts of a representation. But if these autonomous domains express different kinds of linguistic information, and if they use different labels to describe this information, then any interactions between them tend to look like random events. For instance, in Germanic languages such as English and Swedish, aspirated stops can occur syllable-initially but not syllable-finally. That is, the melodic unit which represents aspiration – some form of the |H| element, or otherwise, the feature [constricted glottis] – is associated with a syllable onset rather than a coda. No matter how robust this pattern may be, however, it is difficult for the grammar to express a formal link between a melodic unit |H| and the prosodic unit 'onset'. The problem is that the terms '|H|' and 'onset' belong to different vocabularies, making any relation between them appear like a stipulation. On the other hand, if melody and prosody are described using the same units, then melody-prosody interaction might not appear so arbitrary – at least, both domains would be 'speaking the same language'. PfP takes the view that if the same structural units are present in melodic and prosodic structure, then it is natural to want to integrate the two.

The second point supporting the integration of melody and prosody concerns the use of empty prosodic structure. Empty structure is a characteristic of the Government Phonology tradition (e.g. Charette 1991; Harris 1998; van der Hulst 2003; Scheer 2004; Cyran 2010; Živanović and Pöchtrager 2010), where a nucleus may be pronounced even if it has no melodic units associated with it. An empty (i.e. melodically unspecified) nucleus is pronounced as a default vowel, typically [ə] or [ɨ], under certain conditions. For example, in the English word [ˈwɒtʃɨz] 'watches' the nucleus following [tʃ] is pronounced as a weak vowel [ɨ] even though it is melodically empty – it has no elements in its structure. In feature-based approaches, the idea of pronouncing empty structure seems incongruous because the sound properties associated with a prosodic position are defined by its feature representation – and if there are no features, then logically, the position should be silent. But in the Government Phonology framework, which uses elements to represent segmental structure, there is nothing unusual in realising an empty prosodic position. This is because elements represent marked phonological properties, not phonetic qualities. So, if there are no elements, then simply, there are no marked properties. But an empty nucleus can still be pronounced as an *un*marked vowel. The effect of this is to blur the distinction between melody and prosody, since it means that a prosodic unit (an empty nucleus) is pronounceable in the absence of melodic units (elements). This does not sit comfortably with the familiar assumption that melody is concerned with segmental information while prosody is concerned with organising information. Furthermore, it raises the question of whether it is necessary, or even desirable, to separate melody from prosody at all.

Melody-prosody integration becomes a more realistic option if a common set of structural units is shared by both domains. This idea is central to the PfP program, in which the same elements are present in melody and prosody: they represent melodic properties in the usual way, and in addition, they take on an organising function. As organising units, elements project to higher structural levels, where they behave like prosodic constituents. This then removes the need for prosodic constituents such as onset, nucleus, syllable, and foot. One of the advantages of giving elements this dual role is to facilitate the kinds of interactions mentioned above: in a unified structure, elements at the melodic level interact directly with elements at the prosodic level. This marks a departure from the conventional notion that structural units specify only one kind of information, either melodic or prosodic.

To summarise, phonological representations in PfP refer only to elements. When elements behave as melodic units they have an interpretive function: they are mapped onto the speech signal and express information about segmental properties. By contrast, when they behave as prosodic units they have an organising function: they provide information about the domains within which segmental properties are distributed. This approach highlights a fundamental point about the nature of phonological representations – namely, they are concerned with segments and with the way those segments are arranged in morphemes. And since a morpheme is identified by its melodic (and, of course, semantic) properties, it follows that it ought to be represented solely by structural units that are melodic in character (i.e. by elements).

2.3 A melody-prosody hierarchy

This section describes what a combined melody-prosody representation looks like in the PfP model. To fulfil their organising function, elements project from melodic structure to higher structural levels. But in practice, not all elements do this: it is only the resonance elements |A|, |I| and |U| which have a prosodic function. The reason for this is that, unlike |H|, |L| and |ʔ|, they are associated with nuclei – or more precisely, with prosodic domains that correspond to nuclear domains in conventional descriptions of phonological structure. And it is these nucleus-like domains which act as the building blocks of prosodic structure (cf. onset-like domains, which are largely irrelevant to higher-level prosodic relations). Expressed in familiar terms, a nucleus first projects to a rhyme node, then to a syllable, then to a foot, and so on. And in PfP a similar hierarchical structure is assumed. The difference lies in the units involved: when resonance elements project upwards to function prosodically, they keep their identity as resonance elements rather than being recast as prosodic constituents. Note that, in giving elements a dual melodic-prosodic function, PfP abandons the notion of an interface between the two domains of melody and prosody. (On this point, PfP differs from most element-based representations, in which prosodic structure terminates at the point where it meets/licenses melodic structure.) Instead, PfP considers melody and prosody to be just two different aspects of the same structural hierarchy.

Nothing crucial is lost by discarding traditional prosodic labels like 'onset' and 'syllable', because they are just that – labels. They mark out prosodic domains, and in turn, define the scope of phonological patterns and processes. But when we describe domains, we do so by referring to the segmental strings – and ultimately, the elements – that they contain. That is, there is little difference between describing a prosodic domain (e.g. nucleus) and describing the melodic expressions in that domain (e.g. |A U|). In short, a domain *is* its element structure. And to reflect this, PfP uses elements in place of the usual constituent labels to identify prosodic domains. The result is a shared vocabulary of elements for both melodic and prosodic structure. To illustrate this, (1) shows a partial representation of the word *city* ['sɪti], where the PfP version in (1b) may be compared with the standard version in (1a). Note that PfP favours a strict CVCV approach to prosodic structure (Lowenstamm 1996; Scheer 2004), so no 'rhyme' constituent is shown. The details of the PfP structure in (1b) will be explained below. Also, note that consonant structure is omitted here, as it is not relevant to the discussion at this point.

(1) a. *city* ['sɪti]   b. *city* ['sɪti] (PfP)

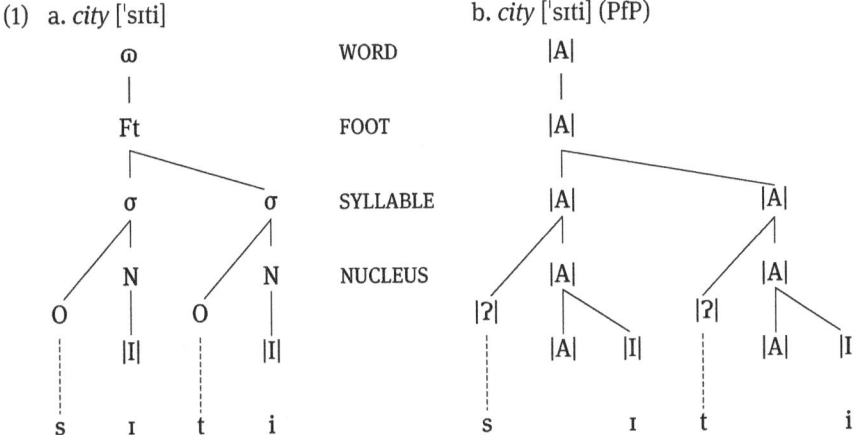

Notice that elements are the only structural units present in (1b), so it follows that they have a dual function: interpretive (melodic) and organisational (prosodic). The prosodic role of elements is described in section 3. That section also introduces another important aspect of PfP representations, namely, that all units at all levels form head-dependent relations with one another. Section 3 is preceded by a brief overview of elements. Readers who are already familiar with the Element Theory approach may prefer to skip section 2.4 and go straight to section 3.

2.4 Overview of elements

Like features, elements are units of melodic structure which represent segmental properties. However, they differ from features by being associated with aspects of the acoustic signal rather than with articulation (Harris and Lindsey 1995, Nasukawa and Backley 2008, Backley 2011, Nasukawa 2017b). Each element represents an acoustic pattern that is thought to carry linguistic information – that is, a pattern which listeners use to identity morphemes. For example, the element |L| represents the pattern of low-frequency periodic energy that is present in nasals, voiced obstruents and low-tone vowels, while the element |U| represents a formant pattern in which sound energy is concentrated at the lower end of the spectrum, as in labials, velars and rounded vowels (Nasukawa and Backley 2008; Backley and Nasukawa 2009; Backley 2011).

Element Theory exists in several versions (Backley 2012). The one described here uses the six elements listed in (2), each shown with its defining acoustic pattern (Harris and Lindsey 1995; Nasukawa and Backley 2008, 2011; Backley and Nasukawa 2009, 2010).

(2) a. Resonance elements
|I| high F2 which converges with F3
|U| concentration of low-frequency energy via formant lowering
|A| high F1 which converges with F2

b. Laryngeal elements
|ʔ| abrupt and sustained drop in amplitude
|H| aperiodic noise energy
|L| periodic noise energy, nasal murmur

As shown in (2), the six elements naturally divide into two subsets. The resonance elements |A|, |I| and |U| are associated with formant structure patterns, so they are primarily associated with vowels. But they also appear in consonants, where they define place properties in consonants. The laryngeal elements |H|, |L| and |ʔ| refer to non-resonance properties of the speech signal such as noise energy and amplitude, so they mainly occur in consonants. But they also represent secondary vowel properties; for example, |ʔ| produces 'creaky voice' while |L| adds nasal murmur.

Elements do not just refer to the physical speech signal, however. They also denote abstract phonological categories. These categories function linguistically to express lexical contrasts, and they are present in native speakers' mental representations of words and morphemes. The main categories represented by each element are shown below.

(3) a. Resonance elements

nuclear	non-nuclear
|I| front vowels	coronal: dental, palatal POA
|U| round vowels	dorsal: labial, velar POA
|A| non-high vowels	guttural: uvular, pharyngeal POA

b. Laryngeal elements

non-nuclear	nuclear
|ʔ| oral/glottal occlusion	creaky voice in laryngealised vowels
|H| aspiration, voicelessness	high tone
|L| nasality; obstruent voicing	nasality; low tone

Unlike standard features, which have a plus and a minus value, elements are monovalent or single-valued. That is, elements have an inherent plus value which indicates the presence of a given marked property. So, in element terms a contrast such as [+continuant] versus [−continuant] is expressed by the presence versus the absence of an element. In this instance the active element is |ʔ|, which roughly corresponds to [−continuant]; stops and affricates (and perhaps also nasals) contain |ʔ| while other segment types have no |ʔ| in their representation, i.e. they are unmarked for non-continuant, so they are produced as continuant sounds.

Another difference between features and elements is that the latter have 'autonomous interpretation' (Harris and Lindsey 1995: 34). That is, an element can be pronounced by itself; it does not need support from other elements in order to be realised phonetically. This means that a representation may contain just one element, which can stand alone as a pronounceable segment. For example, the |ʔ| element adds the property 'occlusion' (i.e. non-continuant) to an expression. But if no other elements are present, then the expression has no other marked properties, i.e. it is unspecified for place and voicing. Speakers can still pronounce an unspecified stop as a glottal closure [ʔ] – in effect, producing bare occlusion. (Compare this to a feature-based representation, where [−continuant] has no autonomous interpretation: it is neither audible nor pronounceable unless other features are also present to provide the necessary phonetic properties to produce a 'full' segment.) Note that, while single-element expressions are well-formed, most segments are represented by element compounds. Section 3 takes up the question of how segments are represented in PfP using hierarchical structures such as (1b).

3 Resonance elements as prosodic constituents

Standard approaches to prosodic structure have always been based on relations between nuclei or rhymes. The same is true of prosodic structure in PfP, where it is only the resonance (vocalic) elements |I|, |U| and |A| that have a prosodic function. These elements encode vowel contrasts in the usual way, but they also define prosodic domains by projecting to higher structural levels. A partial representation of the word *kiss* [kɪs] is shown in (4) with prosodic domains marked using the conventional labels 'nucleus', 'syllable', and so on. The explanation below it focuses on structure within the nucleus. Note that PfP follows Government Phonology (e.g. Harris and Gussmann 1998) in syllabifying a word-final consonant in the onset of a syllable with an empty nucleus Ø, i.e. [kɪ.sØ].

(4) kiss [kɪs]

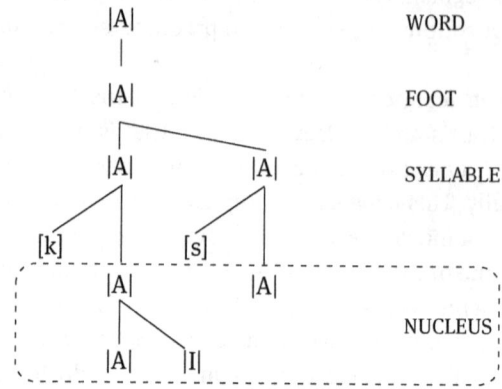

The structure in (4) resembles standard hierarchical representations of prosodic structure in that constituency is based on head-dependent relations: foot structure is binary and asymmetric, and the syllable domain has a vocalic head with a consonant (onset) dependent. The difference is that in PfP head-dependency operates at all levels, including those within melodic structure. Asymmetry between melodic elements will be described below.

The head of a nucleus must be a resonance element, the choice between |I|, |U| and |A| being determined by parameter. For example, nuclei in English are |A|-headed while in Japanese they are |U|-headed. To determine which element is the head or 'base' element, we refer to the phonetic quality of a language's carrier signal. The carrier signal, or 'baseline resonance', is the vowel quality which appears in default or non-contrastive vowels – that is, in nuclei which have no marked properties. The default vowel in English is usually [ə], which is the phonetic realisation of |A| in its weak form (Backley 2011: 50). From this we can infer that |A| is the base element in English. By contrast, in Japanese the neutral vowel is [ɯ], which is represented by |U| in its weak form (Nasukawa 2017b). This is the vowel quality that is heard in loanwords when the phonotactic rules of Japanese require a nucleus to be pronounced, e.g. [bɯrakkɯ] 'black'. Like heads in general, the head of a nucleus can stand alone as a well-formed structure; and when it is pronounced, it has a default vowel quality.

As there are three resonance elements, there are three possible representations of a default vowel, as shown in (5). In each case the base element functions as a prosodic unit – the PfP equivalent of a melodically empty nuclear position. It is because these nuclei are unspecified for melodic content that they have the acoustic quality of baseline resonance and function as non-contrastive vowels.

(5) Nuclear heads as default vowels

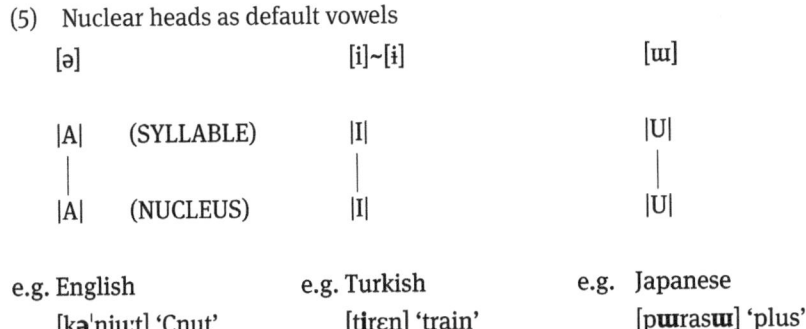

e.g. English e.g. Turkish e.g. Japanese
[kə'nju:t] 'Cnut' [tiɾen] 'train' [pɯrasɯ] 'plus'

These are minimal structures, in that each consists of a domain head and nothing else. And as minimal structures, they convey a minimal amount of linguistic information: they indicate the presence of a nucleus and nothing else. In order to support contrastive vowels, as opposed to default vowels, the nuclear head must have dependent structure. This is because melodic information in PfP is expressed mainly by dependent elements, not by head elements. (6) shows how dependent structure is added to the base element |A| to represent 'full' vowels.

(6) Representing vowel contrasts

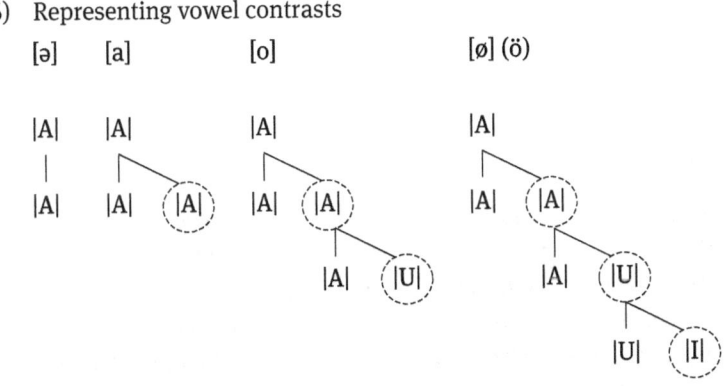

Here, the dependent elements (circled) have a melodic function, while head elements (without circles) have a prosodic function. In principle, there is no restriction on the degree of complexity (i.e. levels of embedding) in a structure. But in practice, representations are never more complex than is necessary: they must be big enough to express the lexical contrasts of a language, but no bigger. So, many languages will not require structures as complex as the one representing [ø] in (6), for example, in which three melodic elements combine. While vowel representations may differ in complexity, they are all structurally similar, comprising chains of binary head-dependency relations holding between the elements |I|, |U| and |A|.

From the structures in (6) we can identify two basic characteristics of structure-building in PfP. First, *all* elements are involved in head-dependency relations, whether their contribution is melodic or prosodic. Second, element concatenation involves structural embedding. That is, when elements combine in an expression, each element occupies its own level of structure. This means that each of the elements in an expression has a different status, since each is positioned at a different 'distance' from the head of the nuclear domain, i.e. at differing levels of embedding. And as (7) shows, the positioning of its elements can affect the way an expression is pronounced. This is because the lower an element is in the hierarchical structure, the more phonetically prominent that element is (Nasukawa and Backley 2019).

(7) Embedding and acoustic prominence

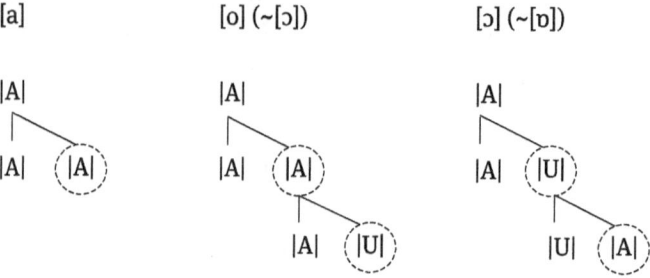

This relation between embedding and phonetic prominence follows from the inherent difference between heads and dependents in PfP. Head elements are concerned with building prosodic structure, not with expressing melodic information. By contrast, dependent elements are all about melodic contrasts which, in spoken language, are communicated via the acoustic signal. It is unsurprising, therefore, that the audibility of an element – its acoustic prominence – increases when that element is more deeply embedded in the dependent structure and further removed from the domain head. This is illustrated by comparing the representations for [o] and [ɒ] in (7), both of which combine the melodic elements |A| and |U|. When |A| is the terminal element the phonetic outcome is a low vowel [ɔ]~[ɒ], since the properties of |A| (i.e. F1 raising, achieved by maximising openness) are more prominent than those of |U| (i.e. formant lowering through lip rounding). By contrast, when |U| is more deeply embedded than |A|, the result is a less open vowel [o]~[ɔ], since the effects of |U| predominate over those of its local head |A|.

In section 2.3 it was noted that PfP adopts a strict CVCV approach to prosodic structure. There is nothing equivalent to a syllable coda, therefore – all consonants are dependents of the 'syllable' constituent. The absence of codas also means that PfP has nothing corresponding to a rhyme. Instead, a nuclear head projects directly to the syllable level, the syllable domain comprising a nucleus and its dependent consonant (if any). Given its adherence to the strict CVCV format, PfP represents long vowels by concatenating two syllable-sized units. These form a head-dependency relation at the 'foot' level, as in (8).

(8) [tuː] 'two'

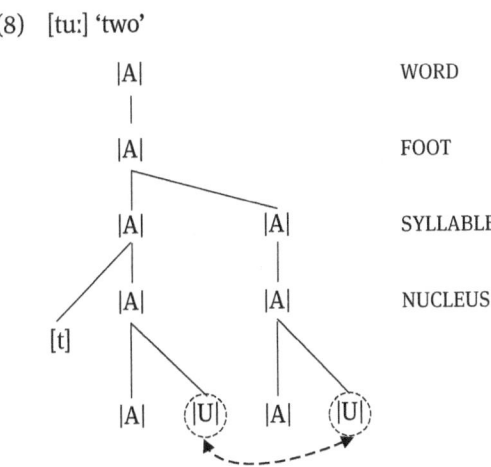

Here, the foot domain – the equivalent of a branching nucleus in standard approaches to syllable structure – defines the scope of melodic agreement, where 'agreement' is achieved through element copying. This assumes that the right-hand syllable in (8) is lexically empty, comprising just the base element |A|. The |U| element in the left-hand syllable is then copied into the vacant slot. Copying is motivated by the fact that the empty syllable carries linguistic information, since it represents the latter portion of a long vowel. And to communicate the information that [tuː] 'two' has a long vowel, speakers must make this empty position audible. Because this dependent position has no melodic properties of its own, however, it must replicate those of its head to create a long vowel [uː].

4 Heads and dependents revisited

Section 3 showed how hierarchical structure is used to capture the melodic-prosodic properties that are encoded in lexical representations. However, examples such as (4) also reveal an inconsistency in the way heads and dependents function in this hierarchical structure. This section describes this inconsistency and then outlines revisions to the proposed model.

It was noted above in relation to (6) that information about melodic contrasts is expressed by dependent elements rather than head elements, while the role of head elements is to build prosodic structure. In this respect PfP runs counter to our expectations, since the usual assumption is that heads contain more segmental information than dependents – notice how the structure in (4) follows this convention. The PfP position, which goes against our instincts regarding the roles of heads and dependents, is motivated in Nasukawa (2016, 2017b) and Backley and Nasukawa (2020). It may be summarised as follows. Heads have a prosodic function: they project to higher structural levels and support dependent structure. In (8), for example, |A| functions as the domain head at every level of prosodic structure from the nucleus up to the word (and beyond). But as prosodic units, heads are not important for expressing melodic information; in (5), for instance, a bare nuclear head is realised as a non-contrastive vowel. On the other hand, dependents have a melodic function: elements in dependent positions are rich in melodic information, allowing them to express lexical contrasts. Dependents also support further levels of dependent structure below them, which introduce yet more contrastive properties to an expression.

For phonologists, this way of understanding the roles of heads and dependents looks like a case of role reversal (Nasukawa and Backley 2015). But for those working in syntax, the approach is a familiar one in which linguistic information is concentrated in dependents while heads play more of a structural role. The examples in (9) illustrate the point.

(9) a. 'drink beer' (VP) b. 'at the end' (PP)

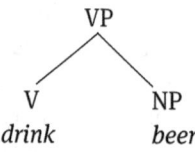
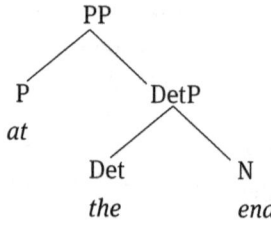

In (9a) the verb *drink* is the head of the VP *drink beer*. And as a head, its function is mainly structural, as it supports the dependent NP *beer*. Notice that it does not contain much lexical information, since the meaning of *drink* is largely predictable from the meaning of *beer* – verb choice is severely limited in this context. By contrast, the dependent *beer* shows the opposite characteristics, as it is unimportant in structural terms but rich in lexical information. And being the semantic focus of the phrase, it bears the main stress: *drìnk béer*. The same pattern can be seen in (9b), where *at* and *the* (the phrasal heads of PP and DetP, respectively) have a low semantic load but they fulfil the prosodic role of supporting dependent structure. Again, it is their dependents which contribute most of the lexical information.

The nature of the inconsistency mentioned above should now be clear: the roles of heads and dependents are reversed between syntax and phonology. That is, in syntactic structure heads are recessive while dependents are informationally rich, whereas in phonological structure the contrastive information is traditionally carried by heads rather than by dependents. One of PfP's aims is to address this inconsistency by generalising the way head-dependency is used in the grammar. Head-dependent relations are a fundamental property of linguistic structure in general, controlling how units combine throughout the grammar. Ideally, then, each module of the grammar should implement head-dependency in the same way. With this in mind, PfP attempts to unify head-dependent behaviour by reassigning the roles of heads and dependents in phonology so that they parallel those of heads and dependents in syntax. This means we need to reorganise head-dependent relations in PfP structures such as (4) and (8). To illustrate this, a revised representation of (4) is given in (10).

(10) *kiss* [kɪs] (revised)

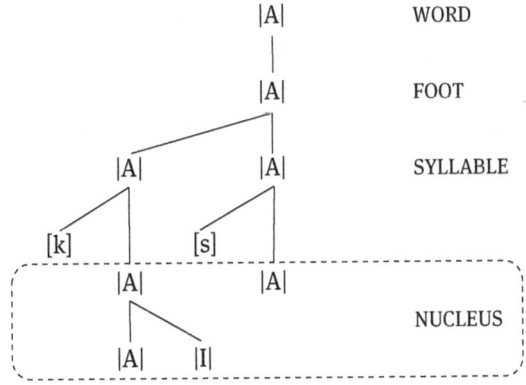

Notice how the head of the word domain is now a projection of an empty nucleus, i.e. a nucleus which has a purely prosodic function – it contains no melodic properties. By contrast, the full vowel [ɪ] is represented by |I|, which is the most deeply embedded element in the structure.

5 Consonant structure

In PfP, consonant representations follow the same principles of structure-building that apply to vowels. The difference is that consonants use the laryngeal elements |H|, |L| and |ʔ| in addition to |A|, |I| and |U|. Like the resonance elements in vowels, the laryngeal elements in consonants have both a melodic function and a prosodic function.

It was shown in section 3 that the base element in a vowel structure is chosen from the |A|-|I|-|U| set. In consonant structure, on the other hand, the base element must be either |H| or |ʔ|.[1] By giving vowel structures and consonant structures different domain heads, PfP makes the point that vowels and consonants are different in kind, but it does so without referring to formal labels such as 'nucleus' or 'onset' (which are not present in PfP representations – see section 2.2). As in vowels, the base element in consonants has a prosodic role and can stand alone as a well-formed structure. By itself it is pronounced as a non-contrastive consonant, typically the kind of consonant that can serve as an onset-filler when the phonotactic rules require it. In many languages including English, French, and Rennellese, this default consonant is [ʔ]; so, it follows that in these systems |ʔ| operates as the base element. But there are also languages such as Wiyot and Yurok in which [h] is the 'epenthetic' consonant (Blevins 2008); in these languages the parametric choice of base element must be |H|. In all cases, the base element |ʔ| or |H| plays a structural role and, in the absence of dependent elements, represents an empty non-nuclear (i.e. onset) position.

To represent consonant contrasts, the base element must have dependent structure because, as with vowels, dependent elements carry melodic information in consonants. And like the vowel structures in (6) and (7), consonant structures also require all elements to form head-dependent asymmetries. Once again, element concatenation always introduces a further level of embedding, as shown in (11). Melodic elements are circled.

---

[1] The reasons why |L| does not function as a consonant head are discussed in Nasukawa and Backley (2018).

(11) Consonant structures in |ʔ|-type languages

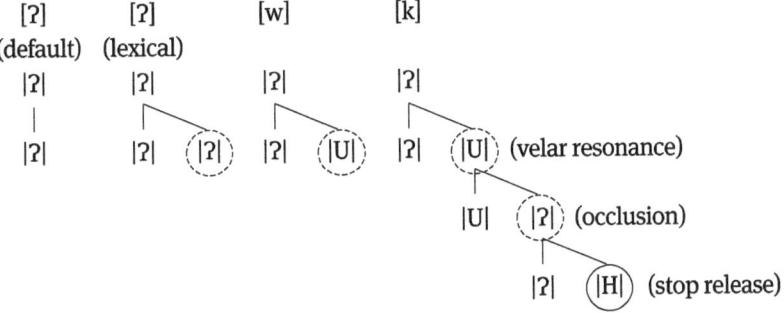

In standard versions of Element Theory there is a lexical contrast between the headed and non-headed forms of an element, e.g. headed |U| for labial resonance, non-headed |U| for velar resonance (Backley and Nasukawa 2009; Backley 2011). These two forms of an element represent different (though related) phonological properties, and each property has a different (though related) phonetic realisation. In general, the headed form has an acoustically more prominent realisation than its non-headed counterpart. For example, non-headed |H| is present in fricatives and released stops, where the aperiodic noise energy associated with |H| is produced as frication and audible plosion, respectively (see (2b) above). By contrast, headed |H| is present in aspirated stops; more generally, it is also a property of fortis obstruents in languages such as English, where voicelessness behaves as an active laryngeal property. And to reflect |H|'s headed status, aperiodic noise is relatively prominent in the speech signal for aspirates and other fortis consonants.

Surprisingly, there is no consensus in standard Element Theory on the question of how to formally express headedness properties in representations, even though the difference between headed and non-headed can be lexically distinctive. The convention has always been to mark headedness using a diacritic such as underlining, e.g. headed |U̱| versus non-headed |U|. This practice has not been carried over into PfP, however. In fact, PfP has no direct equivalent of the headed/non-headed distinction just described; instead, the relative prominence of an element derives from its position in the hierarchical structure, not from any lexically assigned diacritic. There are two ways in which PfP uses structure to give an element prominence. One way is to have the element occupy the lowest part of the hierarchy. This was illustrated in (7), which showed how a more deeply embedded element makes a greater contribution to an expression than one which is located closer to the domain head. Recall that, for example, the structure with |A| as its terminal element is realised as a relatively open vowel [ɔ]~[ɒ] (cf. [o]~[ɔ] when |A| occupies a higher position).

The other way of making an element prominent is to have it occupy two levels of structure as opposed to just one, as the examples in (12) show. In the structure for aspirated [kʰ] there are two tokens of melodic |H| (in addition to the consonant base element, prosodic |H|): the higher |H| represents stop release, as shown in the representation for [k] in (11), while the lower |H| represents aspiration – that is, aperiodic noise in its more prominent, acoustically salient form. Owing to its embedded position, this lower |H| has a status similar to that of a headed element in standard Element Theory. Turning to the structure for [ʃ] in (12), this also has two tokens of melodic |H|: the higher |H| represents aperiodic noise and is realised as frication, whereas the lower |H| is realised as the active voicelessness that characterises fortis obstruents in English and other Germanic languages. Notice also that [ʃ] has two resonance elements |A| and |I|, which are interpreted together as post-alveolar place. The higher element |A| represents coronal as a broad place category, while the |I| element below it specifies palatal as the perceptually more salient resonance property. The strident quality of post-alveolar [ʃ] (as well as of [tʃ dʒ ...]) comes from a combination of prominent |H| (fortis voicelessness) and prominent |I| (palatal resonance), which occupy the lowest two positions in the hierarchy.

(12)   Consonant structures in |H|-type languages

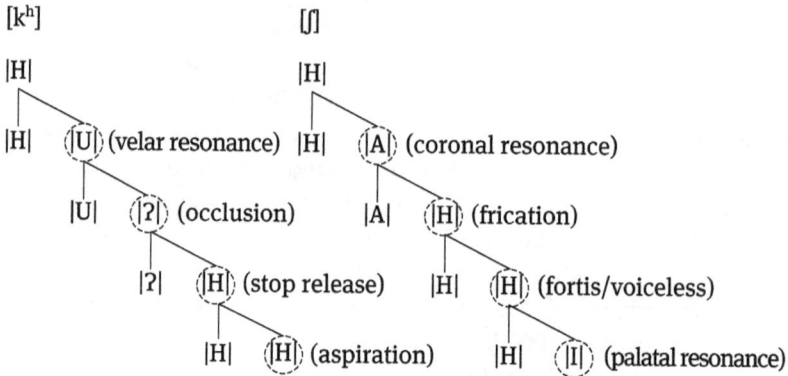

6 Syllable structure

So far, the discussion has focused on melodic structure within vowels and consonants. Finally, this section considers how melody is organised into syllables. In fact, because PfP follows a strict CVCV approach, a syllable-sized domain is nothing more than the concatenation of a single consonant and a single vowel. Note that, although 'syllable' is not a formal label in the PfP vocabulary, it is still necessary to refer to syllable-sized structures as autonomous prosodic units, so that they can be accessed by phonological rules. As will be shown in (13) below, the head of a nucleus is also the head of a CV (syllable) domain, since consonant melody is structurally dependent on vowel melody. For descriptive purposes, the CV domain shown here is split into two sub-domains, a C-domain and a V-domain. In structural terms, however, these are to be understood as two parts of one continuous hierarchy.

In principle, all melodic elements in a PfP representation are realised simultaneously, since PfP is a precedence-free approach – it makes no reference to the linear ordering of segments or segmental properties when a structure is phonetically realised. This is true for [k] in (11) and [ʃ] in (12), for example. But with the aspirate [kʰ] in (12), a simultaneous pronunciation is not possible because the structure contains two incompatible properties which cannot easily be produced or perceived at the same time: upper |H| (stop release) and lower |H| (aspiration). For listeners to perceive aspiration independently of stop release, speakers must stagger these two properties by pronouncing them in succession. The same analysis also applies to affricates such as [tʃ], [ts] and [pf], which contain |ʔ| for occlusion and |H| for frication. Clearly, speakers cannot produce a speech signal which features, at the same time, a sharp drop in amplitude (for |ʔ|) and aperiodic noise energy (for |H|). For speakers to communicate all of the melodic information contained in an affricate, a staggered realisation is required.

(13) CV structure: [ki]

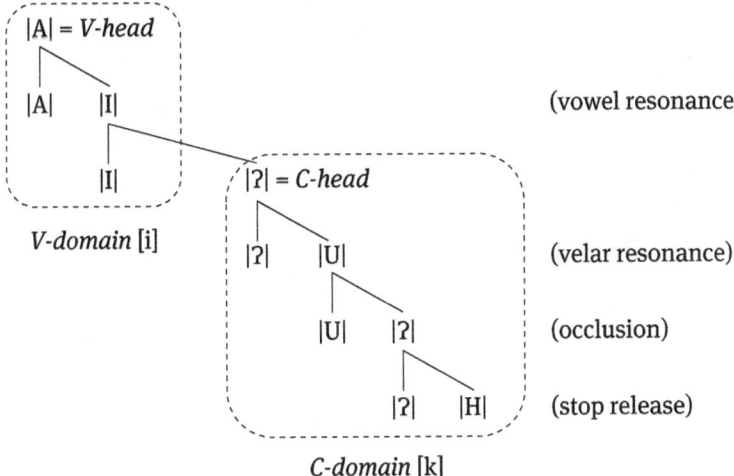

CV structures such as (13) must also be realised as sequences, because they have a resonance (vocalic) portion and a non-resonance (consonantal) portion. These naturally form separate domains owing to the physiological incompatibility between them: vowel production requires spontaneous voicing and a relatively open vocal tract, whereas consonant production involves non-modal voice and an obstruction in the vocal tract. It is this physiological difference which forces speakers to pronounce vowel material and consonant material separately. Notice that speakers are consistent in the way they divide the CV structure into two parts, because this is determined by the structure itself: the incompatibility just mentioned is between the part headed by the resonance element |A| (the V-domain) and the part headed by the non-resonance element |ʔ| (the C-domain). There remains the question of the order in which these two portions are phonetically realised, however. Nasukawa et al. (2019: 634) proposes a general principle of precedence which states that a domain located in a lower position in the hierarchical structure is realised before a domain in a higher position. This means that (13) is produced as CV rather than VC (where VC involves a disyllabic structure [V.CØ]). This principle of precedence is not claimed to be universal, but it does describe the default pattern.

Summary

The preceding pages have shown how elements can play a prosodic role, in addition to their regular melodic role, in phonological representations. By using elements as prosodic units, PfP eliminates the need for traditional prosodic constituents such as nucleus, syllable and foot; and in doing so, it moves towards the integration of melody and prosody into a single hierarchical structure. By characterising prosodic domains in terms of elements, PfP highlights the point that a prosodic domain is essentially melodic in nature, and as such, should be described in melodic terms. Domains are melodic in the sense that they have no substance of their own – they are identified solely by the segments within their scope and the phonological effects operating on those segments, both of which are defined by referring to elements.

In addition to giving elements a prosodic function, PfP sheds light on the roles of heads and dependents in phonological structure. It has been argued that linguistic (lexical) information is conveyed by dependent elements, whereas heads are mainly involved with building and supporting structure. This view contradicts the assumptions found in mainstream approaches to phonology. However, by adopting this position we achieve a closer parallel between phonology and syntax in terms of structure-building. The aim of this paper has been to introduce the basics of PfP representations and to explain the thinking behind the PfP approach. The recent literature contains further discussion of specific aspects of PfP including its treatment of melodic weakening (Nasukawa and Backley 2019), the role of recursion in phonology (Backley and Nasukawa 2020) and the phonetic interpretation of precedence-free structure (Nasukawa et al. 2019).

References

Anderson, John M. & Colin J. Ewen. 1987. *Principles of Dependency Phonology*. Cambridge: Cambridge University Press.
Anderson, John M. & Charles Jones. 1974. Three theses concerning phonological representations. *Journal of Linguistics* 10. 1–26.
Backley, Phillip. 2011. *An introduction to Element Theory*. Edinburgh: Edinburgh University Press.
Backley, Phillip. 2012. Variation in Element Theory. *Linguistic Variation* 12(1). 57–102. DOI: https://doi.org/10.1075/lv.12.1.03bac
Backley, Phillip & Kuniya Nasukawa. 2009. Representing labials and velars: A single 'dark' element. *Phonological Studies* 12. 3–10.
Backley, Phillip & Kuniya Nasukawa. 2010. Consonant-vowel unity in Element Theory. *Phonological Studies* 13. 21–28.
Backley, Phillip & Kuniya Nasukawa. 2020. Recursion in melodic-prosodic structure. In Kuniya Nasukawa (ed.), *Morpheme-internal Recursion in Phonology*, 11–35. Boston & Berlin: Mouton de Gruyter.
Blevins, Juliette. 2008. Consonant epenthesis: Natural and unnatural histories. In Jeff Good (ed.), *Linguistic Universals and Language Change*, 79–107. Oxford: Oxford University Press.
Breit, Florian. 2017. Melodic heads, saliency, and strength in voicing and nasality. *Glossa: A journal of general linguistics* 2(1), 85. 1–35. DOI: 10.5334/gjgl.462
Charette, Monik. 1991. *Conditions on phonological government*. Cambridge: Cambridge University Press.
Cyran, Eugeniusz. 2010. *Complexity scales and licensing in phonology*. Berlin & New York: Mouton de Gruyter.
Harris, John. 1990. Segmental complexity and phonological government. *Phonology* 7. 255–300.
Harris, John. 1998. Licensing inheritance: An integrated theory of neutralisation. *Phonology* 14. 315–370.
Harris, John & Edmund Gussmann. 1998. Final codas: Why the West was wrong. In Eugenius Cyran (ed.), *Structure and interpretation: Studies in phonology*, 139–162. Lublin: Folium.
Harris, John & Geoff Lindsey. 1995. The elements of phonological representation. In Jacques Durand & Francis Katamba (eds.), *Frontiers of phonology: Atoms, structures, derivations*, 34–79. Harlow: Longman.

Hulst, Harry van der. 1995. Radical CV Phonology: The categorical gesture. In Jacques Durand & Francis Katamba (eds.), *Frontiers of phonology: Atoms, structures, derivations*, 80–116. Harlow: Longman.

Hulst, Harry van der. 2003. Dutch syllable structure meets Government Phonology. In Takeru Honma, Masao Okazaki, Toshiyuki Tabata & Shin-ichi Tanaka (eds.), *A new century of Phonology and phonological theory: A festschrift for Prof. Shosuke Haraguchi on the occasion of his sixtieth birthday*, 313–343. Tokyo, Japan: Kaitakusha.

Kaye, Jonathan D., Jean Lowenstamm & Jean-Roger Vergnaud. 1985. The internal structure of phonological elements: A theory of charm and government. *Phonology Yearbook* 2. 305–328.

Kaye, Jonathan D., Jean Lowenstamm & Jean-Roger Vergnaud. 1990. Constituent structure and government in phonology. *Phonology* 7. 193–231.

Kaye, Jonathan D. 2000. A users' guide to Government Phonology (GP). Unpublished Ms. [http://www.unice.fr/dsl/nis01/guideGP.pdf]

Lowenstamm, Jean. 1996. CV as the only syllable type. In Jacques Durand & Bernard Laks (eds.), *Current trends in phonology: Models and methods*, 419–441. Salford, Manchester: ESRI.

Nasukawa, Kuniya. 2014. Features and recursive structure. *Nordlyd* 41(1). 1–19.

Nasukawa, Kuniya. 2015. Recursion in the lexical structure of morphemes. In Marc van Oostendorp & Henk van Riemsdijk (eds.), *Representing structure in phonology and syntax*, 211–238. Berlin and Boston: Mouton de Gruyter.

Naukawa, Kuniya. 2016. A precedence-free approach to (de-)palatalisation in Japanese. *Glossa: A journal of general linguistics* 1(1). 1–21. DOI: http://dx.doi.org/10.5334/gjgl.26

Nasukawa, Kuniya. 2017a. Extending the application of Merge to elements in phonological representations. *Journal of the phonetic society of Japan* 21. 59–70.

Nasukawa, Kuniya. 2017b. The phonetic salience of phonological head-dependent structure in a modulated-carrier model of speech. In Bridget Samuels (ed.), *Beyond markedness in formal phonology*, 121–152. Amsterdam: John Benjamins.

Nasukawa, Kuniya & Phillip Backley. 2008. Affrication as a performance device. *Phonological studies* 11. 35–46.

Nasukawa, Kuniya & Phillip Backley. 2011. The internal structure of 'r' in Japanese. *Phonological studies* 14. 27–34.

Nasukawa, Kuniya & Phillip Backley. 2015. Heads and complements in phonology: A case of role reversal? *Phonological studies* 18. 67–74.

Nasukawa, Kuniya & Phillip Backley. 2017. Representing moraicity in Precedence-free Phonology. *Phonological studies* 20. 55–62.

Nasukawa, Kuniya & Phillip Backley. 2018. |H| and |L| have unequal status. *Phonological studies* 21. 41–48.

Nasukawa, Kuniya & Phillip Backley. 2019. Phonological evidence for segmental structure: Insights from vowel reduction. *Phonological studies* 22. 51–58.

Nasukawa, Kuniya, Phillip Backley, Yoshiho Yasugi & Masatoshi Koizumi. 2019. (Published online 21 November 2018.) Challenging universal typology: Right-edge consonantal prominence in Kaqchikel. *Journal of linguistics* 55(3), 611–641. https://doi.org/10.1017/S0022226718000488

Rosenthall, Samuel. 1994. *Vowel/glide alternation in a theory of constraint interaction*. PhD dissertation. University of Massachusetts at Amherst.

Schane, Sanford A. 1984. The fundamentals of particle phonology. *Phonology Yearbook* 1. 129–155.

Schane, Sanford A. 1995. Diphthongization in particle phonology. In John A. Goldsmith (ed.), *The handbook of phonological theory*, 586–608. Oxford: Blackwell.
Scheer, Tobias. 2004. A lateral theory of phonology. What is CVCV, and why should it be?. Berlin & New York: Mouton de Gruyter.
Živanović, Sašo & Markus A. Pöchtrager. 2010. GP2, and Putonghua too. *Acta linguistica Hungarica* 57(4). 357–380.

B. Elan Dresher
Contrastive hierarchies and phonological primes

Abstract: This paper presents an overview of the main ideas underlying Contrastive Hierarchy Theory (CHT) with a view to identifying important ways in which this theory is similar to and differs from Element Theory (ET). In CHT, contrastive features are computed hierarchically by the Successive Division Algorithm. Two central hypotheses are that only contrastive features can be phonologically active, and that feature hierarchies can vary both synchronically and diachronically. It is argued that CHT overcomes the empirical and conceptual problems faced by innate feature theories; at the same time, it provides an account of why features exist and how many features a language could have that is lacking in many emergent feature theories. I show that CHT and ET both take a middle course between phonetic determinism on one side and substance-free phonology on the other. In both theories, phonological primes are cognitive entities that form a bridge between the mental representations and operations of the phonological component and their external phonetic manifestations. Both theories include markedness as part of the formalism. It is further argued that contrastive hierarchies are not incompatible with ET and have already been implemented in this framework.

Keywords: Contrastive Hierarchy Theory; Element Theory; Successive Division Algorithm; Contrastivist Hypothesis; binary vs. unary features; markedness.

1 Introduction

Contrastive Hierarchy Theory (Dresher 2009, 2018; Hall 2007, 2011) builds on Jakobson's (1941) basic insight that the contrasts of a language are organized in a hierarchical order. Contrastive Hierarchy Theory assumes that phonological primes are binary features, and in this sense parts company with versions of Element Theory and related approaches. Nevertheless, there are a number of

---

Acknowledgements: I would like to thank Graziela Bohn for help with the Brazilian Portuguese analysis and examples, and Harry van der Hulst and William Idsardi for discussion of features. I am also grateful to two reviewers for insightful comments on an earlier draft.

B. Elan Dresher, University of Toronto

https://doi.org/10.1515/9783110691948-003

affinities between Contrastive Hierarchy Theory and Element Theory, and in this paper I will try to highlight what I think are some points in common, as well as some differences.

I will start in section 2 with a review of the main ideas that I take from Jakobson (1941), and briefly mention what became of these ideas in the 1950s and 1960s. In section 3, I set out the main tenets of Contrastive Hierarchy Theory, and in sections 4 and 5 I discuss the status of phonological primes (features in Contrastive Hierarchy Theory, elements in Element Theory) with respect to phonetics and substance-free phonology. I will show that Contrastive Hierarchy Theory and Element Theory have a similar approach to these issues, whether we take the primes to be features or elements. Section 6 focuses on three- and four-vowel systems, where there may or may not be an important difference between Contrastive Hierarchy Theory and Element Theory with respect to contrast. Then section 7 briefly surveys some five-vowel systems with the aim of showing that contrastive hierarchies must be allowed to vary from one language to another. Section 8 makes the same point with a diachronic example, showing how the five-vowel system of West Germanic reorganized its system of contrasts in early Old English. Section 9 considers the issue of binary features versus single-valued elements. Section 10 is a brief conclusion.

2 The acquisition of phonological contrasts

Jakobson (1941) (English translation 1968, French in 1969) advances the notion that contrasts are crucial in phonological acquisition and that they develop in a hierarchical order. In particular, he proposes that learners begin with broad contrasts that are split by stages into progressively finer ones. The acquisition of vowel systems set out in Jakobson (1941) and its sequel, Jakobson and Halle (1956), follows this schema, as shown in (1).

(1) Early stages of vowel acquisition (Jakobson 1941; Jakobson and Halle 1956)

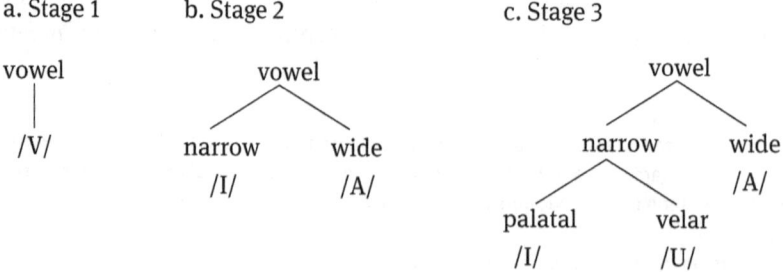

At the first stage (1a), there is only a single vowel. As there are no contrasts, we can simply designate it /V/. Jakobson and Halle write that this lone vowel is the maximally open vowel [a], the "optimal vowel". But we do not need to be that specific: we can understand this to be a default value, or a typical but not obligatory instantiation.

In the next stage (1b) it is proposed that the single vowel splits into a narrow (high) vowel /I/, which is typically [i], and a wide (low) vowel /A/, typically [a]. I will continue to understand these values as defaults; I use capital letters to represent vowels that fit the contrastive labels that characterize them.

In the next stage (1c) the narrow vowel splits into a palatal (front) vowel /I/ and a velar (back or round) vowel /U/, typically [u]. After these first stages, Jakobson and Halle allow variation in the order of acquisition of vowel contrasts. The wide branch can be expanded to parallel the narrow one. Or the narrow vowels can develop a rounding contrast in one or both branches. Continuing in this fashion we will arrive at a complete inventory of the phonemes in a language, with each phoneme assigned a set of contrastive properties that distinguish it from every other one.

I have been trying to reconstruct a history of "branching trees" in phonology (Dresher 2009, 2015, 2016, 2018). Early, though inexplicit, examples can be found in the work of Jakobson ([1931] 1962) and Trubetzkoy (1939) in the 1930s, continuing with Jakobson (1941) and Jakobson and Lotz (1949), then more explicitly in Jakobson, Fant, and Halle (1952), Cherry, Halle, and Jakobson (1953), Jakobson and Halle (1956), and Halle (1959). This approach was imported into early versions of the theory of Generative Phonology; it is featured prominently in the first Generative Phonology textbook by Robert T. Harms in (1968). Nevertheless, for reasons I have discussed (Dresher 2009: 96–104), branching trees were omitted from Chomsky and Halle's *The sound pattern of English* (*SPE*; 1968), and disappeared from mainstream phonological theory for the rest of the century.

In child language studies, however, branching trees continued to be used, for they are a natural way to describe developing phonological inventories (Pye, Ingram, and List 1987; Ingram 1988, 1989; Levelt 1989; Dinnsen et al. 1990; Dinnsen 1992, 1996; see Dresher 1998a for a review). Fikkert (1994) presents observed acquisition sequences in the development of Dutch onsets that follows this general scheme, and Bohn (2015) shows the routes that three children take in acquiring the vowel system of Brazilian Portuguese.

As a general theory of phonological representations, branching trees were revived by Clements, first in the form of an accessibility hierarchy (Clements 2001) and then as a robustness scale (Clements 2009), and independently at the University of Toronto, where they are called contrastive feature hierarchies (Dresher, Piggott, and Rice 1994; Dyck 1995; Zhang 1996; Dresher 1998b; Dresher and Rice

2007; Hall 2007; Dresher 2009; etc.). It is the latter approach I will be presenting here. It has gone under various names: Modified Contrastive Specification (MCS), or "Toronto School" phonology, or Contrast and Enhancement Theory, or Contrastive Hierarchy Theory, which is the name I use here. I do not claim there is any standard version of this theory; in what follows, I will present the theory as I understand it.

3 Contrastive Hierarchy Theory

Contrastive Hierarchy Theory has assumed that phonological primes are features; some Contrastive Hierarchy Theory analyses have used privative features, but I will stick to binary ones. The first major building block of our theory is that contrasts are computed hierarchically by ordered features that can be expressed as a branching tree. Branching trees are generated by what I call the Successive Division Algorithm (Dresher 1998b, 2003, 2009), given informally in (2):

(2) The Successive Division Algorithm
Assign contrastive features by successively dividing the inventory until every phoneme has been distinguished.

What are the criteria for selecting and ordering the features? Phonetics is clearly important, in that the selected features must be consistent with the phonetic properties of the phonemes. For example, a contrast between /i/ and /a/ would most likely involve a height feature like [low] or [high], though other choices are possible, e.g. [front] or [advanced/retracted tongue root]. Of course, the contrastive specification of a phoneme could sometimes deviate from the surface phonetics. For example, as discussed in section 6, in some Inuit dialects an underlying contrast between /i/ and /ə/ is neutralized at the surface, with both /i/ and /ə/ being realized as phonetic [i] (Compton and Dresher 2011). In this case, underlying /i/ and /ə/ would be distinguished by a contrastive feature, even though their surface phonetics are identical.

As this example shows, the way a sound patterns can override its phonetics (Sapir 1925). Thus, we consider as most fundamental that features should be selected and ordered so as to reflect the phonological activity in a language, where activity is defined as in (3), which is adapted from Clements (2001: 77):

(3) Phonological Activity
A feature can be said to be *active* if it plays a role in the phonological computation; that is, if it is required for the expression of phonological regularities in a language, including both static phonotactic patterns and patterns of alternation.

The second major tenet of Contrastive Hierarchy Theory has been formulated by Hall (2007) as the Contrastivist Hypothesis (4):

(4) The Contrastivist Hypothesis
The phonological component of a language L operates only on those features which are necessary to distinguish the phonemes of L from one another.

That is, only contrastive features can be phonologically active. If this hypothesis is correct, then (5) follows as a corollary:

(5) Corollary to the Contrastivist Hypothesis
If a feature is phonologically active, then it must be contrastive.

One final assumption is that the two values of a feature are not symmetrical: every feature has a *marked* and *unmarked* value. I assume that markedness is language particular (Rice 2003, 2007), and is acquired based on phonological patterning. I will designate the marked value of a feature F as [F], and the unmarked value as (non-F). I will refer to the two values together as [±F].

To see how the contrastive hierarchy works, consider a language with three vowel phonemes /i, a, u/. If the vowels are split off from the rest of the inventory so that they form a sub-inventory, then they must be assigned a contrastive hierarchy with two vowel features. Though the features and their ordering vary, the limit of two features constrains what the hierarchies can be. Two possible contrastive hierarchies using the features [back] and [low] are given in (6), and two more hierarchies, using [high] and [round], are shown in (7).

(6) Three-vowel systems with the features [back] and [low]
   a. [back] > [low]   b. [low] > [back]

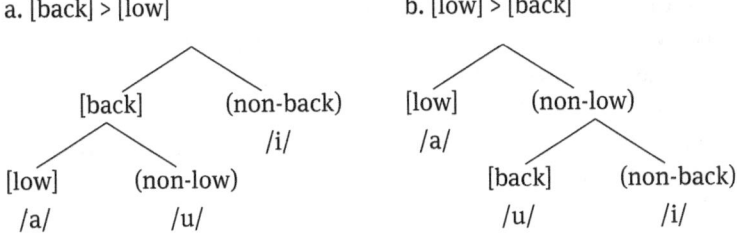

(7) Three-vowel systems with the features [high] and [round]
   a. [high] > [round]   b. [round] > [high]

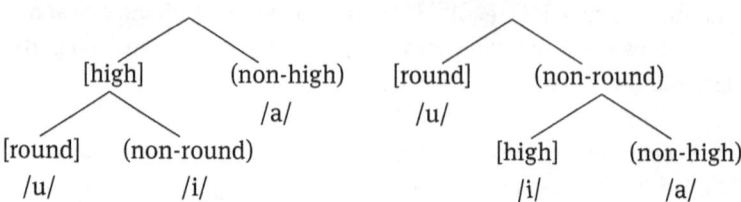

Synchronically, the hierarchy constrains phonological activity, since only contrastive features can be phonologically active. Thus, in (6a) both /a/ and /u/ can potentially trigger backing, since both are contrastively [back]; in (6b), only /u/ is contrastively [back], so we expect that /a/ would not cause backing in the phonology. Similarly, in (7a) we expect that both /i/ and /u/ would be able to cause raising, as they are both [high]; but in (7b), only /i/ is contrastively [high], and is the only potential trigger of a raising rule.

Diachronically, the hierarchy constrains neutralization and merger, as proposed by Ko (2010, 2012) and Oxford (2015):

(8) Diachronic phonological merger in Contrastive Hierarchy Theory
   a. The Minimal Contrast Principle (Ko 2010: 191; 2012: 35–37)
      Phonological merger operates on a minimal contrast – that is, on two segments that share a terminal branching node under a given contrastive hierarchy.
   b. The Sisterhood Merger Hypothesis (Oxford 2015: 314)
      Structural mergers apply to "contrastive sisters".

Given the hypothesis in (8), we expect that /u/ might merge with /a/ in (6a), with /i/ in (6b) and (7a), but that /i/ and /a/ could merge to the exclusion of /u/ in (7b); see Oxford (2015) for examples of merger patterns just like these in the history of the Algonquian languages. Typological generalizations can thus not be found by looking at inventories alone (say, /i, a, u/), or at individual phonemes (/a/), or phones ([a]), without also considering the relevant contrastive feature hierarchy.

Unless a phoneme is further specified by other contrastive features (originating in other phonemes), it is made more specific only in a post-phonological component. Stevens, Keyser, and Kawasaki (1986) propose that feature contrasts can be *enhanced* by other features with similar acoustic effects (see also Stevens and Keyser 1989; Keyser and Stevens 2001, 2006). Hall (2011) shows how the enhancement of contrastive features can result in configurations predicted by

Dispersion Theory (Liljencrants and Lindblom 1972; Lindblom 1986; Flemming 2002). Thus, a vowel that is contrastively [back] and (non-low) can enhance these features by adding {round} and {high}, respectively, becoming [u] – enhancement features are indicated by curly brackets {}. These enhancements are not universal, however, and other realizations are possible (Dyck 1995; Hall 2011).

4 Why are the primes as they are (whatever they are)?

In a volume titled *Where do phonological features come from?* (Clements and Ridouane 2011), most of the papers take the position that phonological features are not innate, but rather "emerge" in the course of acquisition. Mielke (2008) and Samuels (2011) summarize the arguments against innate features:
(a) from a biolinguistic perspective, phonological features are too specific, and exclude sign languages (van der Hulst 1993; Sandler 1993);
(b) empirically, no one set of features have been discovered that "do all tricks" (Hyman 2011 with respect to tone features, but the remark applies more generally);
(c) since at least some features have to be acquired from phonological activity, a prespecified list of features becomes less useful in learning.

But if features are not innate, what compels them to emerge at all? It is not enough to assert that features *may* emerge, or that they are a useful way to capture phonological generalizations. We need to explain why features inevitably emerge, and why they have the properties that they do. In particular, why don't learners, or some learners, simply posit segment-level representations? What controls the number of features – how broad or narrow are they? How many features should learners posit for three vowels, for example? Are there limits?

The contrastive feature hierarchy provides an answer to these questions: learners must arrive at a set of hierarchically ordered contrastive features. Thus, an inventory of three phonemes allows exactly two contrastive features. Two variants are shown in (9), differing in how marked features are distributed. A four-phoneme inventory can have a minimum of two features and a maximum of three, as in (10).

(9) Three-phoneme systems: F1 > F2
   a. Marked value of F1 expands   b. Unmarked value of F1 expands

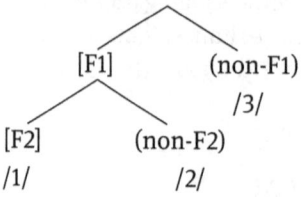 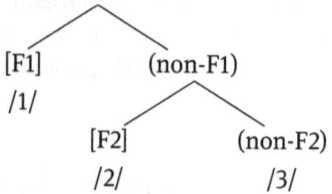

(10) Four-phoneme systems
   a. Minimum number of features: 2   b. Maximum number of features: 3

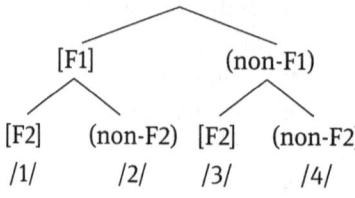 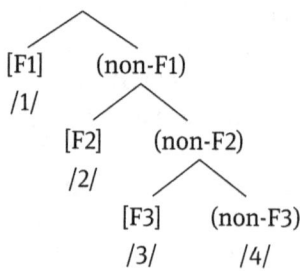

In general, the number of binary features required by an inventory of *n* elements falls in the following ranges: the minimum number of features is equal to the smallest integer greater than or equal to $\log_2 n$, and the maximum number of features is equal to *n*–1. As can be seen in (11), the minimum number of features goes up very slowly as phonemes are added; the upper limit rises with *n*. However, inventories that approach the upper limit are extremely uneconomical. At the max limit, each new segment uses a unique contrastive feature unshared by any other phoneme. It has been proposed that phonological inventories prefer to reuse the same features, producing a tendency toward feature economy (de Groot 1931; Martinet 1955; Ohala 1980; Clements 2003; Lindblom et al. 2011; see Hall 2011 and Mackie and Mielke 2011 for discussion, and Cherry, Halle, and Jakobson 1953 for economy in the context of branching trees).[1]

---

[1] A reviewer writes that, even if we assume feature economy, there are far fewer primes in Element Theory (about six). This indeed is an issue worth studying further; the low number of elements, if it can be sustained empirically, might point to the need to further constrain possible feature systems. For a suggestion, please see the following note.

(11) Number of contrastive features by inventory size

Phonemes	$\log_2 n$	min	max	Phonemes	$\log_2 n$	min	max
3	1.58	2	2	10	3.32	4	9
4	2	2	3	12	3.58	4	11
5	2.32	3	4	16	4	4	15
6	2.58	3	5	20	4.32	5	19
7	2.81	3	6	25	4.64	5	24
8	3	3	7	32	5	5	31

Thus, the contrastive hierarchy and the Contrastivist Hypothesis go a long way toward accounting for why phonological systems resemble each other in terms of representations, without requiring individual features to be innate. For the content of features, learners make use of the available materials relevant to the modality: for spoken language, acoustic and articulatory properties of speech sounds; for sign language, hand shapes and facial expressions. On this view, the concept of a contrastive hierarchy is an innate part of Universal Grammar (UG), and is the glue that binds phonological representations and makes them appear similar from language to language (Dresher 2014a).

It is important to emphasize that, though phonological features may make use of innate auditory dispositions, they are not the same as those, but are cognitive entities created by learners.[2] Thus, the contrasts indicated by features like [back] and [low] may be crosslinguistically common because we have neurons sensitive to formant transitions. So, it appears, do ferrets (Mesgarani et al. 2008). But ferrets do not necessarily have our kind of phonological representations.

5 Form and substance in phonology

I believe that Contrastive Hierarchy Theory and Element Theory are in agreement that phonological primes (features for Contrastive Hierarchy Theory, elements for Element Theory) are cognitive entities that are not determined by phonetics, in contrast to phonetically-based approaches to phonology (Steriade 2001; Flemming

---

[2] There may be constraints on what sort of cognitive features can be created from these auditory dispositions; for example, we do not find "picket fence" features that divide up the acoustic space in discontinuous ways (Heffner, Idsardi, and Newman 2019). Constraints on what a feature can be (perhaps along the lines of the "dimensions" posited by Avery & Idsardi 2001) could bring the set of possible features closer to that of the elements of Element Theory.

2002; Hayes, Kirchner, and Steriade 2004). On the other side, both Contrastive Hierarchy Theory and Element Theory are not as radical as various "substance-free" theories in separating phonological representations from phonetics (Hale and Reiss 2000, 2008; Odden 2006; Blaho 2008; Mielke 2008; Samuels 2011; Reiss 2017). Hall (2014) comments that substance-free theories, whose approach he traces back to Fudge (1967), are actually similar to substance-based theories in relegating the explanation for many aspects of phonology to phonetic factors and diachronic change.

Advocates of substance-free phonology argue that phonology is concerned only with formal notions and not with phonetic substance. However, the line between form and substance is not as clear cut as advocates of substance-free phonology make it out to be. Take markedness, for example. Reiss (2017: 429) writes, "The way forward, in the twenty-first century, is to abandon markedness". He assumes that markedness is not formal, but is part of substance. There are different notions of what markedness is, and some of them might fall under "substance"; but this is not the case for the version assumed in Contrastive Hierarchy Theory.

I have proposed (Dresher 2014a) that the learners' task is to arrive at a set of primes that account for the contrasts and phonological activity of their language. I have assumed that the primes are binary features, but much the same holds if we assume that they are privative features or elements. These primes are not arbitrary diacritics or numbers but have phonetic correlates. I also assume that features are asymmetrical in having a marked and unmarked value. These values, like the features themselves, are acquired by learners based on the evidence of their language. Since markedness, on this view, is inherent in the definition of a feature, I consider it to be a part of the formal side of phonology.

The same holds even more obviously of phonological theories influenced by Kaye, Lowenstamm, and Vergnaud (1985) (KLV). According to Jean-Roger Vergnaud (p. c.), one of the motivations for developing the KLV theory was to incorporate the *SPE* markedness theory directly into representations. For example, in Backley's (2011) *An introduction to Element Theory*, the vowels in a five-vowel system like the one in (12) differ in the complexity of their representations. Reflecting the *SPE* markedness theory (Chomsky and Halle 1968: 409), [e] and [o] have more complex representations than [i, a, u].

(12) Five-vowel system (Backley 2011)

[i]	[e]	[a]	[o]	[u]
|I|	|I A|	|A|	|U A|	|U|

In GP 2.0 (Pöchtrager 2006, 2016; Živanović and Pöchtrager 2010; Kaye and Pöchtrager 2013; Voeltzel 2016) markedness is expressed structurally. The vowel [i] has a relatively simple representation (13a); [e] is essentially an [i] with an additional layer of structure (13b); and [ɛ] is an [e] with a further layer of structure (13c). These structures are formal phonological representations, so are not merely "substance", though they relate to phonetic substance.

Voeltzel (2016) summarizes Pöchtrager's (2016) account of vowel reduction in Brazilian Portuguese employing the representations in (13). In this account, the stressed position of a word has "room" for all three vowels. In the position before the stressed vowel there is no room for the most complex vowel, [ɛ], which reduces to [e]. The most reduction occurs in final unstressed position, where all three front vowels appear as [i].[3] It is an empirical question whether this theory is correct, but I see no grounds for considering it to be a case of "substance abuse".

(13) Vowel representations in GP2.0

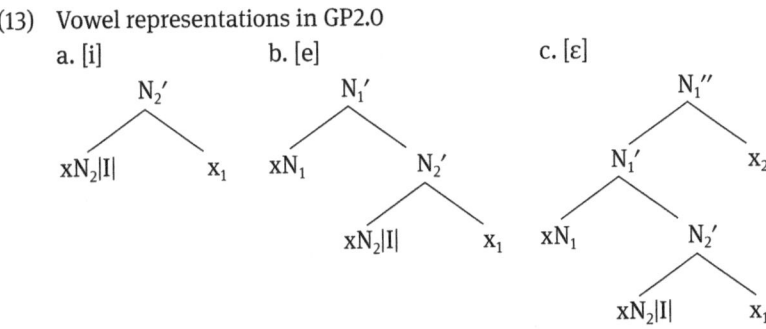

My reservations about this analysis concern variability and the phonetic interpretation of these representations. As mentioned above, I follow Rice (2003, 2007) in assuming that markedness is language particular. Thus, it does not appear to be the case that /e/ is always more marked than /i/ and that /ɛ/ is always more marked than /e/. Indeed, Nevins (2012) writes that Brazilian Portuguese dialects themselves differ with respect to whether [e] or [ɛ] is the result of neutralization. This is not an argument against a structural approach to markedness, but rather an argument that a given structure may have different phonetic interpretations in different systems. Nevins (2012) considers flexibility of interpretation to be a desirable property of Element Theory, in that it allows either /ɛ/ or /e/ to be

---

3 As we shall see in (14), the three front vowels are realized not as [i] but as [ɪ] in final position; thus, it is not obvious that this [ɪ] should be assigned the same representation as stressed [i].

assigned the more marked structure, as the evidence requires.[4] I would argue that the same holds of the relationship between other vowels, such as /i/ and /e/ or /i/ and /u/.

A second caveat is that this analysis equates the phonetic realizations of vowels in unstressed position with certain vowels in stressed position. For example, the above analysis suggests that final unstressed [i] in Brazilian Portuguese, which is the only front vowel in that position, is the same as stressed [i], which contrasts with two other front vowels. One might be able to argue that this is the case in some languages, but in many languages it is clear that the reduced vowels cannot be phonetically equated with particular stressed vowels. That is, neutralization is not always to the unmarked stressed vowel, but may be to a vowel that has a different representation from both the marked and unmarked stressed vowels (Trubetzkoy 1939: 71–72).

This actually appears to be the case in Brazilian Portuguese. According to Barbosa and Albano (2004), a São Paulo speaker had the seven stressed non-nasalized vowels shown in (14). They write (2004: 229) that in pre-stressed position, "the quality of the corresponding stressed vowel is roughly preserved". But this is not the case for unstressed vowels in final position.

(14) Vowels of Brazilian Portuguese, Paulista dialect (Barbosa and Albano 2004)

Stressed position	i	e	ɛ	a	ɔ	o	u
Before the stress	i		e	a		o	u
Final unstressed		ɪ		ɐ		ʊ	

Spahr (2012) proposes a contrastive hierarchy account of Brazilian Portuguese vowel reduction; I have modified his hierarchy to that proposed by Bohn (2015, 2017) for the Paulista dialect. The tree in (15) shows the seven oral vowels in stressed position. The hierarchy is [back] > [low] > [high] > [RTR].[5] Bohn (2015, 2017) motivates this ordering based on the patterns of activity in this dialect (see also Bohn and Santos 2018).

---

[4] Specifically, he proposes that in "Southeastern" dialects the lax-mid vowels [ɛ, ɔ] are represented as headed |I,A|, |U,A| (marked, in our terms) and the tense-mid vowels [e, o] are unheaded (unmarked); in "Northeastern" dialects [e, o] are headed |I,A|, |U,A| and [ɛ, ɔ] are unheaded.
[5] I have changed Bohn's (2015, 2017) [ATR] to [RTR] to reflect the markedness in this dialect.

(15) Paulista Brazilian Portuguese stressed vowels (Bohn 2015, 2017)

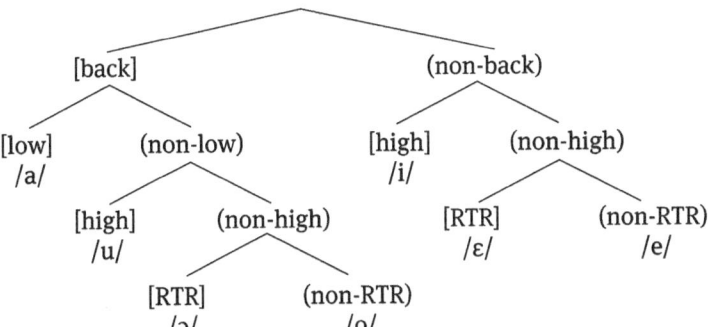

In pre-stress position (16), there are no [±RTR] contrasts under the (non-high) nodes numbered 3. Spahr proposes that these nodes are interpreted as archiphonemes à la Trubetzkoy. The new representations [back], (non-low, non-high) and (non-back, non-high) receive their own phonetic interpretations: in this case [o] and [e], but in other dialects [ɔ] and [ɛ].⁶

(16) Brazilian Portuguese vowels in pre-stress position (based on Spahr 2012)

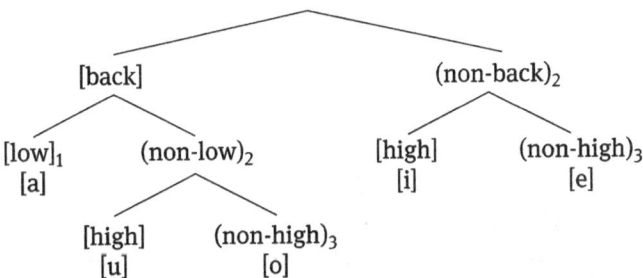

In unstressed final position (17), the contrasts under the nodes numbered 2 are suppressed, and the segments under these nodes receive distinct phonetic interpretations as [ʊ] and [ɪ]. In this new set of contrasts the segment under node 1 also receives a distinct phonetic interpretation, [ɐ].⁷

---

6 In this case it would also be possible to propose that neutralization is to the unmarked member of the /e/ ~ /ɛ/ and /o/ ~ /ɔ/ contrasts. Such an analysis is not possible, however, for unstressed final position.
7 The reduced hierarchies in (16) and (17) are derived by neutralization from underlying segments that are specified with all the features assigned to them by the full contrastive hierarchy in (15); for example, underlying /ɛ/, /ɔ/ appear as [e], [o], respectively, when unstressed, as in [bέlʊ] 'beautiful' ~ [beléze] 'beauty' and [mɔ́rtʃɪ] 'death' ~ [mortáw] 'deadly'. That is, there is a

(17) Brazilian Portuguese vowels in unstressed final position (based on Spahr 2012)

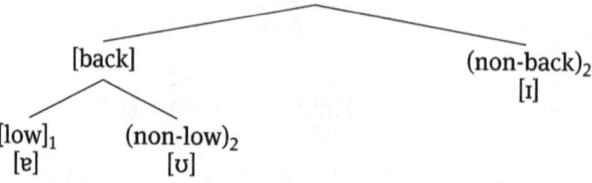

```
        [back]                    (non-back)₂
                                     [ɪ]
   [low]₁    (non-low)₂
    [ɐ]       [ʊ]
```

Like in GP 2.0, this analysis uses representational complexity, though in a different way. In both GP 2.0 and Contrastive Hierarchy Theory, this complexity is part of the formal representational apparatus, though it relates to aspects of phonetic substance. Neither analysis involves "substance abuse". The consequences of remaining completely free of substance in cases like these is that substance-free phonology also frees itself from providing a descriptively adequate account of vowel reduction patterns. Contrary to Reiss (2017), the way forward in the twenty-first century is not to abandon markedness and contrast on *a priori* grounds, but to incorporate them to the extent that they contribute to illuminating accounts of phonological patterns.

6 Contrast and Element Theory: Three- and four-vowel systems

At the Paris Conference on Theoretical Issues in Contemporary Phonology: Reading Tobias Scheer, I attempted (Dresher 2014b) to answer the challenge posed by Scheer (2010), that the contrastive hierarchy "is irrelevant should it turn out that unary primes are the correct approach to melodic representations." I argued there that contrastive hierarchies are relevant to representations made up of unary primes, as instantiated, for example, in Element Theory. Further, I proposed that Element Theory itself inherently relies on contrastive considerations – and hence,

---

single underlying system of hierarchical contrasts. This case should be distinguished from the reduced inventories that can be found in morphologically defined contexts, as in the case of many Romance languages where inflectional suffixes (desinences) use a reduced inventory of vowels as compared with roots. Dyck (1995) and Frigeni (2002) have proposed analyses of such cases that involve separate contrastive hierarchies for the desinential domain. There, different hierarchies are posited underlyingly, not just at the surface.

on contrastive hierarchies – to a greater extent than is often recognized. In this section I review some of those arguments.

With respect to the relevance of contrastive hierarchies, there have been a number of proposals to apply them to unary elements, so this is not a hypothetical possibility. One such is Carvalho (2011). As he points out, "the fundamental idea" of Contrastive Hierarchy Theory is that "infrasegmental structure [. . .] reflects the way features combine and behave in a given language", uniting both representation and computation. Voeltzel and Tifrit (2013) and Voeltzel (2016) apply the hierarchical concept to representations of Scandinavian languages based on Element Theory. Voeltzel (2016) shows that an element-based hierarchy will not necessarily be a simple translation of a feature-based one; nevertheless, I would argue that it should follow the same basic principles of contrast and hierarchy. Van der Hulst (2018) has an extensive discussion illustrating how the Successive Division Algorithm can be applied to the elements of Radical CV Phonology (van der Hulst 1995, 1996, 2005, 2020).

While different versions of Element Theory may have different approaches to the role of contrast, I have proposed that most unary representational systems are based on contrast. I say this even if it may not be stated explicitly, and even if contrastive considerations are not always applied consistently. Consider the analysis of three-vowel systems by Backley (2011: 19). He observes that the vowels of both Tamazight (Berber, Northern Africa) in (18a) and Amuesha (Arawakan, Peru) in (18b) have the representations |I|, |U|, and |A|, despite their phonetic differences.

(18) Three-vowel systems (Backley 2011)
     a. Tamazight   b. Amuesha
     [i]   [u]   [a]   [e]   [o]   [ɐ]
     |I| |U| |A| |I| |U| |A|

Why are Amuesha [e] and [o] not represented as combinations of |I A| and |U A|, respectively, like [e] and [o] in the five-vowel systems shown in (12) above? Presumably, it is because they are not in contrast with other vowels that are represented |I| and |U|, and further, because they do not behave as if they have complex representations. As Backley (2011: 19) remarks, "the vowels [. . .] are tokens of abstract phonological categories, and languages differ in the way they choose to phonetically interpret these categories." That is, it is phonological behaviour and contrast that govern the representations, in addition to phonetics.

In the case of Wapishana (Arawakan, Guyana and Brazil) in (19a), Backley (2011: 31) proposes that [ə] is an unspecified vowel. One reason is that its spectral pattern is different from the patterns typically associated with the basic elements |I|, |U|, and |A|. Again, though, phonetics is not the whole story. For English weak vowels, for example, Backley (2011: 50) proposes the assignments in (19b). Here, [ə] is assigned the element |A|, unlike in Wapishana, and another vowel, [ɨ], is the empty vowel. Which vowels are empty depends on how they behave. Notice also that the Wapishana and English vowel representations are minimally contrastive.

(19) Four-vowel systems (Backley 2011)
    a. Wapishana   b. English weak vowels
    [i]   [u]   [a]   [ə]   [ɪ]   [ʊ]   [ə]   [ɨ]
    |I| |U| |A| | | |I| |U| |A| | |

In fact, the Wapishana vowel inventory is very similar to that of Proto-Eskimo, the ancestor of the Inuit-Yupik languages. Proto-Eskimo is commonly reconstructed to have the vowels */i/, */u/, */a/, and a fourth vowel assumed to be some sort of central vowel which I write schwa */ə/, following Fortescue, Jacobson, and Kaplan (1994). Compton and Dresher (2011) propose that the Inuit-Yupik contrastive hierarchy is [low] > [labial] > [coronal], as shown in (20a).

(20) a. Inuit-Yupik contrastive hierarchy: four-vowel inventory (Compton and Dresher 2011)

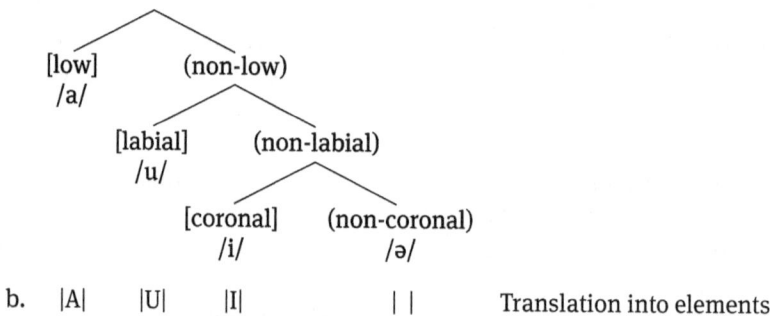

    b. |A| |U| |I| | | Translation into elements

These asymmetric features are not far from a unary system. Indeed, they can easily be translated into elements as shown in (20b): [low] becomes |A|, [labial] becomes |U|, [coronal] becomes |I|, and the unmarked /ə/ becomes the empty element. In fact, exactly this tree and this ordering of elements is proposed for a four-vowel system by van der Hulst (2018).

    Evidence for this type of representation for /ə/ comes from Yupik, which retains the four-vowel system. Though present in the inventory, schwa does not have the same status as the other vowels. According to Kaplan (1990: 147), it "cannot occur long or in a cluster with another vowel"; instead, it undergoes dissimilation or assimilation when adjacent to full vowels. In other dialects underlying /ə/ has merged with /i/ at the surface, but can be distinguished from underlying /i/ by its distinct patterning. In the literature this vowel is known as "weak *i*", as opposed to the "strong *i*" that descends from Proto-Eskimo (P-E) *i. In Barrow Inupiaq (Kaplan 1981: 119), weak *i* changes to [a] before another vowel, but strong *i* does not.

Original */i/ could cause palatalization of consonants, and some Inuit dialects show palatalization (or traces of former palatalization) (Dorais 2003: 33). In the word 'foot' in the North Baffin dialect (21a), *i* (from P-E *i) causes a following *t* to change to *s*. This assibilation is the most common manifestation of palatalization in Inuit dialects. Compare the retention of [t] after weak *i* (from P-E *ə) in 'palm of hand' (21b).

(21) Strong and weak *i* in North Baffin (Dorais 2003)

		Proto-Eskimo		North Baffin	
a.	Strong *i*	*itəyaʁ	>	isiɣak	'foot'
b.	Weak *i*	*ətəmaɣ	>	itimak	'palm of hand'

These examples support attributing a feature to /i/ that can cause palatalization: Compton and Dresher (2011) call it [coronal]. It is very similar to the role played by |I| in Element Theory. Compton and Dresher (2011) argue that there is evidence that the features [low] and [labial] are also phonologically active (participate in phonological processes).

For four-vowel dialects like the ones discussed above, then, Contrastive Hierarchy Theory and Element Theory are mostly in accord: each of /i/, /u/, and /a/ are represented by a single marked feature, and /ə/ is empty (in Element Theory) or completely unmarked (in Contrastive Hierarchy Theory). Now let us turn to three-vowel Inuit dialects.

In many Inuit dialects the distinction between */i/ and */ə/ has been completely lost: these dialects have only three distinct vowels: /i/, /a/, and /u/. Dialects with palatalization or with signs of former palatalization occur across the Inuit region, as do dialects without palatalization. One might suppose that some dialects that once had palatalization would generalize it to occur after all /i/s, including original /i/ from *i and the new /i/ from *ə. But this is not the case. Compton and Dresher (2011) observe a generalization about palatalization in Inuit dialects (22):

(22) Palatalization in Inuit dialects (Compton and Dresher 2011)
Inuit /i/ can cause palatalization (assibilation) of a consonant only in dialects where there is evidence for a (former) contrast with a fourth vowel; where there is no contrast between strong and weak *i*, /i/ does not trigger palatalization.

This generalization follows from the assumption that the feature hierarchy for Inuit and Yupik is [low] > [labial] > [coronal] as in (20). When the fourth vowel is in the underlying inventory, /i/ has a contrastive [coronal] feature that enables it to cause palatalization; but in the absence of a fourth vowel, [coronal] is not a contrastive feature, as shown in (23). By the Contrastivist Hypothesis, if a feature is not contrastive, it may not be active. Therefore, the restriction of a three-vowel inventory to two features, required by the Contrastivist Hypothesis and the Successive Division Algorithm, is supported by evidence from phonological patterning.

(23) Inuit-Yupik contrastive hierarchy: three-vowel inventory (Compton and Dresher 2011)

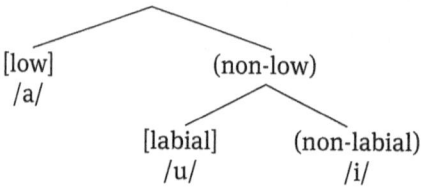

The result of our analysis is that the representation of an /i/ in a three-vowel dialect has no marked features; in this sense, it is closer to the representation of /ə/ in a four-vowel dialect than it is to that of /i/ in a four-vowel dialect, as we can see in (24), and even more noticeably when we list only the marked features, as in (25).[8]

(24) Inuit-Yupik vowel systems
a. Four-vowel inventories
[a]   [u]   [i]   [ə]
[low] ⎡non-low⎤ ⎡non-low ⎤ ⎡non-low   ⎤
       ⎣ labial ⎦ ⎢non-labial⎥ ⎢non-labial ⎥
                  ⎣ coronal ⎦ ⎣non-coronal⎦

b. Three-vowel inventories
[a]   [u]   [i]
[low] ⎡non-low⎤ ⎡non-low ⎤
       ⎣ labial ⎦ ⎣non-labial⎦

(25) Inuit-Yupik vowel systems (marked features only)
a. Four-vowel inventories
[a]   [u]   [i]   [ə]
[low] [labial] [coronal]   [ ]

b. Three-vowel inventories
[a]   [u]   [i]
[low] [labial]   [ ]

---

8 Just to be clear, I assume that unmarked features appear in the representations and are visible to the phonology; I do not assume that features are privative. The point of listing only the marked features in (25) is to show more vividly the way in which [i] in a three-vowel system (25b) is like [ə] in a four-vowel system (25a).

In this light, let us return to Backley's (2011) analysis of three-vowel inventories in (18). He employs three elements, meaning that his analysis is not in accord with the Successive Division Algorithm and the Contrastivist Hypothesis. The prediction of the Successive Division Algorithm, as shown in detail for Element Theory by van der Hulst (2018), is that one vowel in every inventory should be empty. This prediction is supported in three-vowel Inuit dialects. We similarly expect one vowel in Tamazight and Amuesha (not necessarily the same one) to be empty; which one it is needs to be determined by investigating which elements are actually active in these languages.

Backley's analysis of three-vowel inventories does not comport with his practice in systems with four vowels, as in (19). It is also not consistent with his own statement (Backley 2011: 20) that "What counts in E[lement] T[heory] is the way a segment behaves, particularly in relation to natural classes and to other segments in the system. Its behaviour determines its phonological identity, and therefore, its element structure."[9]

7 Variability in contrastive hierarchies: Five-vowel systems

N. S. Trubetzkoy's *Grundzüge der Phonologie* (1939) (translated into French in 1949, into English in 1969, and into Spanish in a new edition in 2019) in some ways anticipated the theory of contrast I have been arguing for here. Trubetzkoy observes that in many five-vowel systems – he gives Latin as an example – the low vowel does not participate in tonality contrasts; "tonality" refers to backness or lip rounding, that is, properties that affect the second formant (F2). In the diagram in (26a), the low vowel /a/ is separated from the other vowels; in terms of contemporary distinctive features, we could say that the line draws the boundary of the feature [±low].

---

9 See also Cyran (2011), who proposes that two dialects of Polish have different phonological laryngeal systems despite having almost identical phonetic realizations. He argues that in Warsaw Polish voiced obstruents have an L-element and voiceless obstruents are unmarked; in Cracow Polish voiceless obstruents have an H-element and voiced obstruents are unmarked (and passively voiced). According to Cyran (2011: 77), "spectrograms are not telling us what type of system we are dealing with. They only provide the information on the phonetic side of the equation." The crucial evidence bearing on the phonological system comes, in our terms, from phonological activity – in this case, the sandhi phenomena in Polish – which show that Cracow Polish is an H-system and Warsaw Polish is an L-system.

(26) Five-vowel systems with different contrastive structures (based on Trubetzkoy 1939)
   a. Latin   b. Archi   c. Japanese

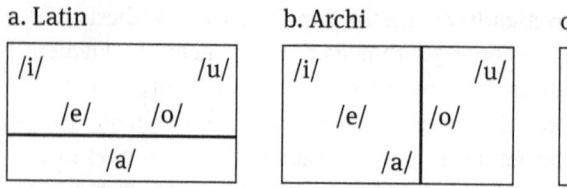

Trubetzkoy observes that other types of five-vowel systems exist. In Archi (East Caucasian), a language of Central Daghestan, a consonantal rounding contrast is neutralized before and after the rounded vowels /u/ and /o/. "As a result, these vowels are placed in opposition with [. . .] unrounded *a, e,* and *i*. This means that all vowels are divided into rounded and unrounded vowels, while the back or front position of the tongue proves irrelevant" (Trubetzkoy 1969: 100–101). In (26b), the dividing line represents the boundary of [±round].

Trubetzkoy argues that neutralization of the opposition between palatalized and non-palatalized consonants before *i* and *e* in Japanese shows that these vowels are put into opposition with the other vowels /a, o, u/ (26c). The governing opposition is that between front and back vowels, "lip rounding being irrelevant" (Trubetzkoy 1969: 101).

Trubetzkoy's discussion of these vowel systems amounts to giving priority to a different contrast in each system: in terms of binary features, to [±low] in Latin, to [±round] in Archi, and to [±front] in Japanese. In other words, these features stand at the top of their respective hierarchies, which can be represented as the partial branching trees in (27). Trubetzkoy does not tell us the details of the other contrasts in each system; what the other two (or, more unusually, three) features are depends on the evidence from each language.

(27) Partial contrastive hierarchies for the vowel systems in (26)
   a. Latin   b. Archi   c. Japanese

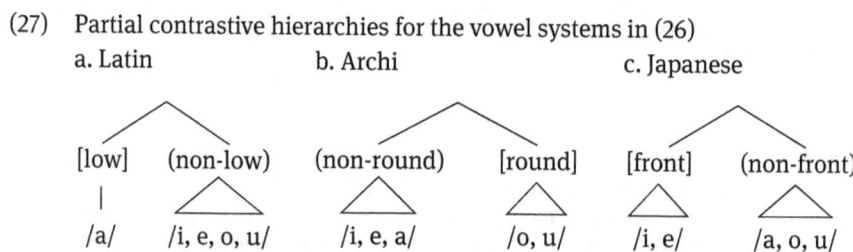

Finally, Trubetzkoy considers systems with five vowels plus a central "indeterminate vowel", often written as /ə/. He writes that in the usual case, this vowel "does not stand in a bilateral opposition relation with any other phoneme of the vowel system", but is "characterized only negatively". If we follow the Latin pattern, /a/ is the only [low] vowel, and /i, e, o, u/ are distinguished by tonality contrasts; in terms of binary features, these are typically [±high], [±front], and one of [±back] or [±round]. /ə/ is thus (non-low, non-high, non-front, non-back/non-round), that is, "characterized only negatively". We can diagram these contrasts as in (28a).

However, Trubetzkoy observes that in Bulgarian, the pairs /i, e/, /ə, a/, and /u, o/ neutralize in unstressed syllables. This suggests that the central vowel has a special relationship with /a/, as shown schematically in (28b), where pairs of vowels that neutralize are separated by a dashed line; see Spahr (2014) for a Contrastive Hierarchy Theory analysis of this system. I conclude that vowel systems show considerable variability in their contrastive feature hierarchies, as shown by their patterns of phonological activity.

(28) Systems with five-vowels plus one (based on Trubetzkoy 1939)
  a. Common pattern   b. Bulgarian

/i/			/u/
	/e/	/ə/	/o/
	/a/		

/i/			/u/
	/e/	/ə/	/o/
	/a/		

In the next section we will see how gradual phonetic changes can eventually trigger a change in the contrastive hierarchy of a five-vowel system.

8 Contrastive hierarchies in diachronic phonology: Old English *i*-umlaut

The rule of *i*-umlaut began in early Germanic as a phonetic process that created fronted allophones of the back vowels when */i(ː)/ or */j/ followed (V. Kiparsky 1932; Twaddell 1938; Benediktsson 1967; Antonsen 1972; Penzl 1972). In the examples in (29), */u/ is fronted to [y] and /oː/ is fronted to [øː]:

(29) Examples of *i*-umlaut
  Gloss   'evil N.S.'   'foot N.P.'
  Early Germanic   *ubil   *foːt+i
  i-umlaut   *ybil   *føːt+i

At a certain time, the West Germanic vowel system had five short and five long vowels (Antonsen 1965; Ringe and Taylor 2014: 106). I will henceforth disregard the latter (see Dresher 2018 for discussion of the long vowels). Inspired by the analysis of Purnell and Raimy (2015), I have argued (Dresher 2018) that at this stage West Germanic had the vowel feature hierarchy [low] > [front] > [high], as in (30). The evidence for these specifications, following Antonsen (1972), is that */a/ could cause lowering of */i/ and */u/,[10] and */i/ ~ */e/ and */u/ ~ */o/ were distinguished by a single feature, [high]. Following Lass (1994), Ringe (2006: 148), and Purnell & Raimy (2015), I assume that the feature that distinguishes */i, e/ from */u/ is [front], because /i/ could cause fronting of back vowels.

(30) West Germanic feature hierarchy (Dresher 2018): [low] > [front] > [high]

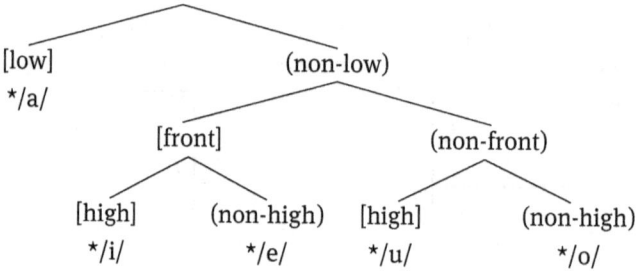

Given our analysis of the West Germanic vowel system, the result of fronting */u, o/ in the contrastive phonology would be to change their (non-front) feature to [front]; this would simply make them identical to */i, e/. But *i*-umlaut crucially preserves the rounded nature of the fronted vowels. It is clear from (30) that the feature [round] is not contrastive at this stage. Therefore, the enhancement feature {round} must be in play at the point that */u, o/ are fronted, so that they become not merely [non-low, front], but also remain {round}, as shown in (31).

(31) *i*-umlaut must involve the enhancement feature {round}

*u	b	i	l	→	*y	b	i	l
(non-low)	(non-low)				(non-low)	(non-low)		
(non-front)	[front]				[front]	[front]		
[high]	[high]				[high]	[high]		
{round}	{non-round}				{round}	{non-round}		

---

10 The phoneme */o/ derives from a lowered allophone of Proto-Germanic */u/ (Twaddell 1948; Antonsen 1972).

This analysis is consistent with the assumption of many commentators, beginning with V. Kiparsky (1932) and Twaddell (1938), that *i*-umlaut began as a late phonetic rule and was not part of the contrastive (lexical) phonology. There is evidence, however, that *i*-umlaut became a lexical rule even while it was still creating fronted allophones of the vowels */u/ and */o/ (Liberman 1991; Fertig 1996; Janda 2003; see P. Kiparsky 2015 for discussion). How could this happen?

Recall that {round} is a non-contrastive enhancement feature in the West Germanic feature hierarchy in (30). However, another hierarchy can be constructed that includes [round] as a contrastive feature. This hierarchy requires demoting [low] to allow [round] to be contrastive over the non-front vowels. The new hierarchy, [front] > [round] > [high], yields the tree in (32).

(32) West Germanic feature hierarchy 2 (Dresher 2018): [front] > [round] > [high]

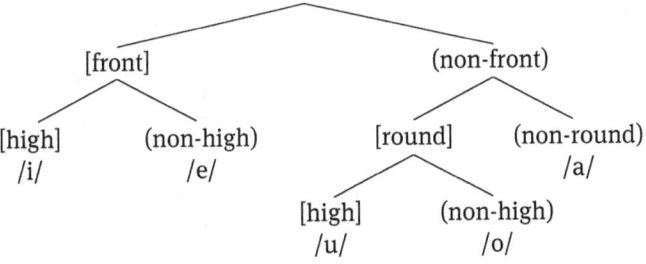

Now changing the (non-front), [round] vowels to [front] results in new front rounded vowels, which begin as allophones (33). They are thus what Moulton (2003) calls "deep allophones": they can arise in the contrastive phonology because they consist only of contrastive features.

(33) Fronting of /u, o/ in West Germanic feature hierarchy 2

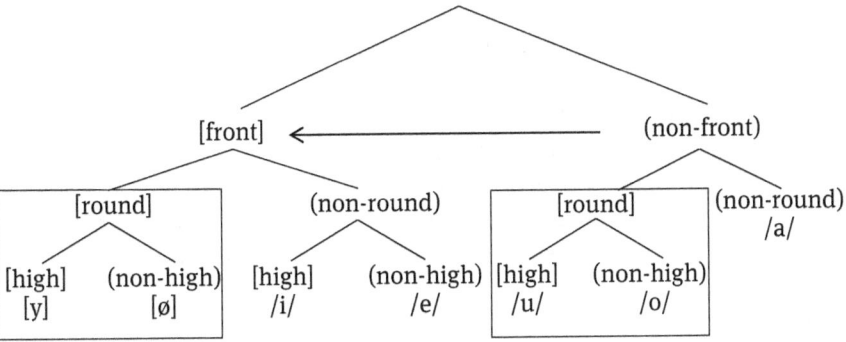

Notice that in the new feature hierarchy /a/ no longer has a [+low] feature. Unlike earlier */a/, I know of no evidence that this West Germanic /a/ – as in Old English, for example – requires an active [low] feature. This kind of connection between contrast and activity is exactly what Contrastive Hierarchy Theory predicts.

9 Binary features versus elements

Before concluding, I would like to briefly consider what might appear to be the most significant difference between Contrastive Hierarchy Theory and Element Theory: namely, the fact that, at least in my version of it, the former utilizes binary features and the latter has privative (single-valued) elements.[11] Conceptually, contrastive specification with a binary feature [±F] can result in a ternary distinction between segments that are specified [F], segments specified (non-F), and segments not specified for F (0 F). In a privative feature system, there is only a binary distinction between [F] and nothing, thus conflating (non-F) with (0 F). One question, then, is whether we ever need to distinguish between these two.

As reviewed in Dresher (2014b), this distinction is relevant in the analysis of the co-occurrence restrictions discussed by Mackenzie (2009, 2011, 2013). For example, in Ngizim (Chadic), pulmonic (plain) obstruents must agree in voicing (34a), but implosives may co-occur with both voiceless and voiced obstruents, as illustrated in (34b).

(34) Ngizim voicing harmony (Mackenzie 2013: 301, citing Schuh 1997)

a. Pulmonic consonants			b. Pulmonic and implosive consonants	
gâːzá	'chicken'	*k...z	kìːɗú	'eat (meat)'
dəbâ	'woven tray'	*t...b	fə́ɗú	'four'
kútər	'tail'	*g...t	pəɗə́k	'morning'
tásáu	'find'	*d...s	dəɓú	'give water'

Mackenzie proposes that Ngizim obstruents are specified by two laryngeal features, [±voice] and [±constricted glottis] ([±c.g.]); the features are ordered [c.g.] > [voice], which results in implosives being unspecified for [±voice], as shown in (35a). Given these representations, voicing harmony in Ngizim can be seen to require that obstruents may not have different values of [±voice]; obstruents

---

[11] I have discussed this issue in more detail in Dresher (2009: 32–34) and Dresher (2014b). I note again that there are versions of Contrastive Hierarchy Theory that do not assume binary features.

unspecified for [±voice] do not participate in the harmony. On this analysis it is necessary to distinguish between (non-voice), which participates in harmony, and (0 voice), which does not.

(35) Three laryngeal classes (Mackenzie 2009, 2013)
   a. Ngizim   b. Hausa

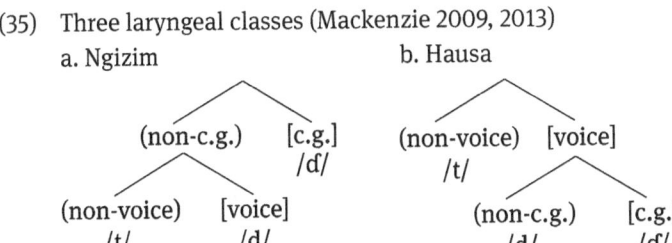

A defender of single-valued features or elements could point out that it is possible to replicate an analysis that uses both values of a binary feature by adding another unary feature (see Dresher 2012 for a similar comparison between binary features and feature-geometric dependencies). For example, one could propose that a unary |voice| element is a dependent of some element like |pulmonic| which applies to /t, d/ but not /ɗ/. The unary representations would have to be flexible enough to accommodate the facts of Hausa (Newman 2000), another Chadic language in which voiced consonants must agree with respect to [±c.g.], but a voiceless pulmonic consonant can co-occur with an implosive. Mackenzie proposes that in Hausa the laryngeal features are ordered [voice] > [c.g.] as in (35b); now, harmony applies to obstruents with a specification for [±c.g.].

It is worth trying to discover under what conditions binary-feature analyses can be replicated with elements, and vice-versa, as a way of determining what the empirical differences between these theories really are. Depending on what other constraints are put on representations, the issue of one value versus two values may not turn out to be as significant as it might appear.

10 Conclusion

To sum up, many phonologists have had the intuition that the phonological systems of the world's languages use a limited set of primes, be they features or elements. I have argued that this is because Universal Grammar requires speakers to construct contrastive feature hierarchies, and these hierarchies limit the number of primes available to the phonology. It follows that feature hierarchies show considerable crosslinguistic variability. In this respect, Element Theory posits fewer primes than Contrastive Hierarchy Theory; if this position can be maintained, it would suggest that there are more constraints on possible features than those imposed by contrast.

I have also proposed that Contrastive Hierarchy Theory and Element Theory have in common that they take a middle course between phonetic determinism on one side and substance-free phonology on the other. In both theories, phonological primes are cognitive entities that form a bridge between the mental representations and operations of the phonological component and their external phonetic manifestations. Both theories (Element Theory a bit inconsistently) posit a connection between contrastive representations and phonological activity: as in the vowel systems of Inuit-Yupik and West Germanic, changes in one are associated with changes in the other.

References

Antonsen, Elmer H. 1965. On defining stages in prehistoric Germanic. *Language* 41. 19–36.
Antonsen, Elmer H. 1972. The Proto-Germanic syllabics (vowels). In Frans van Coetsem & Herbert L. Kufner (eds.), *Toward a grammar of Proto-Germanic*, 117–140. Tübingen: Max Niemeyer.
Avery, Peter & William J. Idsardi. 2001. Laryngeal dimensions, completion and enhancement. In T. Alan Hall (ed.), *Distinctive feature theory*, 41–70. Berlin-New York: Mouton de Gruyter.
Backley, Phillip. 2011. *An introduction to Element Theory*. Edinburgh: Edinburgh University Press.
Barbosa, Plínio A. & Eleonora Cavalcante Albano. 2004. Brazilian Portuguese. *Journal of the International Phonetics Association* 34. 227–232.
Benediktsson, Hreinn. 1967. The Proto-Germanic vowel system. In *To honor Roman Jakobson: Essays on the occasion of his seventieth birthday, 11 October 1966*. Vol. 1, 174–196. The Hague & Paris: Mouton.
Blaho, Sylvia. 2008. *The syntax of phonology: A radically substance-free approach*. Tromsø: University of Tromsø dissertation.
Bohn, Graziela. 2015. *Aquisição das vogais tônicas e pretônicas do Português Brasileiro*. São Paulo: University of São Paulo dissertation.
Bohn, Graziela Pigatto. 2017. The acquisition of tonic and pre-tonic vowels in Brazilian Portuguese. *Journal of Portuguese Linguistics* 16(7), 1–5. DOI: https://doi.org/10.5334/jpl.184
Bohn, Graziela Pigatto & Raquel Santana Santos. 2018. The acquisition of pre-tonic vowels in Brazilian Portuguese. *Alfa: Revista de Linguística* (São José do Rio Preto) 62(1). 191–221.
Carvalho, Joaquim Brandão de. 2011. Contrastive hierarchies, privative features, and Portuguese vowels. *Linguística: Revista de Estudos Linguísticos da Universidade do Porto* 6. 51–66.
Cherry, E. Colin, Morris Halle & Roman Jakobson. 1953. Toward the logical description of languages in their phonemic aspect. *Language* 29. 34–46.
Chomsky, Noam & Morris Halle. 1968. *The sound pattern of English*. New York, NY: Harper & Row.

Clements, George Nick. 2001. Representational economy in constraint-based phonology. In T. Alan Hall, (ed.), *Distinctive feature theory*, 71–146. Berlin: Mouton de Gruyter.

Clements, George Nick. 2003. Feature economy in sound systems. *Phonology* 20. 287–333.

Clements, George Nick. 2009. The role of features in speech sound inventories. In Eric Raimy & Charles E. Cairns (eds.), *Contemporary views on architecture and representations in phonological theory*, 19–68. Cambridge, MA: MIT Press.

Clements, George Nick & Rachid Ridouane (eds.). 2011. *Where do features come from? Cognitive, physical and developmental bases of distinctive speech categories*. Amsterdam: John Benjamins.

Compton, Richard & B. Elan Dresher. 2011. Palatalization and "strong *i*" across Inuit dialects. *Canadian Journal of Linguistics/ Revue canadienne de linguistique* 56. 203–228.

Cyran, Eugeniusz. 2011. Laryngeal realism and laryngeal relativism: Two voicing systems in Polish? *Studies in Polish Linguistics* 6. 45–80.

Dinnsen, Daniel A. 1992. Variation in developing and fully developed phonetic inventories. In Charles A. Ferguson, Lisa Menn & Carol Stoel-Gammon (eds.), *Phonological development: Models, research, implications*, 191–210. Timonium, MD: York Press.

Dinnsen, Daniel A. 1996. Context-sensitive underspecification and the acquisition of phonetic contrasts. *Journal of Child Language* 23. 31–55.

Dinnsen, Daniel A., Steven B. Chin, Mary Elbert & Thomas W. Powell. 1990. Some constraints on functionally disordered phonologies: Phonetic inventories and phonotactics. *Journal of Speech and Hearing Research* 33. 28–37.

Dorais, Louis-Jacques. 2003. *Inuit uqausiqatigiit: Inuit languages and dialects (second, revised edition)*. Iqaluit: Nunavut Arctic College.

Dresher, B. Elan. 1998a. Child phonology, learnability, and phonological theory. In Tej Bhatia & William C. Ritchie (eds.), *Handbook of language acquisition*, 299–346. New York: Academic Press.

Dresher, B. Elan. 1998b. On contrast and redundancy. Presented at the annual meeting of the Canadian Linguistic Association, Ottawa. Ms., University of Toronto.

Dresher, B. Elan. 2003. Contrast and asymmetries in inventories. In Anna-Maria di Sciullo (ed.), *Asymmetry in grammar, volume 2: Morphology, phonology, acquisition*, 239–257. Amsterdam: John Benjamins.

Dresher, B. Elan. 2009. *The contrastive hierarchy in phonology*. Cambridge: Cambridge University Press.

Dresher, B. Elan. 2012. Is harmony limited to contrastive features? In A. McKillen & J. Loughran (eds.), *Proceedings from Phonology in the 21st Century: In Honour of Glyne Piggott. McGill Working Papers in Linguistics* 22 (1), 16 pages. https://www.mcgill.ca/mcgwpl/archives/volume-221-2012.

Dresher, B. Elan. 2014a. The arch not the stones: Universal feature theory without universal features. *Nordlyd* 41 (2). 165–181.

Dresher, B. Elan. 2014b. Contrastive hierarchies in Element Theory. Presented at the Conference on Theoretical Issues in Contemporary Phonology: Reading Tobias Scheer, École des Hautes Études en Sciences Sociales (EHESS), Paris, February 2014. Posted at https://sites.google.com/site/rtsfrench/.

Dresher, B. Elan. 2015. The motivation for contrastive feature hierarchies in phonology. *Linguistic Variation* 15. 1–40.

Dresher, B. Elan. 2016. Contrast in phonology 1867–1967: History and development. *Annual Review of Linguistics* 2. 53–73.

Dresher, B. Elan. 2018. Contrastive feature hierarchies in Old English diachronic phonology. *Transactions of the Philological Society* 116 (1). 1–29.

Dresher, B. Elan, Glyne L. Piggott & Keren Rice. 1994. Contrast in phonology: Overview. *Toronto Working Papers in Linguistics* 13 (1). iii-xvii.

Dresher, B. Elan & Keren Rice. 2007. Markedness and the contrastive hierarchy in phonology. https://dresher.artsci. utoronto.ca/~contrast/.

Dyck, Carrie. 1995. *Constraining the phonology-phonetics interface, with exemplification from Spanish and Italian dialects.* Toronto, ON: University of Toronto dissertation.

Fertig, David. 1996. Phonology, orthography, and the umlaut puzzle. In Rosina L. Lippi-Green & Joseph C. Salmons (eds.), *Germanic linguistics: Syntactic and diachronic*, 169–184. Amsterdam/Philadelphia: John Benjamins.

Fikkert, Paula. 1994. *On the acquisition of prosodic structure (HIL Dissertations 6).* Dordrecht: ICG Printing.

Flemming, Edward S. 2002. *Auditory representations in phonology.* New York, NY: Routledge.

Fortescue, Michael, Steven A. Jacobson & Lawrence D. Kaplan. 1994. *Comparative Eskimo dictionary with Aleut cognates.* Fairbanks: Alaska Native Language Center.

Frigeni, Chiara. 2002. Metaphony in Campidanian Sardinian: A domain-based analysis. *Toronto Working Papers in Linguistics (Special Issue on Contrast in Phonology)* 20. 63–91.

Fudge, Erik C. 1967. The nature of phonological primes. *Journal of Linguistics* 3. 1–36.

Groot, A. W. de. 1931. Phonologie und Phonetik als Funktionswissenschaften. *Travaux du Cercle Linguistique de Prague* 4. 116–147.

Hale, Mark & Charles Reiss. 2000. "Substance abuse" and "dysfunctionalism": Current trends in phonology. *Linguistic Inquiry* 31. 157–169.

Hale, Mark & Charles Reiss. 2008. *The phonological enterprise.* Oxford: Oxford University Press.

Hall, Daniel Currie. 2007. *The role and representation of contrast in phonological theory.* Toronto, ON: University of Toronto dissertation.

Hall, Daniel Currie. 2011. Phonological contrast and its phonetic enhancement: Dispersedness without dispersion. *Phonology* 28. 1–54.

Hall, Daniel Currie. 2014. On substance in phonology. *Actes du congrès annuel de l'Association canadienne de linguistique 2014/Proceedings of the 2014 annual conference of the Canadian Linguistic Association.* Posted at https://cla-acl.artsci.utoronto.ca/actes-2014-proceedings/.

Halle, Morris. 1959. *The sound pattern of Russian: A linguistic and acoustical investigation.* The Hague: Mouton. Second printing, 1971.

Harms, Robert T. 1968. *Introduction to phonological theory.* Englewood Cliffs, NJ: Prentice-Hall.

Hayes, Bruce, Robert Kirchner & Donca Steriade (eds.). 2004. *Phonetically based phonology.* Cambridge: Cambridge University Press.

Heffner, Christopher C., William J. Idsardi & Rochelle S. Newman. 2019. Constraints on learning disjunctive, unidimensional auditory and phonetic categories. *Attention, Perception, & Psychophysics* 81. 958–980. https://doi.org/10.3758/s13414-019-01683-x.

Hulst, Harry van der. 1993. Units in the analysis of signs. *Phonology* 10. 209–241.

Hulst, Harry van der. 1995. Radical CV phonology: The categorial gesture. In Jacques Durand & Francis Katamba (eds.), *Frontiers of phonology*, 80–116. Essex: Longman.

Hulst, Harry van der. 1996. Radical CV phonology: The segment-syllable connection. In Jacques Durand & Bernard Laks (eds.), *Current trends in phonology: Models and methods*, 333–361. Salford: ESRI.

Hulst, Harry van der. 2005. The molecular structure of phonological segments. In Philip Carr, Jacques Durand & Colin J. Ewen (eds.), *Headhood, elements, specification and contrastivity: Phonological papers in honour of John Anderson*, 193–234. Amsterdam: John Benjamins.

Hulst, Harry van der. 2018. *Asymmetries in vowel harmony – A representational account*. Oxford: Oxford University Press.

Hulst, Harry van der. 2020. *Principles of Radical CV Phonology: A theory of segmental and syllabic structure*. Edinburgh: Edinburgh University Press.

Hyman, Larry M. 2011. Do tones have features? In John A. Goldsmith, Elizabeth Hume & W. Leo Wetzels (eds.), *Tones and features*, 50–80. Berlin: Mouton De Gruyter.

Ingram, David. 1988. Jakobson revisited: Some evidence from the acquisition of Polish phonology. *Lingua* 75. 55–82.

Ingram, David. 1989. *First language acquisition: Method, description and explanation*. Cambridge: Cambridge University Press.

Jakobson, Roman. [1931] 1962. Phonemic notes on Standard Slovak. In *Selected writings I. Phonological studies*, 221–230. The Hague: Mouton (1962). [In Czech in *Studies presented to Albert Pražak*. Bratislava: Slovenská Miscellanea, 1931.]

Jakobson, Roman. 1941. *Kindersprache, Aphasie, und allgemeine Lautgesetze*. Uppsala: Uppsala Universitets Arsskrift.

Jakobson, Roman. 1968. *Child language, aphasia, and phonological universals*, translated from German by A. R. Keiler. The Hague: Mouton, 1968.

Jakobson, Roman. 1969. *Langage enfantin et aphasie*, translated from English and German by Jean-Paul Boons & Radmila Zygouris. Paris: Les Éditions de Minuit.

Jakobson, Roman, C. Gunnar M. Fant & Morris Halle. 1952. *Preliminaries to speech analysis*. MIT Acoustics Laboratory, Technical Report, No. 13. Reissued by MIT Press, Cambridge, Mass., Eleventh Printing, 1976.

Jakobson, Roman & Morris Halle. 1956. *Fundamentals of language*. The Hague: Mouton.

Jakobson, Roman & John Lotz. 1949. Notes on the French phonemic pattern. *Word* 5. 151–158.

Janda, Richard D. 2003. "Phonologization" as the start of dephoneticization – or, on sound change and its aftermath: Of extension, generalization, lexicalization, and morphologization. In Brian D. Joseph & Richard D. Janda (eds.), *The handbook of historical linguistics*, 401–422. Oxford: Blackwell.

Kaplan, Lawrence D. 1981. *Phonological issues in North Alaskan Inupiaq*. Fairbanks: Alaska Native Language Center.

Kaplan, Lawrence D. 1990. The language of the Alaskan Inuit. In Dirmid R. F. Collis (ed.), *Arctic languages: An awakening*, 131–158. Paris: UNESCO.

Kaye, Jonathan, Jean Lowenstamm & Jean-Roger Vergnaud. 1985. The internal structure of phonological elements: A theory of charm and government. *Phonology Yearbook* 2. 305–328.

Kaye, Jonathan & Markus A. Pöchtrager. 2013. GP 2.0. *SOAS Working Papers in Linguistics* 16. 52–64.

Keyser, Samuel Jay & Kenneth N. Stevens. 2001. Enhancement revisited. In Michael J. Kenstowicz (ed.), *Ken Hale: A life in language*, 271–291. Cambridge, Mass.: MIT Press.

Keyser, Samuel Jay & Kenneth N. Stevens. 2006. Enhancement and overlap in the speech chain. *Language* 82. 33–63.

Kiparsky, Paul. 2015. Phonologization. In Patrick Honeybone & Joseph Salmons (eds.), *The handbook of historical phonology*, 563–579. Oxford: Oxford University Press.

Kiparsky, Valentin. 1932. Johdatusta fonologiaan. *Virittäjä* 36. 230–250.
Ko, Seongyeon. 2010. A contrastivist view on the evolution of the Korean vowel system. In Hiroki Maezawa & Azusa Yokogoshi (eds.), *MITWPL 61: Proceedings of the Sixth Workshop on Altaic Formal Linguistics*, 181 – 196.
Ko, Seongyeon. 2012. *Tongue root harmony and vowel contrast in Northeast Asian languages*. Ithaca, NY: Cornell University dissertation. [Published 2018, Wiesbaden: Harrassowitz Verlag.]
Lass, Roger. 1994. *Old English: A historical linguistic companion*. Cambridge: Cambridge University Press.
Levelt, Clara C. 1989. *An essay on child phonology*. M.A. thesis, Leiden University.
Liberman, Anatoly. 1991. Phonologization in Germanic: Umlauts and vowel shifts. In Elmer H. Antonsen & Hans Henrich Hock (eds.), *Stæfcræft: Studies in Germanic Linguistics*, 125–137. Amsterdam: John Benjamins.
Liljencrants, Johan & Björn Lindblom. 1972. Numerical simulation of vowel quality systems: The role of perceptual contrast. *Language* 48. 839–862.
Lindblom, Björn. 1986. Phonetic universals in vowel systems. In John J. Ohala & Jeri J. Jaeger (eds.), *Experimental phonology*, 13–44. New York: Academic Press.
Lindblom, Björn, Randy Diehl, Sang-Hoon Park & Giampiero Salvi. 2011. Sound systems are shaped by their users: The recombination of phonetic substance. In George Nick Clements & Rachid Ridouane (eds), *Where Do Phonological Features Come From?: Cognitive, physical and developmental bases of distinctive speech categories*, 67–97. Amsterdam/Philadelphia: John Benjamins.
Mackenzie, Sara. 2009. *Contrast and similarity in consonant harmony processes*. Toronto, ON: University of Toronto dissertation.
Mackenzie, Sara. 2011. Contrast and the evaluation of similarity: Evidence from consonant harmony. *Lingua* 121. 1401–1423.
Mackenzie, Sara. 2013. Laryngeal co-occurrence restrictions in Aymara: Contrastive representations and constraint interaction. *Phonology* 30. 297–345.
Mackie, Scott & Jeff Mielke. 2011. Feature economy in natural, random, and synthetic inventories. In George Nick Clements & Rachid Ridouane (eds), *Where Do Phonological Features Come From?: Cognitive, physical and developmental bases of distinctive speech categories*. 43–63. Amsterdam/Philadelphia: John Benjamins.
Martinet, André. 1955. *Économie des changements phonétiques*. Berne: Francke.
Mesgarani, Nima, Stephen V. David, Jonathan B. Fritz & Shihab A. Shamma. 2008. Phoneme representation and classification in primary auditory cortex. *Journal of the Acoustical Society of America* 123. 899–909.
Mielke, Jeff. 2008. *The emergence of distinctive features*. Oxford: Oxford University Press.
Moulton, Keir. 2003. Deep allophones in the Old English laryngeal system. *Toronto Working Papers in Linguistics* 20. 157–173.
Nevins, Andrew. 2012. Vowel lenition and fortition in Brazilian Portuguese. *Letras de Hoje*, Porto Alegre 47 (3). 228–233.
Newman, Paul. 2000. *The Hausa language: An encyclopedic reference grammar*. New Haven: Yale University Press.
Odden, David. 2006. Phonology ex nihilo. Presented at the Phonology Get-Together, Universitetet i Tromsø, December 2006. Handout available online at https://sites.google.com/view/oddenlinguistics/home.

Ohala, John J. 1980. Introduction to the symposium on phonetic universals in phonological systems and their explanation. In *Proceedings of the 9th International Congress of Phonetic Sciences*, Vol. 3, 181–185. University of Copenhagen: Institute of Phonetics.

Oxford, Will. 2015. Patterns of contrast in phonological change: Evidence from Algonquian vowel systems. *Language* 91. 308–357.

Penzl, Herbert. 1972. Methods of comparative Germanic linguistics. In Frans van Coetsem & Herbert L. Kufner (eds.), *Toward a grammar of Proto-Germanic*, 1–43. Tübingen: Max Niemeyer.

Pöchtrager, Markus A. 2006. *The structure of length*. Vienna: University of Vienna dissertation.

Pöchtrager, Markus A. 2016. Vowel reduction: Sawing off the branch you're sitting on. Séminaire P3, Laboratoire de Linguistique de Nantes, June 2016.

Purnell, Thomas & Eric Raimy. 2015. Distinctive features, levels of representation and historical phonology. In Patrick Honeybone & Joseph Salmons (eds.), *The handbook of historical phonology*, 522–544. Oxford: Oxford University Press.

Pye, Clifton, David Ingram & Helen List. 1987. A comparison of initial consonant acquisition in English and Quiché. In Keith E. Nelson & Ann Van Kleeck (eds.), *Children's language (vol. 6)*, 175–190. Hillsdale, NJ: Erlbaum.

Reiss, Charles. 2017. Substance-free phonology. In Stephen J. Hannahs & Anna R. K. Bosch (eds.), *The Routledge handbook of phonological theory*, 425–452. New York, NY: Routledge.

Rice, Keren. 2003. Featural markedness in phonology: Variation. In Lisa Cheng & Rint Sybesma (eds.), *The second Glot International state-of-the-article book: The latest in linguistics*, 387–427. Berlin: Mouton de Gruyter.

Rice, Keren. 2007. Markedness in phonology. In Paul de Lacy (ed.), *The Cambridge handbook of phonology*, 79–97. Cambridge: Cambridge University Press.

Ringe, Donald. 2006. *A history of English: From Proto-Indo-European to Proto-Germanic (A linguistic history of English, Vol. 1)*. Oxford: Oxford University Press. Oxford Scholarship Online (www.oxfordscholarship.com).

Ringe, Donald & Ann Taylor. 2014. *The development of Old English (A linguistic history of English, Vol. 2)*. Oxford: Oxford University Press.

Samuels, Bridget D. 2011. *Phonological architecture: A biolinguistic perspective*. Oxford: Oxford University Press.

Sandler, Wendy. 1993. Sign language and modularity. *Lingua* 89. 315–351.

Sapir, Edward. 1925. Sound patterns in language. *Language* 1. 37–51.

Scheer, Tobias. 2010. How to marry (structuralist) contrast and (generative) processing (review of Dresher 2009). *Lingua* 120 (10). 2522–2534.

Schuh, Russell G. 1997. Changes in obstruent voicing in Bade/Ngizim. Ms., University of California, Los Angeles.

Spahr, Christopher. 2012. Positional neutralization in the Contrastive Hierarchy: The case of phonological vowel reduction. Ms., University of Toronto.

Spahr, Christopher. 2014. A contrastive hierarchical account of positional neutralization. *The Linguistic Review* 31 (3–4). 551–585.

Steriade, Donca. 2001. Directional asymmetries in place assimilation: A perceptual account. In Elizabeth V. Hume & Keith Johnson (eds.), *The role of speech perception in phonology*, 219–250. San Diego, CA: Academic Press.

Stevens, Kenneth N. & Samuel Jay Keyser. 1989. Primary features and their enhancement in consonants. *Language* 65. 81–106.

Stevens, Kenneth N., Samuel Jay Keyser & Haruko Kawasaki. 1986. Toward a phonetic and phonological theory of redundant features. In Joseph S. Perkell & Dennis H. Klatt (eds.), *Symposium on invariance and variability of speech processes*, 432–469. Hillsdale, NJ: Lawrence Erlbaum.
Trubetzkoy, N. S. 1939. *Grundzüge der Phonologie*. Göttingen: Vandenhoek & Ruprecht.
Trubetzkoy, N. S. 1949. *Principes de phonologie*, translated from German by J. Cantineau. Paris: Klincksieck.
Trubetzkoy, N. S. 1969. *Principles of phonology*, translated from German by Christiane A. M. Baltaxe. Berkeley: University of California Press.
Trubetzkoy, N. S. 2019. *Principios de fonología*. New translation and critical edition by Esther Herrera Zendeyas & Michael Herbert Knapp. Mexico City: El Colegio de México, Centro de Estudios Lingüísticos y Literarios.
Twaddell, W. Freeman. 1938. A note on OHG umlaut. *Monatshefte für deutschen Unterricht* 30. 177–181.
Twaddell, W. Freeman. 1948. The prehistoric Germanic short syllabics. *Language* 24 (2). 139–151.
Voeltzel, Laurence. 2016. *Morphophonologie des langues scandinaves. Hiérarchie segmentale et complexité syllabique*. Nantes: Université de Nantes dissertation.
Voeltzel, Laurence & Ali Tifrit. 2013. From binary features to elements: The case of Scandinavian. Paper presented at Features in Phonology, Morphology, Syntax and Semantics: What are they? CASTL, University of Tromsø, Oct.–Nov. 2013.
Zhang, Xi. 1996. *Vowel systems of the Manchu-Tungus languages of China*. Toronto, ON: University of Toronto dissertation.
Živanović, Sašo & Markus A. Pöchtrager. 2010. GP 2, and Putonghua too. *Acta Linguistica Hungarica* 57 (4). 357–380.

Eric Raimy
Privativity and ternary phonological behavior

Abstract: Privative approaches to phonological representations provide a challenge to phonological theory. The main challenge is that ternary phonological behavior appears to require binary features. The laryngeal phonology of Polish demonstrates such ternary behavior (Rubach 1996). We assume modified contrastive specification and add superordinate marking from Purnell, Raimy, and Salmons (2019). These assumptions provide the structure for strictly privative representations to account for ternary phonological behavior. We apply this approach to the laryngeal phonology of Polish and additionally demonstrate the importance of modularity between phonology and phonetics. The end result is a strictly privative approach to phonological representations that accounts for ternary phonological behavior and connects it to aspects of modularity. This approach also serves as a response to substance free phonology by introducing the alternative view of *substance impoverished phonology*.

Keywords: laryngeal realism; distinctive features; contrastive hierarchy; modularity; substance impoverished phonology.

1 Introduction

Kaye, Lowenstamm and Vergnaud (1985, 1990) set the stage for contemporary approaches in Element Theory. One of the defining characteristics of Element Theory based analyses is the assumption that phonological representations are privative in nature where segments are interpreted based on the presence or absence of particular elements in different structural configurations. The desire

---

Acknowledgements: I would like to thank the participants at the Elements: State of the Art and Perspectives conference and two reviewers for helpful discussion of the content of this chapter. Peter Avery, Elan Dresher, Keren Rice, Bill Idsardi and Tom Purnell have all played both a direct and indirect roll in the formation of these ideas whether they realized it or not. They should be given credit for any successes in this work but all flaws are my own. This research has been supported by both the Nancy C. Hoefs and the Marjorie and Loren Tiefenthaler Professor of English chairs at the University of Wisconsin-Madison.

Eric Raimy, University of Wisconsin-Madison

https://doi.org/10.1515/9783110691948-004

to use privative representations goes beyond Element Theory and has proponents in Particle Theory (Schane 1984) and Dependency Phonology (Anderson and Jones 1974, Anderson and Ewen 1987) which made fundamental proposals in the 1970's. Privative representation is generally understood to be a more restrictive representation than binary features (Lombardi 1995, Oxford 2015). These representations are more restrictive because they make specific and strong claims about phonological activity and substance in phonology. We will be focusing on general questions of privative representations as opposed to any particular implementation of Element Theory, Particle Theory, or Dependency Phonology and hope our contributions deepen the general understanding of the nature of privative representations.

Concerns about whether privative representations are able to reach descriptive adequacy (Chomsky 1965) has caused contemporary researchers to either retreat from the strong position of privativity on phonological substance or to simply reject privative features for binary ones. Rubach (1996) uses the data from Polish laryngeal phonology to make an argument against privative features. Cyran (2011) represents the rejection of phonological substance claims in privative representation. Beckman et al (2011) raise questions about how specified phonological representations are which provides a link between the points raised by Rubach (1996) and Cyran (2011). A key aspect of rejecting the strong position on privative representations is that phonology appears to require a ternary distinction in phonological activity. Ternary phonological activity has deep implications for phonological representations.

We will address the questions about privative representations raised above in section 2 by starting with discussing how opposition or contrast is encoded, more specifically, how the non-specified side of a contrast or opposition should be represented. In section 3, we will present the superordinate marking proposal in Purnell, Raimy, and Salmons (2019, henceforth PRS) that implements a new way of providing phonological substance to the unmarked side of an opposition or contrast with a privative representation. This will explain our positions on substance and overspecification in phonetics and phonology. An analysis of the Polish laryngeal phonology that defends a strong interpretation of privative representations will be presented in section 4. Section 5 will address the concerns raised by Rubach (1996), Cyran (2011), and Beckman et al (2011) by expanding the Laryngeal Realism (Iverson and Salmons 1995) framework to cover all distinctive features. To conclude, section 6 will discuss how compatible the present findings are with Element Theory in general.

2 Nothing

The use of the concept of 'nothing' is ubiquitous throughout phonology. A likely universal but unmentioned assumption in any proposed phonological computation or representation is that omission of specification should be assumed to represent 'nothing'. In other words, absence is nothing. This background assumption is the source for the idea that privative representations are more constrained because phonology only has an opposition of something vs. nothing. Stanley (1967) showed that binary representations allowed for three different options for opposition, [+] vs. [−] vs. Ø. To restate this difference, binary features allow phonological activity to distinguish between marked, unmarked, and underspecified representations (Calabrese 2009) while privative representations can only distinguish between marked and unspecified representations. The invocation of markedness here (see Rice 1999ab for an overview of markedness in phonology) suggests that there is a question of phonological substance involved for binary approaches. A substance free view of binary features is well known to be problematic since Chapter 9 of SPE (Chomsky and Halle 1968). A naive interpretation of binary features is that there should be no difference between the [+] value and [−] value for a feature but this doesn't match what we know about phonological activity.

A way to rethink this conundrum of ternary power in phonological representations is to change the focus from asking how the two marked values of a binary feature are different, to how the two unmarked values are different. One way to ask this is whether there can be two kinds of unmarked representations? Or, can there be two kinds of unspecified representations? Looking towards math and logic provides useful inspiration on these questions.

The number zero sheds light on how we can think about phonological representations. Zero has at least two roles in math with one being a place holder and the second being a number. The place holding role is a familiar one for any person who understands place notation in numbers.

(1) Place notation

2	0	2	0	2
ten-thousands	thousands	hundreds	tens	ones

(1) shows how place notation works with the order of magnitude listed across the bottom. With the assumption of place notation, we can interpret the number 20202 as consisting of 2 ten thousands, 0 thousands, 2 hundreds, 0 tens, and 2 ones which we collapse to twenty thousand two hundred and two. Here zero simply marks the skipping of an order of magnitude which allows a distinction among 222, 2022, 2202, 22002, etc. to be maintained. This form of zero as a place holder occurred first in historical records (Kaplan 1999) and is similar in nature to unspecified features in a phonological representation. The second role that zero plays is as a number that has certain properties as discussed in the entry for Zero in the Encyclopedia of Mathematics. A key part of this entry is that zero has different definitions and characteristics based on which kind of math is being considered.

Privative representations in phonology act as a specification or mark in opposition to something else. The classic interpretation of this something else can be understood as zero as a place holder. There is no substance or characteristics of the representation in opposition to a privative item. This limits phonological activity to only a two way distinction based on the presence or absence of a privative item. Ternary phonological activity requires a representation that is different from the basic privative item and the absence of it. The next section will present the solution to this puzzle developed in Purnell, Raimy, and Salmons (2019).

3 Superordinate marking as a kind of zero

Purnell, Raimy, and Salmons (2019) adopt the general assumptions of Modified Contrastive Underspecification (Dresher, Piggott, and Rice 1994, henceforth MCU) which define some of the crucial assumptions about phonological representation and substance that are important in understanding the multiple oppositions to a privative item. One key concept is that greater phonological representation leads to greater phonetic substance (Rice 2009). This traditionally plays out by having each distinctive feature (the unit of representation in MCU) adding phonetic substance so more features equal more substance. PRS further develops the representation equals substance position by reinterpreting feature geometry (Clements 1985, Sagey 1986, Halle 2005, etc.) as a semantics for phonological segments as opposed to a structural configuration of distinctive features. Further explanation of these points is best done with an example.

Let us consider a three vowel system consisting of phonetic [ɪ], [ʊ], and [ɐ] and assume the general articulatory descriptions of these vowels in (2).

(2) Hypothetical three vowel system
[ɪ] short high front unrounded monophthong
[ʊ] short high back rounded monophthong
[ɐ] short low central unrounded monophthong

MCS takes the position that the phonological representations for these vowels will be underspecified and only posit enough structure to encode the necessary oppositions or contrasts among the vowels. Since there are three vowels to distinguish, a privative approach within MCS will require two features to accomplish this task. If we treat the phonetic features used to describe the vowels in (2) as potential phonological features, there are nine distinct phonetic features that could be used: short, high, low, front, back, central, rounded, unrounded, and monophthong. This is clearly more than necessary and is the result of phonetic representations being overspecified from a phonological perspective. Two of these features, *short* and *monophthong*, are uniform across all of the vowels and thus can be eliminated from consideration. If some phonological substance is associated with the phonetic features, two more features can be eliminated because they are articulatory defaults and do not represent active gestures. One of these is *central* which is just a default articulatory setting of the tongue position which is neither *front* nor *back*. Another is *unrounded* which is the default articulatory setting of the lips which is neither *rounded* nor *drawn*. Considering the articulatory aspects of phonetic description allows for a biologically based substance to be introduced in phonological representations which has the above effect of reducing the hypothesis space for learning. Using phonetic substance to reduce the hypothesis space for a learner is a good thing.

MCS representations are commonly derived from Dresher (2009)'s *successive division algorithm* (henceforth SDA). The visual representation of the SDA assigning features as part of the process of developing a phonemic inventory is a tree diagram. Following PRS, we will call this tree diagram a *contrastive hierarchy*. The contrastive hierarchies in (3) present some of the different ways the hypothetical three vowel inventory can be phonologically encoded. Each hierarchy has as its title a *contrastive ranking* which indicates the order of features used. We will assume the naïve phonetic features used in (2) as the source of features the SDA pulls from for this example.

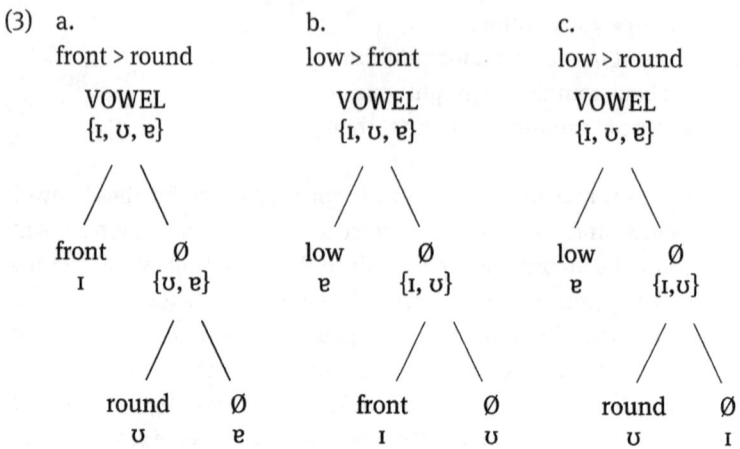

The three contrastive hierarchies in (3) demonstrate the placeholder use of zero to indicate the unmarked side of a privative contrast or opposition. The representations in (4) are what phonological computations operate on so we can see that the zeros in (3) are just place holders and do not add any structure or content to the segments themselves.

(4) a. front > round

ɪ	ʊ	ɐ
front	round	

b. low > front

ɪ	ʊ	ɐ
front		low

c. low > round

ɪ	ʊ	ɐ
	round	low

(4) presents *contrastive segments* which are the results of the SDA and shows both the restrictiveness of privative approaches to representation and also the potential draw backs. Restrictiveness follows from each of the phonological inventories only positing two active features. In (4a), only the features of front and round exist in the phonology making /ɐ/ an inert, default, or empty vowel. This inventory would match a language that has alternations stemming from the spreading of a front or round feature or the deletion of these features. This vowel system would be unable to support phonological backing or lowering rules though the spreading of features. The systems in (4b) and (4c) have similar pros and cons

modulo the features that are posited. One common thing across all MCS type systems is that there will be an item that is fully underspecified. Remember that these MCS type representation are phonological ones and not phonetic ones. Hall (2011) argues that these underspecified phonological representations are filled with more phonetic specification as part of the phonological derivation.

Purnell, Raimy, and Salmons (2019) argue for a reinterpretation of how the unmarked side of a contrast is treated based on feature geometry in general and a particular approach to distinctive features based on proposals by Avery and Idsardi (2001). One of the reasons PRS adopts the approach to distinctive features proposed by Avery and Idsardi (2001) is that this system takes a completely privative position on the distinctive features themselves. The full feature geometry of Avery and Idsardi (2001) can be found in the appendix but we present the relevant subpart to encode the vowel systems under discussion in (5).

(5)   Avery and Idsardi Oral Place Feature Geometry

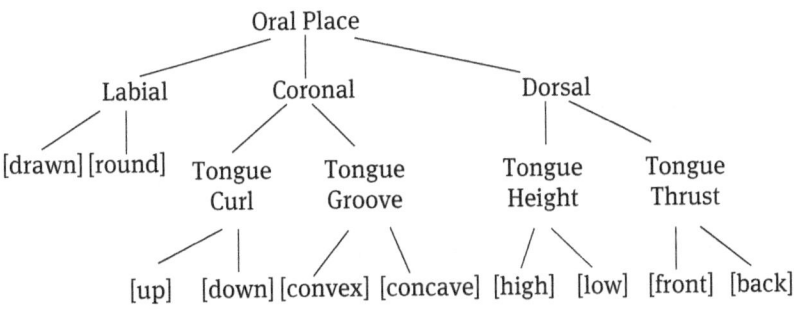

Although the graphic presentation of feature geometry suggests a structural interpretation, PRS argues that feature geometry should be understood as a semantic organization that specifies the relationships among different pieces of phonological representations (e.g. Halle (2005)'s bottle brush model). We assume that phonological representations for spoken language act as a link between articulatory and acoustic representations (signed phonologies link visual and hand based articulatory representations) and Avery and Idsardi (2001) adopt an articulator based model of feature geometry (Sagey 1986, Halle 2005, et seq).

The articulator based approach provides a biological basis for the semantic organization with superordinate and subordinate relations. (5) presents the Oral Place category of articulators which covers much of the supralaryngeal cavity and is sufficient for distinguishing the vowel systems in (3). Oral Place as a category includes the lips and tongue as articulators with the tongue being split into two parts. This gives us the categories of Labial, Coronal, and Dorsal. Oral Place is the superordinate category for all three and each of the three are a subordinate category of Oral Place. We can derive a difference in phonetic substance based on the super vs. sub ordinate relationship with the superordinate category having less substance because it is a more general and broader category and the subordinate category having more substance because it is a narrower more specific category.

There is additional biologically based structure in the Avery and Idsardi (2001) feature system. The terminal nodes in (5) are enclosed in brackets to indicate they represent specific articulatory gestures. Gestures come in antagonistic pairs which are dominated by an organizational node called a *dimension*. For example, the gestures [front] and [back] indicate moving the dorsum of the tongue either forward or backward and are dominated by the dimension Tongue Thrust. Note that it is physically impossible to move the dorsum of the tongue both forward and backward at the same time and this is part of the role that the dimension node plays. Dimension nodes encode this antagonistic relationship and are thus more abstract and have less phonetic substance than the phonetic gestures themselves. Avery and Idsardi propose that a modular difference between phonology and phonetics is that phonological representations consist of dimensions while phonetic representations consist of gestures. Dimensions are converted to gestures through a completion rule which is one step in the derivation from phonological representations to phonetic ones.

With this background we can return to the example vowel inventory in (2) and see how PRS use aspects of the Avery and Idsardi system to provide a different way to interpret the null symbols in (3). We will revise the contrastive rankings, hierarchies, and segments in (3) and (4) using Avery and Idsardi dimensions in (6). Note that we will be assuming that the height contrast in these vowel systems is controlled by Tongue Height for clarity but see Purnell and Raimy (2015) for arguments that Tongue Root can also encode low vowels.

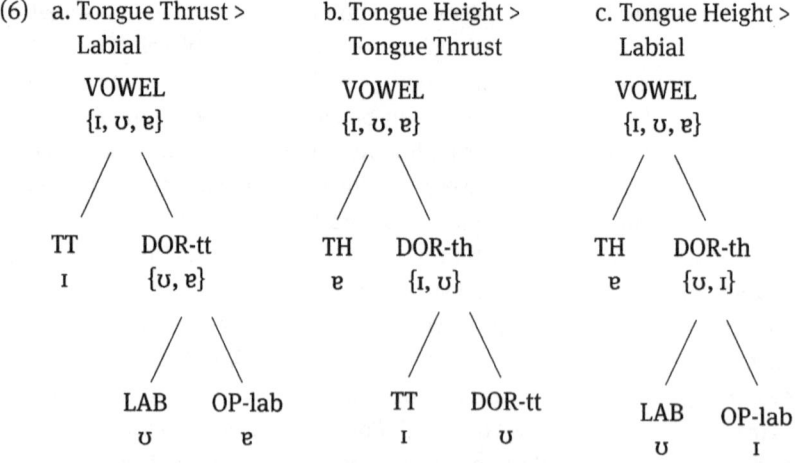

The contrastive hierarchies in (6) demonstrate what PRS calls *superordinate marking*. Each branching of the hierarchy indicates a contrast with the marked side of the opposition specified with a dimension and the unmarked side with the superordinate category which contains the dimension (see the Appendix for the whole category structure). In (6a), the first dimension used is Tongue Thrust and this marks the front vowel /ɪ/ in opposition to the other non-front vowels [ɐ] and [ʊ] which are consequently marked with DOR-tt (e.g. Dorsal-Tongue Thrust). Dorsal is the superordinate category that includes both Tongue Height and Tongue Thrust and we add the initials of what dimension is posited as the basis for the contrast. (6a) then uses the dimension Labial to mark /ʊ/ which then leaves /ɐ/ marked with OP-lab (e.g. Oral Place-Labial) as the superordinate category. The other two contrastive hierarchies in (6) operate in the same way and demonstrate how the choice of dimension and the order of the choice can support different phonological representations from the same surface inventory of segments.

There are two immediate advantages created by PRS's super ordinate marking proposal over the traditional privative and binary features that can be seen when the contrastive segments are considered. (7) presents the contrastive segments for the three different vowel systems.

(7) Avery and Idsardi based contrastive segments

	ɪ	ʊ	ɐ
ranking/hierarchy (6a)	Tongue Thrust	Dorsal-tt Labial	Dorsal-tt Oral Place-lab
ranking/hierarchy (6b)	Dorsal-th Tongue Thrust	Dorsal-th Dorsal-tt	Tongue Height
ranking/hierarchy (6c)	Dorsal-th Oral Place-lab	Dorsal-th Labial	Tongue Height

The first advantage is that all of the vowels in each inventory get some phonological specification as opposed to the traditional privative feature MCS approach in (4). This avoids the problem of phonological activity that fully or partially unspecified segments pose. This point will be fully explored in sections 4 and 5.

The second advantage is that distinctions among different types of phonological activity and modularity can be derived directly from the representations. To see this, let's show how the representations in (7) for the ranking and hierarchy in (6a) are converted to more surface phonetic forms.

(8) Phonology to phonetics derivation in PRS

		/ɪ/	/ʊ/	/ɐ/
a.	*phonology dimensions*	Tongue Thrust	Dorsal-tt Labial	Dorsal-tt Oral Place-lab
b.	*phonology-phonetics completion*	[front]	Dorsal-tt [round]	Dorsal-tt Oral Place-lab
c.	*underspecified phonetics*	{i, ɪ, e, ɛ, æ...}	{u, ʊ, o, œ...}	{ʌ, ɯ, a, ɑ...}
d.	*categorical phonetics enhancement fill-ins*	[front] [high] short ...	[high] [round] [back] short ...	[low]
e.	*surface phonetics*	[ɪ]	[ʊ]	[ɐ]

The table in (8) has added steps in the phonological derivation that show where additional phonetic substance is added to the phonological representations. (8a) shows the beginning phonological representations consisting of only dimensions and superordinate categories. These features will drive certain phonological activity but not others. Detailed examples of these will be presented in section 4. (8b) shows how the representations change through the application of completion rules (Avery and Idsardi 2001) which will exchange a dimension for one of the two subordinate articulatory gestures. In this example, Tongue Thrust is completed with [front] and Labial is completed with [round]. The row in (8c) is a purely expository step to highlight the abstractness and vagueness of the level of representation in (8b). All of these segments are underspecified for most phonetic substance with the substance being present being demarcated through contrast and opposition. /ɪ/ at this point is defined by frontness and could be any vowel that has this phonetic substance. /ɐ/ is defined completely through opposition. It can be any vowel that is 'not front' or 'not round'. This position is not unique to the present proposals and is available to any approach that has a sufficiently articulated and complex theory of the phonology-phonetics interface (see Hamann 2013 for discussion). See Kwon (in prep) for the role these kinds of representation play in second language acquisition and perception. (8d) likely conflates multiple levels of representation that support enhancement and fill in rules. These levels and processes add phonetic specification to create a categorical phonetics level which can be interpreted by the phonetics module. (8e) presents rough IPA transcriptions of the actual surface phonetic targets with the understanding that how wide or narrow the targets actually are is dependent on the categorical phonetic level is interpreted in a language specific context. For example, the low vowel [ɐ] may or may not vary in front/backness depending on the language. Hall (2011) explicitly discusses the relationship between underspecified contrastive representations and enhanced surface phonetic representation that show dispersion effects. Hall's conclusion is that this approach successfully grounds both views of phonology. A key aspect of Hall's findings is that it should be expected that underlying underspecified contrastive representations end up being overspecified in the phonetics based on enhancement. This observation will be key in understanding the laryngeal phonology of Polish in section 4.

The modular structure of the derivational levels in (8) is complex but beneficial. The complexity is from there being multiple possible explanations to be considered in analyzing a phenomenon of interest to phonology. There could be purely a phonological explanation, a purely phonetic explanation, or a mixed explanation depending on which level (or levels) of representation provide explanation. This complexity is beneficial because the representations that are involved in an explanation will identify which level of representation is involved. Each level will have particular characteristics that help differentiate among them. Phonological level representation provides discrete categorical type explanations and phonetic level representation provide continuous variable type explanations. There are of course mixed explanations available too. This flexibility in providing explanations will be used in section 4 when discussing the Polish data.

Given the proposals by PRS, we have a privative feature system that can distinguish among three different types of features: marked~superordinate~unspecified. This provides an approximation of the expressive power of a binary feature system with +, −, and Ø. There is an inherent difference between the two approaches though. The superordinate marking system has an implicit specific vs. general relationship between the marked and superordinate category which derives different phonological behaviors from the two types of categories as presented in (8). Binary systems must keep a separate list of which value for which feature should behave as marked or unmarked (Calabrese 2009, Nevins 2015). Consequently, a privative system can produce ternary phonological behavior like a binary system but is not equivalent to a binary system.

The introduction and background to PRS's approach to privative features provides the backdrop for the analyses of Polish which we turn to in the next section.

4 Laryngeal phonology in Polish

Polish presents a well-documented and intricate pattern of laryngeal phonology which is well summarized by Rubach (1996). The data from Polish provide information about the nature of features covering both the topics of binary vs. privative approaches (Rubach 1996) and phonological substance (Cyran 2011). (9) presents the obstruent inventory in Polish so as to demonstrate the basic laryngeal contrast. We do not add any new empirical data and rely on Rubach's survey of the relevant phonological activity in Polish that is summarized and reorganized in (10). We will only touch on Rubach's specific claims about prosodic structure and derivational levels as needed and agree with them in a general way. We use general descriptive terms to describe the phonological activity and will develop and discuss the technical aspects of the actual analysis in turn.

(9) Laryngeal Contrast in Polish Obstruents (Gussman 2007)
  voiceless /p, pʲ, t, tʲ, c, k, f, fʲ, s, sʲ, ɕ, ʃ, ʃʲ, t͡s, t͡ɕ, t͡ʃ, t͡sʲ, t͡ʃʲ, ç, x/
  voiced   /b, bʲ, d, dʲ, ɟ, g, v, vʲ, z, zʲ, ʑ, ʒ, ʒʲ, d͡z, d͡ʑ, d͡ʒ, d͡zʲ, d͡ʒʲ/

(10) a. Phonological activity in Polish (Rubach 1996: 70–72)
  Voice Assimilation: voiced obstruents cause preceding obstruents to become voiced

kos + i + ć	'mow'	koś + b + a	'mowing'
[ɕ]		[ʑ + b]	
licz + y + ć	'count'	licz + b + a	'number'
[t͡ʃ]		[d͡ʒ + b]	
nos + i + ć	'carry'	noś + że	'do carry'
[ɕ]		[ʑ + ʒ]	(imperative)
szlak + u	'route'	szlak bojowy	'war route'
[k]		[g + b]	
rosłaby	'she would grow'	rósłby	'he would grow'
[s]		[zwb]	
litr + y	'liters'	litr wody	'liter of water'
[t]		[dr v]	
cykl	'cycle'	cykl biologiczny	'biological cycle'
[k]		[gl b]	
pieśn + i	'song'	pieśń bojowa	'war song'
[ɕ]		[ʑɲ b]	
pomysł + y	'ideas'	pomysł zawodów	'the idea of the games'
[s]		[zw z]	

b. Word Final Devoicing: obstruents are devoiced in word final position

sad + y [d]	'orchards'	sad [t]	(nominative singular)
koz + a [z]	'goat'	kóz [s]	(genitive plural)
praw + o [v]	'law'	praw [f]	(genitive plural)
zubr + y [b]	'bisons'	zubr [pr]	(nominative singular)
mog + ł + a [g]	'she could'	mog + ł [kw]	'he could'
mielizn + a [z]	'shallow water'	mielizn [sn]	(genitive plural)
mechanizm + y [z]	'mechanisms'	mechanizm [sm]	(nominative singular)

c. Voiceless Assimilation: voiceless obstruents cause preceding obstruents to become voiceless

dech [d]	'breath'	tch + u [tx]	(genitive plural)
młod + y [d]	'young'	młod + sz + y [t + ʃ]	'younger'
ryb + a [b]	'fish'	ryb + k + a [p + k]	(diminutive)
pokład + y [d]	'boards'	pokład statku [t + st]	'board of ship'
wykaz + y [z]	'lists'	wykaz pism [s p]	'list of journals'
Jędrek [jendrek]	'Andy'	Jędrk + a [jentrk + a]	(genitive singular)
mog + ł + a [g]	'she could'	mog + ł + sz + y [k + w + ʃ]	'having been able'
kadr + a [d]	'staff'	kadr fachowych [tr f]	'professional staff' (gen plural)

d. Cracow Voice Assimilation: voiceless obstruents are voiced before sonorants

	Warsaw Polish	Cracow Polish
somochód lśni 'the car is shining'	[t lɕ]	[d lɕ]
somochód Leona 'Leon's car'	[t l]	[d l]
somochód Romana 'Roman's car'	[t r]	[d r]
somochód nasz 'our car'	[t n]	[d n]
somochód ojca 'father's car'	[t o]	[d o]
brat Leona 'Leon's brother'	[t l]	[d l]
brat Romana 'Roman's brother'	[t r]	[d r]
brat nasz 'our brother'	[t n]	[d n]
brat ojca 'father's brother'	[t o]	[d o]

To begin, (9) presents the obstruents of Polish (Gussman 2007) which indicates it has a laryngeal contrast in stops, affricates, and fricatives with the surface phonetics suggesting that it is a voicing system. (10a) demonstrates the presence of a Voice Assimilation process where voiceless obstruents become voiced when a voiced obstruent follows. Word Final Devoicing is shown in (10b) where a voiced obstruent becomes voiceless at the end of a prosodic word. Both of these processes have wrinkles in them due to the transparency of nonsyllabic sonorants but by following Rubach's work, these issues can be accounted for. (10c) presents data that show Voiceless Assimilation where a voiced obstruent becomes voiceless when it is followed by a voiceless obstruent. Finally, (10d) presents a dialectal difference in Polish where sonorants do not cause Voice Assimilation across a word boundary in the Warsaw dialect but sonorants do in the Cracow dialect. The Cracow dialect raises questions on how to understand the phonological representation of sonorants. Cracow Voice Assimilation suggests that voiced obstruents and sonorants both trigger voice assimilation which would mean that they should have the same phonological specification which is contrary to the longstanding position that sonorants are unspecified for voice in the lexicon (Kiparsky 1985). Our analysis of this constellation of phonological activity is presented in the next section.

4.1 Contrast and laryngeal assimilation

The Avery and Idsardi (2001) feature system subscribes to Laryngeal Realism (Iverson and Salmons 1995) with a particular commitment to the articulatory phonetics. The relevant part of the overall semantics of the feature system for laryngeal features is in (11).

(11) Laryngeal features

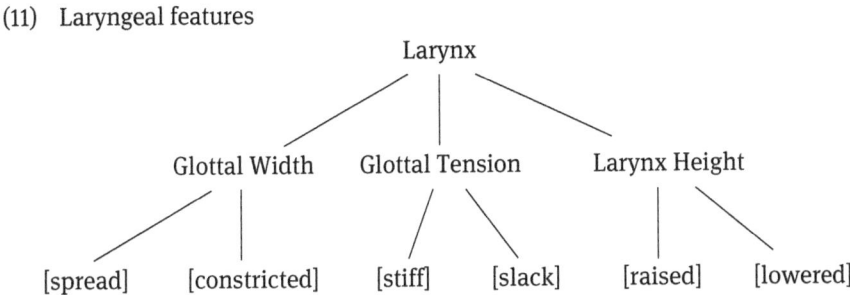

The organization of the laryngeal part of the Avery and Idsardi system is based on the now well understood functional anatomy of the larynx (see Zemlin 1998). Overall, the larynx has three affordances that are represented by the dimensions Glottal Width, Glottal Tension, and Larynx Height. Glottal Width controls the width of the glottis by either abducting the vocal folds, [spread], or adducting them, [constricted]. Glottal Tension controls the position of the thyroid cartilage and rocking the thyroid cartilage forward causes lengthening and stiffening of the focal folds, [stiff], and rocking the thyroid cartilage backwards toward the spine shortens and slackens the vocal folds, [slack]. Larynx Height controls the position of the larynx in general by either moving it upwards, [raised], or downwards, [lowered]. The three dimensions provide the building blocks for phonological representation of laryngeal systems and the six gestures provide the articulatory phonetics categories.

We interpret Laryngeal Realism as understanding that the translation of acoustic correlates to articulatory gestures is context dependent. This will be a very important point in understanding fundamental differences between Voice Assimilation from (10a) and our analysis of Cracow Voice Assimilation in (10d). A first step in understanding the parsing of acoustic information into articulatory gestures is to distinguish phonation from a phonological 'voice' feature. Phonation is the physical vibration of the vocal folds and is understood through the myoelastic-aerodynamic theory (Berg 1958) where vocal fold vibration is the result of a combination of laryngeal position and air pressure in the vocal tract. Articulator free distinctions as encoded in acoustic landmarks (Stevens 2002, Slifka 2007) such as obstruent (stops, affricates, and fricatives) vs. sonorants (nasals and approximants) provide contexts for interpreting laryngeal activity.

For obstruents, the default language ready laryngeal state produces a plain phone, [t] or [s], which undergoes phonation based on the neutral vocal tract. For stops, a short lag voice onset time is produced in post pausal word initial preapproximant contexts and variable voicing occurs in interapproximant contexts. Fricatives show partial voicing in initial and final position and almost complete voicing in intervocalic contexts. Plain obstruents following these descriptions are the 'voiced' (sic) series in General American English for many speakers. Laryngeal Realism takes the position that deviation from these acoustic descriptions require active manipulation of the larynx to alter the phonation behavior.

A voice system, as we understand Polish to be an example of, invokes the manipulation of Glottal Tension, specifically the [slack] gesture, to increase phonation in obstruents. The slackening of the vocal cords promotes phonation which leads to prevoicing on stops in initial position and full phonation on intervocalic stops and fricatives in all positions. Laryngeal Realism provides the possibility of a fairly transparent phonetics-phonology interface because manipulation of the larynx can be read off of the acoustics in a fairly straightforward manner with contextual information. Consequently, the phonological representation of the voiced vs. plain series in obstruents in Polish is in (12).

(12) Laryngeal representation in Polish
    voiced = Glottal Tension
    voiceless = Larynx-gt

The voiced series in Polish (as representing a voicing language) is marked with the Glottal Tension dimension and consequently the voiceless series is marked with Larynx-gt by following the superordinate marking proposal of PRS. The completion rule for Glottal Tension in Polish exchanges it for the gesture [slack] which produces the proper phonetic representation. The phonetic interpretation of the Larynx-gt specification for the voiceless series will turn out to be more complicated than commonly thought and we will expand on this in section 4.3.

A novel interpretation of the non-syllabic analysis of Polish laryngeal phonology proposed by Rubach (1996) allows a tier based analysis of both the voice assimilation (10a) and voiceless assimilation (10c) data. The general idea is that Polish projects a Glottal Tension tier which includes the superordinate Larynx-gt marking and this tier is broken into constituents by brackets (Idsardi 1992, 2009) also being projected. Syllabic nuclei project right brackets that create constituents on the Glottal Tension tier. (13) provides the basics of the representations involved in this analysis. Note that 'g' indicates Glottal Tension and 'l' indicates Larynx-gt.

(13) Grid based domains
   a. li<u>cz</u> + y + ć [t͡ʃ]   li<u>cz</u> + b + a [d͡ʒ + b]
       'count'   'number'
   i.   ii.   iii.

```
      )  1  )  1       *     )  1     g  )           )  g     g  )
   x  x  x  x  x          x  x  x     x  x        x  x  x     x  x
   l  i  tʃ  ɨ  tɕ        l  i  tʃ    b  a        l  i  d͡ʒ    b  a
```

b. litr + y [t]   litr wody [dr v]
    'liters'   'liter of water'
i.   ii.   iii.
) l   ) *   ) l   g) g)   ) g   g) g)
    x x x x x   x x x x x x x x   x   x x x   x   x x x
    l i t r ɨ   l i t r v o d ɨ   l   i t r   v   o d ɨ

c. ryb+a [b]   ryb + k + a [p + k]
    'fish'   'fish' (diminutive)
i.   ii.   iii.
) g)   *   ) g   l)   ) l   l)
    x x x x   x x x x x x   x x   x x
    r ɨ b a   r ɨ b k a r   ɨ p   k a

d. mog + ł + a [g]   mog + ł + sz + y [k + w + ʃ]
    'she could'   'having been able'
i.   ii.   iii.
) g   )   *   ) g   l)   ) l   l)
    x x x x x   x x x   x x   x x x   x x x
    m o g w a   m o g   w ʃ ɨ   m o k   w ʃ ɨ

e. brak + rdzy [k + r + d]
    'lack'+ 'rust' > 'lack of rust'
i.   ii.   iii.
    g   ) l) g) * g   ) l   g) * g   ) g   g)
    x x x x x x x   x x x x x x x   x x x x x x x
    b r a k r dz ɨ   b r a k r dz ɨ   b r a g r dz ɨ

The representations in (13) provide the opportunity to posit one generalization for the data which is that the feature next to the open side of the right bracket determines the featural content of the whole constituent. Each of the examples in (13) provides the relevant case to support this generalization. (13a) shows voice assimilation where a voiceless obstruent in (13ai) becomes voiced to meet the generalization in (13aiii). The series in (13b) shows that non-syllabic sonorants are transparent to this process because they do not project onto the Glottal Tension tier. (13c) presents the case where there is devoicing because the feature next to the right bracket is Larynx-gt and (13d) demonstrates that non-syllabic sonorants are still transparent. (13e) presents a case where a non-syllabic sonorant is not transparent and we follow Rubach (1996)'s analysis that these sonorants are adjoined to prosodic structure late in the derivation and become a syllabic nucleus which causes them to project a right bracket. In the end, the incorporation of these blocking sonorants may require some revision as to how we understand what segments project brackets but we leave this for future research.

We will take the standard position that marked features can be phonologically active and thus spread or copy. This allows the Voice Assimilation Rule to be formulated in (14) to account for some of the data in (13).

(14) Voice Assimilation
      Larynx-gt → Glottal Tension / _ Glottal Tension

The rule in (14) assumes that it operates only on the Glottal Tension tier which accounts for the sonorant transparency effects and that it only operates within the domains created on the Glottal Tension tier by the projected right brackets. Without providing a full proof, these characteristics should place the rule in the *tier based strictly local* computational realm (Jardine and Heinz 2016). The simplicity of the rule will allow it to be translated to parochial versions of phonological theory with ease if the current feature system is adopted. This will account for the data in (13a) and (13b). We will follow Lombardi (1995) in assuming that what appears to be surface spreading of an unspecified or unmarked feature (a superordinate category in this system) is the result of a licensing or deletion rule. We will account for the data in (13c) and (13d) as part of the next section.

4.2 Word final devoicing and voiceless spread

The common terms used to refer to aspects of Polish laryngeal phonology that are used in this section's title are misnomers in the context of the analysis we develop. The domain based analysis that accounts for Glottal Tension spreading can be extended to voiceless spread and word final devoicing for the most part. The way to do this is to require Glottal Tension to be licensed by being next to a right bracket. Given how we have developed the structure of the Glottal Tension tier, this can be expressed equally well in either a positive manner in a precedence grammar (Heinz 2010) or a negative fashion as a constraint.

(15) Glottal Tension Licensing
   a. positive: precedence grammar

$$G = \begin{cases} GT\,) \\ GT\, GT \\ Larynx\text{–}gt) \\ Larynx\text{–}gt\, Larynx\text{–}gt \\ Larynx\text{–}gt\, \% \end{cases}$$

   b. negative: constraint
      *GT Larynx-gt
      *GT %

The precedence grammar in (15a) states that on the Glottal Tension tier the only sequences that are permitted are a Glottal Tension feature followed by either a right bracket or another Glottal Tension feature, or a Larynx-gt feature followed by a right bracket, another Larynx-gt feature, or the end of a word (indicated by %, Raimy 2000). The constraints in (15b) state that a sequence of Glottal Tension followed by a Larynx-gt feature or the end of a word are penalized. The robustness of this generalization across approaches to phonological computation is an argument in its favor in our opinion.

(15) is silent on what to do with representations that are not licensed and there are new questions about phonological operations given the proposals of PRS. Established phonological operations of spreading and deletion are still available but due to the semantic organization of the features we can add an operations of *feature widening* and *feature narrowing* as possibilities (Tom Purnell, personal communication). The notions of wider and narrower are based on whether the feature gains or loses phonetic specificity by moving higher or lower in the semantic space of the Avery and Idsardi feature geometry. Changing Glottal Tension to Larynx-gt is an example of feature widening and changing Larynx-gt to Glottal Tension is feature narrowing.

We argue that the elimination of Glottal Tension when it is not licensed is an example of feature widening. This means that Glottal Tension changes to Larynx-gt as opposed to being deleted. There are two main aspects of this argument. One is based on the phonetics of the voiceless series of obstruents in Polish and the other is based on the dialectal difference between the Warsaw and Cracow dialects of Polish. We develop these points in the next two sections.

4.3 The phonetics of polish voiceless obstruents

Keating (1984) and Keating, Mikoś, and Ganong (1981) provide acoustic measurements of Polish and English stops in initial and medial position. This comparison is important because both English and Polish are two-way laryngeal systems that differ in how the contrast is marked. Polish is a Glottal Tension system and English is a Glottal Width system (Iverson and Ahn 2007). Both of these systems share the unmarked category which is superordinately marked with Larynx. A transparent phonology-phonetics interface would have the Larynx category be the same across the two systems modulo some language specific phonetic target tuning. Both Polish and English have their plain Larynx category described as phonetically voiceless unaspirated (Keating 1984). When actual acoustic measurements are considered, especially with contextual variance, the two languages appear to implement the Laryngeal category differently. (16) presents data from Keating (1984).

(16) Voice onset times (VOT) for stops in Polish and English

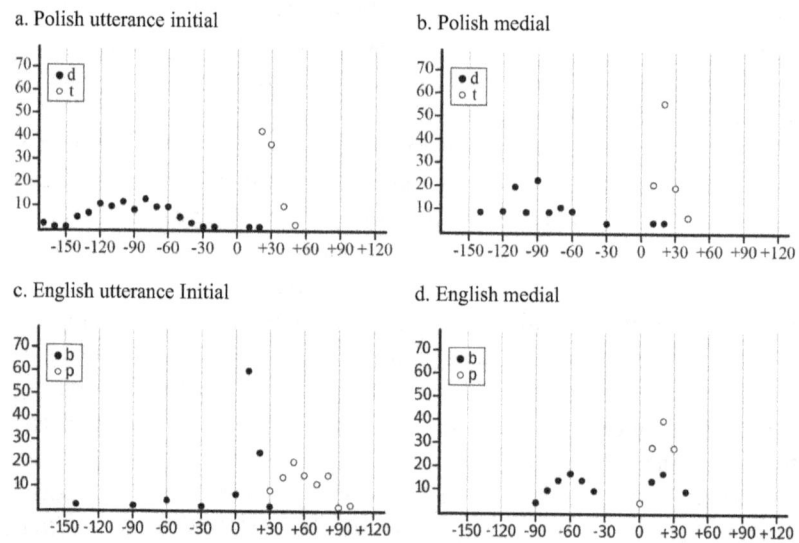

The panels in (16) allow for a direct comparison of the acoustic phonetics of the laryngeal systems of Polish and English. (16a) presents alveolar stops in utterance initial position in Polish and (16c) right below presents English labial stops in utterance initial position. Viewing these two graphs allows one to see the difference between a Glottal Tension system vs. a Glottal Width system. Polish, (16a) shows that voiced stops are prevoiced having a negative VOT (dark dots) in contrast to the plain voiceless unaspirated stops that have a short lag VOT (white dots). English in

(16c) has aspirated stops (more properly transcribed as /pʰ/) with a long lag VOT (white dots) contrasted with plain short lag stops (more properly transcribed as /p/, dark dots). The distribution of VOTs for the plain voiceless unaspirated stops in Polish and English overlap (light dots for Polish and dark dots for English) and look very similar but are not quite identical. The distribution of Polish short lag stops appear to have a VOT just a bit longer than the English ones.

The panels (16b) for Polish and (16d) for English show the same stops in a word internal environment (i.e. interapproximant). It is now clear that the Larynx category in these two languages must behave differently for some reason. In Polish, (16b), there is little change to the acoustic phonetics in the system. Glottal Tension marking still entails prevoicing and the unmarked Laryngeal category remains short lag VOT. English presents a different case though. The Laryngeal category in English changes from a short lag VOT (as in 16c) in post pausal position to become prevoiced in an intersonorant position while the Glottal Width category remains long lag but has reduced the overall VOT.

We believe that the phonetics of the English Larynx category represent a truly underspecified articulatory category. The variation in VOT for these stops in English can be understood and predicted assuming a language ready larynx setting from the myoelastic theory of phonation (Berg 1958, Laver 1994). Phonation is the vibration of the vocal folds and is the result of the Bernoulli effect acting on language ready vocal folds where imbalances in air pressure above and below the glottis cause the vocal folds to be blown apart and then pulled back together again. The variation between short lag VOT in post pausal initial position and fully prevoiced VOTs between vowels is directly predicted by modelling the larynx (Westbury and Keating 1986). In short, the phonological representation of the unmarked laryngeal category as phonetically underspecified provides a direct and transparent phonology-phonetics interface. The change from short lag VOT to full prevoicing can be fully understood simply as a change in context.

Based on this understanding of English, Polish requires the unmarked Larynx category to be different in some way. We reject a substance free position where phonological categories have arbitrary lookup in the phonetics module (Scheer and Cyran 2017) and instead pursue an enhancement (Keyser and Stevens 2006, Hall 2011) based approach.

Within the Avery and Idsardi (2001) feature system, one of the main roles phonology plays is the conversion of the phonological dimension based representation into a phonetic gesture based representation (for production, and vice versa for perception). For marked dimension features, a completion rule will exchange a dimension for one of the two dependent gestures. The application of completion rules will create a level of representation that is mixed between unmarked superordinate categories and gestures (see ex 8b). We refer to this step in the phonological derivation as the phonology-phonetics level. Although some bare superordinate categories, such as the major place categories Coronal, Labial, and Dorsal, can be directly interpreted by the phonetics, it is very common for phonologies to further specify them with gestures which produces overspecified phonetic representations. After all enhancement and fill in rules are applied a categorical phonetic representation exists which is further processed by the phonetics module. Our claim about Polish is that the Larynx-gt superordinate category undergoes an enhancement rule which exchanges it for the gesture [spread]. This is the basis for the difference in how the 'plain voiceless' category behaves in Polish and English. [spread] is straight forward for general 'voiceless' according to Laver (1994:187) and this is echoed by Borden & Harris (1980:90) who state, "The simplest adjustment of the vocal folds during speech is the one made for voiceless consonants. The folds abduct . . . the PCA [posterior cricoarytenoid] is the only muscle that acts to abduct the vocal folds." Westbury and Keating (1986:151) also support this general idea and state " . . . a medial stop . . . may be made fully voiceless if articulatory adjustments occur at the level of the larynx, which make the vocal folds less susceptible to oscillation, and/or which hasten neutralization of the pressure drop across them . . . Abduction of the vocal folds . . . may have both effects." (17) presents the steps in how the phonological representations are converted into categorical phonetics ones for Polish and English.

(17) Derivational steps in the laryngeal phonology of Polish and English

	Polish voiced	Polish voiceless unaspirated	English voiceless unaspirated	English aspirated
phonology dimensions	Glottal Tension	Larynx-gt	Larynx-gw	Glottal Width
phonology-phonetics completion	[slack]	Larynx-gt	Larynx-gw	[spread]
categorical phonetics enhancement fill-ins	[slack]	[spread]	Larynx-gw	[spread]
utterance initial surface phonetics	prevoiced	'mid' lag VOT	short lag VOT	long lag VOT
interapproximant surface phonetics	prevoiced	'mid' lag VOT	prevoiced	long lag VOT

Specifying the plain voiceless series in Polish with a [spread] gesture in the phonetics explains why voiceless stops do not change based on context like in English but it raises the question as to why Polish does not have full blown aspirated long lag obstruents. Kim (1970)'s proposals on how to understand aspiration indicates that the [spread] gesture is under control of the phonetic module and does not always produce the surface puff of air commonly recognized as aspiration. This observation is the key element in Iverson and Salmon (1995)'s analysis of the distribution of aspiration in English. The specific point is that the amount of glottal opening that the [spread] gesture causes is dependent on context in English. Full glottal abduction occurs in word and foot initial position and results in long lag VOT surface aspiration and partial abduction occurs elsewhere which results in a VOT less than a long lag without the puff of air recognized as aspiration. Polish appears to only take advantage of this medium glottal abduction interpretation of the [spread] gesture resulting in the stable 'short/mid' lag VOT plain voiceless across contexts.

Additional evidence for the presence of [spread] on the voiceless series in Polish comes from the discussion on whether sonorants are transparent to the devoicing of obstruents. Castellví-Vives (2003) documents sonorant devoicing and variability in transparency in obstruent-sonorant-obstruent clusters. The fact that sonorants can devoice in these clusters is direct evidence that there is a [spread] gesture present. A [spread] gesture is required here because it is the articulatory mechanism that devoices (i.e. prevents phonation) a nasal or approximant segment (Lombardi 1991, Cho 1993, Bombien 2014). Castellví-Vives (2003:2768) states, "In phonological analyses transparency cannot be taken as a regular process in Polish either, unless sonorant devoicing and elision are regarded as cases of transparency which are explained by phonetic implementation." which is the exact analysis we are pursuing here.

Exchanging Larynx-gt specification for [spread] gestures as part of the categorical phonetics module forces the explanation of sonorant devoicing and elision towards a phonetic one. A phonetic explanation of variation in sonorant devoicing matches the analysis of Tsuchida (1994) in high vowel devoicing of Japanese. Japanese is a Glottal Tension laryngeal system like Polish so an enhancement of [spread] on the Larynx-gt series is needed, the devoicing of high vowels is variable, and the devoicing has a grammatical component to it because it is only high vowels that undergo the process. Japanese is also not reported as having aspirated voiceless stops like Polish (but see the analysis in Avery and Idsardi 2001:53–54). These three characteristics match the general results of Castellví-Vives (2003) but not the particular details of Polish which is fine. We leave the full development for the phonetic analysis to future work but see Strycharczuk (2012) for some of the complexities involved.

To summarize this section, we propose that the voiceless series of obstruents in Polish are enhanced with a [spread] gesture which does not necessarily cause surface aspiration. The presence of the [spread] gesture in the phonetics ensures that medial voiceless obstruents in Polish do not alternate to voiced obstruents as happens in English. Additionally, the [spread] gesture also provides an explanation for sonorant devoicing (and possibly elision) in Polish as documented by Castellví-Vives (2003).

4.4 Cracow voicing

The final piece of our analysis of Polish laryngeal phonology is to account for the difference between Warsaw and Cracow dialects of Polish. We repeat the data from (10d) below.

(18) Dialect variation in Polish

	Warsaw Polish	Cracow Polish
somochód lśni 'the car is shining'	[t lɕ]	[d lɕ]
somochód Leona 'Leon's car'	[t l]	[d l]
somochód Romana 'Roman's car'	[t r]	[d r]
somochód nasz 'our car'	[t n]	[d n]
somochód ojca 'father's car'	[t o]	[d o]
brat Leona 'Leon's brother'	[t l]	[d l]
brat Romana 'Roman's brother'	[t r]	[d r]
brat nasz 'our brother'	[t n]	[d n]
brat ojca 'father's brother'	[t o]	[d o]

The analysis developed so far in section 4 will account for and produce the Warsaw data once we remember to invoke and formalize the Word Final Devoicing rule. Word Final Devoicing is the process that causes feature widening where a Glottal Tension specification is widened to Larynx-gt as in (19) which is basically Rubach (1996:77)'s final devoicing rule.

(19) Word Final Devoicing
Glottal Tension → Larynx-gt / ___)$_{PW}$

Following Rubach, the specification of the Prosodic Word edge is a complexity required to accommodate word final obstruent-sonorant clusters. For the Warsaw data, the rule in (19) will devoice (more properly featurally widen) the /d/ in *samochód* and then there are no Glottal Tension segments (sonorants are unspecified for Glottal Tension) following in the domain to 'revoice' it via the Voice Assimilation rule in (14).

The Cracow dialect can now be accounted for by a modified version of the Word Final Devoicing rule in (19). Instead of featurally widening the Glottal Tension feature, the Cracow final devoicing rule, (20), deletes the Glottal Tension feature.

(20) Cracow Final Devoicing
Glottal Tension → ∅ / ___)$_{PW}$

Deleting the Glottal Tension feature on an obstruent will result in a plain voiceless segment such as found in English. (20) deletes the Glottal Tension feature which prevents the voiceless series from being enhanced with [spread]. Cracow voicing is then understood as a phonetic effect where the plain voiceless obstruent undergoes contextual voicing (i.e. phonation) due to being between two approximants since the obstruents have not been enhanced. In other words, it behaves like English voiceless plain segments in medial position as in (16d). This completes our analysis of the data in (10) with the dialectal difference between Warsaw and Cracow Polish coming down to whether the word final devoicing rule featurally widens Glottal Tension to Larynx-gt or outright deletes it.

4.5 Summary of polish laryngeal phonology

We have developed an analysis of the laryngeal phonology of Polish in this section. This particular data from Polish is important because it has been the source of arguments about privative vs. binary features and the substance of phonology. The approach presented here is entirely based on the privative features from Purnell, Raimy, and Salmons (2019). This analysis has a complex relationship with Rubach (1996) because it replicates the general results but does so with privative features. We have posited equivalents of Voice Assimilation and Word Final Devoicing rules and assumed Rubach's general position on the prosodic aspects of these rules.

One novel finding of our proposed analysis is the presence of the enhancement of voiceless obstruents in Polish with the insertion of a [spread] gesture. This point plays an important role in explaining the phonetics of voiceless stops in word medial position and the phonetics surrounding 'transparent' sonorants. Additionally, dialectal variation in the formation of the word final devoicing rule affects whether the enhancement rule applies or not. Warsaw Polish is a dialect where the Word Final Devoicing rule feeds the enhancement rule. Word Final Devoicing in Cracow Polish actually deletes the laryngeal feature which bleeds the enhancement rule. This accounts for the Cracow voicing rule as a case of passive voicing due to a conducive phonetic environment.

The whole analysis is fairly banal once the proposals from Purnell, Raimy, and Salmons (2019) are adopted. The superordinate marking proposal allows a fully privative feature system to encode ternary phonological behavior. This along with a modular approach to phonology and phonetics is all that is needed to understand Polish laryngeal phonology.

5 Featural realism: Binary features and phonological substance

The Polish laryngeal phonology data has been used by various scholars to make arguments about the nature of phonological representations. Rubach (1996) uses this data to argue for binary features. Cyran (2011) makes arguments about phonological substance which interact with arguments from Beckman et al (2011) to produce opposing positions spanning from substance free phonology (Reiss 2017) to phonetic determinism. We discuss both of these topics in turn in this section and then propose the position of *Featural Realism* as a way to reconcile all of this work within the proposals of PRS.

5.1 Rubach (1996): Binary features

Although we are very much in debt to Rubach (1996)'s analysis of the data covered in section 4 and basically replicate his analysis, the proposals from PRS nullify the need for binary features. Rubach (1996) makes a specific claim that binary features are required in order to explain why obstruent clusters (initial and word internal) must agree in laryngeal features. Rubach achieves this effect through a combination of two processes: Obstruent Delinking and Spread.

(21) a. Obstruent Delinking   b. Spread

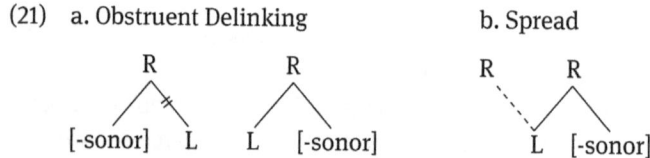

Once the specific details of Rubach's analysis are considered, one can see the indebtedness that we have to it. The operation of the Obstruent Delinking and Spread rules enforce uniformity of laryngeal specification in obstruent clusters by first delinking (i.e. deleting) the laryngeal specification of any obstruent that occurs before another obstruent, (21a), and then spreading the laryngeal specification of the obstruent at the end of the cluster to preceding obstruents, (21b). This is very similar to the analysis we proposed in section 4.1. with our Voice Assimilation rule, (14), doing the majority of the work.

Rubach (1996)'s argument that binary features are needed is based on transparency effects in obstruent-sonorant-obstruent clusters. The representative example of this according to Rubach (1996) is in (22).

(22) Binary vs. privative voice

```
                    Binary Voice              Privative Voice
                    j  e  n  d  r  k  a       j  e  n  d  r  k  a    [jentrka]
                    |  |  |  |                |  |  |  |  |  |                |
        laryngeal   L  L  L  L                L  L  L  L  L  L                L
                    +  +  +  +                -  +  +  +  +  +                +
                    v  v  v  v                v  v  v  v  v  v                v
```

Rubach's argument is that a privative approach to voice would not specify the voiceless /k/ in *jendrka* 'Andy (genitive singular)' with any laryngeal node which would then prevent it from triggering the Obstruent Delinking rule, (21a), which then amplifies the problem because the Spreading rule, (21b), would have no laryngeal content to spread. This is a standard classic argument against privative features based on surface activity of the unspecified feature.

The analysis we have developed in section 4.1 directly addresses this type of argument against privative features through the superordinate marking procedure. This provides the 'unmarked' side of a contrast with some phonological substance that behaves in the proper way for locality calculations which Rubach's concerns. Furthermore, these word internal cases are covered by the analysis already proposed in sections 4.1 and 4.2. The one place where our analysis is undeveloped is the question as to when a sonorant consonant is transparent or opaque with respect to Voice Assimilation in (14) as shown in the near doublets in (23).

(23) Sonorant opacity vs. transparency (Rubach 1996:71–72)
   a. transparent (Obstruent-Sonorant#Obstruent)
      litr + y [t] 'liters'   litr wody   [dr#v]   'liter of water'
   b. opaque (Obstruent#Sonorant-Obstruent)
      odgłos [s] 'sound'   odgłos rżenia   [s#rʒ]   'sound of neighing'
                                           *[z#rʒ]

Rubach (1996) states that whether a sonorant is transparent or opaque to Voice Assimilation is dependent on both sonority cline and where the word boundary is. (23a) is a case where the obstruent-sonorant cluster is at the end of a word and the sonorant acts as transparent for the purposes of Voice Assimiliation and Word Final Devoicing. (23b) is a case where the sonorant-obstruent cluster is at the beginning of the word with a resulting aberrant sonority change. These cases have the sonorant acting as opaque to Voice Assimilation so in the particular example the [s] at the end of *odgłos* does not become voiced from the [ʒ] in the following word (*rżenia*) when it is added. The difference between (23a) and (23b) hinges on prosodic effects which are orthogonal to our main points. We assume that Rubach (1996) is on the right track in connecting this to whether and when the sonorant consonant is associated to prosodic structure (see discussion of (13e) in section 4.1). We leave developing this point further in a contemporary Distributed Morphology (Newell 2017) framework to future research.

5.2 Phonological substance

Avery and Idsardi (2001) focuses mainly on laryngeal phonology but the appendix to their article includes a full feature geometry that we repeat in the Appendix to this article. This is a suggestion that our understanding of laryngeal phonology and Laryngeal Realism can and should be expanded to cover all phonological features. The potential benefits from this expansion can be demonstrated once some common misunderstandings about Laryngeal Realism are discussed. To begin this discussion, we present a table from Iverson and Ahn (2007) which we have updated to include superordinate marking and some other languages.

(24) Laryngeal representation based on contrast in Laryngeal Realism

	/p~b/	/b/	/pʰ/	/p'/	/bʰ/
a. Hawaiian	[ ]				
b. K'ekchi	Larynx-lh			Larynx Height	
c. French (Polish)	Larynx-gt	Glottal Tension			
d. English (Swedish)	Larynx-gw		Glottal Width		
e. Thai	Larynx-gt & Larynx-gw	Glottal Tension	Glottal Width		
f. Hindi	Larynx-gt & Larynx-gw	Glottal Tension	Glottal Width		Glottal Tension & Glottal Width

The updates to Iverson and Ahn in (24) are fairly straight forward addition of Larynx superordinate specifications with one complexity. For (24a-c) there is only a single contrast in the laryngeal system so there will only be a single superordinate marking. The examples from Thai (24e) and Hindi (24f) both have multiple superordinate markings of Larynx due to having three or four contrasts respectively. The marked categories in these systems may have an additional superordinate marking resulting from the order of features in the respective contrastive ranking. The vowel examples from (6) and (7) demonstrate this point. We omit these markings in (24) for purely visual and expository reasons but note that there will be multiple different configurations based on particular contrastive rankings. We leave these aside for this chapter since they will not impact the following arguments. (24) is accurate enough in the representations to discuss two misunderstandings about privative representations and their role in featural realism.

5.2.1 Misunderstanding overspecification

The first misunderstanding of the import of the proposals on representation in (24) is represented by Beckman et al (2011)'s arguments for overspecified phonological representations. Beckman et al provide evidence that both [spread] and [slack] gestures are represented in Swedish because of surface phonetics and more importantly because of an interaction between speaking rate and the surface implementation of [spread] and [slack] gestures. Simply put, only specified categories are affected by changes in speech rate with both [spread] (aspiration in Swedish) and [slack] (prevoicing in Swedish) gestures increasing in duration in slower speech. We agree with Beckman et al (2011) on the interpretation of speech rate and specified categories but disagree with them on what level of representation is responsible for these effects. Our disagreement is likely based on Beckman et al (2011) only considering the representations in (24) which are the phonological level and not considering the later level of categorical phonetics which is presented in (25).

(25) Categorial phonetics representations

	GT completion	Larynx enhancement	GW completion	Phonological Activity (spreading)
Polish	[slack]	[spread]		GT
Swedish		[slack]	[spread]	GW
English A		Larynx-gw	[spread]	GW
English B		[slack]	[spread]	GW

(25) is organized to show the generally agreed upon phonological organization for each language in the header row as either a GT 'voicing' language or a GW 'aspiration' (sic) language. The following rows present the categorical phonetics representation for different languages based on what completion rules have operated on dimensions and what enhancement rules have applied. Polish,

Swedish, and English B all end up being phonetically overspecified while English A retains a plain underspecified phonetic segment. English B represents some Southern dialects of American English as documented by Hunnicutt and Morris (2016). English A is the commonly assumed General American English that was discussed in section 4.3 and it is the outlier in the table.

The last column in (25) represents the identified phonological activity of the laryngeal feature in each language. We follow Avery and Rice (1989) and adopt the strong position that phonological representations are learned/determined based on phonological evidence such as featural activity and not surface phonetics. This allows the results of completion vs. enhancement rules to be distinguished. Surface phonetic gestures arising from completion rules indicate phonological dimensions that are related to phonological activity. Thus, the GW languages in (25) use the phonological activity of GW spread as a cue to treat the phonetic [spread] gesture as an indicator of phonological representation (and thus substance). Ringen and Helgason (2004) demonstrate that there is no spreading of the specified [slack] gesture which confirms that the phonetic overspecification in Swedish results from enhancement. There is no need to posit a Glottal Tension dimension in the phonology of Swedish. The same goes for Glottal Width in Polish here and in (25). The examples in (25) which are phonetically overspecified then have the other phonetic gesture treated as phonetically inert and thus relegated to an enhancement rule. Note that enhancement rules need to be learned as evidenced in the difference between English A and English B. Our view has phonological representations determined by phonological considerations.

Beckman et al (2011) in their work on Swedish argue that there is a direct link between categorical phonetic representations and phonological representations. Their proposal specifically argues that phonetic overspecification causes phonological overspecification. Translating this position into the current representations this would mean that the phonetic contrast of [spread]~[slack] in Swedish (and presumably English B) causes a GW~GT phonological contrast. This position eliminates the connection between phonological activity and phonological representation because both active (GW in Swedish and EnglishA,B) and inactive (GT in Swedish and English B) phonological features exist. Even though Beckman et al (2011) do traffic in privative laryngeal representations, specifying both active and inactive features in the phonology reduces the attraction of privative features. Overspecified representations, whether privative or binary, cannot encode markedness or any other asymmetry in phonological activity and thus, require a look up table to represent this information in line with proposals of Calabrese (2009). We consequently do not see any advantage in Beckman et al (2011)'s proposals over the present ones.

To conclude this section, overspecification in phonetic representation is a common phenomenon that has not had due attention paid to it in our opinion. Beckman et al (2011) should be given credit of providing concrete evidence that phonetic overspecification exists from a new methodology. Westbury and Keating (1986) point out that the plain or default representation in laryngeal systems is commonly specified in intrasonorant position which would be a result of overspecified phonetics. Finally, place of articulation is almost always phonetically overspecified which should tell phonologists that seeing laryngeal representation being phonetically overspecified is not surprising. Even with the phonetic overspecification of place of articulation, there are good arguments for underspecification (see Rice 2009 for a good summary) that we consider converging evidence for the proposals in this chapter.

5.2.2 Misunderstanding phonological substance

Part of the misunderstanding of phonetic overspecification discussed in the previous section is positing phonological structure based on phonetic structure. This can be understood as *phonetic determinism* which we clearly do not think is a good idea. Cyran (2011) argues for the polar opposite interpretation of the relation between phonological representation or substance and phonetic structure based on the Polish data analyzed in this chapter. Cyran (2011:59) states, "The hypothesis I would like to put forward at this stage is that indeed there is a fair degree of relativity in that a phonetically 'voicing' language may in fact be defined by the presence of |H| (this is [spread] or GW in the Avery & Idsardi system, ER), where the marked series shows no appreciable aspiration at all, while the unmarked series is realized with full voice (VOT lead)." This is a complex proposal and we agree with the general approach and shape of Cyran (2011)'s analysis but disagree on the overall conclusion about phonological substance.

For the Warsaw Polish dialect Cyran (2011) proposes an analysis that is almost identical to the one proposed here with two technical differences. The first difference is that Cyran works in Element Theory so uses different features than we do. The representations that will be relevant for discussion and comparison are the |L| and |H| elements which are standardly used to represent 'voicing' and 'aspirating' laryngeal contrasts respectively. Warsaw Polish is thus a standard 'voicing' language where the laryngeal contrast in the obstruents is encoded as |L|~Ø. (26) presents how Cyran (2011) handles Final Obstruent Devoicing (FOD) which is representative of his approach for Warsaw Polish.

(26) Warsaw Polish Final Obstruent Devoicing (Cyran 2011:70)

lexical representation		phonological representation FOD		phonetic interpretation	
/vᴸagᴸ/	=	/vᴸagᴸa/	>	[vaga]	'scale, nom.sg.'
/vᴸagᴸ/	=	/vᴸag°/	>	[vak]	'scale, gen.pl.'
/bᴸik°/	=	/bᴸik°a/	>	[bɨka]	'bull, gen. sg.'
/bᴸik°/	=	/bᴸik°/	>	[bɨk]	'bull, nom. sg.'

Cyran (2011) indicates the specification of obstruents by superscript with an obstruent with an |L| element having a superscript ᴸ and an unmarked or unspecified obstruent with a superscript °. The data in (26) demonstrate that FOD in Cyran (2011) is accomplished by deleting the |L| element in the word final context. This means that the stem *vag* 'scale' retains a voiced velar obstruent when suffixed with a vowel, *vaga* 'scale, nom.sg.' but the velar obstruent is devoiced to [g°] when in word final position with it occurring as a voiceless velar stop, [k], at the surface. The stem *bik* 'bull' does not show this alternation because the stem final /k/ is already unmarked.

(27) presents Cyran (2011)'s analysis for FOD in the Cracow Polish dialect. Cyran 'flips' the laryngeal representations on the obstruents so the 'voiced' series is unmarked and the 'voiceless' series is now marked with |H|.

(27) Cracow Polish Final Obstruent Devoicing (Cyran 2011:71)

lexical representation		phonological representation FOD		phonetic interpretation	
/v°ag°/	=	/v°ag°a/	>	[vaga]	'scale, nom.sg.'
/v°ag°/	=	/v°ag°/	>	[vak]	'scale, gen.pl.'
/b°ikᴴ/	=	/b°ikᴴa/	>	[bɨka]	'bull, gen. sg.'
/b°ikᴴ/	=	/b°ik°/	>	[bɨk]	'bull, nom. sg.'

Cyran argues that the computation is the same in Warsaw and Cracow Polish so the FOD produces neutralization by deleting the marked laryngeal element, |L| for Warsaw and |H| for Cracow, in word final position. Cracow Polish then neutralizes the laryngeal contrast in word final position to unmarked, [g°/k°], which is interpreted as 'voiceless' and maintains the laryngeal contrast in other contexts with obstruents specified with |H| being voiceless unaspirated and unspecified obstruents being 'voiced'.

The difference in representation between Warsaw and Cracow Polish provides the basis for the explanation of Cracow Voicing. This is presented in (28) which is simplified from the autosegmental representations in Cyran and modeled on the format in (26–27).

(28) Cracow sandhi voicing (Cyran 2011:75–76, modified)
    a. Warsaw Polish

lexical representation	phonological representation |L| delinking	phonetic interpretation	
/rzᴸutº/	/rzᴸutº#ɔkºa/	utº#ɔ > [t]	*rzut oka* 'glimpse'
/radᴸ/	/radº#ɔjtsɔjskʲix/	adº#ɔ > [t]	*rad ojcowskich* 'fatherly advice, gen. pl.'

    b. Cracow Polish

lexical representation	phonological representation |H| delinking	phonetic interpretation	
/rzºutᴴ/	/rzºutº#ɔkᴴa/	utº#ɔ > [d]	*rzut oka* 'glimpse'
/radº/	/radº#ɔjtsɔjskʲix/	adº#ɔ > [d]	*rad ojcowskich* 'fatherly advice, gen. pl.'

The key to Cyran's analysis and claims about laryngeal relativism is that both the Warsaw and Cracow Polish dialects end the phonology with the laryngeal contrast neutralized in word final position. At this point different phonetics take over in the two dialects. Warsaw Polish, (28a), interprets an unspecified obstruent at the end of the word followed by a vowel initial word (VØ#V) as voiceless while Cracow Polish, (28b), interprets it as voiced. To fully appreciate the possible variation in phonetic interpretation in Cyran's analysis, the table in (29) summarizes how the elements |L|, |H|, and the unspecified category are interpreted by the phonetics.

(29) Phonetic interpretation for Cyran (2011)

Representation	Context	Warsaw	Cracow
|L|	all	voiced	N/A
|H|	all	N/A	voiceless
Ø	_V	voiceless	voiced
Ø	_# (FOD)	voiceless	voiceless
Ø	_#V	voiceless	voiced

The table in (29) sheds light on the limits of laryngeal relativity. The elements themselves, |L| and |H| in this instance, appear to not be 'relative' in that they are uniformly phonetically interpreted as 'voiced' or 'voiceless' in all contexts. It is only the unspecified category that has relativistic interpretation. In the Warsaw dialect, the unspecified category is always interpreted as 'voiceless'. We agree with the general point here but note that in our analysis this results because the 'unspecified' category is actually marked with LarynxGT which is then enhanced with [spread] thus enforcing the phonetic voiceless category. The Cracow dialect, on the other hand, has a contextual interpretation of the unspecified category where it is voiceless in word final position but is voiced when followed by a vowel regardless of whether there is a word boundary or not.

Cyran (2011) is absolutely correct that given the representations used in his proposed analysis it is entirely reasonable to conclude that phonetic interpretation can do what it will with an unspecified category and thus result in laryngeal relativity. Clearly, we disagree with the necessity of this conclusion and section 4 demonstrates how we arrive at the exact opposite position. The superordinate marking hypothesis posits structure for unspecified (but contrastive) categories. This underspecified structure provides a scaffolding for phonetics to further specify the representation. As argued, this provides the ability for ternary distinctions to be made which is the key insight in Cyran's analysis. A simple binary contrast is not sufficient to understand Polish laryngeal phonology but a ternary one is.

We believe Cyran (2011)'s laryngeal relativism proposal is due to misunderstanding phonetic overspecification. Cyran (2011) assumes that an underspecified phonology determines an underspecified output for phonetics to interpret. Because the output of the phonology is still extremely underspecified, the phonetics must be very powerful and appears to be arbitrary. An unconstrained mapping between phonology and phonetics enables Cyran to flip the phonological representation in Polish from an |L| voice language for the Warsaw dialect to an |H| language for the Cracow dialect. Phonetic interpretation then cleans up the fundamental phonological difference between the two dialects to create a surface similarity that only diverges based on the presence or absence of Cracow Voicing.

A feature of Cyran (2011)'s analysis of Polish is that even while flipping the representations from marking |L| for Warsaw Polish to |H| for Cracow Polish it claims that the computational rules remain the same. Remember that Rubach (1996) posits both voice and voiceless spreading but we argue that there is only 'voice' GT spreading (10a) with the appearance of voiceless spreading actually being the results of licensing restrictions on GT (15). Cyran (2011) claims that Cracow Polish can be viewed of the mirror of this where voiceless spreading is the actual spreading of the |H| element and then voice spreading is a licensing effect. This approach will cause problems for the question of sonorant transparency effects though. If a sonorant is transparent to this process then it should be fully devoiced (or deleted if suggestions by Castellvi-Vives 2003 are followed) as the |H| element is spread and shared by the flanking obstruents. This appears to be incorrect with the available facts about sonorant transparency indicating that it is a phonetically variable process. Cyran (2011) should have it as a categorical phonological alternation though. Either the sonorant is transparent and devoices as part of the spread of |H| or the sonorant is opaque (like a vowel) and blocks the spread.

Our proposal agrees with Cyran (2011) that the beginning of phonology is underspecified and with Beckman et al (2011) that the end of phonetics is (mostly) overspecified. Both Cyran (2011) and Beckman et al (2011) lose the connection between phonological activity and phonological representation. In (25) there is a direct connection between phonological activity as expressed by the spreading of a dimension (in our system) and the basic marking of phonological substance. English (both A and B) and Swedish provide strong evidence for the spreading of GW which is the evidence for the learner that they are a GW system. Ringen and Helgason (2004) argue that Swedish does not have a rule spreading [slack] as a feature so there is no entailment between phonetic [slack] and a 'voice assimilation' rule. This is exactly what we expect with our proposals. Phonetic enhancements do not entail phonological activity consequently, as the learner determines what phonological activity is present, this affects what side of an overspecified opposition is marked phonologically. Both Swedish and English B, (25), provide surface phonetic evidence of either [spread] (to be GW) or [slack] (to be GT) as the marked category for the phonology. The presence of the GW spreading cues the learner to memorize the GW type system. English A doesn't provide this type of ambiguity in laryngeal phonology since [slack] as a phonetic feature doesn't appear which provides only [spread] (to be GW) as the option to encode the contrast in the phonology. Our view on substance in phonology is that phonology is *substance impoverished*, not substance free (Reiss 2017) nor phonetically determined. We will discuss this point further in the next section.

Our final concern with the proposed representations in (29) is how we should treat and understand dialectal variation in phonological representations. It appears that the only difference between the Warsaw and Cracow dialects of Polish is the presence of the Cracow Voicing, (18). Cyran (2011) takes this one difference as sufficient to flip the phonological representation of the laryngeal contrast from a 'voice' system to an 'aspiration' system (GT to GW in our terms). While a substance free or laryngeal relativism approach to the phonology-phonetics interface can produce this grammar, it only raises questions of how we should think about structural similarity between closely related dialects. We have the opinion that the Cracow and Warsaw dialects are very similar and only differ in the Cracow Voicing rule and thus should be structurally very similar. The analysis in section 4 argues that the difference between these two dialects is found in the Word Final Devoicing rule and whether it deletes or widens the GT dimension. A minimal difference between dialects should be accounted for by a minimal difference in grammar. Cyran (2011) does not share this view and proposes fundamentally different phonological representations for the Cracow and Warsaw dialects. Great changes in representations require strong arguments and the analysis in section 4 demonstrates that a great change in representation is not necessary to understand the difference between Cracow and Warsaw dialects of Polish. Consequently, we do not find the arguments in Cyran (2011) for laryngeal relativism and a substance free phonology-phonetics interface to be convincing.

5.3 Featural realism

Our analysis of Polish is an intermediate position between the positions taken on the relationship between phonetics and phonology exemplified by Beckman et al (2011) in section 5.2.1 and Cyran (2011) discussed in sect 5.2.2. To review, Beckman et al (2011) can be viewed of representing a phonetically driven phonology where all surface phonetic representation is recapitulated in the phonology. We will refer to this as the *substance full* position. Cyran (2011) can be viewed as representing the exact opposite perspective where there is no connection between surface phonetics and the underlying phonology. This is the *substance free* position espoused by Reiss (2017). As indicated in the previous section, we believe there is a third position that we refer to as *substance impoverished* phonology and we believe that this is the natural position for the combination of proposals by Dresher et al (1994), Dresher (2009), Avery and Idsardi (2001) and Purnell, Raimy, and Salmons (2019). Without speaking for all of these authors or seeking their countenance, we will dub this synthesis of proposals on phonological representations *Featural Realism*.

Featural Realism expands the general position of Laryngeal Realism (Iverson and Salmons 1995) to cover all segmental features and the general tenets of this position are listed in (30).

(30) Featural Realism
   a. distinctive features are innate
   b. phonological structure is underspecified
   c. phonological structure is substance
   d. phonological structure is markedness

    e. phonological structure is learned
    f. phonetic surface representations are generally overspecified
    g. the phonological derivation is hyper-modular

For (30a), we believe that distinctive features and the general semantic organization of them as presented in the Appendix are innate. Mesgarani et al (2008) shows that the spectrotemporal receptive fields in ferrets can support either the precursors to or the actual processing of human speech based on what we would recognize as distinctive features. We assume that if ferrets have these cognitive structures then they are preserved in mammals, especially in humans who actually use them in language. Clearly more work needs to be done to fully understand this point within cognitive neuroscience but that work would merely confirm existing work on distinctive features within phonology. Claims of innateness are not fashionable these days outside of the biological sciences but the evidence we have supports this particular claim.

The presence of a mammalian fairly general innate ability to process speech sounds via distinctive features raises the question of how humans are different. We believe that humans have some extra module to connect the acoustic perception of distinctive features to the articulatory plans required to produce speech in something akin to proposals by Liberman and Mattingly (1985). Poeppel et al (2008) and Poeppel and Idsardi (2011) provide a contemporary view on how cognitive neuroscience is working on this question. The point we are interested in here is that the categories that phonology use to build representations are 'organic' to the cognitive system. They will be substantive because they are drawing on other representations that are substantive in other perception and production modules.

(30b) is based on both linguistic and non-linguistic considerations. General cognitive science results suggest that representation is memory and vice versa (Murray et al 2017). Chechile (2018) demonstrates that memory is not completely veridical which means not all aspects of perceptual input are encoded in memory. This indicates that memory is in general underspecified which makes all cognitive representations underspecified. From the linguistics perspective, the Successive Division Algorithm proposed by Dresher (2009) will always produce underspecified representations in line with Modified Contrastive Specification (Dresher et al 1994).

Our take on markedness is a narrow interpretation based on proposals from Avery and Rice (1989) where phonological specification equals markedness. We recognize that this is not the only way markedness is conceived of (see Rice 1999ab for an overview). This means that markedness can be read directly off of a phonological representation based on what is specified and how much phonetic substance has been posited by phonological features. This position covers (30c) and (30d).

(30e) requires the most explication because it helps reach across the span between the substance free and substance full approaches to phonology. As already mentioned, phonological representations will be underspecified due to how the successive division algorithm (SDA, Dresher 2009) operates and this is good because it matches our general knowledge about memory and representation. The SDA will begin encoding contrast based on the pool of distinctive features present in the overall vowel inventory. This was discussed in section 3 and it should be noted that based on tenet (30a) the overall hypothesis space is closed both by the features being innate and the ambient language specific vowel inventory. (6) presented three possible ways to encode the vowel inventory of /ɪ, ʊ, ɐ/ which demonstrates learning segmental inventories via the SDA prevents surface level phonetics from completely determining the underlying phonological representations. If this position is true, then this will explain why cross linguistic comparison of segmental inventories and their phonological processes present the illusion of being substance free. Two surface identical segmental inventories can provide conflicting evidence about substance in phonology which clearly argues against substance full or phonetically determined models of phonology. The substance free (Reiss 2017) position overinterprets this situation though by concluding there is absolutely no phonetic substance because not all phonetic substance is encoded in the representation.

Empirical facts drive (30f). The discussion of how vowel systems are encoded in section 3 quickly shows how additional enhancement and fill in rules are required to account for the surface phonetics of contrast in vowel systems. Hall (2011) provides the foundational document on this point where he outlines how MCS type representations can easily and straightforwardly account for surface dispersion type effects once enhancement and fill-in rules are considered. This tenet highlights the necessarily modular nature of Featural Realism because the phonological level of representation will only account for so much. One important aspect of the discussion in section 5.2.1 are the parallels between the issues of overspecification in consonants and in vowels.

Finally, we follow the general suggestion from Carruthers (2006) that a more profligate attitude towards modules in cognitive systems is beneficial which matches (30g). The outline of the derivation in (8) presents an unusual number of levels of representation when compared with other approaches. Murray et al (2017) presents a viewpoint that there are multiple memory systems in mammals with each distinct memory system defining a cognitive module with proprietary representations. We follow this point of view and assume that each change in representation through phonological rule, completion rule, enhancement rule, fill-in rule, etc. defines a change in modules. Another aspect of our approach to hyper-modularity is that we do not ascribe to the position that modular transition is governed by arbitrary look up tables as suggested by Scheer and Cyran (2017). Arbitrary lists are not likely candidates for a cognitive system given that there is a growing consensus that the general format for a cognitive representation is a map (Bellmund et al 2018). Maps have a geometry and metric scale that relates the entries stored in the representation. Consequently, map to map, i.e. module to module, transition is far more principled and constrained than suggested by the look up table assumption of Scheer and Cyran (2017) and substance free phonology (Reiss 2017) in general.

The tenets in (30) lay out a perspective on phonology that has not been formalized before as far as we are aware. We believe they provide a useful guide for a research program that helps navigate many contemporary issues in phonology.

6 Elements and conclusion

This chapter started by referencing the foundational work in Element Theory of Kaye, Lowenstamm and Vergnaud (1985, 1990). A casual view of the work presented here when compared to contemporary work in Element Theory may suggest that there is no connection between the two. But if the 'ground rules' of Kaye et al (1990) are considered then we can see that there is great affinity. (31) presents these ground rules and we will discuss each in turn as a conclusion to this chapter.

(31) 'Ground Rules' of Kaye et al (1990:194)
    a. Privativeness
       Phonological oppositions that are privative at the level of lexical representation remain privative at all levels
       Consequences:
       No default rules to 'fill in' missing features.
       Only univalent spreading (harmony) processes.
       'You can't spread something that isn't there.'
       Unmarked values never spread directly.
       In Trubetzkoyan terms, privative oppositions do not get converted to equipollent ones in the course of a derivation.

b. Universality
The set of available phonological processes behaves like a function mapping initial representations onto final representations.
Consequences:
The same physical object will receive uniform interpretation across phonological systems.
Markedness conventions are universal.

c. Non-arbitrariness
There is a direct relation between a phonological process and the context in which it occurs.
Example:
Consider a process that converts a high tone into a rising tone following a low tone. An autosegmental treatment of this phenomenon satisfies the non-arbitrariness condition; a rule based treatment does not.

(31a) presents the rule of privativeness. Evaluating whether the proposals in this chapter follow this rule is complicated because it is unlikely that Kaye et al (1990) shares the same assumptions as Featural Realism does on modularity. If only the phonological level of representation (dimension vs. superordinate category) is considered then (31a) is completely met but this would strictly limit what counts as phonological phenomena to be accounted for. (31b) is universalness which in our interpretation Featural Realism follows quite strongly if we again limit the interpretation to the phonological level. Any object that is posited at the phonological level has the same interpretation cross linguistically. The complexity here is that later levels of representation and processing can obscure this fact. Note that the implication that there is 'uniform interpretation' suggests that substance free phonology (Reiss 2017) should be anathema to Element Theory. Non-arbitrariness, (31c) as the last ground rule, is also followed in general by Featural Realism. The superordinate marking proposal complicates this a bit because of licensing effects but the general mechanism of spreading marked features remains as the main active component of phonology.

To conclude, privative features should be the standard form of distinctive features in any phonological theory. The details of different phonological theories may obscure similarities but privative features may provide a standard form to see true similarities and differences among theories.

References

Anderson, John & Colin Ewen. 1987. *Principles of Dependency Phonology*. Cambridge University Press.

Anderson, John & Charles Jones. 1974. Three theses concerning phonological representations. *Journal of Linguistics* 10(1). 1–26. https://doi.org/10.1017/S0022226700003972.

Avery, Peter & William J. Idsardi. 2001. Laryngeal dimensions, completion and enhancement. In T. Alan Hall (ed.), *Distinctive Feature Theory*. Berlin, Boston: DE GRUYTER. https://doi.org/10.1515/9783110886672.41.

Avery, Peter & Keren Rice. 1989. Segment Structure and Coronal Underspecification. *Phonology* 6(2). 179–200.

Beckman, Jill, Pétur Helgason, Bob McMurray & Catherine Ringen. 2011. Rate effects on Swedish VOT: Evidence for phonological overspecification. *Journal of Phonetics* 39(1). 39–49. https://doi.org/10.1016/j.wocn.2010.11.001.

Bellmund, Jacob L. S., Peter Gärdenfors, Edvard I. Moser & Christian F. Doeller. 2018. Navigating cognition: Spatial codes for human thinking. *Science* 362(6415). eaat6766. https://doi.org/10.1126/science.aat6766.

Berg, Janwillem van den. 1958. Myoelastic-aerodynamic theory of voice production. *Journal of Speech and Hearing Research* 1(3). 227–244.

Bombien, Lasse. 2014. Voicing alterations in Icelandic sonorants. https://www.researchgate.net/profile/Lasse_Bombien/publication/208032994_Voicing_alternations_in_Icelandic_sonorants-a_photoglottographic_and_acoustic_analysis/links/0deec5306d358e1498000000.pdf

Borden, Gloria J. & Katherine S. Harris. 1980. *Speech Science Primer*. Baltimore Williams & Watkins.

Calabrese, Andrea. 2009. Markedness Theory versus Phonological Idiosyncrasies in a Realistic Model of Language. In Eric Raimy & Charles E. Cairns (eds.), *Contemporary Views on Architecture and Representations in Phonology*, 260–303. The MIT Press. doi:10.7551/mitpress/9780262182706.003.0013.

Carruthers, Peter. 2006. *The Architecture of the Mind*. Oxford University Press.

Castellvi-Vives, Joan. 2003. Neutralization and Transparency Effects in Consonant Clusters in Polish. In Maria-Josep Solé & Joaquin Romero (eds.), *15th International Congress of Phonetic Sciences*, 4.

Chechile, Richard A. 2018. *Analyzing Memory: The formation, retention, and measurement of memory*. MIT Press.

Cho, Young-mee Yu. 1993. The Phonology and Phonetics of "Voiceless" Vowels. *Proceedings of the Nineteenth Annual Meeting of the Berkeley Linguistics Society*. 64–75.

Chomsky, Noam. 1965. *Aspects of the theory of syntax*. MIT Press.

Chomsky, Noam & Morris Halle. 1968. *The sound pattern of English*. Harper & Row.

Clements, George Nick. 1985. The geometry of phonological features. *Phonology Yearbook* 2(1). 225–252. doi:10.1017/S0952675700000440.

Cyran, Eugeniusz. 2011. Laryngeal realism and laryngeal relativism: Two voicing systems in Polish? *Studies in Polish Linguistics* 6. 45–80.

Dresher, Elan. 2009. *The contrastive hierarchy in phonology*. Cambridge University Press.

Dresher, Elan, Glyne Piggott & Keren Rice. 1994. Contrast in phonology: overview. *Toronto Working Papers in Linguistics* 13. https://twpl.library.utoronto.ca/index.php/twpl/article/view/6331.

Gussman, Edmund. 2007. Sounds, Letters and Theories. In *The Phonology of Polish*. 1–20. Oxford, UK: Oxford University Press.

Hall, Daniel Currie. 2011. Phonological contrast and its phonetic enhancement: dispersedness without dispersion. *Phonology* 28(1). 1–54. https://doi.org/10.1017/S0952675711000029.

Halle, Morris. 2005. Palatalization/Velar Softening: What It Is and What It Tells Us about the Nature of Language. *Linguistic Inquiry* 36(1). 23–41.

Hamann, Silke. 2013. Phonetics-Phonology Interface. In Nancy C. Kula, Bert Botma & Kuniya Nasukawa (eds.), *The Bloomsbury Companion to Phonology*, 202–224. Bloomsbury Publishing Plc.

Heinz, Jeffrey. 2010. Learning Long-Distance Phonotactics. *Linguistic Inquiry*. 41(4). 623–661.

Hunnicutt, Leigh & Paul A Morris. 2016. Prevoicing and Aspiration in Southern American English. *University of Pennsylvania Working Papers in Linguistics* 22(1). 215–224.

Idsardi, William. 1992. *The computation of prosody*. MIT Ph.D.

Idsardi, William J. 2009. Calculating Metrical Structure. In Eric Raimy & Charles E. Cairns (eds.), *Contemporary Views on Architecture and Representations in Phonology*, 190–211. The MIT Press. https://doi.org/10.7551/mitpress/9780262182706.003.0009.

Iverson, Gregory K. & Sang-Cheol Ahn. 2007. English Voicing in Dimensional Theory. *Language sciences (Oxford, England)* 29(2–3). 247–269. https://doi.org/10.1016/j.langsci.2006.12.012.

Iverson, Gregory K. & Joseph C. Salmons. 1995. Aspiration and Laryngeal Representation in Germanic. *Phonology* 12(3). 369–396.

Jardine, Adam & Jeffrey Heinz. 2016. Learning Tier-based Strictly 2-Local Languages. *Transactions of the Association for Computational Linguistics* 4. 87–98. https://doi.org/10.1162/tacl_a_00085.

Kaplan, Robert. 1999. *The nothing that is a natural history of zero*. Oxford University Press.

Kaye, Jonathan, Jean Lowenstamm & Jean-Roger Vergnaud. 1985. The internal structure of phonological elements: a theory of charm and government. *Phonology Yearbook* 2(1). 305–328. doi:10.1017/S0952675700000476.

Kaye, Jonathan, Jean Lowenstamm & Jean-Roger Vergnaud. 1990. Constituent structure and government in phonology. *Phonology* 7(1). 193–231. doi:10.1017/S0952675700001184.

Keating, Patricia A. 1984. Phonetic and Phonological Representation of Stop Consonant Voicing. *Language* 60(2). 286. https://doi.org/10.2307/413642.

Keating, Patricia A., Michael J. Mikoś & William F. Ganong. 1981. A cross-language study of range of voice onset time in the perception of initial stop voicing. *The Journal of the Acoustical Society of America* 70(5). 1261–1271. https://doi.org/10.1121/1.387139.

Keyser, Samuel Jay & Kenneth N. Stevens. 2006. Enhancement and Overlap in the Speech Chain. *Language* 82(1). 33–63. https://doi.org/10.1353/lan.2006.0051.

Kim, Chin-Wu. 1970. A Theory of Aspiration. *Phonetica* 21. 107–116.

Kiparsky, Paul. 1985. Some consequences of Lexical Phonology. *Phonology Yearbook* 2(1). 85–138. https://doi.org/10.1017/S0952675700000397.

Kwon, Joy. In prep. *Defining perceptual similarity with phonological levels of representation: Feature (mis)match in Korean and English*. University of Wisconsin-Madison Ph.D.

Laver, John. 1994. *Principles of phonetics*. Cambridge University Press.

Liberman, Alvin M. & Ignatius G. Mattingly. 1985. The motor theory of speech perception revised. *Cognition* 21(1). 1–36. https://doi.org/10.1016/0010-0277(85)90021-6.

Lombardi, Linda. 1991. *Laryngeal features and laryngeal neutralization.* Amherst, MA: University of Massachusetts Ph.D.

Lombardi, Linda. 1995. Laryngeal neutralization and syllable wellformedness. *Natural Language and Linguistic Theory* 13(1). 39–74. doi:10.1007/BF00992778.

Mesgarani, Nima, Stephen V. David, Jonathan B. Fritz & Shihab A. Shamma. 2008. Phoneme representation and classification in primary auditory cortex. *The Journal of the Acoustical Society of America* 123(2). 899–909. https://doi.org/10.1121/1.2816572.

Murray, Elisabeth A., Steven P. Wise & Kim S. Graham. 2017. *The Evolution of Memory Systems: Ancestors, anatomy, and adaptions.* Oxford University Press.

Nevins, Andrew. 2015. Triumphs and limits of the Contrastivity-Only Hypothesis. *Linguistic Variation* 15(1). 41–68. doi:10.1075/lv.15.1.02nev.

Newell, Heather. 2017. The syntax-phonology interface. In Stephen J. Hannahs & Anna R. K. Bosch (eds.), *The Routledge Handbook of Phonological Theory.* 197–225. Routledge.

Oxford, Will. 2015. Patterns of contrast in phonological change: Evidence from Algonquian vowel systems. *Language* 91(2). 308–357. doi:10.1353/lan.2015.0028.

Poeppel, David & William Idsardi. 2011. Recognizing words from speech: The perception-action-memory loop. In M. Gareth Gaskell & Pienie Zwitserlood (eds.), *Lexical representation: a multidisciplinary approach* (Phonology and Phonetics 17), 171–196. Berlin ; New York: De Gruyter Mouton.

Poeppel, David, William J. Idsardi & Virginie van Wassenhove. 2008. Speech perception at the interface of neurobiology and linguistics. *Philosophical Transactions of the Royal Society B: Biological Sciences* 363(1493). 1071–1086. https://doi.org/10.1098/rstb.2007.2160.

Purnell, Thomas & Eric Raimy. 2015. Distinctive Features, Levels of Representation, and Historical Phonology. In Patrick Honeybone & Joseph Salmons (eds.), *The Oxford Handbook of Historical Phonology.* Oxford University Press. https://doi.org/10.1093/oxfordhb/9780199232819.013.002.

Purnell, Thomas C., Eric Raimy & Joseph Salmons. 2019. Old English vowels: Diachrony, privativity, and phonological representations. *Language* 95(4). e447–e473. doi:10.1353/lan.2019.0083.

Raimy, Eric. 2000. *The phonology and morphology of reduplication.* Mouton de Gruyter.

Reiss, Charles. 2017. Substance Free phonology. In Stephen J. Hannahs & Anna R. K. Bosch (eds.), *The Routledge Handbook of Phonological Theory,* 425–452. 1st ed. Routledge. https://doi.org/10.4324/9781315675428-15.

Rice, Keren. 1999a. Featural Markedness in Phonology: Variation-Part I. *Glot International* 4(7). 3–6.

Rice, Keren. 1999b. Featural Markedness in Phonology: Variation-Part II. *Glot International* 4(8). 3–7.

Rice, Keren. 2009. Nuancing Markedness: A Place for Contrast. In Eric Raimy & Charles E. Cairns (eds.), *Contemporary Views on Architecture and Representations in Phonology,* 310–321. The MIT Press. doi:10.7551/mitpress/9780262182706.003.0015.

Ringen, Catherine & Pétur Helgason. 2004. Distinctive [voice] does not imply regressive assimilation: Evidence from Swedish. *International Journal of English Studies* 4(2). 53–71.

Rubach, Jerzy. 1996. Nonsyllabic Analysis of Voice Assimilation in Polish. *Linguistic Inquiry* 27(1). 69–110.

Sagey, Elizabeth. 1986. *The representation of features and relations in non-linear phonology.* MIT Ph.D.

Schane, Sanford A. 1984. The fundamentals of particle phonology. *Phonology Yearbook* 1. 129–155. https://doi.org/10.1017/S0952675700000324.

Scheer, Tobias & Eugeniusz Cyran. 2017. Interfaces in Government Phonology. In Stephen J. Hannah & Anna R. K. Bosch (eds.), *The Routledge Handbook of Phonological Theory.* 293–324. Routledge.

Slifka, Janet. 2007. Acoustic Cues, Landmarks, and Distinctive Features: a Model of Human Speech Processing. *ECTI Transactions on Computer and Information Technology (ECTI-CIT)* 2(2). 91–96. https://doi.org/10.37936/ecti-cit.200622.53277.

Stanley, Richard. 1967. Redundancy Rules in Phonology. *Language* 43(2). 393. doi:10.2307/411542.

Stevens, Kenneth N. 2002. Toward a model for lexical access based on acoustic landmarks and distinctive features. *The Journal of the Acoustical Society of America* 111(4). 1872–1891. https://doi.org/10.1121/1.1458026.

Strycharczuk, Patrycja. 2012. Sonorant transparency and the complexity of voicing in Polish. *Journal of Phonetics* 40(5). 655–671. https://doi.org/10.1016/j.wocn.2012.05.006.

Tsuchida, Ayako. 1997. *Phonetics and phonology of Japanese vowel devoicing.* United States – New York: Cornell University Ph.D.

Westbury, John R. & Patricia A. Keating. 1986. On the Naturalness of Stop Consonant Voicing. *Journal of Linguistics* 22(1). 145–166.

Zemlin, Willard R. 1998. *Speech and hearing science: Anatomy and Physiology* 4th ed. Pearson.

Zero. *Encyclopedia of Mathematics.* URL: http://encyclopediaofmath.org/index.php?title=Zero&oldid=35962

Appendix

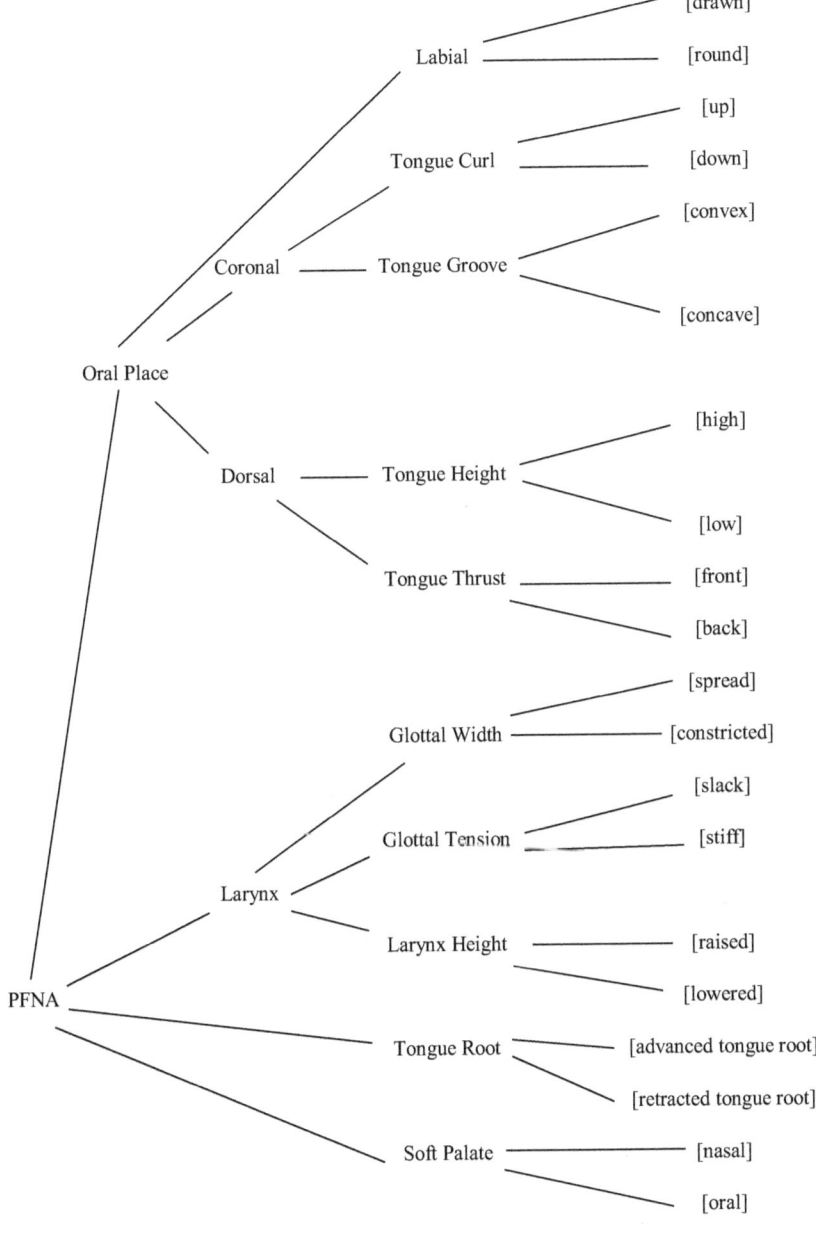

Harry van der Hulst
A guide to Radical CV Phonology, with special reference to tongue root and tongue body harmony

Abstract: In this article, I provide an outline of Radical CV Phonology (RCVP). This model covers segmental structure and syllabic structure. Key properties of this model are the use of dependency relations, and a reduction of the set of phonological elements to just two unary elements: |C| and |V|. Each of those two elements correlates with different although related phonetic interpretations (which are expressed by individual features in traditional feature systems), depending on their positions in the segmental and syllabic structure and on their status as heads or dependents. The model is supported by typological studies on phonemic contrast, as well as affinities between traditional features that are usually captured in terms of stipulative redundancy rules. This article is faithful to the 2020 version of the model in van der Hulst (2020), although some alternatives to the 2020 model are considered with regard to tongue root distinctions.

Keywords: elements; dependency; minimal specification; The Opponent Principle; syllable structure.

1 Introduction

My goal in this article is contribute to the discussion about different perspectives on element theory. To this end, I provide an outline of my perspective, which is captured in a model that I have been developing over many years, called Radical CV Phonology (RCVP). This model covers segmental structure as well as syllabic structure. A book-length exposition of this model is offered in van der Hulst (2020), to which I must refer readers for more details, and empirical support from typological studies on phonemic contrast, as well as insights that the model provides about affinities between traditional features that are usually captured in terms of

Harry van der Hulst, University of Connecticut

stipulative redundancy rules.[1] Such affinities are 'built in' into the model, which uses only two elements that, given their structural position in an intrasegmental dependency structure, express all 'features' that are necessary to capture all phonemic contrasts that have been attested. While this chapter contains a brief comparison between RCVP and two other models (Contrastive Hierarchy Theory and versions of Government Phonology), the book devotes a chapter to comparison to many other theories of segmental structure. I also show in this book how the principles of RCVP can be applied in the domain of sign phonology. An extensive application of how the model can deal with vowel harmony systems can be found in van der Hulst (2018), which combines the RCVP perspective on vowel structure with a notion of licensing of 'variable elements' to account for vowel harmony patterns in both relatively simple and more complex cases that involve transparent and opaque vowels. Inevitably, the model has gone through different versions. This article is faithful to the 2020 version, with the exception of how I here propose to deal with distinctions that are traditionally captured by features such as [ATR], [RTR], [low and high]. Section 2 briefly states my background assumptions about some central issues in phonology. Section 3 then provides an outline of the RCVP model. Sections 4 and 5 discuss comparisons with Contrastive Hierarchy Theory and Government Phonology. In section 6 I consider some alternatives to the 2020 model with regard to tongue root distinctions. I offer some conclusions in section 7.

2 Basic assumptions

2.1 What does phonology cover?

Phonology studies the truly observable (indeed perceived) level of languages with full consideration of the articulatory and psycho-acoustic properties –which is often referred to as 'phonetics'– but also mind-internal levels, including one which represents only those properties of the signal that are 'linguistically relevant' or contrastive, and thus 'phonemic'. I assume here that an additional shallower, i.e. more fully specified level (which I call the *word level*), is also required. The minimally specified level and the word level form what I call the grammatical phonology. I assume here that *grammatical phonology* is related to the perceived signal and the articulatory actions on the one hand and the shallowest internal

---

[1] See https://edinburghuniversitypress.com/book-principles-of-radical-cv-phonology-hb.html. This article is based on a presentation at the conference: Elements – State of the Art and Perspective, held in Nantes (France) on June 14–17, 2018.

representation (which I call *utterance phonology*, which is 'post-grammatical') by a system of phonetic implementation.

2.2 Five theses concerning phonological primes

2.2.1 Are features based on perception or articulation?

I suggest a compromise view and argue that there is no need to exclude articulation from the grammar (as is assumed explicitly in Government Phonology), but rather that both acoustics and articulation deliver cognitive substances that provide the 'raw material' that phonological elements categorize. To include articulation as a cognitive substance, we do not have to rely on the motor-theory of speech perception. I hypothesize that, alongside percepts of the acoustic speech signal, speakers also have *proprioceptions*, which refer to the sense of the relative position of one's own body parts and strength of effort needed for their movement.[2]

2.2.2 Are features innate?

Adopting the view that features are responsible for allowing the expression of contrast, I suggest that features for spoken languages and for sign languages (or for any other modality that can be used for the expression of a human language) are not innate but instead result from an innate categorization principle that splits phonetic substances into two opposing categories. Van der Hulst (2015b) calls this the *Opponent Principle*. This principle need not be thought of as being specific to language, being part of the capacity that is called categorical perception.

2.2.3 Are features, or is phonology in general, substance-free?

I assume with John Anderson (Anderson 2011) that features are substance-based, arising during the process of language acquisition, based on perceptions of the acoustic signal (to which I add proprioceptions) and guided by the recursive splitting process. I therefore would not accept features that are 'purely abstract' (that are phonetically 'meaningless', as proposed in Foley (1977)), nor that structures can arise that are 'phonological unicorns', i.e. structures that are not pho-

---

[2] Section 2.2 is based on van der Hulst & van de Weijer (2018) and van der Hulst (2020: chapter 1).

nologizations of actual phonetic events that occur in human languages. The substance-based approach that I adopt apparently stands in contrast to so-called substance-free theories proposed in Hale & Reiss (2000) and Blaho (2008), but there is no disagreement about the fact that (grammatical) phonology makes no direct reference to phonetic substance.

2.2.4 Are phonological representations fully specified?

I adopt Anderson's view that phonological representations are minimally specified and that the criterion for specification is *contrast*.[3] Using unary elements dramatically reduces the need for underspecification, but this notion is still relevant if only contrastive element specifications are postulated in lexical representations (see van der Hulst (2016, 2018)), which means that we need a system that recognizes only contrastive elements. However, minimal specification does not entail a system of rules that fill in redundant information. I assume that minimally specified representations are mostly directly phonetically implementable and implemented, albeit with the intervention of *enhancement rules* that may activate redundant elements at the word level (see van der Hulst (2015a, 2018, 2020)).

2.2.5 Is there such a thing as a segment inventory?

Anderson assumes that contrast (and ultimately the notion of segmental inventory) is relative to syllabic positions and refers to this as the idea of *polysystematicity*, a view originating in Firth's prosodic phonology (Firth (1948)), which rejects the notion of a phoneme as a unit that generalizes over sets of segments that occur in different syllabic positions (unless the contrastive possibilities are exactly the same). I am doubtful that there would be no 'reality' to a unifying notion of say, the phoneme [l] (as a unit that subsumes the l-sounds in English *lip, blink, silly, health, already* and *pill*, which all differ in phonetic details, being, as such, in complementary distribution), despite the fact that phonemes will not be specified with the same degree of complexity in all positions in lexical entries, because minimal specification will indeed require that in positions in which there is neutralization of contrast fewer specifications are necessary. For example, in *blink*, [l] only contrasts with [r], whereas in final position it contrasts with a much larger set of segments, at least in English. I suggest that this would not prevent

---

3 See Dresher (2009) for a perspective on minimal specification using binary features; see section 3.

the adoption of a unified phoneme /l/ as a psychologically real entity, but I do see the 'danger' that such a notion can be reinforced, some would say created, by the adoption of a spelling symbol <l> for all of them; see Anderson (2014).

2.2.6 Is phonology different?

Fundamental to Anderson's work is the *Structural Analogy Assumption*, which holds that structural relations and principles are the same in both planes of grammar, syntax and phonology. The planes therefore primarily differ in terms of the sets of their basic units, i.e. their alphabets, which are determined by the interface with phonetic substance (for the expression plane) and conceptual meaning (for the content plane). The assumption of structural analogy has roots in Louis Hjelmslev's theory of glossematics (e.g. Hjelmslev (1943 [1953])). It might seem that this assumption runs counter to the modularity assumption that is prevalent in Generative Grammar (and Cognitive Science in general), but this is only true if we assume that recognizing different modules (of grammar or of the mind) somehow entails that these modules must have radically different internal organizations. I suggest that the opposite is more likely, allowing the mind to use the same 'tricks' in different modules, perhaps as many as possible, even across very different cognitive domains.

3 An outline of Radical CV Phonology

Radical CV Phonology is a theory of segmental and syllabic structure. Based on a series of previous articles, notably van der Hulst (1995, 2005), it is fully developed in van der Hulst (2020), henceforth VDH20, on which this section draws heavily.

3.1 Segmental structure

Roughly, RCVP shares its basic principles, as expressed in (1), with Dependency Phonology (DP) which introduced at least six important innovations, several of which date back to early publications by John Anderson and Charles Jones (Anderson & Jones 1972, 1974):[4]

---

[4] A prepublication appeared in 1972 in *Edinburgh Working Papers in Linguistics*. This paper did not propose the second principle in (1), which was introduced later, following Lass & Anderson (1975).

(1) Fundamental principles of RCVP:
  a. Phonological primes are unary (they are called *elements*[5])
  b. Elements are grouped into units ('gestures' or 'class nodes')[6]
  c. Each class is populated by the same two elements, C and V
  d. When combined, elements enter into a head-dependency relation
  e. All elements are used for both consonants and vowels
  f. Some primes may occur in more than one class
  g. Representations are minimally specified

The idea to use only two elements, C and V, is the hallmark of RCVP, although the seeds for using the same elements in different element classes were clearly planted in Anderson and Ewen (1987). RCVP takes this idea to the extreme.

In (2) I represent the full RCVP geometry:[7]

(2) The 'geometry' of elements in RCVP

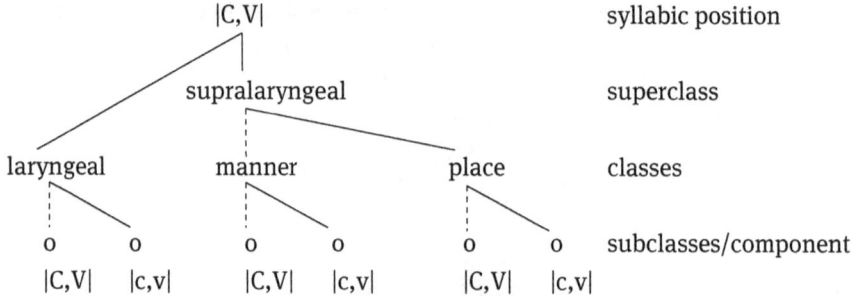

- Vertical broken lines dominate heads.
- Vertical closed lines indicate subjunction (showing the same unit to be a head at multiple levels).
- Slant lines connect dependents to their heads.

---

[5] DP uses the term *component*, but I adopt the GP term element. Schane (1984) uses the term *particle*.
[6] The idea of acknowledging element classes occurs in the earliest version of DP (e.g. see Anderson & Jones (1974)). The same idea later led to versions of what was called 'Feature Geometry' (see Clements (1985)). In van der Hulst (2020, chapter 11) I discuss various FG models.
[7] The left-to-right arrangement in this diagram does not imply any notion of linear order. This geometry deviates somewhat from the one adopted in AE and bears a close resemblance to the original geometry that was proposed in Clements (1985). In VDH20, chapter 11 this model is compared to other models with which it shares certain properties. The notation |C,V| or |c,v| stands for 'C or V'; it does *not* represent a combination of C and V. In VDH20, § 3.2.2 I discuss the question as to whether we need a separate C/V characterization for major class distinctions. For the moment I will assume that these distinctions are encoded in terms of the syllabic structure.

I will refer to element specifications in head subclasses as primary specifications and specifications in the dependent class as secondary specifications.[8] Both subclasses contain the two elements C and V; for convenience, the elements in the dependent are given in lower case when we explicitly consider them in secondary subclasses; when I refer to elements in general I will use upper case. Within each class, elements can occur alone or in combination (with dependency). A general characteristic of elements that are heads is their perceptual salience.

The motivation for regarding manner as the head class comes from the fact that manner specifications, specifically primary specifications, are determinants of the syllabic distribution of segments and of their sonority (which is of course related to syllabic distribution). Their relevance for sonority also correlates with the role of heads in perceptual salience. Additionally, taking mobility ('spreadability') to be characteristic of dependents, I suggest that relative stability (resistance to 'spreading') is also a sign of heads.[9] This same criterion then also motivates the laryngeal and place classes as dependent classes, given the 'mobility' of laryngeal elements (specifically tone) and place elements.[10] Another property of heads is obligatoriness. All segments thus must have a manner property. The laryngeal class is taken to be the outer dependent ('the specifier' in the 'X-bar' type of organization in (2)) because of its greater optionality (especially when interpreted as tone) and its greater mobility than the place elements, again clearly evident not only from the mobility of tonal elements, but also from phonation properties like voicing. Clements (1985) also proposed the three classes that RCVP acknowledges, with the same grouping of the classes, albeit without imposing a head-dependency relation. In later work in 'FG' the manner node was removed on the argument that there are no processes that treat manner features as a group (see, e.g. McCarthy (1988)). However, group behaviour can also be demonstrated by relevance to phonotactic distribution and in this respect manner features do

---

8 Since in § 5 I makes some comparisons between RCVP and Government Phonology (GP), I note here that in terms of formal power, one might argue that GP's distinction between headed and non-headed elements is comparable to RCVP's distinction between primary and secondary elements. However, the details of how these distinctions are applied to distinctive properties are very different.
9 See Gordon (2016, chapter 6) for a study showing that spreading processes involving major class or manner features are rare.
10 In autosegmental approaches, mobility amounts to 'spreading' (adding association lines). My own approach to mobility in as far as it falls within phonology proper uses the notion of licensing (of variable elements); see van der Hulst (2018).

act like a group. I thus reject the argument that only 'processes' support grouping which it typical of work in the FG-tradition.[11]

While (2) contains labels for element classes, a proper representation of segmental structure can omit all the labels that were provided in (1); that is, the various labels for the classes are for convenience only, having no formal status in. Each unit in the structure can be defined in purely structural terms:

(3)
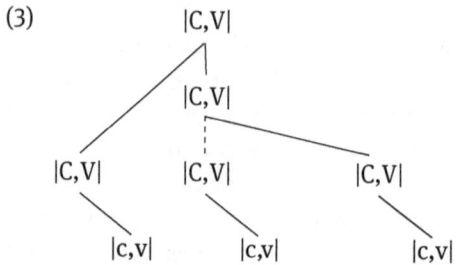

It is important to see that (2)/(3) is meant as a pure dependency structure and thus not as a constituent structure, in line with the essence of dependency grammar approaches which replace constituency by head-dependent relations, rather than augment the latter to the former.[12]

The two elements C and V[13] (upper or lower case) are strictly formal units, which, depending on their position in the segmental structure (and their role as head or dependent), correlate with specific phonetic properties (as encoded in a set of interpretation functions; see (9) below). Additionally, their interpretation is also dependent on the syllabic position of the entire segmental structure, which means that both elements have different (albeit related) interpretations for each syllabic position in all three classes. The choice of the symbols ('C' and 'V', rather than, say 'א' and 'ƥ') for the two basic primes is motivated by the fact that within each class node, one element is favoured in the syllabic onset head position (the preferred locus of Consonants), while the other is favoured in the

---

[11] In fact, if automatic processes are accounted for in the phonetic implementation, their relevance for grouping is dubious.

[12] It is worth pointing out that in a dependency approach (which does not recognise constituents) there is no distinction between 'merging' and 'labelling'. In a dependency approach, the unit that a dependent adjoins to is automatically the head of the construction, which thus has the identity of the head unit. The issue of labelling simply does not exist in a dependency approach and is thus a non-issue.

[13] When referring to these two elements, I will *not* consistently place them between vertical lines.

rhymal head position (the preferred locus of Vowels). In other words, the labels are mnemonic aids to the traditional idea that consonants and vowels are optimal segments in onset and rhymal head positions, respectively. (In § 3.2, I show how the C/V notation extends to syllable structure.) Since vowels are more sonorous than consonants and thus have greater perceptual salience, we can interpret the C/V opposition as standing for relative perceptual salience, with V indicating higher perceptual salience. Indeed, this interpretation of the element opposition makes the C/V labelling notation arbitrary, which becomes especially clear when I apply RCVP to sign language phonology (see VDH20, chapter 10). Nevertheless, I will continue to use the C/V labelling, having taken note of the notational arbitrariness.

It cannot be left unnoticed that RCVP derives the traditional classes of 'features' (laryngeal, manner, place and major class) from an 'X-bar' type macrostructure. I speculate that this particular organisation, which appears to be shared between (pre-Merge versions of) syntax and phonology, in which heads can have two types of dependents ('complements' and 'specifiers/modifiers'), is perhaps not accidental, but rather reflects a 'deep' structural analogy between syntax and phonology; see den Dikken & van der Hulst (2020) for a strong defence of this view. X-bar theory was introduced as a constituent-based theory, augmented with the notion of headedness; see Kornai & Pullum (1990) for a critical discussion of some aspects of this idea, albeit with acceptance of the central notion of headedness. Following DP, the head-dependency relation in RCVP is seen not as an augmentation of a constituent structure, but rather as replacing constituent structure. Nevertheless, to distinguish between two types of dependents, a similar claim to that of X-bar theory is being made.

Within each of the six subclasses in (2), in principle, an element can occur alone or in combination. This allows for a four-way distinction in which two structures are formally complex in combining two elements that enter into a dependency relation:[14]

(4)   C   C;V   V;C   V

In earlier accounts of RCVP, I would say that the maximal set of four structures results from a two-way (i.e. recursive) splitting of the phonetic space that correlates with a phonological element class:

---

[14] Following DP (Anderson and Ewen 1987) 'x;y' indicates that x is the head and y is the dependent. Other notational convention to distinguish heads from dependents have also been used, e.g., x⇒y. In Government Phonology, the head is underlined: 'x̲,y'.

(5) a.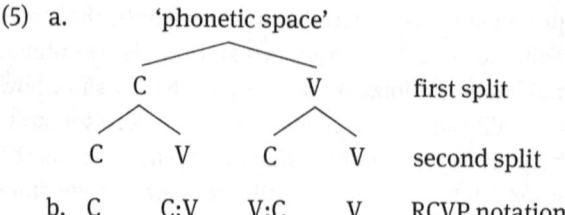

b.   C   C;V   V;C   V   RCVP notation

The first split produces two opposed categories that can be characterised with a single element, C or V. For example, in the head manner class for onset heads (when occupied by obstruents[15]), this split would produce stops and fricatives. A second split creates two 'finer' categories, one of which is characterized by an element combination. For example, still within the same class, a second split of the C category delivers plain stops, C, and fricative stops (affricates), C;V.

Even though this notation has intuitive appeal, it is important to note that this two-way splitting diagram is *not*, as such, part of the representation of the segmental structure. It merely depicts how the splitting procedure *recursively* delivers four potentially distinctive phonetic categories that are formally represented as a single C or V or as combinations of these two elements, with a dependency relation imposed. Recursive splitting is due to what van der Hulst (2015b) calls *the Opponent Principle*. This principle (which is rooted in categorical perception; Harnad (1990)) directs a specific categorisation of phonetic substance that 'produces' feature systems for spoken and signed languages in the course of ontogenetic development.[16]

Assuming that each subclass in (1) correlates with a 'phonetic space or dimension', C and V correlate with (and phonologize) opposite phonetic categories within such a dimension. The opposing categories comprise two non-overlapping 'intervals' within which certain 'prototypical' phonetic events are optimal in terms of achieving maximal perceptual contrast with minimal articulatory effort.[17] While the elements are thus strictly formal cognitive units, they do correlate with

---

[15] In VDH20, § 3.2.2 discuss the theoretical position which allow only obstruents in the onset head position.

[16] Theoretically, each of the four categories could be split once more into two opponent categories. The phonetic differences between categories would then become very subtle and it is apparently the case that natural languages do not require going into such subtle differences to achieve phonemic contrast. Additionally, it may be that such subtler differences will be increasingly hard to distinguish perceptually, and to make articulatorily. For this point and some additional discussion of the four-way split, I refer to VDH20, § 3.2.2.

[17] A phonetic category thus has a prototype character with optimal members, prototypes, and suboptimal members. This prototype functions as a perceptual magnet; see Kuhl (1991).

phonetic events (or phonetic categories, covering a subrange of the relevant phonetic dimension). In fact, we can think of elements as (subconscious) cognitive percepts and propriocepts that correlate with such phonetic categories.[18]

It is important to stress that while the Opponent Principle delivers the maximally opposed elements C and V for each phonetic dimension, it does not as such deliver all the phonological categories that are needed for the analysis of all possible contrasts. For that, we need not only the two opposed elements, but also their combinations. This clearly shows that to explain phonological categorisation more is needed than the Opponent Principle alone. Crucially, we also need a Combinatorial Principle, and, moreover, a Dependency Principle, the last as an obligatory aspect of 'combinations'.

As shown in (2) and (3), the two elements can also occur in a secondary (dependent) subclass in each class, which, if we allow a four-way distinction there as well, leads to the following set of possible structures for each element class:

(6) a. Plane primary (head) structures:
C C;V V;C V

b. Primary structures with added secondary (dependent) structures:[19]
{{C}c} {{C;V}c} {{V;C}c} {{V}c}
{{C}c;v} {{C;V}c;v} {{V;C}c;v} {{V}c;v}
{{C}v;c} {{C;V}v;c} {{V;C}v;c} {{V}v;c}
{{C}v} {{C;V}v} {{V;C}v} {{V}v}

Note that RCVP admits, as one would expect, that the absence of a dependent *secondary* specification can be contrastive with the presence of such a specification. Dependents are never obligatory.[20] The 'option' of having structures that

---

[18] As mentioned in § 1.2.1, I assume that elements have both an acoustic correlate (a percept) and an articulatory plan (a propriocept). We could also call these mental units *concepts*, but because that term is usually associated with 'semantic' concepts, I will use the term *percepts* for mental units that correlate with phonetic substance.

[19] Recall that as a matter of notational convention, I will use lower case symbols for the dependent class elements, following Anderson (2011). I will also use the brace notation when a distinction between primary and secondary elements is made.

[20] In specific segmental systems it is possible in principle that a dependent is 'phonetically' present in a certain class and for a certain segment type, although in such cases the presence of the dependent is always predictable and thus absent in a minimal-contrastive representation. An example would be the requirement that high vowels are advanced. See VHH20, chapter 9 where 'underspecification' is discussed.

lack a head class element, which would create four additional possibilities, is simply not available as part of the RCVP syntax (because dependents cannot be more complex than heads and, moreover, because dependents need a head). As a consequence, elements in dependent nodes can only be activated when elements in corresponding head nodes have been activated.[21] RCVP also rules out a completely unspecified class node as a contrastive option.[22]

In (6a), the four-way distinction regards the combinations of elements within the head class, while (6b) represents a combination of each of these four options and one or two elements in the dependent class. The full array of structural possibilities in (6b) is unlikely to be exploited in any language. Moreover, as we will see, there is a strong tendency for the dependent class to only require the two simple structures c and v. The only reason for formally permitting complex dependent structures is that this may be required in the manner class for obstruent consonants and vowels (both syllabic heads), as I show in van der VDH20, chapters 4 and 5. This means that the two middle rows in (6b) are mostly not used. That the dependent class tends to be non-complex can be seen as a trademark of dependent units. As a general head/dependency principle, in any structure, the dependent unit can never be more complex than its head; see Dresher and van der Hulst (1998).

It turns out that structures for vowels are much more restricted than structures for consonants, with one exception. There is only limited use for a dependent class in vowel place, and secondary vowel manner is typologically rare.[23] However, in the case of the laryngeal class, consonants are more limited than vowels. In consonants, as motivated in VDH20, chapter 6, element combinations

---

21 The idea that *within a class*, the head component elements must be activated before we get to the dependent elements correlates with the fact that within the segmental structure as a whole the manner class (more specifically its head elements, which account for aperture) must be activated before we get to the place component elements. It has been shown in typological studies of vowel systems that a minimal system would use only manner (i.e. aperture), leading to a so-called *vertical vowel system*, found in some northwest Caucasian languages (Kabardian, Adyghe); see Lass (1984). But there are no vowel systems that only use place distinctions. This further motivates the head status of the manner class (which expresses aperture for vowels and stricture for consonants).
22 In van der Hulst (2020, chapter 7) I reject the notion of 'empty nucleus', which might qualify as a possible candidate for the representation of a completely unspecified segment.
23 The greater complexity of consonantal units is seemingly in contradiction with the head/dependency principle, which precludes dependent from being more complex than heads, since vowels are head of syllables. However, the greater need for consonantal distinctions is motivated by the independent factor that consonants play a greater role in lexical phonemic contrast, i.e. in the identification of differences between morphemes and words than vowels.

are excluded in *both* the head and the dependent dimension.[24] For vowels, tonal properties do require combinations of the head laryngeal elements, which can be supplemented by a dependent class element (representing register differences[25]). For these various points about asymmetries between head and dependent structures, I must refer to VDH20.

The fact that combinations are (typically) allowed in head classes but not in dependent classes is perfectly 'natural' in a dependency approach, where, in fact, we expect to find complexity asymmetries between heads and dependents of precisely this kind. As mentioned, heads allowing greater complexity than dependents is a typical manifestation of head/dependent asymmetries. For example, while manner and place allow complex structures in their head classes, this is not required for the laryngeal class, at least for consonants.[26] Both laryngeal and place are dependent classes, but the place class is included in the super class supralaryngeal. Thus, the fact that the place class (especially for consonants) allow more structures than the laryngeal class is, once more, an example of an expected head/dependent asymmetry.

The proposal to represent contrastive segments in terms of element structures does not entail that phonemic[27] contrast must always be represented in terms of different, positively specified C/V structures. One might argue that a strictly minimal way of representing contrast can make use of the 'zero option', that is, the absence of an element specification. Thus, a contrast within a given class could perhaps be expressed in terms of C versus zero or V versus zero, and one would expect that this choice would have implications for which category is deemed 'marked'. For example, if a language has a simple tonal contrast between

---

[24] Both laryngeal and place are dependent classes, but the place class is included in the super class, supralaryngeal. Thus, the fact that the place class allows more structures than the laryngeal class is, once more, an example of an expected head/dependent asymmetry.

[25] The notion of register has also been invoked to explain the occurrence of four tone heights in Yip (1980). I restrict the use of register to the dependent class elements; see VDH20, § 6.3.

[26] It should be noted that this does not square with the fact that consonants generally allow more contrast. The fact of the matter is that languages can allow a four-way tonal contrast in the primary laryngeal class, especially Asian tone languages. This richness is not matched by phonation contrasts among consonants, at least not given the way in which RCVP represents phonation contrast, where the primary class only contrasts voicing with 'non-voicing' (which I refer to as 'tenseness'); see VDH20, chapter 6 for details.

[27] Since I use the term 'phonological' as comprising the study both of contrastive or distinctive units at the cognitive level and of phonetic categories (as well as the relation between them) at the utterance level, I will often refer to the level of cognitive ('symbolic' or 'formal') representations as 'phonemic', whereas the utterance level will be called 'phonetic'; this follows the terminological practice of American structuralists; see van der Hulst (2013, 2015b, 2016b).

H (= C in the laryngeal head class) and L (= V in the laryngeal head class), one could conceivably specify only one of them. In many analyses of tonal systems, phonologist have argued that only the H tone is literally marked. I discuss the use of non-specification in this sense in VDH20, chapter 9. However, in RCVP use of the zero option is limited in various ways; for example, the zero option cannot be used in the head manner class, since a manner specification is obligatory for each segment.

While the elements are formal and as such 'substance-free', elements do of course correlate with phonetic 'events' (phonetic categories); in John Anderson's terms, the primes of phonology are *substance-based* (see Anderson (2011)); see § 1.2.3. The relation between formal units such as elements and phonetic events is often referred to in terms like 'phonetic implementation', although phonetic implementation comprises much more, by also accounting for co-articulatory, allophonic effects. Here I focus on the phonetic correlates of elements as they occur in syllabified segments, assuming that elements, given their structural context, have more or less invariant phonetic correlates.[28] Since the elements C and V occur in many different structural positions, they correlate with several different (albeit related, at least in principle) phonetic events. I will refer to these correlates as the phonetic interpretations or simply correlates of elements; other phonological approaches use the term 'exponents'. I do not think that it is possible to assign a very global 'phonetic meaning' to C and V 'out of context'. Rather, out of context, these two elements account for a general bias that each occurrence of them shares. The bias of C is that each occurrence of this element is preferred in a syllable position that itself has this label ('a syllabic onset') and the reverse holds for the V element ('a syllabic nucleus'). I will explain this further after having discussed the RCVP account of syllable structure in § 3.2; VDH20, chapter 8 provides a detailed account of this idea of preference. Also, as mentioned earlier, an even more abstract interpretation of the C and V categories refers to their relative perceptual salience, with C being less salient than V.

We will thus see that each of the two elements C and V have a variety of phonetic 'meanings' or interpretations, which with a plus or minus value, in traditional binary feature systems are usually associated with different distinctive features, or with opposing unary features or element, such as H (tone) and L (tone). It is in this sense that RCVP provides a 'metatheory' of phonological

---

28 One reason for not excluding articulations as correlates of elements is that in several cases, while there is an invariant articulatory correlate, an invariant acoustic property can be hard to find locally in the segment; see Taylor (2006).

primes, albeit consistently unary primes.[29] Of course, RCVP cannot accommodate 'all features that have ever been proposed'. My claim is that it accommodates precisely those feature proposals that are the best motivated empirically and therefore most widely used.

In (7), I indicate some of the interpretation functions that assign phonetic correlates to the elements in their various structural positions (here only stated as a mix of articulatory terms and, as for the tones, perceptual terms). The inclusion of 'onset head' or 'nucleus head' implies that interpretation is dependent not only on the elements subclass (the head class in (7)), but also, as mentioned, on syllabic position:

(7) Phonetic Interpretation Functions for elements in manner (Man) and laryngeal (Lar) *head* classes when occurring in syllabic head positions:[30]

PI (Man: C, head class, onset head)	=	⟦stop⟧
PI (Man: C, head class, nucleus head)	=	⟦high⟧
PI (Man: V, head class, onset head)	=	⟦fricative⟧
PI (Man: V, head class, nucleus head)	=	⟦low⟧
PI (Place: C, head class, onset head)	=	⟦palatal⟧
PI (Place: C, head class, nucleus head)	=	⟦front⟧
PI (Place: V, head class, onset head)	=	⟦labial⟧
PI (Place: V, head class, nucleus head)	=	⟦round⟧
PI (Lar: C, head class, onset head)	=	⟦tense⟧
PI (Lar: C, head class, nucleus head)	=	⟦high tone⟧
PI (Lar: V, head class, onset head)	=	⟦voiced⟧
PI (Lar: V, head class, nucleus head)	=	⟦low tone⟧

---

29 That said, RCVP captures the idea of binarity by reducing all contrast to a binary opposition between C and V, whose phonetic interpretations often resemble the interpretation of the two values of traditional binary features. The questions as to how many rimes there are and whether or not they are binary is answered by RCVP as follows: there are only two primes which are polar opposites. This is not the same as having one feature with two values, because the two primes can be combined, where (at least as usually understood) one cannot combine the '+' and the '-' because that leads to a contradiction. That said, one can take C and V to be values of attributes that are captured by the various classes.

30 I focus here on articulatory interpretations. There are also (psycho-)acoustic interpretations; see § 1.2.1. The '⟦ . . . ⟧' indicate 'phonetic interpretation/implementation'. It cannot escape our attention that the labels for these phonetic interpretations look a lot like traditional binary feature labels, while the use of double brackets is borrowed from a common usage for the representation of meanings that are assigned to syntactic objects.

The phonetic details of interpretations are, to some extent, language-specific. The property 'rhotic', for example, which will be expressed as a manner distinction for *sonorant* consonants, has rather different phonetic manifestations in different languages, so much so that it has been argued that there is no unifying phonetic property. This issue is discussed in detail in Navarro (2018), who makes a convincing argument for the claim that there is nonetheless a unifying phonological representation for this seemingly heterogeneous class of sounds. Another extreme example concerns [[ATR]], which is represented in RCVP by a C element in the dependent place class of vowels (see § 5). Different languages show rather different phonetic correlates of this element, which means that the label ATR is only a rough indication of the articulatory mechanisms that can be involved in expanding the pharyngeal cavity. It has been observed that the acoustic goals of the expanded correlate can be achieved in multiple ways, including lowering the larynx, expansion of the pharyngeal wall or activity of the epiglottis, for example; see Lindau (1979) and Moisik (2013). This specific example is discussed in detail in van der Hulst (2018, chapter 3).

In conclusion, the phonetic interpretation of an element is dependent on:

(8) a. Being a C or V element
 b. Being a head or a dependent in a subclass
 c. Occurring in a head or dependent subclass
 d. Its syllabic position

The reduction of a set of phonetic properties that correspond to different features in traditional feature systems to either C or V is reminiscent of reducing a set of phonetic segments to a single phoneme. Such a reduction (albeit not uncontested; see § 1.2.5) is possible when phonetic segments occur in *complementary distribution*, for instance by occupying different structural positions in the syllable, foot or word. My claim is that the phonetic interpretations of C and V are likewise in complementary distribution. For example, the elements in the head laryngeal class are interpreted as tonal properties when they occur in the syllable head (nucleus), whereas they are interpreted as phonation properties when they occur in the onset head. In this sense tonal properties and phonation properties are in complementary distribution. The idea that tonal and phonation properties are interpretations of the same set of primes was originally proposed in Halle & Stevens (1971), and RCVP accommodates this proposal in a strong form, by claiming that tone and phonation are in complementary distribution.[31] Likewise, in the

---

[31] This claim is not without empirical challenges, which I discuss in VDH20, § 6.4.4.

manner class, stricture in consonants (as captured by the binary feature [±continuant]) is claimed to be in complementary distribution with height (aperture) in vowels.

We expect the different interpretations of elements in different positions to be phonetically related (just as allophones of a phoneme are supposed to be phonetically similar) and we also expect phonological generalisations to express correlations between instances of the same element that occur in different classes and syllabic positions. As an example, I mention the fact that V correlates with the property of being a sonorant in the syllabic V position ('the nucleus'), whereas it correlates with voicing in the laryngeal head class for consonants. The correlation between [+sonorant] and [+voice] has often been noted. It is captured by a redundancy rule in binary systems:

(9) [+sonorant] → [+voice]

In RCVP the same redundancy reflects the general fact that the implied dependency holds between occurrences of the same element in different structural positions:

(10) [Syllabic: V] → [Laryngeal: V]

A similar dependency can be observed between [+high] and [+ATR], which in RCVP are also interpretations of the same element C (in the manner head class and the dependent place class, respectively). It is thus a gain of RCVP that it is possible to reduce to a general format all redundancy statements which in a traditional feature system essentially express random correlations between formally different features, as:

(11) X:α → Y:α

Here 'X' and 'Y' are variables for structural positions, while 'α' ranges over C and V. In VDH20, chapter 9 I present a systematic exploitation of the 'universal redundancy or preference rule' in (11), which expresses what I call Harmony (or Bias).

As discussed in § 1.2.6, a guiding principle of DP is the Structural Analogy Assumption (SAA), which states that representations in phonology and syntax differ mostly due to the fact that these two planes have different sets of basic categories (the so-called 'alphabets'), given that they are grounded in different substances. Since phonology and syntax categorise different cognitive substances (phonetic percepts/propriocepts and semantic concepts, respectively), we expect their sets of basic categories to be different, both in number and in nature, i.e. what they correlate with. What the SAA states is that phonological structure and syntactic structure display identical *structural relations*, such as, in particular, the relation of dependency between head and dependents, recursion and perhaps also maximal binarity of structure.[32] However, I assume that structural analogy also promotes 'replication' of the same structures *within* planes. RCVP postulates that the various classes within the segment are structurally analogous to the extent that all make use of the same C/V structures (namely those in (8)).

3.2 Syllable structure

Faithful to the basic premise of RCVP, the syllable itself is a combination of a C and a V-unit, which, if no further splitting applies, delivers the core CV syllable structure that is present in all languages. If languages allow a larger repertoire of syllable structures, this results from splitting the C and/or V unit which produces binary branching onsets and rhymes, respectively:

(12)   Syllabic positions

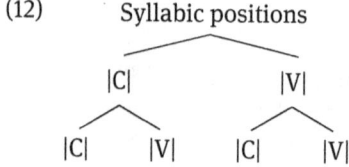

|C| |V|

|C| |V| |C| |V|

While the four-way division as such implies no linearization, when combined into a syllable structure, there will be linear sequencing as dictated by some version of the well-known 'Sonority Sequencing Principle' which will require less sonorant segments to precede more sonorant segments in the onset and the reverse in the rhyme unit.

A proper dependency representation of a syllable structure that contains all four syllabic categories is as follows.[33] In (13) I added convenient unit names for

---

[32] See den Dikken & van der Hulst (2020) for the strong claim that there is only one type of syntax, which generalises over phonology and 'syntax'.

[33] Perhaps there is a resemblance between seeing all syntagmatic relation in terms of dependency and seeing them in terms of 'lateral licensing', as in Scheer (2004), among others.

each construction and for each of the four segmental positions, but these labels have no theoretical status:[34]

(13) a.

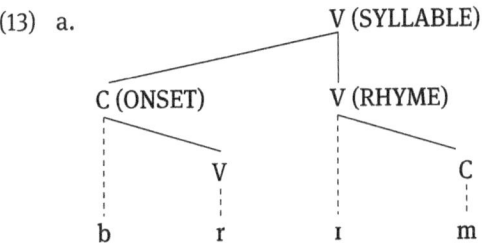

b. EDGE   BRIDGE   NUCLEUS   CODA
c. obstruents sonorant cons. vowels   sonorant cons.

In VDH20 I propose that the types of segments that can occur in each syllabic position are determined by the C/V structure of these positions. As indicated in (13c), only obstruents are allowed in onset heads, while only vowels are allow in the nucleus. Both dependent positions only allow sonorant consonants. This proposal makes very strong predictions about the maximal complexity of syllables and which segment types can occur in syllabic positions. Both onset and rhyme can be maximally binary branching. In addition, we disallow onsets consisting of two obstruents, two sonorant consonants and sonorant consonant followed by an obstruent. We also disallow obstruents to function as nuclei and as codas. A similarly strict view was adopted by proponents of GP (see Kaye, Lowenstamm and Vergnaud 1990). I refer to VDH20, chapter 3 for a more detailed discussion of syllable structure, including onsets and rhyme of greater complexity, as well as how to accommodate sonorant consonants as onset head or nuclei; see also van der Hulst (to appear) for an account of recursive structure in onsets and rhyme.

3.3 The full segmental structure

In VDH20 I propose phonetic interpretations for all primary and secondary C/V structures in the manner, place and laryngeal class in all four syllabic positions. I here provide a summary structure for the onset and rhyme positions (omitting some special cases; × = allows combinations; ⊗ = does not allow combinations):

---

[34] I assume that syllable structure is recursive, but I do not discuss this here; see van der Hulst (2010, to appear) and den Dikken & van der Hulst (2020).

(14)

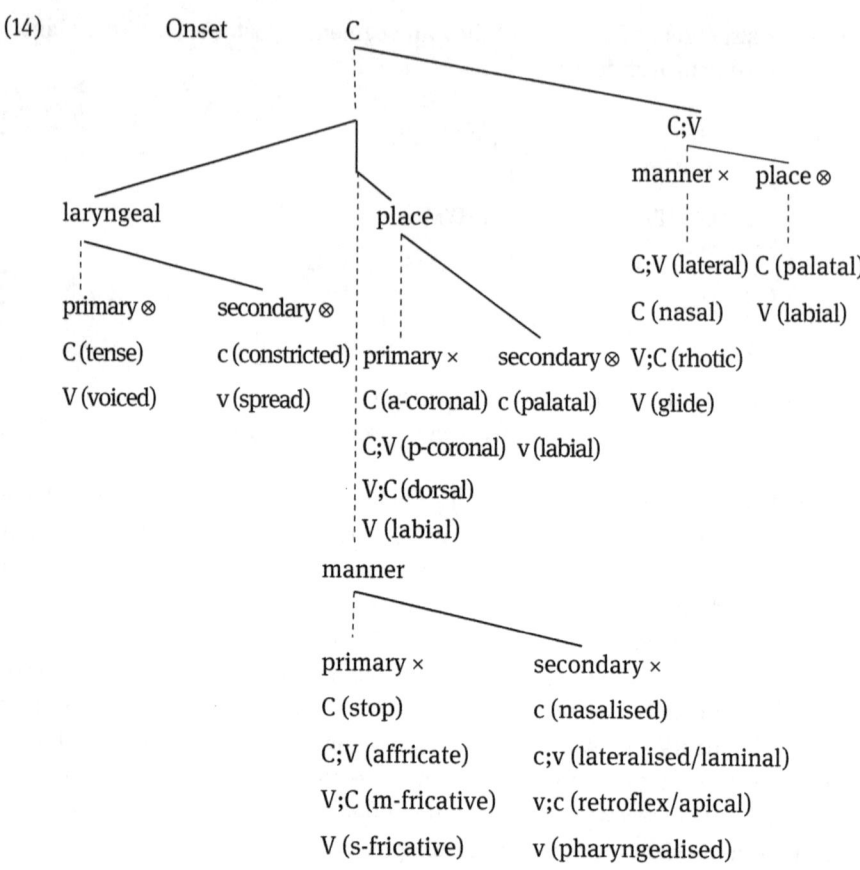

(15) Rhyme[35]

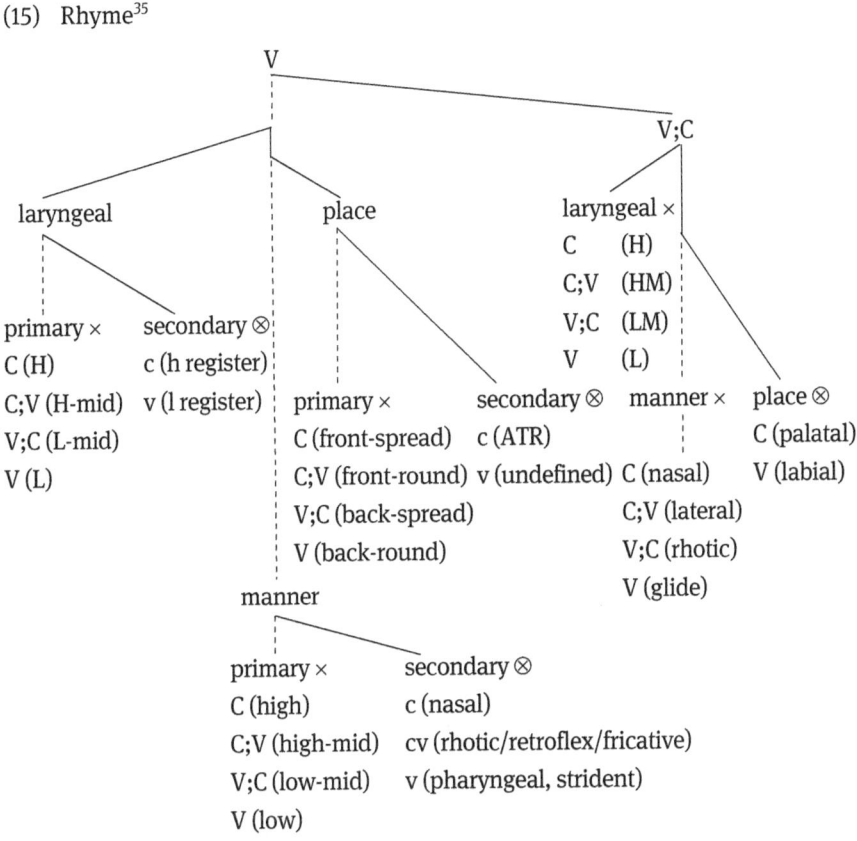

I refer to VD20 for extensive discussion and empirical documentation of all the assigned interpretations which are here given in mostly articulatory terms that resemble traditional binary features in many cases. The structure in (14) and (15) make clear in which sense RCVP can be regarded as a *meta-theory* of distinctive features, here understood as phonetic categories that can be used contrastively. The interpretations for the secondary intermediate cv manner for the rhyme head ('vowels') are especially tentative. In § 5 I single out for further discussion the secondary vowels manners c (nasal) and v (pharyngeal) for discussion, as well as the secondary place specification c (ATR).[35]

While in principle all four syllabic positions could expand the full segmental structure in (13), (14) and (15) show that place and laryngeal specifications in dependent position (bridge and coda) are limited. To account for this, Kehrein &

---

[35] In section 5 of this article I propose an alternative structure for vowel manner and place.

Golston (2004) suggest that place and laryngeal specifications are properties of syllabic units (for them, onset, nucleus and coda). I incorporate this insight by restricting place and laryngeal specifications to onset and rhyme heads (with minor exceptions that I discuss in VDH20). As shown in (14) and (15) the dependent onset and rhyme positions allow limited place specifications and, in the coda, also limited tone specifications, indicated in italic.

(13) seems to restrict the position of sonorant consonant to dependent syllabic positions. But sonorant consonants can also occur as onset or rhyme heads; in the latter case they are called 'syllabic'. In such cases the syllabic structure is as follows:

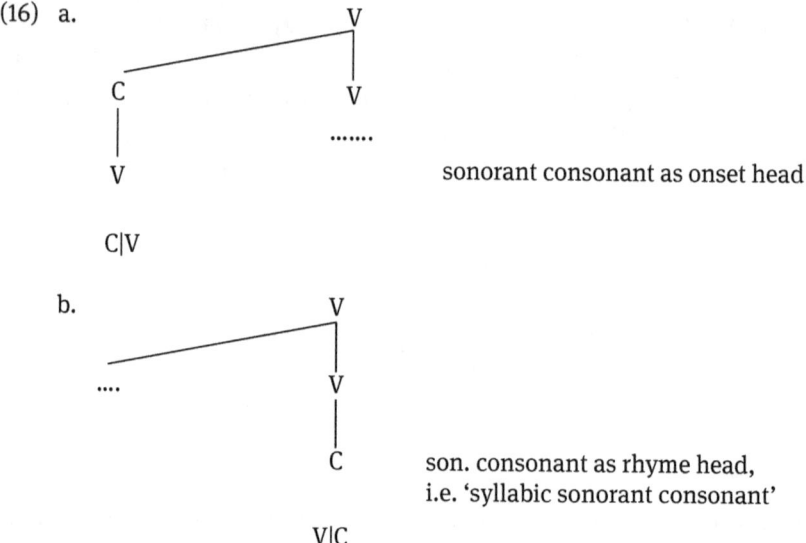

The structure in (16a) and (16b) involve *subjunction*, rather than adjunction. A distinction between subjunction and adjunction is permitted in a dependency-based grammar, although it would be formally incoherent in a constituent-based formalism (see Böhm 2018). (17) show the two possibilities for /r/ in onset dependent and onset head respectively:

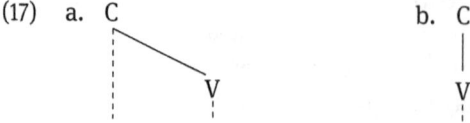

The structure in (17a) can be mapped on a linearly ordered string (b>r; following the sonority sequencing generalization), whereas the structure in (17b) cannot.

When sonorant consonants occur as head, the manner interpretation are the same as when they occur in dependent positions.

4 The Successive Division Algorithm delivers minimal specification

Dresher (2009) proposes a way of assigning a minimal feature specification to segments based on a *Successive Division Algorithm* that follows a language-specific ranking of features and stops when every segment in the inventory is distinguished from all others. In van der Hulst (2018) I use this algorithm with a *universal* ranking of manner and place elements. This universal ranking is implicit in the structure of the manner and place class and can be derived by assigning an asterisk to each head at both levels within which does not differentiate between the dependent elements:[36]

(18) a.   V   (syllabic V-position, i.e. nucleus)

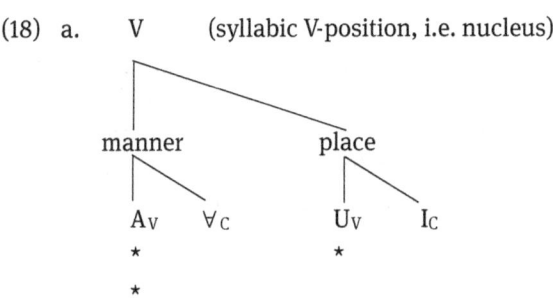

  b. $A_V > U_V > I_C/\forall_C$

In this ranking |I| and |∀| have equal 'prominence'. In van der Hulst (2018: 75) I suggest that "|I|, which denotes a more salient phonetic event, takes precedence over |∀|, unless this element is non-distinctive and/or occurs in a 'mixture' with the U-element (as in Finnish, where [i] and [e] are so-called neutral vowels and front rounded vowels [ü] and [ö] are present)"; see van der Hulst (2018: 88–89)

---

[36] The method for assigning asterisks is the same that Liberman & Prince (1977) propose for deriving a grid from a metrical tree: at the lowest layer assign an asterisk to each head; at the next layers assign another asterisk to the ultimate head of each head, etc.

for further discussion. Given the SDA and the universal ranking (per syllabic position[37]), elements will be specified depending on contrast.

If there is no vowel contrast (a frequent situation in unstressed syllable that display complete neutralization of vowel contrast, as in English), the default element is the manner |A| element. |A| is the unmarked choice in a syllabic V-position (i.e. the nucleus) because the syllabic V-position (rhyme head) prefers V-elements (as opposed to the onset head, which is a syllabic C-unit and thus prefers C elements, i.e. stops; see 14).

If a contrast is detected it will be a contrast between |A| and |∀|. A binary contrast within a vowel set, producing a so-called vertical vowel system, is thus a manner contrast; place does not yet come into consideration. Contrast in manner precedes contrast in place (color), which is expected given that manner is the head class. An additional contrast could involve allowing a *combination* of the manner element, creating a vertical vowel system with multiple heights. The other possible route is to introduce color by activating a place element. What happens if the learner is confronted with a low vowel [a] and a high vowel with a specific color (rather than being central, as in a vertical system)? Firstly, we need to consider the possibility that the color is simply a 'phonetic effect', which results in the high vowel being either [u]-ish or [i]-ish. Color could also arise under the influence of neighboring consonants, as has been claimed for Kabardian (Kuipers 1960). We can only be sure that color is contrastively present if there is a color contrast between [u] and [i]. This then implies that we minimally have a three-vowel system [a u i]. We then expect the specification to be as in (19), assuming that the binary color contrast only requires activation of one of the color elements, let us say |U|, because that is a V-type element:

(19) [a]   [i]   [u]
      A
            ∀   ∀
                  U

In (20) and (21), I demonstrate how contrast is minimally specified in a three- and five-vowel system, respectively:

---

[37] The ranking in (18) holds when elements occur in the V-syllabic unit (the rhyme). In the onset, the ranking would be $|\forall|_C > I_C > U_V/A_V$, which ranks stops over fricatives and coronal over labials; both rank over dorsals which combine the I and U element; see (14).

(20) A three-vowel system (iua): A > U > I
   a.
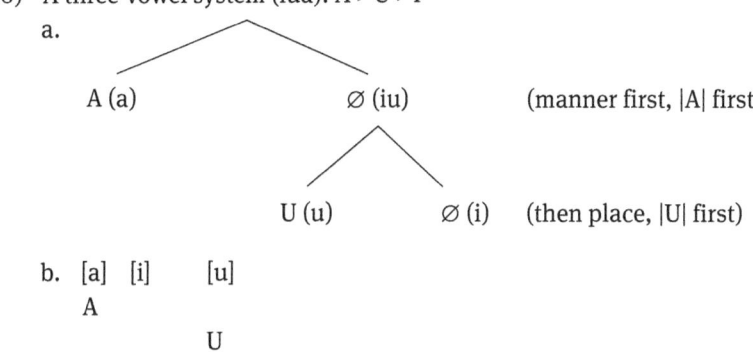

   b. [a] [i] [u]
      A
          U

Note that (20b) differs from (19) in omitting a manner element for high vowels. The same result obtains for a five-vowel system:

(21) A five-vowel system (iueoa): A > U > I/∀
   a.
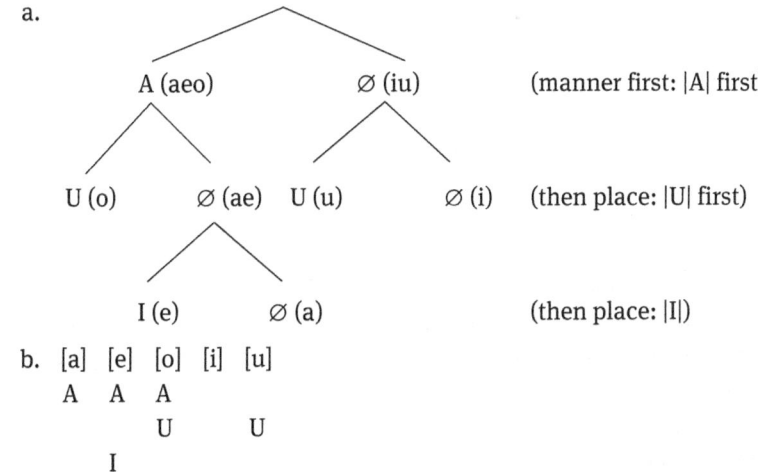

   b. [a] [e] [o] [i] [u]
      A   A   A
              U   U
          I

However, we now have to resolve a paradox which goes unnoticed in van der Hulst (2018). The fact that in a three- and five-vowel system high vowels are specified in (20) and (21) *without* a manner element |∀|, means that they are specified without *any* manner element. This seems inconsistent with the claim that manner, being the head class, cannot remain unspecified in a segment. To resolve this problem, I will simply assume that the |∀| is the 'place-holder' element which automatically appears if the manner node is unspecified due to the SDA.[38] The most direct way to achieve this is to say that when the highest-ranking element |A| is activated, its antagonistic counterpart |∀| is as well. Thus (21) must be replaced by (22):

(22) A five-vowel system (iueoa): A/∀ > U > I

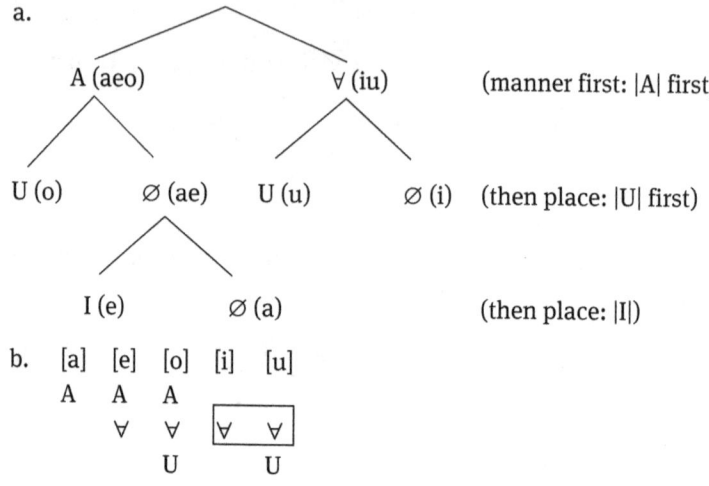

We must note that the 'parsing trees' are not an independent level of representation. They merely depict how phonological segments are minimally represented, given the ranking of elements in (16b). In fact, the parsing tree in (22) is a combination of the recursive splitting diagram that I introduced as showing how learner parse the phonetic spaces that are relevant for phonemic contrast. Rather than following each recursive splitting for all three element classes in sequences (for example Manner > Place > Laryngeal), the available spaces for phonetic contrast are parsed in accordance with a 'Balancing Principle', which favors that the first parse, which is the first manner parse into V (=|A|) vs. C (=|∀|), is followed by the first parse for place (with activating V (=|U|) before C (=|I|)), which for a very complex phoneme system can then be followed by the second manner parse which leads to a combination of |A| and |∀|, plus a dependency relation, and so on. At some point, if the language it tonal, we would expect a tonal element is activated, presumably after vowels have been distinguished in terms or aperture and color.

---

[38] In this function the |"|-element is similar to the 'cold vowel' that was used in Kaye, Lowenstamm and Vergnaud (1985), which was in fact similar in terms of its 'phonetic content', being specified in this model as [+high].

The RCVP segmental structure and the ranking that can be derived from it thus predicts a learning path. In acquisition, the first step is to assume a *sequential* CV unit (which is already established at the babbling stage), i.e. the syllable. Before any contrast is established, the single segment (that represents all segments in the target language) will have the expected C or V elements, depending on the C or V nature of its syllabic position. In the rhyme unit, the elements that is activated is V (=|A|), which predict that at that point the only vowel will be an [a]-like vowel. When contrast is established this will first activate the C and V element in the head/primary manner, which produces a high/closed vowel and a low/open vowel. When additional contrast is detected this likely (following the balancing principle) involves activated of the place element V (=|U|).

The same parsing logic predicts an 'order' in which attested vowel system increase in complexity:

(23) Ranking:
1-vowel system: A_V (by default)
2-vowel system (no place): A_V vs $\forall_C$
3-vowel system without place: A_V vs $\forall_C > A_V + \forall_C$
3-vowel system with place: A_V vs $\forall_C > U_V$
5-vowel system: A_V vs $\forall_C > U_V > I_C$
More complicated systems: A_V vs $\forall_C > U_V > I_C > A_V + \forall_C$

I refer to van der Hulst (2018, § 2.3) for further details.

5 Comparison to government phonology1.0

Having outlined the RCVP model, I will now draw attention to some specific differences between RCVP and (standard) DP and GP, as well as some commonalities. As I will show, there is a sense in which the choice of only two elements in RCVP converges with a particular version of GP that only adopts six elements (as assumed in Backley 2011). Government Phonology, though developed independently from DP, has important characteristics in common with the latter approach.[39]

---

[39] I pointed the 'resemblance' out to J.R. Vergnaud in 1982 when he presented these ideas at a GLOW workshop in Paris. A statement in Kaye, Lowenstamm and Vergnaud (1985: 310) that their molecular approach to segmental structure bears some degree of resemblance to earlier work by Anderson and Jones signals an awareness of the similarities.

Later developments in GP were aimed at reducing the number of elements. The overall result of the reduction program was a set of six elements, which Backley (2011) discusses and applies to segmental inventories and processes. He proposes a system of six elements with no further structure imposed on this set; also see Scheer & Kula (2018) and Backley (2011). GP continues to do without any concept of elements grouping. However, in the last chapter, Backley discusses two ways of classifying the six elements.

(24) | variable | relevant values | elements | |
|---|---|---|---|
| | | dark | light |
| resonance | resonant vs. non-resonant | [A] | [ʔ](~ [∀])[40] |
| frequency | low vs. high frequency | [L] | [H] |
| color | dark vs. bright | [U] | [I] |

By grouping the elements in antagonistic pairs, Backley says that we reveal "three variables that are even more basic than the acoustic patterns associated with the elements themselves". He continues:

"We can think of the perceptual variables in [(24)] as the fundamental properties of spoken language – properties which humans instinctively pay attention to during communication. Now, because contrast is based on acoustic differences, it makes sense for languages to exploit cues that are maximally different, since these are the easiest to distinguish. The cues that are relevant to phonology are therefore the cues that identify the most extreme values of the three variables. In other words, the elements in each pair are opposites" (p. 195)

Backley asserts that the variables are not formal units of grammar, nor are the labels 'dark' and 'light'. This is precisely where my model differs from GP element theory. The structure in (25) gives a simplified version of the RCVP structure in (2). Note that the three classes correspond to Backley's variables (added in parentheses in (25)). Within each class, RCVP will locate the same two elements, C and V, which correlate with different interpretations in each class which expressed that, in Backley's words: "the elements in each pair are opposites". This, in a way, delivers a six-way element distinction which corresponds to the six elements that GP ended up with:

---

[40] Instead of 'ʔ' I use the symbol '∀'.

(25) The 'geometry' of elements in Radical cv Phonology

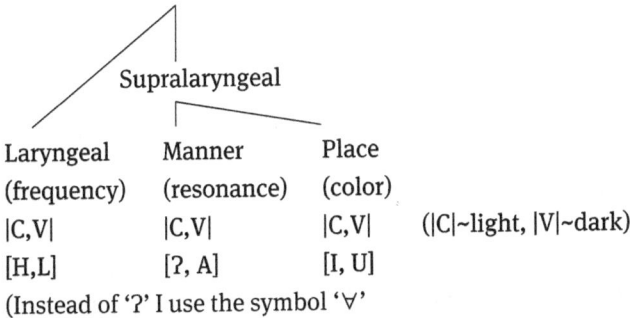

Laryngeal   Manner   Place
(frequency)   (resonance)   (color)
|C,V| |C,V| |C,V| (|C|~light, |V|~dark)
[H,L]   [?, A]   [I, U]
(Instead of '?' I use the symbol '∀'

Backley's light/dark opposition correlates with the C/V nature of each element. Backley's reasoning to keep the distinctions in (24) that he recognizes as important outside the formal grammar is not entirely clear to me. I note that if he *would* have added these distinctions to his formal system, his theory would have ended up being nearly identical to the RCVP model. RCVP can reduce the set of six to one pair of opposing elements, because, unlike GP, RCVP formally recognizes the notion of element grouping that Backley refers to as 'variables' in (24).

Note that the C/V labeling captures the original insight behind *Charm Theory* (proposed in Kaye, Lowenstamm and Vergnaud (1985): C corresponds to negative charm and indeed: C values are unmarked in onset positions. V corresponds for positive charm, and V values are favored in nuclear positions. The correspondence is not perfect. Kaye, Lowenstamm and Vergnaud (1985, 1990) took U and L to be negatively charmed.

It is also the case that DP and GP make somewhat different usage of the dependency relation. RCVP rigidly applies the head-dependency relation, which means that I do not recognise structures in which elements stand in a relationship of 'mutual dependency', as is possible in DP, nor do I use the diacritic headed/non-headed distinction of GP. Thus, I only allow (26a) and (26b) and exclude the possibilities in (24c):

(26) a. A is the head of B.
     b. B is the head of A.
     c. i. DP: A and B are 'mutually dependent'.
         ii. GP: Elements can be headed or non-headed.

In contrast to (26c), RCVP uses headedness *obligatorily* to acknowledge the asymmetry that arises from merging (maximally two) elements per class node; mono-elemental structures are headed by default. Thus, in RCVP, |A| (or its RCVP 'full' equivalent) cannot be distinct from |A|, nor is |AI| distinct from either |AI| or |AI|.[41]

Another apparent significant difference between RCVP and GP (also Backley's version) lies in RCVP's adoption of the element |∀| (although Kaye, Lowenstamm & Vergnaud (1985) originally proposed an element very much like it, |ʜ|, which was abandoned in favor of contrastive use of headedness, as mentioned above). In GP, there is no theoretical reason for pairing up the element |A| with an antagonistic partner, as there is in RCVP. The crucial availability of the element |∀| is supported in van der Hulst (2018). However, as shown in (25), the |∀| corresponds to the '?' elements in GP, so the adoption of |∀| merely makes explicit that the 'closure' element has an equal role to play in vowels (representing high or 'non-low') and in consonants (representing 'non-continuancy'). The |∀| also bears a resemblance to the 'cold vowel' that was proposed in Kaye, Lowenstamm and Vergnaud (1985) in that |∀| is the default manner element that must be present if |A| is not specified, as was discussed in section 3.

Finally, we need to ask whether *elements have an independent realization*. In GP each element is supposed to be independently pronounceable. This means that each element, occurring alone, characterizes a complete segment. While this was certainly also the case in the DP approach, especially for the 'aiu' set, DP does not adopt this requirement for all elements. RCVP takes the view that this property only applies to the *head occurrence* of elements, although it must be added that no head element is interpretable in the absence of a manner element, since manner, being the head of the segmental structure, is an obligatory unit.

6 ATR, RTR and nasality

In this section, I will discuss the representation of tongue root distinctions and nasality which, for me at least, have always been hard to capture in RCVP in a fully satisfactory way. I have gone back and forth between different proposals. To prove this point, I will here discuss some of these alternatives. By discussing the motivations for choosing between these various alternatives, I hope to give the reader a perspective on the 'logic' of RCVP, that is, the considerations that

---

[41] This does not preclude leaving the dependency relation unspecified when in a class only one combination of the two elements is needed. If, for example, this concern mid vowels, the dependency is predictable from the phonetic properties of the mid series which can be [e/o] or [ɛ/ɔ].

have led me to embrace certain structures and interpretations, while rejecting others.[42]

In 'older' work on RCVP (e.g. van der Hulst 2005), I have considered the structure in (27), which, using more current terminology, adopts ATR and RTR as secondary manner elements:

(27) V (rhyme)

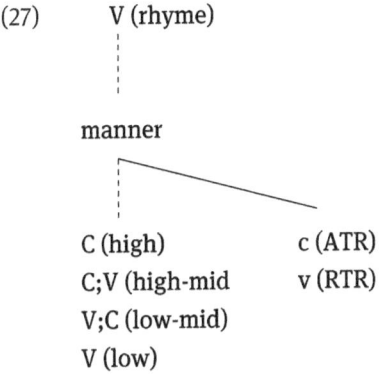

manner

C (high)   c (ATR)
C;V (high-mid)   v (RTR)
V;C (low-mid)
V (low)

The motivation for taking these interpretations of secondary c and v is that it expresses a direct and formal correlation between tongue height and TR position: high (C) correlates with ATR (c) and low (V) correlates with RTR (v). These correlations are well motivated because high vowels prefer to be advanced while low vowels prefer to be retracted. In VDH20, chapter 8 I show in detail that these kinds of correlations are expected given the RCVP notation. However, there are two problems with (27). Firstly, it does not reserve a place for nasality in the manner class. The class of nasal consonants is represented as C in the manner head class when the segmental structure occurs in the onset dependent position, but that does not account for nasality as a *secondary* property of vowels or consonants. Perhaps, nasality can be expressed elsewhere? GP analyzes nasality as a possible interpretation of the L-element as a dependent, which also covers low tone when it is a head. This would require a revision of the laryngeal class which

---

42 I realize that some might take going back and forth between alternatives, or find new ones, as a sign of the fact that the RCVP is misguided in trying to 'squeeze' all contrastive phonetic properties in a uniform model that seeks structural analogy between the class nodes, and is based on a few 'first principles'. For me, however, this has always been the most interesting and intriguing part of the enterprise which was led by a conjecture that phonological structure at the segmental and syllabic level (and perhaps higher level too) can be reduced to two basic units which, given their antagonistic nature, are perfectly suited to capture the notion of contrast which is fundamental to the phonology.

in VDH20 does not accommodate nasality. A second problem with (27) is that it allows for a contrast between RTR and ATR vowels which remains unattested.[43]

In van der Hulst (2018) I adopt a different proposal which captures the mutual exclusivity of ATR and RTR:

(28) V (rhyme)

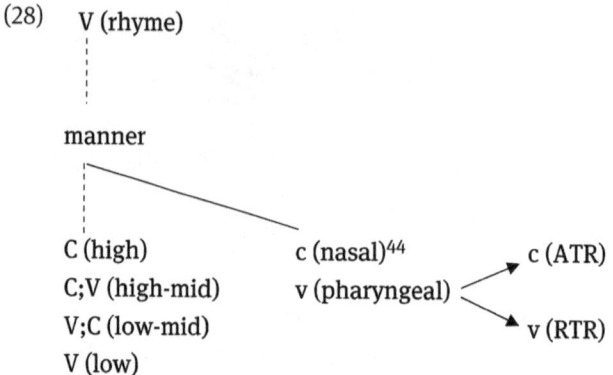

C (high)   c (nasal)[44]   c (ATR)
C;V (high-mid)   v (pharyngeal)
V;C (low-mid)   v (RTR)
V (low)

Here 'pharyngeal' refers to the pharyngeal cavity, but not specifically to either ATR or RTR, which are taken to be two non-contrastive phonetic choices. The motivation for needing both RTR and ATR comes most clearly from a broad typological study of tongue harmony in African languages in Casali (2003, 2008, to appear). Casali convincingly shows that languages with TR harmony in which there is a TR contrast among high vowels are best analysed by taking ATR as the active harmony property. Casali then also argues that languages that only have a contrast for mid vowels require activation of the feature RTR because in those cases the lower mid vowels act as the dominant class; see also Leitch (1996), who confirms this approach in a typological study of vowel harmony in Bantu languages. In van der Hulst (2018: chapter 7) I refer to these findings as 'Casali's Correlation'.[45]

---

[43] Certain Kru languages might qualify, however, for using both ATR and RTR; see Newman (1986) and Singler (2008); but the nature of the vowel contrast and the harmony facts in these languages are not entirely clear to me.

[44] As in DP, nasal(ity) is seemingly expressed twice in the model. However, we need to understand that the manner C element expresses that nasal consonants are stops and not their nasality, which is a side effect given that the nasal cavity is used as an escape route for the egressive airstream. Nasal consonants are universally provided with a secondary manner c element to capture their nasality. This relation is an instance of the universal redundancy rule in (11) which in this case applies obligatorily.

[45] Additional motivation for recognizing both RTR and ATR will be discussed below with reference to vowel harmony patterns in Tungusic and Mongolic languages.

Even though, as shown in Wood (1979, 1982) these two actions involve different muscles: the genioglossus and the hyoglossus, respectively, I proposed that secondary v is phonetically ambiguous, thus allowing the phonetic distinction between ATR and RTR to be a non-contrastive *phonetic split* of the pharyngeal element, with ATR representing a *phonetic* c element and RTR a *phonetic* v element, the choice being determined by the structure of the vowel system, following Casali's Correlation. This proposal then makes the occurrence of ATR and RTR mutually exclusive within a single language.

However, even though in this proposal RTR is available for a language that shows an RTR relation among mid vowels, I actually do not recruit RTR for the analysis of such seven vowel systems. Rather I proposed that (a) the mid vowels are A-headed (i.e. V;C or A;∀), whereas high-mid vowels are non-headed (CV or ∀A) and that (b) in the presence of low-mid vowels, high-mid vowels will become A-headed, which accounts for the harmony. The argument for representing high-mid vowels as non-headed is that the head manner C element is 'defective', a claim that is motivated at length in van der Hulst (2018),[46] one manifestation of its defectiveness being that it cannot be a head. I here quote from page 244 of that work (section references are to sections in the book):

"I will argue that while we find convincing cases of lowering in terms of licensing of the variable element (A), cases of raising in terms of licensing (∀) are limited. I will show that the element |∀| is regularly involved only if its licensing role is itself licensed by stress. I propose that the rarity of |∀|-harmony is based on a deficiency of the |∀| element, which does not have an independent articulatory correlate. Its presence in the system of elements is enforced by the opponent principle and as such it plays a role in representing mid vowels. From a formal point of view, the deficiency of |∀| lies in its inability to be a head. As a result, this element cannot be a head in a complex aperture structure, as well as in a licensing relation, except when 'fortified' by stress."

The defectiveness of the |∀|-element, which is extensively motivated in van der Hulst (2015), explains why low-mid vowels are dominant, transferring their headedness specification to high mid vowel, this turning them into low-mid vowels.

---

[46] The crucial point is that manner C for vowels does not have an independent phonetic interpretation, there being no articulatory basis for 'high'; see also van der Hulst (2015). The defectiveness of this element is reminiscent of the defective character of the element [ɨ] in Government Phonology (Kaye, Lowenstamm and Vergnaud 1985). In van der Hulst (2018: § 6.6.2.2.2 I make the argument that the ∀ is only involved in stress-dependent harmony (i.e. metaphony).

By adopting the headedness mechanism for harmony among mid vowels in seven-vowel systems and by allowing RTR as a phonetic interpretation of the pharyngeal element, my 2018 model creates an ambiguity in the analysis of such seven-vowel systems. To avoid this ambiguity, I proposed that the choice between RTR as secondary v or a A-headedness depends on the structure of the vowel system.

In van der Hulst (2018: § 10.1–3) I discuss a group of languages that have a so-called 'double triangular system', for which it has been claimed that RTR is the active and often 'dominant' feature in terms of harmony, making them 'diagonal harmony systems' (a term used in Kim (1978)). My idea was that only in such language the active harmonic element is RTR as secondary manner v, while A-headedness harmony would apply in seven-vowel systems with two series of mid vowels. An example of a double triangular systems with RTR dominance is Nez Perce:

(29) double triangular system (Nez Perce)

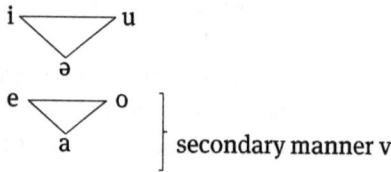 secondary manner v

However, the prediction that double triangular system will select secondary manner v as the active element is contradicted by vowel harmony in Gaam [tbi] (Eastern Sudanic, Eastern Jebel in Sudan) as reported in Kutch Lojenga (to appear), based on Stirtz (2009).[47] This language has six contrastive vowels and an active dominant/recessive vowel-harmony system with ATR dominance. The vowel system is as follows:

(30) double triangular system (Gaam)

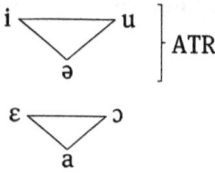 ATR

---

[47] This report is based on data from Stirtz (2009).

The following examples (31) to (33) showing left-to-right and right-to-left spreading are from Stirtz (2009: 78 and 79):

(31) Rightward spreading to plural suffix *-ɛɛg*, which changes to *–iig* after [+ATR] roots.

Noun SG	Noun PL				
cèèr	cèèr-ɛ̄ɛ̄g	'singer'	jííl	jííl-íīg	'locust'
ḍààr	ḍààr-ɛ̀ɛ̀g	'eagle'	ə̀ər	ə̀ər-ììg	'sheep'
cɔ́ɔ́l	cɔ́ɔ́l-ɛ̄ɛ̄g	'donkey'	gùùr	gùùr-īīg	'stone tool'

(32) Rightward spreading to plural suffix *-aag*, which changes to *-əəg* after [+ATR] roots.

Noun SG	Noun PL				
tɛ́ɛ̀l	tɛ́ɛ́l-ààg	'anchor'	îl	íl-ə̀əg	'horn'
kásán	kásán-áāg	'friend'	ə̀nḍə́ə́r	ə̀nḍə́ə́r-ə̄əg	'tree'
bɔ́n	bɔ̀n-āāg	'heart'	kūūð	kūūð-ə́əg	'shadow'

(33) Leftward spreading from the [+ATR] plural suffix *–əg*, whereby [-ATR] vowels in the root change to [+ATR] (Stirtz 2009: 81, 84).

Noun SG	Noun PL	
tɛ̄ɛ̄nḍ	tīīnḍ-əg	'riddle(s)'
wɛ́ɛ́(s)	wís-sə̄g	'house(s)'
fānḍ	fə̄nḍ-əg	'cheek(s)'

It should, however, be noted that the alternation between the low mid vowels and the high vowels in Gaam seems to amount to more than just ATR; the low mid vowels also contain the A-element, which must be removed when they become ATR. Alternatively, we could say that the alternation reveals that the mid vowels in Gaam are *phonologically* high, i.e. /ɪ/ and /ʊ/ (so that they do not in fact contain the A-element, which would then be added in the phonetic implementation):

(34) double triangular system (Gaam)

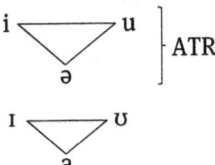

If this is a possible analysis, Gaam would fall under Casali's Correlation and be predicted to use ATR as the active element.[48]

While, thus, the idea that usage of secondary v or A-headedness for RTR harmony may be dependent on the structure of the vowel system, in the 2020 model, being dissatisfied with the dual phonetic split of secondary v, I adopt (35), which restricts the interpretation of secondary v to pharyngeal *constriction*, RTR. This of course raises the question how ATR as an active element is accounted for. To give this element a 'place' in the RCVP segmental structure, I returned to an 'old' idea that I had proposed in van der Hulst (1988a, 1988b), which was to identify ATR with a dependent usage of the I-element (in the place class). There is good reason to link ATR to the I element, since both draw on activity of the genioglossus muscle which pulls the tongue forward as a consequence of raising and fronting the tongue body.[49] Also note that the affinity with high vowels, i.e. C manner, is still expressed because the I-element is also a C element (in the place class).[50] With this proposal, we no longer need to say that the secondary manner element v correlates with two opposing phonetic properties. This secondary element always correlates consistently with RTR:

---

[48] But perhaps we should not make too much of differences in transcriptions in this case. Various studies of African harmony systems note that the two transcriptions are often both used by different authors for the same languages; see van der Hulst (2018: § 6.3.1.2.1 on Kikuyu).
[49] This affinity is perhaps also the cause of a shift from palatal harmony to ATR harmony which has been said to occur in some Mongolian languages; see Svantesson (1985). Although Ko (2011) argues for the opposite development, this does not take away from the fact that palatal harmony and ATR harmony are closely related.
[50] See van der Hulst (2016) for a discussion of the correlations with reference to Wood (1975, 1979, 1982). In Wood's system, his feature [palatal] applies to all high vowels, not just [i]. In the proposal in (35), this would only be the case for the secondary use of the element I ([ATR]).

(35)   V (rhyme)

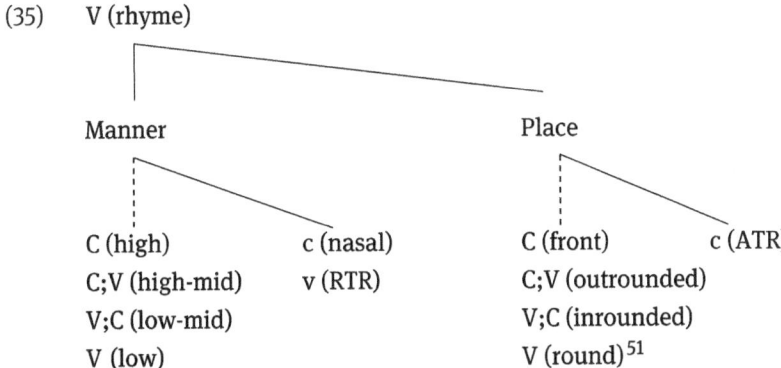

Manner		Place	
C (high)	c (nasal)	C (front)	c (ATR)
C;V (high-mid)	v (RTR)	C;V (outrounded)	
V;C (low-mid)		V;C (inrounded)	
V (low)		V (round)[51]	

The appears to be no secondary version required of the place V element, which is of course slightly unsatisfactory, given the strong insistence in RCVP on structural analogy between the element classes.[52]

A consequence of this proposal (like the one in 27) is that we no longer rule out a language having both pharyngeal harmony and ATR harmony, at least not on formal grounds.

There is, however, a further ambiguity that is noted in van der Hulst (2018). A double triangular system in which the 'lower vowels' are dominant (thus unlike what we find in Gaam) could also be analysed in terms of the primary element V (i.e. as 'A-harmony'), i.e., as a 'lowering' effect.[53] In van der Hulst (2018: 410) I do not offer a solution to avoid this ambiguity and I simply admit that the alternations in Nez Perce can be represented with secondary v or with primary V (=|A|), allowing (29) and (36) as possible analyses:

---

[51] There appears to be no secondary version required of the place V element, which is of course slightly unsatisfactory, given the strong insistence in RCVP on structural analogy between the element classes.

[52] In VDH20 I analyze 'rhotic(ized)' as a secondary manner property involving a combination of c and v; see (15) where this proposal is incorporated. Interestingly, this property (variously described as 'retroflex' and 'rhotacized') can occur harmonically in a number of languages, such as Yurok, Kalasha and Serrano, although Smith (to appear) regards these as a variety of RTR harmony. A possible avenue to explore would be to analyse the relevant property as secondary v in the place node. Roundness of vowels and retroflexion share an acoustic property that Jakobson and Halle (1956) captured with their feature [flat] which they used for round vowels and for the secondary articulation in consonants including labialization and retroflexion.

[53] I note that this was in fact the proposed analysis in van der Hulst (1988). However, a comparison between the 1988 model and later models is complicated because in the 1988 model there was no distinction between primary and secondary classes.

(36) double triangular system (Nez Perce)

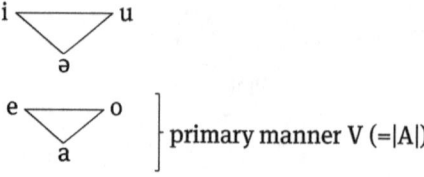
primary manner V (=|A|)

Lowering harmony in term of the A-element is well-motivated. In van der Hulst (2018, chapter 6) I discuss various cases of lowering harmony, mainly in Bantu languages (Hyman (1999), in terms of A-harmony (i.e. with reference to the primary occurrence of this element), which are reported as involving lowering of high vowels /i/ and /u/ to mid vowels /e/ and /o/.

(37) Seven-vowel system with lowering harmony

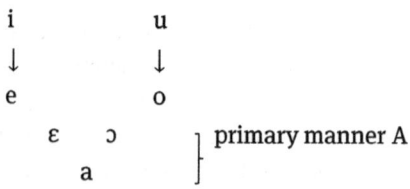
primary manner A

In contrast, harmony between the two mid series in seven-vowel systems cannot simply analyzed in terms of the element |A| because both series contain this element to begin with. This is why I have proposed to employ the mechanism of A-*headedness* for such systems, although as we have seen, an analysis in terms of secondary manner v is also possible, but perhaps only chosen in double triangular systems of the Nez Perce type and not available for seven-vowel systems.[54]

We need to ask however, whether the analysis using secondary v in (29) really works for Nez Perce. If secondary manner v represents RTR, then why do high vowels /i/ and /u/ turn into the mid vowels /e/ and /o/, rather than /ɪ/ and /ʊ/? If the dominant non-high vowels are truly mid vowels than the analysis in terms the A-element is more 'direct' since it directly captures the difference between the vowels /i/ and /u/ vs. /e/ and /o/.

Given then that RTR is not required for harmony among mid vowels in seven-vowel systems and given that it does not even seem adequate for cases like

---

[54] We do not want to say that in such system the high mid vowels are in fact 'ɪ' and 'ʊ' because that would predict, as per Casali's Correlation that such a system would have ATR-harmony among the two high series, as in the language Lugbara; see Casali (2003: 326 ff) and van der Hulst (2018: 297 ff.).

Nez Perce, it would seem that the move in (35) to reduce the interpretation of the pharyngeal element to RTR was wrong. We only need ATR, which we could then 'move back' to the secondary manner class.

However, simply getting rid of RTR causes problems. As usual, making changes in one class typically creates problems elsewhere in the system, which testifies to the fact that 'everything is connected' in the RCVP system; there are no local changes without global consequences! Removing RTR creates a problem because we lose the characterization of pharyngealized consonants or pharyngealized vowels as having a secondary manner v, interpreted as pharyngealization; see (14).

For this reason, I feel compelled to stick with (35), which means that we have to live with the fact that secondary manner v, when being harmonic, 'competes' with A-headedness harmony (unless we can restrict v-harmony to double triangular systems) as well as with A-harmony (where the account in terms of A-harmony is in fact more accurate). Perhaps then the conclusion should be that secondary manner v represents a 'local property', i.e. pharyngealization of consonants and vowels, but not one that engages in harmonic relations. Or, when it acts non-locally, it involves both consonants and vowels, as in the case of emphatic harmony in varieties of Arabic (Khan, to appear). Interestingly, a similar characteristic is displayed by nasal harmony (Botma, to appear).

Now that I have suggested that secondary manner v plays a rather limited role in genuine vowel harmony processes, it is necessary to address a specific argument for allowing both RTR and ATR as active harmonic elements, based on the claim that languages simple have a choice to use either ATR or RTR as the active element for vowel harmony.[55] Opposed to this view, I argue in van de Hulst (2018) that most cases that have been analysed as RTR harmony should in fact be analysed as ATR harmony.

As explained in Lindau (1979), phonetically speaking, a distinction between the relative size of the pharyngeal cavity can be made in three different ways:

(38) Set 1: larger pharynx: Set 2: smaller pharynx:
    a. Advanced = dominant neutral
    b. Neutral retracted = dominant
    c. Advanced retracted

---

[55] Since no language seems to use both, this actually supports the idea to see these two phonetic properties as realization of a single element. This was captured in 2018 model.

This finding has led some phonologists to the conclusion that if (39a) obtains, the active phonological feature is ATR, which is the common choice for African languages. In contrast, if (39b) obtains, the active feature would be RTR. Various authors analysing vowel harmony in Asian languages belonging to the Tungusic and Mongolian language families, have established that a TR distinction is made in terms of tongue retraction, (28b); see van der Hulst (2018: § 9.2.).To support 'RTR' analyses, Li (1996), Zhang (1996), and Ko (2011, 2012) all note that (in the relevant cases) the retracted vowels have generally been described as involving articulatory effort, indicating that the active gesture is tongue root retraction.[56]

In the theory proposed in van der Hulst (2018), while RTR is available as an element (namely secondary manner v), I reject this possibility for the Tungusic and Mongolian languages because this would make the wrong predictions for how neutral vowels behave in harmony systems. I argue at length that the facts regarding the behaviour of neutral vowels in *both* African and Asian languages must lead to the conclusion that the set with the larger cavity (whether positively resulting from advancement of the tongue or negatively resulting from the absence of TR retraction) is the dominant set in all vowel harmony systems that fall under Casali's Correlation, that is, in which there is a TR contrast for high vowels. A comparison between African and Asian languages with TR-harmony in Li (1996: 318 ff) makes clear, the Asian languages that have TR-root harmony do indeed often have two series of high vowels which, as per Casali' Correlation would suggest that ATR is the active element. Given the current proposal, namely to analyse ATR as secondary |I|, all these African and Asian languages that have two series of high vowels must be analysed with harmony in terms of this element. For Tungusic and Mongolian languages in which the non-ATR vowels have active TR retraction, I would argue that this retraction merely enhances the phonetic difference between advanced and non-advanced vowels. Such enhancement might, in fact, also occur in African languages, as shown in Lindau (1975, 1976). In the model proposed here (in 24), the RTR is not even available for the Asian systems, despite the phonetic appearance of RTR being active. In conclusion, I suggest that there is no RTR element that plays a role in vowel harmony systems.

I guess, the reader now realizes the point of this section: the saga never ends... but for this chapter, I *will* end with the following structure:

---

[56] This is also stated in Ladefoged and Maddieson (1996: 306) with reference to the Tungusic language Even.

(39)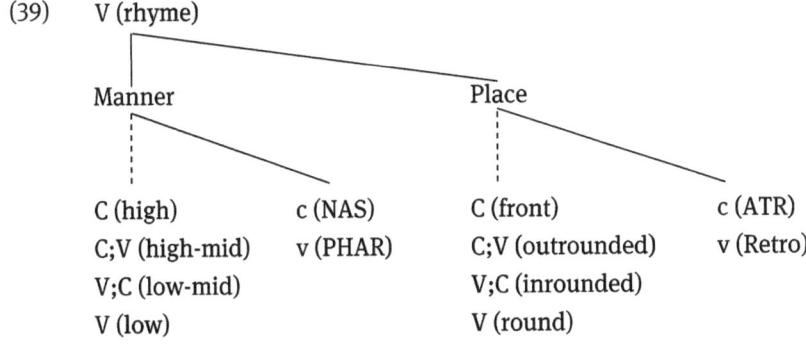

Raising harmony   Nasal harmony   Palatal harmony ATR harmony
Lowering harmony   Emphatic harmony   Labial harmony   Retroflex harmony
Headedness harmony

The two secondary manner c properties in the manner and place class each activate an extra resonating cavity, the nasal cavity the pharyngeal cavity, respectively. Both secondary v elements can occur in harmonic processes of a limited kind (typically involving both consonants and vowels, which suggest that their locality is defined with respect to the segmental ('skeletal') level. We have also noted that raising harmony is limited due to the defectiveness of the C elements in manner (i.e. |∀|), perhaps only occurring under conditions of stress. The odd man out is headedness harmony which captures RTR harmony, not in terms of an active element, but in terms of A-headedness. The suggestion to capture retroflex harmony in term of secondary place v is very tentative.

7 Conclusions

This article summarizes the basic structure of the RCVP model as presented in VDH20 which is the result of considering and rejecting many previous versions. To give the reader a flavor of the struggles that he gone into developing the model, I discuss various alternatives for the representation of contrast that involve activity in the pharyngeal cavity. What emerges from this demonstration is a proposal that is slightly different from the proposal in VDH20, mostly by attributing a reduced role to pharyngealization in vowel harmony processes, appealing only to A-headedness harmony as a mechanism to express what Casali (2003) and Leitch (1996) refers to as RTR harmony in seven-vowel systems with two series of mid vowels, and to A-harmony in the double triangular cases. Nevertheless, there is a role for secondary manner v in non-local harmony (typically involving both consonants and vowels), comparable to a similar role of secondary c (nasality).

References

Anderson, John M. 2011. *The substance of language, Volume III: Phonology-syntax analogies.* Oxford: Oxford University Press.
Anderson, John M. 2014. Graphophonology and anachronic phonology. Notes on episodes in the history of pseudo-phonology. Folia Linguistica Historica 35 (2014). 1–53.
Anderson, John M. & Colin J. Ewen. 1987. *Principles of Dependency Phonology* (Cambridge Studies in Linguistics 47). Cambridge: Cambridge University Press.
Anderson, John M. & Charles Jones. 1972. Three theses concerning phonological representations. *Edinburgh Working Papers in Linguistics* 1. 92–115.
Anderson, John M. & Charles Jones. 1974. Three theses concerning phonological representations. *Journal of Linguistics* 10. 1–26.
Avery, Peter & Keren Rice. 1990. Segment structure and coronal underspecification. *Phonology* 6.2. 179–200.
Backley, Phillip. 2011. *An introduction to Element Theory.* Edinburgh: Edinburgh University Press.
Backley, Phillip. 2012. Variation in Element Theory. *Linguistic Variation* 1.1. 57–102.
Blaho, Sylvia. 2008. *The syntax of phonology: A radically substance-free approach*. PhD dissertation, University of Tromsø.
Böhm, Roger. 2018. Just for the record: Dependency (vs. constituency) for the umpteenth time – A concise guide for the confused with an appended how-(not)-to-read Tesnière's *Éléments*. In Roger Böhm & Harry van der Hulst (eds.), *Substance-based grammar: The (ongoing) work of John Anderson* (Studies in Language Companion Series 204), 261–310. Amsterdam and Philadelphia: John Benjamins.
Botma, Bert. to appear. Nasal harmony. In Nancy Ritter & Harry van der Hulst. eds. *The Oxford Handbook of Vowel Harmony. Oxford*: Oxford University Press.
Casali, Roderic F. 2003. [ATR] value asymmetries and underlying vowel inventory structure in Niger-Congo and Nilo-Saharan. *Linguistic Typology* 7. 307–82.
Casali, Roderic F. 2008. ATR harmony in African languages. *Language and Linguistics Compass* 2.3. 496–549.
Casali, Roderic. to appear. Tongue root harmony and vowel inventory structure. In Nancy Ritter and Harry van der Hulst. eds. *The Oxford Handbook of Vowel Harmony.* Oxford: Oxford University Press.
Clements, George Nick. 1985. The geometry of phonological features. *Phonology* 2. 225–52.
den Dikken, Marcel & Harry van der Hulst. 1988. Segmental hierarchitecture. In Harry van der Hulst & Norval Smith (eds.), *Features, segmental structure and harmony processes*, vol. 1, 1–59. Dordrecht: Foris.
den Dikken, Marcel & Harry van der Hulst. 2020. On some deep structural analogies between syntax and phonology. In Phillip Backley & Kuniya Nasukawa (eds.), *Morpheme-internal recursion in phonology*, 57–114. Berlin and New York: Mouton de Gruyter.

Dresher, B. Elan. 2009. *The contrastive hierarchy in phonology* (Cambridge Studies in Linguistics 121). Cambridge: Cambridge University Press.
Ewen, Colin & Harry van der Hulst. 2001. *The phonological structure of words*. Cambridge: Cambridge University Press.
Firth, J. R. 1948. Sounds and prosodies. *Transactions of the Philological Society* 47.1. 127–52. Repr. in F.R. Palmer (ed.), Prosodic analysis, 1–26. London: Oxford University Press.
Foley, James. 1977. *Foundations of theoretical phonology*. Cambridge: Cambridge University Press.
Gordon, Matthew K. 2016. *Phonological typology* (Oxford Surveys in Phonology and Phonetics 1). Oxford: Oxford University Press.
Gordon, Matthew & Ian Maddieson. 1999. The phonetics of Ndumbea. *Oceanic Linguistics* 38/1. 66–90.
Hale, Mark & Charles Reiss. 2000. 'Substance period' and 'dysfunctionalism': Current trends in phonology. *Linguistic Inquiry* 31.1. 157–69.
Hjelmslev, Louis. 1943 [1953]. *Prolegomena to a theory of language*. Baltimore, MD: Waverly Press.
Hyman, Larry M. 1972. Nasals and nasalization *Studies in African Linguistics* 3/2. 167–205.
Hyman, Larry M. 1995. Nasal consonant harmony at a distance: The case of Yaka. *Studies in African linguistics* 24/1. 5–30.
Hyman, Larry M. 1999. The historical interpretation of vowel harmony in Bantu. In Jean-Marie Hombert & Larry M. Hyman (eds.), *Bantu Historical Linguistics: Theoretical and Empirical Perspectives*, 235–95. Stanford: CLSI publications.
Kaye, Jonathan, Jean Lowenstamm & Jean-Roger Vergnaud. 1985. The internal structure of phonological elements: A theory of charm and government. *Phonology Yearbook* 2. 305–28.
Kaye, Jonathan, Jean Lowenstamm & Jean-Roger Vergnaud. 1990. Constituent structure and government in phonology. *Phonology* 7.2. 193–231.
Kehrein, Wolfgang & Chris Golston. 2004. A prosodic theory of laryngeal contrasts. *Phonology* 21.3. 325–57.
Khan, Geoffrey. to appear. Harmonic phenomena in Semitic. In Nancy Ritter & Harry van der Hulst. eds. *The Oxford Handbook of Vowel Harmony*. Oxford: Oxford University Press.
Kim, Chin Wu. 1978. 'Diagonal' vowel harmony? Some implications for historical phonology. In Jacek Fisiak (ed.), *Recent developments in historical phonology*, 221–36. The Hague: Mouton.
Ko, Seongyeon. 2011. Vowel contrast and vowel harmony shift in the Mongolic languages. *Language Research* 47.1. 23–43.
Ko, Seongyeon. 2012. Tongue root harmony and vowel contrast in Northeast Asian languages. PhD dissertation, Cornell University.
Kornai, András & Geoffrey K. Pullum. 1990. The X-bar theory of phrase structure. *Language* 66.1. 24–50.
Kuhl, Patricia K. 1991. Human adults and human infants show a 'perceptual magnet effect' for the prototypes of speech categories, monkeys do not. *Perception & Psychophysics* 50.2. 93–107.
Kuipers, Aert. 1960. *Phoneme and Morpheme in Kabardian*. Janua Linguarum: Series Minor, Nos. 8–9. 's-Gravenhage: Mouton and Co.

Kutsch Lojenga, Connie. to appear. Vowel harmony in Nilo-Saharan languages. In Nancy Ritter & Harry van der Hulst. eds. *The Oxford Handbook of Vowel Harmony*. Oxford: Oxford University Press.

Ladefoged, Peter & Ian Maddieson. 1996. *The sounds of the world's languages*. Oxford: Blackwell.

Lass, Roger & John M. Anderson. 1975. *Old English phonology*. Cambridge: Cambridge University Press.

Leitch, Myles F. 1996. *Vowel harmonies of the Congo Basin: An Optimality Theory analysis of variation in the Bantu zone C*. PhD dissertation, University of British Columbia.

Li, Bing. 1996. *Tungusic vowel harmony: Description and analysis*. PhD dissertation, University of Amsterdam.

Liberman, Mark & Alan Prince. 1977. On stress and linguistic rhythm. *Linguistic Inquiry* 8.2. 249–336.

Lindau, Mona. 1975. A phonetic explanation to reduced vowel harmony systems. *UCLA Working Papers in Phonetics* 11. 43–54.

Lindau, Mona. 1976. Larynx height in Kwa. *UCLA Working Papers in Linguistics* 31. 53–61.

Lindau, Mona. 1979. The feature [Expanded]. *Journal of Phonetics* 7. 163–76.

Malmberg, Bertil. 1951. *Svens fonetik*. Lund: Gleerup.

Mascaró, Joan. 1984. Continuant spreading in Basque, Catalan and Spanish. In Mark Aronoff & Richard T. Oehrle (eds.), *Language sound structure*, 287–98. Cambridge, MA: MIT Press.

McCarthy, John J. 1988. Feature geometry and dependency: A review. *Phonetica* 43. 84–108.

Moisik, Scott R. 2013. *The epilarynx in speech*. PhD dissertation, University of Victoria.

Nasukawa, Kuniya. 2005. *A Unified Approach to Nasality and Voicing*. Berlin and New York: Walter de Gruyter.

Piggott, Glyne L. 1992. Variability in feature dependency: The case of nasality. *Natural Language & Linguistic Theory* 10.1. 33–77.

Sagey, Elizabeth C. 1986. *The representation of features and relations in non-linear phonology*. PhD dissertation, Massachusetts Institute of Technology.

Schane, Sanford A. 1984. The fundamentals of Particle Phonology. *Phonology Yearbook* 1. 129–55.

Scheer, Tobias. 2004. *A lateral theory of phonology: What is CVCV, and why should it be?* Berlin: Mouton de Gruyter.

Scheer, Tobias & Nancy C. Kula. 2018. Government Phonology: Element theory, conceptual issues and introduction. In Stephen J. Hannahs & Anna R. K. Bosch (eds.), *The Routledge handbook of phonological theory* (Routledge Handbooks in Linguistics), 226–61. London: Routledge.

Smith, Norval. to appear. Rhotic harmony. In Nancy Ritter & Harry van der Hulst. eds. *The Oxford Handbook of Vowel Harmony*. Oxford: Oxford University Press.

Stirtz, Timothy M. 2009. [ATR] Vowel Harmony in Gaahmg; a Six-vowel System. *Journal of African Languages and Linguistics* 30. 73–95.

Taylor, John R. 2006. Where do phonemes come from? A view from the bottom. *International Journal of English Linguistics* 6.2. 19–54.

Thráinsson, Hoskuldur. 1978. On the phonology of Icelandic pre-aspiration. *Nordic Journal of Linguistics* 1.1. 3–54.

van der Hulst, Harry. 1988a. The dual interpretation of |i|, |u| and |a|. *Proceedings of the North East Linguistic Society (NELS)* 18. 208–22.

van der Hulst, Harry. 1988b. The geometry of vocalic features. In Harry van der Hulst & Norval Smith (eds.), *Features, segmental structure and harmony processes*, vol. 2, 77–125. Dordrecht: Foris.

van der Hulst, Harry. 1995. Radical CV Phonology: The categorial gesture. In Jacques Durand & Francis Katamba (eds.), *Frontiers of phonology: Atoms, structures, derivations*. 80–116. London: Longman.

van der Hulst, Harry. 2005. The molecular structure of phonological segments. In Phil Carr, Jacques Durand & Colin J. Ewen (eds.), *Headhood, elements, specification and contrastivity*, 193–234. Amsterdam and Philadelphia: John Benjamins.

van der Hulst, Harry. 2010. A note on recursion in phonology. In Harry van der Hulst (ed.), *Recursion in human language*, 301–42. Berlin: Mouton de Gruyter.

van der Hulst, Harry. 2015a. The laryngeal class in RCVP and voice phenomena in Dutch. In Johanneke Caspers et al. (eds.), *Above and beyond the segments*, 323–49. Amsterdam and Philadelphia: John Benjamins.

van der Hulst, Harry. 2015b. The opponent principle in RCVP: Binarity in a unary system. In Eric Raimy & Charles Cairns (eds.), *The segment in phonetics and phonology*, 149–79. London: Wiley-Blackwell.

van der Hulst, Harry. 2016. Monovalent 'features' in phonology. *Language and Linguistics Compass* 10.2. 83–102.

van der Hulst, Harry. 2013. The discoverers of the phoneme. In Keith Allan (ed.), *The Oxford handbook of the history of linguistics* (Oxford Handbooks in Linguistics), 167–91. Oxford: Oxford University Press.

van der Hulst, Harry. 2017. Deconstructing tongue root harmony systems. In Geoff Lindsey & Andrew Nevins (eds.), *Sonic signatures; Studies dedicated to John Harris* (Language Faculty and Beyond 14), 74–99. Amsterdam and Philadelphia: John Benjamins.

van der Hulst, Harry. 2018. *Asymmetries in vowel harmony – A representational account*. Oxford: Oxford University Press.

van der Hulst, Harry. 2020. *Principles of Radical CV Phonology – A theory of segmental and syllabic structure*. Edinburgh: Edinburgh University Press.

van der Hulst, Harry. to appear. Recursive syllable structure in RCVP. Ms. University of Connecticut [to appear in a Festschrift]

van der Hulst, Harry. in prep. A Guide to Dependency and Government Phonology. Ms, University of Connecticut.

van der Hulst, Harry & Jeroen van de Weijer. 2018. Dependency Phonology. In Stephen J. Hannahs & Anna R. K. Bosch (eds.), *The Routledge handbook of phonological theory* (Routledge Handbooks in Linguistics), 325–59. London: Routledge.

Wood, Sidney A. J. 1975. Tense and lax vowels: Degree of constriction or pharyngeal volume? *Working Papers of the Phonetics Laboratory, Department of General Linguistics, Lund University* 11. 109–33.

Wood, Sidney A. J. 1979. A radiographic analysis of constriction locations for vowels. *Journal of Phonetics* 7.1. 25–43.

Wood, Sidney A. J. 1982. X-ray and model studies of vowel articulation. *Working Papers of the Phonetics Laboratory*, Department of General Linguistics, Lund University 23. 1–49.

Yip, Moira. 2002. *Tone*. Cambridge: Cambridge University Press.

Zhang, Xi. 1996. *Vowel systems of the Manchu-Tungus languages of China*. PhD dissertation, University of Toronto.

Markus A. Pöchtrager
English vowel structure and stress in GP 2.0

Abstract: This contribution looks at the English vowel system (Received Pronunciation) from the point of view of Government Phonology 2.0. It builds on the analysis of tenseness/laxness in Pöchtrager (2020) and forms part of the ongoing development of the hypothesis that the old element **A** be replaced by structure. This substitution has repercussions not only for the representation of vowel quality, but also affects the interaction with prosodic structure, explored in the second half of this article.

Keywords: internal structure of vowels; openness; phonological length; tense/lax; stress and vowel quality.

1 Basic parameters

When looking at what is possible in a stressed nucleus in Received Pronunciation (RP), we usually find charts such as the one in (1), following Wells (1982: 119) in the transcriptions. (We will look at unstressed nuclei in section 3.) The chart is divided into two disjoint sets labelled "L-type/T-type", which will be explained anon.

(1)   a. L-type   b. T-type

		[ɪə]	fear	[ʊə]	sure
[ɪ]	bit	[iː]	beat	[uː]	boot
[e]	bet	[eɪ]	bait	[əʊ]	boat
[æ]	bat	[ɛə/ɛː]	bare	[ɔː]	bought
[ʊ]	put	[ɜː]	dirt	[ɑː]	part
[ʌ]	but			[aɪ]	bite
[ɒ]	pot			[aʊ]	bout
				[ɔɪ]	void

In going through these charts, there are three aspects that require discussion: (i) vowel quality, (ii) length, and (iii) tenseness/laxness. Of these, (ii) and (iii) are sometimes treated as one (or one instead of the other), yet must be considered

Markus A. Pöchtrager, University of Vienna

https://doi.org/10.1515/9783110691948-006

separately. We will quickly look at each one and give a brief preview of how they are represented in Government Phonology (GP) 2.0; the more complete discussion will follow in section 2.

As for quality, **I** and **U** represent frontness and roundedness, as in basically all other flavours of GP.[1] **A** however, both in consonants (coronality) and vowels (openness), is replaced by structure in GP 2.0. This conjecture is based on the repeated observation that **A** interacts with structure, cf. Pöchtrager (2006, 2010, 2012, 2013, 2018a). As we shall see in section 3, this replacement is not achieved directly, such that one primitive of the theory is replaced by another, but rather more indirectly by reference to the total amount of room, where this "room" can come about in more than one way.

For vowel length, we must distinguish between what we can call lexical length and phonological length, two categories which cross-classify. The vowels in pairs like *bit/beat* differ in lexical length (for tenseness see below), independently of the right-hand context, i.e. the final consonant. Pairs like *bit/bid*, on the other hand, differ in phonological length (with no accompanying difference in tenseness), and there is a trade-off between the length of the vowel and that of the following consonant. The phenomenon of phonological length is of course well known in the literature, referred to as (lack of) "pre-fortis clipping" (Crystal & House 1988; Denes 1955; Heffner 1937; Klatt 1976; Lehiste 1970; Lisker 1957; Luce & Charles-Luce 1985; Luce, Charles-Luce & McLennan 1999; Peterson & Lehiste 1960; Rositzke 1939; Umeda 1975). But since there is such a trade-off, i.e. since phonological length is predictable from the following consonant (in the same "syllable"), it is usually treated as "purely" allophonic (hence irrelevant) in discussions of English phonology. Accordingly, it is also absent from charts like the ones in (1). But phonological theory is to provide the means to characterise any human language. As argued in Pöchtrager (2006), by taking phonological length in English into account we will, as a side-product, create the framework to explain more "exotic" length systems such as that of Estonian with its three degrees of length. As a matter of fact, there is nothing exotic about it; the distribution of the various degrees of length follows principles similar to those we see in English. Accordingly, both types of length are to be represented phonologically, also in English. Together, they yield four logical combinations, *bit/bid/beat/bead*.[2] (2) tabulates this.

---

[1] Scheer (1996) being an exception for **U**.
[2] Measurement of appropriate pairs of isolated words in the Oxford Acoustic Phonetic Database (Pickering & Rosner 1993) shows the effects of phonological length to be more dramatic, leading to an increase of about 90% in *bit/bid* or *beat/bead*, while lexical length only leads to an increase of about 45%.

(2)

		phonologically	
		short	long
lexically	short	*bit*	*bid*
	long	*beat*	*bead*

Lexical length is also linked to the third characteristic, tenseness/laxness. A pair like *bit*/*beat* differs not only in lexical length but also opposes a lax vowel (*bit*) to a tense one (*beat*). The labels "tense/lax" (and the implications they carry) have a troubled history, and no alternative (long/short, free/checked) is completely without problems, cf. the more detailed discussion in Pöchtrager (2020). In order to avoid the problems associated with traditional labels I will use the relatively neutral terms L-type and T-type (as in Pöchtrager 2020). Those types refer to the entire nucleus, independently of whether it is a monophthong (like [iː]) or diphthong (like [aɪ]). Neutral labels also emphasise the fact that the two types are based on behaviour, and not on a consistent articulatory or acoustic property: L-type nuclei are disallowed finally (3a) and pre-hiatus (3b), but occur freely before coda-onset clusters (3c).

(3) a. *[bɪ], *[zʊ], but *bee* [biː], *zoo* [zuː]
 b. *l[ɪ]o, *rod[e]o, but l[iː]o, rod[eɪ]o
 c. *limp* [lɪmp], *[liːmp]; *whimper* [wɪmpə], *[wiːmpə]

2 The bipartite structure of a nucleus

Phonological representations in GP 2.0 have a hierarchical, syntax-like organisation. Individual positions (x-slots) are grouped together in x-bar structures at subsequently higher levels in order to express various constituency relations. Unlike many other models, the same kind of constituency continues inside of what is traditionally seen as the endpoint of (syllabic) constituency, "segments".[3] That is, something as simple as a [p] is embedded in a larger structure and is itself made up of an x-bar structure with a head position at its core. Given this all-permeating structure encompassing the entire representation, "segments" as such are epiphenomenal at best. This shows, amongst other things, in the idea that one "segment" can borrow room from another, as we shall see in section 2.1.

---

[3] There is a certain similarity to Nasukawa & Backley's Precedence-Free Phonology and van der Hulst's Radical CV Phonology, cf. Nasukawa (2015), van der Hulst (2020) for recent expositions.

Those x-bar structures group individual x-slots (positions), which can be empty or annotated by elements.[4] Some of those x-slots are designated as heads, and at the current stage of the theory four kinds are employed, or rather two sets of two kinds: The nuclear heads xn and xN (more on which anon), and the onset heads xo and xO (cf. Pöchtrager 2021). I assume that each head can (but does not have to) project up to two times, forming an x-bar-like structure with two levels of dependents.

Nuclei in GP 2.0 have a maximally bipartite structure, i.e. they consist of maximally two heads, xn and xN, with xn on top of xN, if both are present. That is, not both of them will always be present (though at least one of them will have to be), and we shall see how this helps us to express both the full range of vowel qualities as well as the link between vowel quality and stress. That two nuclear heads are employed might be surprising, but is in line with the leading idea in GP 2.0, viz. that structure (vis-à-vis melody) takes on more importance than assumed so far. The reinterpretation of **A** (section 2.3) in particular requires more complex structures whose internal organisation can take over the role that old **A** used to play, and more. In section 3 we will elaborate on the way this extra structure does more than just replace **A**.

Since each head can project maximally twice, we derive (4) as the maximal structure of a nucleus. We will encounter this structure and various substructures of it repeatedly. Note that instead of x's we could have projections of other heads embedded.

---

[4] The theory currently employs only three elements: **I, U, L**. One reviewer inquires about elements used in other flavours of GP, such as **N** (nasality), **@** (neutral) or **R** (coronality), all of which (and more) employed in Harris (1994), for example. There is no consensus on the correct set of elements, and I cannot go into detail for each proposal. Suffice it to say that I assume (along with Backley 2011; Nasukawa 1998; Ploch 1999) that **L** expresses true voicing, nasality and low tone. Also, the coronal element **R** had already been merged (for some) with **A** (Broadbent 1991; Cyran 1997; Goh 1997) and this (new) **A** is then replaced by structure in GP 2.0. Neutral **@**, which Harris uses in velar consonants and lax vowels, is replaced in various ways; velar consonants lack a place-defining element in GP 2.0; for the tense/lax distinction cf. section 2.2.

(4) Maximal structure of a nucleus

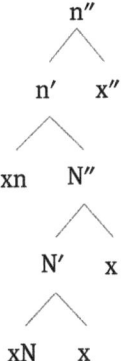

We will now build up from this, still focusing on the stressed position for now.

2.1 Length

We begin with the simple structures in (5), which represent [iːf] as in *leaf* and [iːːv] as in *leave*. This will exemplify the treatment of lexical and phonological length, following (and slightly updating) the account of Pöchtrager (2006: ch. 3.3). In both examples the stressed nucleus consists of only one nuclear head, xn. For our purposes we will focus on the nucleus and the following consonant, ignoring the remainder of the representation. This following consonant is embedded as a daughter of n″, which allows vowel and consonant to interact due to their closeness. Note that onsets, like nuclei, can consist of up to two heads, xo and xO. The final labial here is a projection of xo, cf. Pöchtrager (2021) for details.

(5) a. [iːf] (*leaf*)   b. [iːːv] (*leave*)

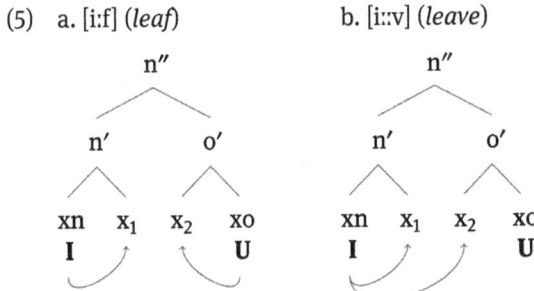

(5a–b) share the same structure, yet differ in crucial details in the distribution of individual positions. What both (5a–b) share is that the nuclear head xn claims its complement x_1 by a relationship called m-command, which ensures that the m-commandee receives the same interpretation as the m-commander.[5] This allows us to express lexical length; the vowels in both words are lexically long. The head xn is annotated with **I** and both xn and its sister receive the same interpretation; that of a long, high front vowel.

(5a–b) differ in their final consonants, fortis [f] vs. lenis [v]. Their representation requires some more explanation. In GP 2.0 the fortis/lenis contrast is taken as structural, while most other models would distinguish the two sets by a melodic property ([±spread glottis], presence or absence of **H**). Yet such a melodic characterisation would not explain why we find a longer vowel before a lenis consonant and a shorter one before a fortis consonant, given that length in general is expressed structurally. This structural reinterpretation of (old) **H** (abandoned in GP 2.0) is yet again effected by m-command. In (5a) the final consonant is fortis, as x_2 is m-commanded by xo. In (5b), on the other hand, we have a final lenis consonant. Lenis consonants are characterised by a non-head position that is not m-commanded by the head, i.e. x_2 in this case. This position is available and can therefore be claimed by the preceding xn, which allows for a non-arbitrary expression of phonological length. In other words, the vowel in (5a) is lexically (but not phonologically) long, while (5b) has a vowel that is lexically and phonologically long. In Pöchtrager (2006) this is also referred to as long (quantity 2, Q2) vs. overlong (Q3), which brings out the parallels to Estonian also in nomenclature.

By conceptualising the fortis/lenis contrast as structural, i.e. by how many positions are taken up by the onset head, we can model the trade-off in vowel length that we find in pairs like *leaf/leave*. This is an advantage over many previous and contemporary models, where the fortis/lenis difference is usually seen as a difference in quality, with the length difference of the preceding vowel left unexplained.[6] Note also that the total amount of room that is to be distributed between xn and xo in (5a–b) stays the same; what differs is who gets how much.

---

[5] M-command is short for "melodic command" and has nothing to do with its syntactic namesake, i.e. it is not a relationship defined on the geometry of the tree. Since the length of the vowel is a lexical property, I assume that m-command is already part of the lexical representation. There is a crucial difference between m-command and spreading in autosegmental accounts: m-command is a relationship between positions. Unlike spreading, it does not depend on there being melody in the m-commander. A position without melody can m-command, but there can be no spreading if there is nothing to spread. A detailed discussion and justification is found in Pöchtrager (2006: 67ff, 80–84).

[6] The present proposal also differs somewhat from so-called virtual geminates (Larsen 1994; Ségéral & Scheer 2001; Scheer 2003; van der Hulst 1984, 1985) which have been posited to explain why consonants in certain languages behave as phonologically long despite the lack of

2.2 T-type/L-type

T-type/L-type are defined by behaviour, with L-type nuclei barred from final position and pre-hiatus. Put differently, an L-type nucleus must be followed by a consonant. The Trubetzkoyian notion of "Silbenschnittkorrelation" (Trubetzkoy 1938: 165ff), Wells's term "checked" (Wells 1982: 119f) and Anderson's "transitive" (Anderson 2004: 273ff) are meant to capture exactly that. Note that phonological length is independent of L-type/T-type: The nuclei in both *bid* and *bit* are L-type, though the first one is phonologically long. Lexical length, in contrast, always guarantees that the nucleus is of the T-type: Both *bead* and *beat* are lexically long and T-type. (Irrespective of the fact that *bead* is also phonologically long.) The same is true of *leaf/leave* in (5a–b). The question is then: How to represent T-type/L-type such that the connection to lexical length as well as the distributional differences are captured? The proposal in Pöchtrager (2020), inspired by Polgárdi (2012), was that T-type/L-type share the same basic structure, i.e. both have a nuclear head and a complement; but they differ in the fate of that complement position. (6) gives [iːf] (*leaf*, repeated from (5a)) and [ɪf] (*riff*) to illustrate.

(6) a. [iːf] (*leaf*)   b. [ɪf] (*riff*)

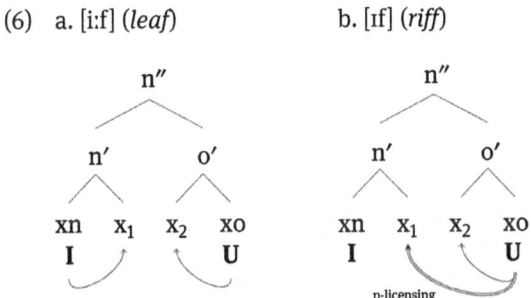

The consonant at the end of the word is identical in both cases. Since it is fortis, xo must m-command x_2. In (6a) x_1 is m-commanded by xn, as stated before. In (6b) xn does not m-command x_1. The following consonant cannot m-command it, as that would yield a geminate, which English does not allow.[7] Instead, I assume that the final consonant p-licenses x_1, keeping x_1 uninterpreted. (I will use a double arrow for p-licensing throughout, while a single arrow represents m-command.) The vowel in (6b) is lexically and phonologically short (quantity 1,

---

a measurable difference to their short counterparts: The fortis/lenis distinction is in no sense virtual but quite real, of course.

7 Unlike Estonian. For the structure of Estonian (and Italian) geminates and the lack thereof in English, cf. Pöchtrager (2006: ch. 4, ch. 5.4).

Q1). The p-licensing relationship (Pöchtrager 2006) extends the Empty Category Principle (ECP) that has formed a central part of GP since the beginning (Charette 1991; Kaye, Lowenstamm & Vergnaud 1990; Kaye 1990). Obviously, whether x_1 is m-commanded by its head or p-licensed by the following consonant is a lexical property: The difference between *leaf* and *riff* (or *bit* and *beat*) is not predictable but lexically stored. (Thus "lexical" length.) Note also that x_1 cannot be claimed by both neighbours at the same time. In section 2.5 we will look at cases where there is neither m-command by the preceding nuclear head nor p-licensing by a following consonant.[8]

(5–6), the representations of *leaf/leave/riff*, cover three out of four logical possibilities that result from lexical length cross-classifying with phonological length. (7) gives the fourth possibility, *give*, with a vowel that is lexically long but phonologically short.

(7)   [ɪːv] (*give*)

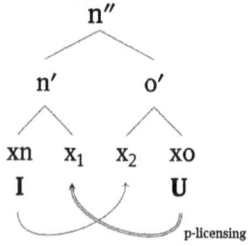

Again, as before, the final lenis consonant comes with an unclaimed position (x_2), which can therefore be m-commanded by xn, leading to phonological length. At the same time xo p-licenses x_1, as we are dealing with an L-type nucleus.[9] The

---

8 Two remarks on p-licensing: Firstly, the p-licensing relationships used here go from an onset head to within a nucleus. Pöchtrager (2006: sections 3.4, 4.3) has cases of p-licensing from a nuclear head to within an onset. In neither case does p-licensing stay within the constituent whose head it emanates from. It is unclear to me whether this is accidental or systematic. Secondly, if we allow a nucleus to p-license (a position in) a preceding nucleus (similar in spirit to Charette 1991), will we predict L-type nuclei in pre-hiatus position? (After all, a p-licensing nucleus could target the sister of the preceding nuclear head.) I assume, in line with Charette (2003: 467f), that p-licensing cannot cross an empty onset which itself needs to be p-licensed. This implies that the two vowels in a hiatus are not strictly adjacent but separated by an empty onset, which is p-licensed and thus cannot p-license itself, as generally assumed in the ECP.
9 (7) might be surprising in that m-command and p-licensing go across each other. Estonian has a similar case which requires two relationships of m-command to cross one another (Pöchtrager 2006: 190ff). Such representations might be somewhat instable and prone to being lost: Words like *bad, mad* represent this type of lexically short but phonologically long, and in many

result is a nuclear head that m-commands one non-head position, x_2 (the sister of xo), while xn in *leaf* (5a, 6a) also m-commands one non-head position, but this time x_1 (its own sister). The vowel of *live* is lexically short and phonologically long, that of *leaf* lexically long but phonologically short. Both are Q2, but differ in their "composition" (which positions are involved).

The idea that the L-type nuclei in (6b) and (7) involve p-licensing by a following consonant has a number of positive consequences. Firstly, it captures the requirement that there be a following (realised) consonant.[10] Wells's notion of 'checking' is expressed by tools that we already have in our theory: Constituents (here: nuclei) have internal structure, and part of that structure can be claimed by other constituents (a following consonant in the present case). The ungrammaticality of L-type nuclei in final position and in hiatus position, cf. (3a–b) follows, since such forms would require a consonant after the vowel in question to p-license the nuclear complement position, but in those cases there is no consonant. Accordingly, those forms are out.

Secondly, the durational difference (in terms of lexical length) between T- and L-type nuclei also follows from this account. L-type means that part of the nucleus is claimed by a following consonant unlike the T-type. The longer duration of the T-type as a whole can be read off the structures employed. (Recall that phonological length and lexical length are independent of one another.)

Thirdly, the ban on T-nuclei preceding coda-onset clusters as in (3c) can also be accounted for. (8a) gives a simplified representation of the word *limp*, alongside a schematised representation of *lip* and *leap* (8b–c). The consonants are abbreviated as 'o' everywhere.[11]

North-American varieties the low vowel has undergone tensing, which eliminates this cross-over. (At least for the low vowel.) My own variety of Austrian German, where final devoicing seems lexicalised if existent at all, systematically disallows the possibility in (7) but has the other three (lexically & phonologically long *red!* 'speak', lexically long & phonologically short *bet!* 'pray', and lexically & phonologically short *Bett* 'bed').

10 'Realised', since an empty onset that is itself p-licensed (and thus silent) will not qualify, cf. footnote 8.

11 I leave open whether the *m* in *limp* has the same structure as that of the final *m* in *limb*. The latter form shows the final sonorant to be lenis, which leads to phonological length. If the *m* in *limp* has the same structure we need to make sure that the available position that comes with this lenis consonant is not accessible to the preceding nuclear head. If the structure of consonants in "true" coda positions (in the sense of Kaye 1990) is different (as attempted in Pöchtrager 2010), however, such that there is no available position to begin with, the problem evaporates.

(8) a. [ɪmp] (*limp*)   b. [ɪp] (*lip*)   c. [iːp] (*leap*)

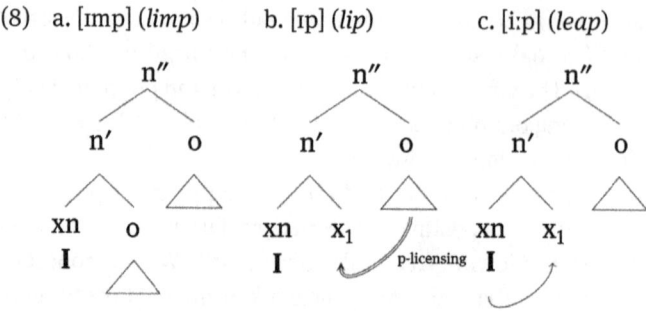

T-type [iː] (8c) is characterised by the nuclear head xn m-commanding its sister. In (8a) this position of the sister is occupied by the nasal *m*, preventing a preceding T-type nucleus. (8b) is like (6b), with the final consonant p-licensing the complement of xn. Given the inaccessibility of that complement position for xn in (8a–b), we can only find L-type nuclei.[12]

In order to account for these properties of L-type nuclei we have created a representation whose size is quite constant. In all the cases considered so far the total amount of positions to be distributed between xn and xo is identical; the forms differ in how the available positions are divided up. We have also seen that in English, an onset heads cannot m-command outside its own projection (i.e. there are no geminates), but the same restriction does not hold for p-licensing. This differs from Estonian, where m-command by an onset head can go outside the immediate projection, cf. footnote 7, while on the other hand m-command within an onset is somewhat more limited in Estonian than in English (Pöchtrager 2006: 188ff).

That there is always the same amount of room to be distributed is due to two factors: (i) All consonants come with a position to express fortis/lenis[13] and (ii) all heads of the type xn expand to their maximum in English. With this maximal expansion of xn in mind we can now look at cases where there is no final consonant, such as *fee*, which bars L-type nuclei and only allows the T-type, which in addition has to be overlong. This, too, follows from the general set-up so far.

---

[12] T-type nuclei are possible before coronal clusters such as *fiend*, *wound* etc., cf. the next subsection.

[13] This excludes glides (Pöchtrager 2006: 91, 162ff); diphthongs are taken to be fully contained in the nucleus in this model, and not as sequences of nucleus plus glide, cf. also section 2.5.

(9) [iː] (*fee*)

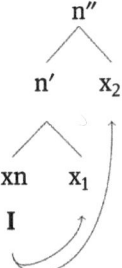

In (9), there are two non-head positions since xn, as in all the other cases, projects up to its highest level, n″. There is no final consonant to p-license any position, so xn can m-command both x_1 and x_2, giving us a vowel that is lexically and phonologically long, even though the third position is not occupied by a lenis consonant.

In order to complete the account of T-type/L-type, we will need to look at cases of diphthongs, which in turn requires that we understand the representation of openness first. This will be the subject matter of the following subsection.

2.3 Openness

Up to now we have focused on only one T-type/L-type pair, the front high vowels. Practically all other versions of GP assume that openness in vowels is expressed by the element **A**,[14] which enjoys the same combinatorial possibilities as any other element. GP 2.0, on the other hand, assumes that **A** had better be replaced by structure. This is based on the repeated observation that **A** behaves quite differently from the other elements and interacts in subtle ways with structure, suggesting that it is itself structure (Pöchtrager 2010, 2013, 2021). More precisely, **A** interacts with (constituent) structure by providing more room than otherwise allowed. The upper size limit of English monosyllabic words illustrates this: Normally, the maximum is reached with a lexically long vowel (or diphthong) plus a single consonant (VV + C: *meet, boot, boat*) or a short vowel and a cluster of two consonants (V + CC: *mint, lift, pact*). However, this limit can be exceeded to yield VVCC or VCCC, on the condition that the last consonant be coronal (Fudge

---

14 There is disagreement what **A** (or its successor) in consonants should represent; I take the position that it should be coronality, in line with Broadbent (1991); Cyran (1997); Goh (1997); Ploch (1999); cf. Pöchtrager (2010, 2013, 2021) for further arguments and also Backley (2011) for an opposing view.

1969; Halle & Vergnaud 1980), i.e. contain **A**: We find *fiend* (no **fiemp*, **fienk*), *count* (no **coump*, **counk*), *east* (no **easp*, **eask*) etc. Those data would allow for the generalisation to be narrowed down even further, since both consonants are coronal. However, such a more restrictive generalisation is not possible if we want to include words like *traipse*, *coax* (diphthong+cluster where only the last member is coronal, more specifically, *s*) as well as *mulct*, *jinx* (three consonants, where again only the last one is coronal).[15]

That **A** provides extra room can not only be seen in English, but also in German and Finnish (Pöchtrager 2012). Such consistent interaction with structure is atypical for an element. It seems more likely that something interacting with structure should be structural itself. One proposal (Pöchtrager 2006, 2010, 2012, 2018a; Kaye & Pöchtrager 2009, 2013) is that expressions which were thought to contain **A** are structurally bigger than those without. Such bigger structures would contain empty positions that can be claimed by adjacent vowels and consonants and give rise to sequences that are bigger than normally allowed, similar to how an empty position inside a lenis consonants can be claimed by a preceding nuclear head.[16]

In this text I will choose an implementation that is a further development from earlier proposals (Pöchtrager 2006, 2010; Kaye & Pöchtrager 2013) and in line with Pöchtrager (2018a, 2020). This is where the bipartite structure of nuclei mentioned at the beginning of section 2 comes into play: Recall that nuclei consist of maximally two heads, xn and xN, with xn on top of xN if both are present. So far we have only seen cases of a projection of xn. We will now move on to projections of xN. This will allow us to express what old **A** used to express. It is important to note, however, that this will go beyond a simple replacement of old **A**, as section 3 will show.

To illustrate, (10) gives the structures of monophthongal front vowels (in different varieties) of English; the diphthongs will follow shortly. (10a) repeats and

---

15 Southern British English adds a further pattern, making the generalisation yet loser: Nuclei containing **A** by itself can appear before *s*C-clusters as long as either one of the final consonants is coronal (contains **A**): *clasp*, *task*, *draft*, but no **cleesp*, **toosk*, **dreeft*. Here the vowel seems to make up for the insufficiency of the cluster. In any case, what unites all these cases is that **A** in certain position(s) provides extra room. Note also that onomatopoeia defy that generalisation, however stated: *oink*, *boink*.

16 When inviting guests to dinner they might drink more than expected, as a result of which the host ends up with their alcohol supply depleted. But some guests bring their own bottle and might not even drink their share, so the host ends up with more than what they started out with. This is what the replacement of old **A** does: One might argue that **A** should be replaced with something very small, of which more can fit in (e.g. more consonants than expected in a phonological string), but there is an alternative conceptualisation such that **A** is bigger, but that (part of) the extra structure it comes with is unused.

collapses both (8b–c), while (10b–c) show close mid and open mid/low vowels, respectively.[17]

(10) a. [ɪ/iː] *bit*/*beat*   b. [e/eː] *bet*/*bait* (Northern)   c. [æ/ɛː] *bat*/(*bare*,) *bad* (NYC)

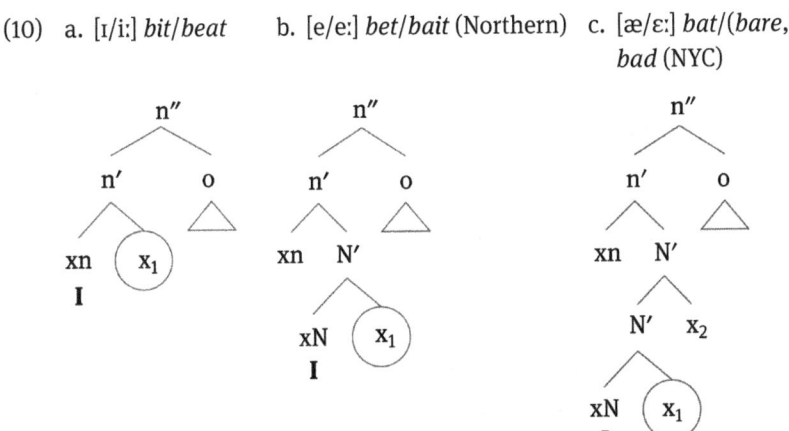

All nuclei in (10) are front since they carry the element I. I will assume that elements stay low down (i.e. within the lowest projection), though cf. section 2.5. (10b–c) represent non-high vowels, where openness is expressed by additional structure in the shape of another nuclear head (xN) and its projection; xn sits on top of xN, i.e. the projection of xN is embedded inside that of xn. The fate of x_1 (circled) will consistently decide between T- and L-type, for all structures in (10). That is, as before, L-type/T-type will depend on whether x_1 is m-commanded by the nuclear head it is a complement of or p-licensed by the following consonant (abbreviated as 'o'). Note that while x_1 is the complement of xn in (10a), but of xN in (10b–c), i.e. it is more deeply embedded in the latter two.[18]

Since many T-type nuclei in RP are diphthongs while L-type nuclei are not, finding matching pairs that differ in T-/L-type only is not always possible. For

---

[17] The reader is reminded that phonetic symbols are only ever approximate indications of an acoustic impression. The representations in (10), as indeed all my representations, are not meant to suggest that every time we encounter a particular symbol in a language we simply assume that it is the same representation as what is given for a particular vowel of English. This might seem obvious, but symbols like [ɛ] are often taken to imply much more than cardinal vowel 3: laxness, –ATR etc.

[18] This suggests that there are languages where this difference is linguistically significant, where the T/L-type distinction for high vowels differs in some way from that for non-high vowels. This is in fact the case in Québec French (Walker 1984), where tenseless/laxness of high vowels depends on the righthand context unlike in non-high vowels, cf. Pöchtrager (2018b) for a preliminary analysis in the present model.

example, the difference between [e/eː] (10b) as in *bet* vs. (Northern, non-RP) *bate* lies in whether x_1 is m-commanded by xN (*bate*) or p-licensed by the following consonant (*bet*). The reader eager to know how to represent RP [eɪ] then is referred to section 2.5. Lastly, (10c) gives [æ/ɛː]. The first vowel is that of *bat* (L-type). The corresponding T-type is what we have in RP *hair, bare*, which does not occur before a final consonant in simplex words. North-American varieties (e.g. New York City English) have that same vowel in *bad, mad*, where it is always lexically and phonologically long, cf. Kaye (2012) for dicussion.[19]

Three further aspects need to be pointed out since they will be important later on as well: Firstly, note that all the nuclei in (10) occur in stressed position and all of them contain xn. We will capitalise on this formal property in section 3. Secondly, vowel height correlates with structural complexity, though this will be qualified somewhat. Thirdly, while it seems that old **A** has simply been replaced by xN, i.e. one primitive replaced by another, we shall see in section 3 that xN and its projection has another important role to play.

2.4 Back & central monophthongs

Replacing **I** by **U** will obviously give us the (back) rounded monophthongs that we need. This is illustrated in (11). English does not exploit the full range of possibilities here, i.e. there is no back counterpart to [æ/ɛː] (10c), i.e. no vowel where an xN labelled with **U** projects all the way up to N″. Again it is the complement to the lowest nuclear head x_1 (circled) that expresses the T-type/L-type distinction.

(11)   a. [ʊ/uː] *put/boot*   b. [ɒ/ɔː] *pot/bought*

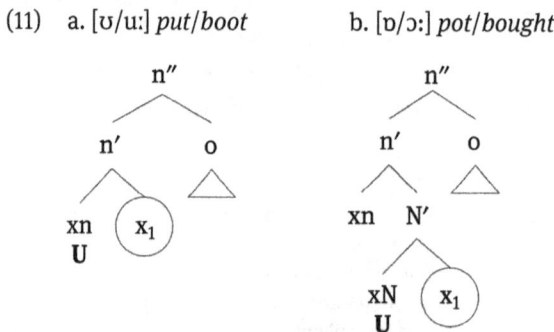

---

[19] Wells (1982) transcribes the vowel in *bare* as [ɛə] but points out that there is really only very little change in quality throughout the vowel. Other authors have [ɛː]. Centering diphthongs and monophthongisations will be addressed in section 2.5. Note also that the role of x_2 in (10c) is still unclear to me.

So far all the vowels we have seen contain some melody somewhere, but with **A** replaced by structure we should of course expect to find more vowels that lack melody altogether than before.[20] (12) presents the monophthongal vowels that have neither **I** nor **U**.

(12) a. [ʌ] *but*   b. [ɜː] *curt*   c. [ɑː] *cart*

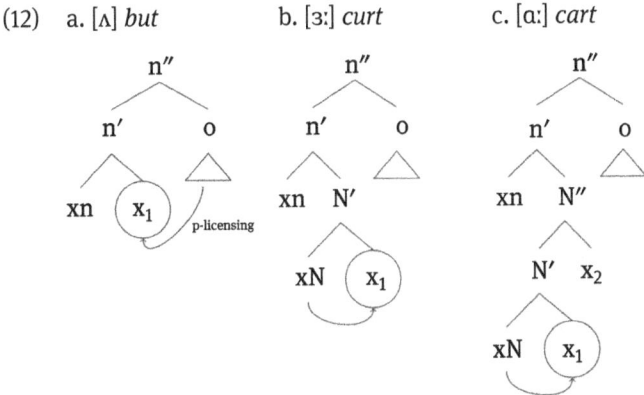

There is an interesting asymmetry here that follows the fault line between structures where we only have the nuclear head xn (12a) and those where a projection of xN is embedded inside that of xn (12b–c): The vowel in (12a) only occurs as lexically short (L-type), while those in (12b–c) are always lexically long (T-type). This suggests that Québec French (cf. footnote 18) is far from the only case where the presence of a second head has implications for the T/L-type distinction, though what exactly the link is is still unclear.

The representations in (12) also show how our characterisation of openness can be refined. (12a), [ʌ], is not usually classified as high, yet it has the same amount of structure as [ɪ/iː] or [ʊ/uː], which count as high. But note that (12a) has an empty head position, and if we take the number of empty positions as an indication of openness, then [ʌ] will have one more than [ɪ/iː/ʊ/uː] (where the head position is not empty), allowing for a more reliable translation.[21]

---

[20] Earlier treatments of the English vowel system within GP also had nuclei devoid of melody: Kaye (2004) takes [ʌ] to be an empty nucleus. But with **A** gone the number of vowels with no melody will obviously increase.

[21] Sadly, that will still not do, since we saw in the representation of *limp* in (8a) that instead of an empty x in complement position we can also find a consonant. This does not make the *i* in *limp* any less of a high vowel. These problems might be indicative of a more deep-seated issue, viz. the inherent danger of translating phonological notions into traditional articulatory terminology. Phonetic terms like "high", "mid", "low" etc. are notoriously imprecise: Both [i] and [u]

A last note on [ʌ]. Following Szigetvári (2016, 2017, 2020) I will assume that schwa (in unstressed position) and [ʌ] (in stressed position) are *mutatis mutandis* the same phonological object, i.e. they have the same amount of structure.

2.5 Diphthongs

In section 2.3, where we looked at [eː], we already had to leave the confines of RP, since many nuclei in English are diphthongs, including RP [eɪ]. Building and elaborating on the representation of diphthongs in Pöchtrager (2015) and Živanovič & Pöchtrager (2010), I will assume that a diphthong has a non-head position annotated with melody. (With the exception of centering diphthongs, more on which below.) I will assume that in terms of structure (number of layers) [eɪ] is like [eː] in (10). What is different is the position of **I**: In [eː] the nuclear head xN is annotated with **I**, while in [eɪ] it is the nuclear complement. The two representations are juxtaposed in (13), with (13a) a repetition of (10b).

(13)   a. [eː]   b. [eɪ]

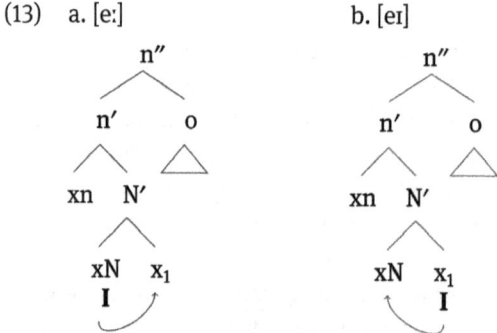

In (13b) x_1, the complement of xN, is annotated with **I**. This gives us the offglide transcribed as [ɪ]. Since the first part of the diphthong is also a front vowel, the **I** must be passed on from the complement to the head xN via m-command. We are dealing with a T-type nucleus here, since x_1 is neither p-licensed by the following consonant nor occupied by a consonant itself (as in the example of *limp* above).

Let us compare this now to the representation of [əʊ] as in *boat* in (14).

---

are both classified as high, yet the latter is nowhere near as high as the former (Ladefoged & Johnson 2010: 21). Articulation will not give a definite answer how to carve up the vowel space (Ladefoged & Maddieson 1996: 282ff).

(14) [əʊ] *boat*

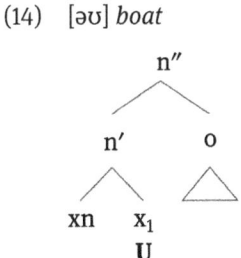

In (12a) we looked at the representation of [ʌ] and said that it was basically the stressed counterpart of schwa, to be addressed in section 3. The vowel in *boat* builds on that, but is obviously diphthongal, i.e. there is melody in the non-head position x_1. There is no m-command from x_1 to xn and thus no colouring of schwa. That fact that the representation of [əʊ] is quite small and does not involve a(n embedded) projection of xN will allow us to account for the inventory of vowels in unstressed position (section 3).

Just as with [əʊ], there are further diphthongs in English where there is no m-command from the complement to the head. (15) gives [aɪ], [aʊ], and [ɔɪ].

(15) a. [aɪ] *bite*   b. [aʊ] *bout*   c. [ɔɪ] *choice*

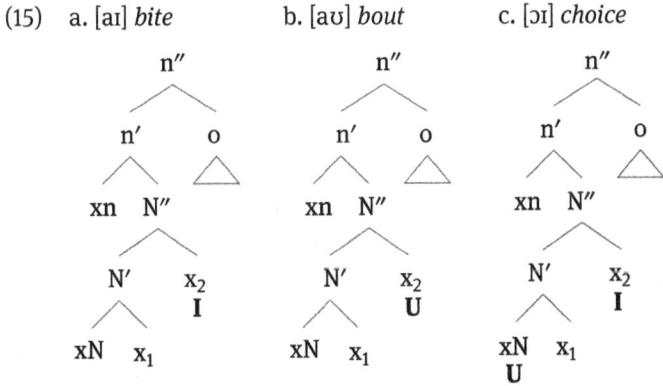

(15a–b) are like the representation of [ɑː] in (12c) with **I** and **U**, respectively, added in non-head position. (15c) also employs the same maximal structure, in order to guarantee that the conditions on phonological binding (Živanovič & Pöchtrager 2010; Pöchtrager 2015) can be met, whereby **U** must not c-command **I**. This precludes the two elements from sitting in sister positions (where they would c-command each other), but also correctly excludes diphthongs like *[eʊ], which would require a structure like (15c) but with **I** and **U** interchanged and thus **U** c-commanding **I**.

Let us finally complete our survey with the so-called centering diphthongs [ɪə], [ʊə] as in *fear* or *poor*. In the discussion of T-type/L-type we derived the ungrammaticality of an L-type nucleus preceding hiatus (e.g. *l[ɪ]o) from the lack of a consonant following the L-type nucleus: There is no consonant to p-license the complement of the nuclear head. There are cases, however, where that generalisation seems to be violated: We find *th*[iːə]*tre* alongside *th*[ɪə]*tre*, and bisyllabic *id*[ɪə] has all but replaced older trisyllabic *id*[iːə] (Wells 1982: 215). There is an important difference between the two variants, however: Those with [iːə] involve hiatus (i.e. two separate nuclei in a row) and conform to the claim that we only find T-type nuclei preceding hiatus. Those with [ɪə], on the other hand, display a (centering) diphthong, i.e. one complex nucleus.[22] (16) gives the representation of [ɪə] as in *idea* or *beard*.

(16) [ɪə]

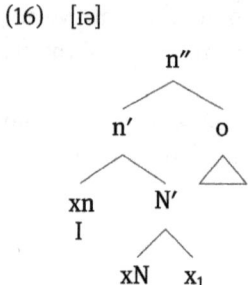

Here, the higher head xn is annotated with **I**. Its complement, N′, contains two empty positions (head and complement). As we had seen in (12a), two empty positions is also what we find in [ʌ/ə]. This expresses the idea that [ɪə] is basically a high vowel with a schwa embedded into it. What is new about (16) is that the element **I** sits in the higher head xn. Neither xn nor xN m-command x_1, and I will assume that any following consonant also fails to p-license, presumably blocked by melody in xn. The result is that x_1 is neither m-commanded nor p-licensed, and the entire substructure N′ gets spelled out as schwa in accordance with the Empty Category Principle (Charette 1991; Kaye 1995). The reader is referred to Pöchtrager (2020: 65ff) for further discussion.

---

22 Centering diphthongs can also be found before *r*, even in non-rhotic varieties where the rhotic has been lost and only the vowel sequence remains (*fear*, *beard*). This shows that the diachronic origin of the schwa is irrelevant synchronically.

3 Vowel quality, prosody, and size

The internal organisation of vowels also has a link to prosodic structure in English. In unstressed position we find schwa (*bitt<u>er</u>*, *sof<u>a</u>*) as well as the high vowels [ɪ/iː] (*attic*, *city*) and (very marginally, often in variation with [ə]) [ʊ/uː] (*album*, *issue*), irrespective of lexical length. In the present system, these are exactly the vowels that are very small in size, and we will explore that relationship now. A reference to vowel quality is also found in Burzio (1994: 17), who countenances weak syllables, containing "consonantal (sonorant) nuclei [and the] high vowels *i*, *u*". (For him this does not follow from anything but is simply assumed as given.) In his system, such weak syllables are restricted to the peripheral positions of the word, and count as extraprosodic in foot-structure. Accordingly, we can find pre-antepenultimate stress in words like *áccuracy* because the final vowel is weak and the preceding material forms a ternary foot (Burzio 1994: 16, ex. 2a).[23] Likewise, in *álligàtor* we have two feet, with main stress on the first foot because the second (and final) foot ends in a weak syllable and thus counts as weak itself (Burzio 1994: 16, ex. 3e).[24]

While we will not be concerned with foot formation or the inventory of feet, we will look at the connection between vowel quality and prosodic weakness/strength. This was also the subject matter of a number of recent papers by Szigetvári (2016, 2017, 2020), who presents a very elegant and symmetric system representing the (British) English vowel inventory.[25] There are two aspects of that account that we need to look at: The representation of vowels and their prosodic properties. In what follows we will quickly sum up Szigetvári's account and then see how some of the insights he presents are actually easily derivable from the model assumed here. In what follows the phonological objects that he employs will be set in boldface.

Szigetvári argues for 6 basic (short) vowels, **i e a o u ə**. Stressed schwa is equated with [ʌ]. The remaining long vowels and diphthongs are based on that set: The vowel in *fee* is taken as a diphthong **ij**, that in *fear* as a long monophthon-

---

[23] Other accounts treat that final *-y* as extrametrical (e.g. Liberman & Prince 1977: 293).
[24] Burzio takes *álligàtor* to end in a syllabic rhotic, which in the variety we are looking at here corresponds to schwa. Since the stress pattern is the same, we have to conclude that schwa patterns with the other vowels allowed in a weak syllable.
[25] This symmetry comes at a price, in the shape of some leeway between (some) phonological objects and their phonetic interpretation. For example, the vowels in *trap* and *start* are treated as the same in quality, differing in quantity only. In contrast, the representations that I have employed here try to straddle phonetic interpretation and phonological behaviour; they are meant to combine our understanding of the behaviour and the realisation of a phonological object.

gal **iː**, *foe* is **əw** etc. The correspondence between the symbols we have been using and Szigetvári's system is shown in (17), which is divided into four sectors (ai, aii, bi, bii), which we will need to look at individually.

(17)   i.   ii.

a.	**i** [ɪ]	**ij** [iː]			**iː** [ɪə]	
	ə [ʌ/ə]		**əw** [əʊ]	**əː** [ɜː]	
	u [ʊ]		**uw** [uː]	**uː** [ʊə]	
b.	**e** [e]	**ej** [eɪ]			**eː** [ɛː/ɛə]	
	a [æ]	**aj** [aɪ]	**aw** [aʊ]	**aː** [ɑː]	
	o [ɒ]	**oj** [ɔɪ]			**oː** [ɔː]	

Szigetvári distinguishes between stress and accent. His notion of accent corresponds to what we have been calling stress; it has to do with the organisation of rhythm, every (non-functional) word has to have one and accent is to some extent movable, as in *thirtéen* vs. *thírteen mén*. In contrast, what Szigetvári calls stress is an inherent property of a vowel. Stress is immutable (it cannot be lost, gained, or shifted), is not (directly) involved in rhythmical organisation, and the stress of a given vowel does not have an effect on that of neighbouring vowels.

In the interest of clarity, I will keep our notion of stress (Szigetvári's "accent"), and refer to Szigetvári's binary dichotomy "stressed/unstressed" as "strong/weak" (with "strength" as the overarching category) in what follows. Strength is not completely independent of the vowel in question: There are implicational relationships such that vowels marked by ː must be strong; this covers all of (17ii). Also, **e a o** are always strong, no matter if there is a glide following or not: The second vowel in *látex* (**e**) counts as strong (though not stressed), as does the only vowel in *face* (**ej**), though this time stressed and followed by a glide. This covers all of (17b) and with that, three out of the four sectors in (17) have been dealt with. The one remaining sector, (17ai), contains **i ə u** (by themselves or followed by glides). They can be either strong or weak: The vowels in both *bee* (**ij**) and *bit* (**i**) are both strong (and stressed), showing that the presence of a glide in the first word is immaterial. The idea that **i ə u** may be either strong or weak can be illustrated with the initial vowels in *úgly* (strong and stressed) as opposed to *agrée* (weak and unstressed). What is usually transcribed as a difference in quality, [ʌ] in *ugly* vs. [ə] in *agree*, is simply strong vs. weak **ə**, respectively. In a similar fashion, *manatee* and *vanity* both end in **ij**, which is strong in the first word and weak in the second. We will look at evidence for the alleged difference in just a moment.

Stress can only fall on a strong vowel (leaving aside stress under focus), but being strong does not guarantee stress. This also means that the position of stress, though often dependent on context, will have to be marked to some extent: In *átoll* and *antíque* both vowels in each word are strong, yet stress falls in different positions in the two in isolation. Other authors (e.g. Hayes 1995; Giegerich 1992) see this as a difference in stress levels: *átòll* (primary–secondary) vs. *àntíque* (secondary–primary).

Strength leads to a difference in phonetic quality for ɐ; [ʌ] when strong, [ə] when weak.[26] Other than that, strength does not involve a difference in vowel quality. In order to establish then whether, say, an [ɪ] (**i**) is strong or weak (it could be either), other tests will have to be employed,[27] e.g. tappability of a preceding d/t. (British English is of course not the best variety for that.) Words like *áutism/náutilus* have a strong first vowel (**o:**, strong by definition), both times followed by **i**. Yet this **i** is strong in the first word but weak in the second, and accordingly tapping is blocked in *autism* but not in *nautilus*. Further criteria point in the same direction.[28]

Being mainly interested in description, Szigetvári does not go into a decomposition of the vowels in terms of phonological building blocks. For him, it remains a stipulation that certain vowels are inherently strong, while others can be either strong or weak. In contrast, the representational format that we have set up to deal with openness, length, and the T-type/L-type distinction provides, as a side-effect, the means to distinguish between strong and weak. Szigetvári's stipulations of strength can be derived from the bipartite structure of nuclei, and at the same time we can explain why strength is an inherent property of a vowel as he assumes.

We begin with two crucial observations to show this. Firstly, weak vowels correspond to small structures in our system: More precisely, they only require one nuclear head, not the two that our model provides in principle. Being weak implies having only one head. This is true of all the vowels in (17ai), which can (but do not have to) be weak. Secondly, vowels corresponding to big structures (more than one nuclear head) are automatically strong. All the vowels in (17aii, bi, bii) will require more than one nuclear head, which implies that they are strong.

Obviously (and crucially) the converse of the two statements does not hold: Not all vowels with only one head are automatically weak, and not all strong

---

26 Assuming that there is a big phonetic difference to begin with, which Szigetvári, following Fabricius (2007), denies.
27 Similar to the criteria Hayes (1995: ch. 2) uses to argue for the existence of stress (primary/secondary) to begin with.
28 Tapping before (weak) schwa is of course also possible.

vowels will automatically have two heads. The contrast between *áutism/náutilus* illustrates exactly that, in that the [ɪ] in *áutism* is small (one head) but strong.[29] The crucial question is then: How to represent a vowel that is small but strong? Recall that nuclei in our system have a bipartite structure of up to two heads, xn and xN. Each head can project up to twice. This gives us a maximum of four layers of structure if both heads are present. For the representation of the stressed vowels in *leaf/leave* (5) two layers of structure were sufficient to express lexical length and T-type (by using the sister of the head), and to incorporate following material (the final consonant). We assumed that those two layers were both a projection of xn, but out of four potential layers in total (those of the projection of xn and xN) there are actually three ways that two adjacent layers could be picked: Both from xn, both from xN, or one from each.[30] Any vowel bigger than that would have fewer "choices" by necessity; the biggest structure would have no choice at all. Put differently, given the way our system is set up, vowels which are structurally smaller can be represented in different ways, and the number of possibilities decreases the bigger the vowel becomes. (Think of a small boat in a narrow canal which can manoeuvre quite easily and stay further to the left, to the right or in the centre, while a large cruise ship might take up all the space there is.) That is, we already have the means to distinguish strong and weak [ɪ/iː]. (18a) repeats (10c), as a baseline for comparison. (18b) repeats (6a–b), collapsed into one. (18c) gives a new addition: Weak [ɪ/iː].

(18) a. [æ/ɛː]   b. [ɪ/iː]   c. [ɪ/iː]
      strong (by necessity) strong   weak

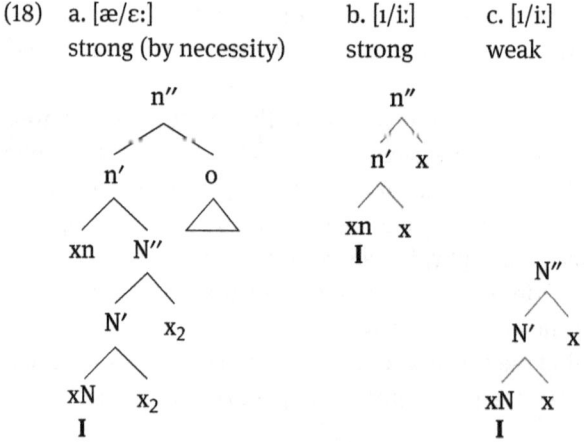

---

29 Some speakers treat *veto/Vito* with final [əʊ] like *áutism/náutilus* when it comes to tapping, which shows that the very small structure we posited for [əʊ] in (14) was on the right track.
30 If the four potential layers are numbered 1–4 (in either direction), then we can pick 1+2, 2+3, or 3+4.

Both (18b–c) have the same amount of layers, but differ in which head those two layers are a projection of. In (18b), both layers are a projection of xN, but in (18c) both are a projection of xn. This assumes that the two heads xn and xN are independent, to the extent that one can occur without the other. This allows us to give a precise definition of strong/weak and assign a "meaning" to (at least) xn: A vowel is strong if and only if xn is present. "Strong" means that xn is present (and possibly xN, too), while "weak" means that only xN is present (but xn is not).

Note also that the bipartite structure of nuclei fulfils two roles simultaneously: It allows for a characterisation of strong/weak and makes possible a structural reinterpretation of old **A**. But comparison of (18a, c) also makes clear that we cannot simply say that the projection of either head by itself is designated as the replacement of **A**, since we want to group neither (18b), which contains xn, nor (18c), which contains xN, with vowels that used to contain old **A**. The properties of the system in total allow for the expression of what was captured by old **A**, but there is not one particular head or position that can be pinpointed. This difference is subtle but important. What can be said, however, is that xn corresponds to metrical strength. (Where authors like Giegerich and Hayes assign secondary stress.)

Besides capturing the strong/weak dichotomy, there are two further advantages of the structural similarity between (18b) and (18c): Firstly, the sister of the head (xn or xN, respectively) could be m-commanded by the head or not, i.e. we expect to find four possibilities depending on which head we are dealing with and if there is m-command: strong T-type (*tea*, *manatee*), weak T-type (*vanity*), strong L-type (*autism*), and weak L-type (*nautilus*). All four cases exist.

Secondly, both strong and weak vowels allow for coda consonants: *Addict* has a weak [ɪ] followed by the coda-onset cluster [kt]. Weakness is established by the fact that tapping is possible. In *edict* no tapping occurs and we conclude that the vowel is strong, and it is followed by the same cluster [kt]. Also the vowel in *Pict* is stressed and (therefore) strong and presents the same cluster as before. The representations in (18b–c) provide a position for that coda [k] in every single case: As a sister to the head.

4 What's next?

This article has attempted to provide a comprehensive account of the RP vowel system, where length (both lexical and phonological), the T/L-type distinction, openness, and the connection between prosodic weakness and structural size all find their place. With respect to the last point, there is still one issue that needs to be addressed.

Vowel reduction is an important piece of evidence for the representation of openness as size. Pöchtrager (2018a) proposed that unstressed positions limit the size of the vowels they allow. Imposing a cap guaranteed that only vowels up to a certain size could occur in prosodically unfavourable position. This will apply to distinctions of length as well as openness and unites quantitative restrictions with qualitative ones; both occur in weak position. Vowels exceeding that limit would be cut to size when stress is removed from them. As a simple example, Italian distinguishes [e] and [ɛ] in stressed position, but only allows [e] in unstressed postion. In a derivational account such as that of Pöchtrager (2018a), taking (stressed) [ɛ] to (unstressed) [e] meant the actual removal of a layer of structure.[31]

For English, Szigetvári argues that vowel alternations in English are never phonological, but really just historical relics of sound changes.[32] This includes alternations involving strength (and thus possible locations of accent); compare the (identical) stressed vowels in *idiótic* and *robótic* (both [ɒ]) to their bases where the corresponding vowels are unstressed, but one time weak [ə] (*idiot*), the other time strong [ɒ] (*robot*). Those alternations are not phonological since there is no procedure that could reliably take one form to the other. This does not affect the fact that in unstressed weak position there are restrictions on what we can find: Only vowels that lack xn.

The same might in fact be true of the cases discussed in more detail in Pöchtrager (2018a), viz. Brazilian Portuguese (Belo Horizonte) and Eastern Catalan. For the former, Cristófaro Alves da Silva (1992: 73ff) points out that reduction in pre-tonic position is peculiar in that it can lead to derived contrasts: In stressed position we find seven vowels ([i e ɛ a ɔ o u]), but in pre-tonic position ([ɛ ɔ]) fail to occur. It is tempting to posit a process of vowel reduction changing [ɛ ɔ] to [e o] once they move from tonic to pretonic position. However, lack of [ɛ ɔ] in pre-tonic position can only be observed for (morphologically) underived forms. In (analytically) derived forms, on the other hand, we do find [ɛ ɔ]. Any putative process of reduction in pre-tonic position would have to be blocked in those cases, suggesting that this is not a phonological process to begin with. However, that does not change the fact that vowels that find themselves in unstressed position lexically are still restricted to five out of seven possible vowels. This can be adequately expressed by reference to size. Further research will have to show what the adequate interpretation of stress shifts is.

---

[31] More precisely, removal of a position and with it the layer it is dominated by, since the theory has no single daughters.
[32] I agree, with the exception of phonological length (*leave* with its Q3 vowel alternating with Q2 in *leaving*), cf. Pöchtrager (2006) for discussion.

References

Anderson, John. 2004. Contrast in phonology, structural analogy, and the interfaces. *Studia Linguistica* 58(3). 269–287.
Backley, Phillip. 2011. *An Introduction to Element Theory*. Edinburgh: Edinburgh University Press.
Broadbent, Judith M. 1991. Linking and Intrusive r in English. *UCL Working Papers in Linguistics* 3. 281–301.
Burzio, Luigi. 1994. *Principles of English stress*. Cambridge: Cambridge University Press.
Charette, Monik. 1991. *Conditions on phonological government*. Cambridge: Cambridge University Press.
Charette, Monik. 2003. Empty and pseudo-empy categories. In Stefan Ploch (ed.), *Living on the Edge. 28 Papers in Honour of Jonathan Kaye*, 465–479. Berlin & New York: Mouton de Gruyter.
Cristófaro Alves da Silva, Thaïs. 1992. *Nuclear Phenomena in Brazilian Portuguese*. London: University of London/School of Oriental and African Studies dissertation.
Crystal, Thomas H. & Arthur S. House. 1988. Segmental durations in connected-speech signals: Current results. *Journal of the Acoustical Society of America* 83(4). 1553–1573.
Cyran, Eugeniusz. 1997. *Resonance Elements in Phonology. A Study in Munster Irish*. Lublin: Wydawnictwo Folium.
Denes, Peter. 1955. Effect of Duration on the Perception of Voicing. *Journal of the Acoustical Society of America* 27(4). 761–764.
Fabricius, Anne. 2007. Variation and change in the trap and strut vowels of RP: A real time comparison of five acoustic data sets. *Journal of the International Phonetic Association* 37(3). 293–320.
Fudge, Erik C. 1969. Syllables. *Journal of Linguistics* 5. 253–286.
Giegerich, Heinz J. 1992. *English phonology. An introduction*. Cambridge, New York, Melbourne: Cambridge University Press.
Goh, Yeng-Seng. 1997. *The Segmental Phonology of Beijing Mandarin*. Crane Publishing Co., Ltd: Taipei.
Halle, Morris & Jean-Roger Vergnaud. 1980. Three dimensional phonology. *Journal of Linguistic Research* 1(1). 83–105.
Harris, John. 1994. *English Sound Structure*. Oxford et al.: Blackwell.
Hayes, Bruce. 1995. *Metrical Stress Theory. Principles and Case Studies*. Chicago & London: The University of Chicago Press.
Heffner, Roe-Merrill S. 1937. Notes on the Length of Vowels. *American Speech* 12(2). 128–134.
Kaye, Jonathan. 1990. 'Coda' Licensing. *Phonology* 7(2). 301–330.
Kaye, Jonathan. 1995. Derivations and interfaces. In Jacques Durand & Francis Katamba (eds.), *Frontiers of Phonology: Atoms, Structures, Derivations*, 289–332. London & New York: Longman.
Kaye, Jonathan. 2004. Current Issues in Phonological Theory. Lecture series, University of Vienna.
Kaye, Jonathan. 2012. Canadian Raising, eh? In Eugeniusz Cyran, Henryk Kardela & Bogdan Szymanek (eds.), *Sound, Structure and Sense. Studies in memory of Edmund Gussmann*, 321–352. Lublin: Wydawnictwo KUL.
Kaye, Jonathan, Jean Lowenstamm & Jean-Roger Vergnaud. 1990. Constituent structure and government in phonology. *Phonology* 7(2). 193–231.

Kaye, Jonathan & Markus A. Pöchtrager. 2009. GP 2.0. Paper presented at the Government Phonology Round Table, Piliscsaba, 25 April.
Kaye, Jonathan & Markus A. Pöchtrager. 2013. GP 2.0. *SOAS Working Papers in Linguistics & Phonetics* 16. 51–64.
Klatt, Dennis H. 1976. Linguistic uses of segmental duration in English: Acoustic and perceptual evidence. *Journal of the Acoustical Society of America* 59(5). 1208–1221.
Ladefoged, Peter & Keith Johnson. 2010. *A Course In Phonetics*. 6th edn. Boston: Wadsworth.
Ladefoged, Peter & Ian Maddieson. 1996. *The Sounds of the World's Languages*. Oxford & Cambridge, Mass.: Blackwell.
Larsen, Uffe Bergeton. 1994. *Some Aspects of Vowel Length and Stød in Modern Danish*. Paris: Université Paris 7 MA thesis.
Lehiste, Ilse. 1970. *Suprasegmentals*. Cambridge, Mass. & London, UK: MIT Press.
Liberman, Mark & Alan Prince. 1977. On Stress and Linguistic Rhythm. *Linguistic Inquiry* 8(2). 249–336.
Lisker, Leigh. 1957. Closure Duration and the Intervocalic Voiced-Voiceless Distinction in English. *Language* 33(1). 42–49.
Luce, Paul A. & Jan Charles-Luce. 1985. Contextual effects on vowel duration, closure duration, and the consonant/vowel ratio in speech production. *Journal of the Acoustical Society of America* 78(6). 1949–1957.
Luce, Paul A., Jan Charles-Luce & Conor McLennan. 1999. Representational specificity of lexical form in the production and perception of spoken words. In John Ohala (ed.), *Proceedings of the XIVth International Congress of Phonetic Sciences*, 1889–1892. San Francisco: Berkeley.
Nasukawa, Kuniya. 1998. An integrated approach to nasality and voicing. In Eugeniusz Cyran (ed.), *Structure and Interpretation. Studies in Phonology*, 205–225. Lublin: Wydawnictwo Folium.
Nasukawa, Kuniya. 2015. Recursion in the lexical structure of morphemes. In Henk van Riemsdijk & Marc van Oostendorp (eds.), *Representing Structure in Phonology and Syntax*, 211–238. Berlin: Mouton de Gruyter.
Peterson, Gorden E. & Ilse Lehiste. 1960. Duration of Syllabic Nuclei in English. *Journal of the Acoustical Society of America* 32(6). 693–703.
Pickering, John & Burton Rosner. 1993. *The Oxford Acoustic Phonetic Database*. Oxford: Oxford University Press.
Ploch, Stefan. 1999. *Nasals on My Mind. The Phonetic and the Cognitive Approach to the Phonology of Nasality*. London: University of London/School of Oriental and African Studies dissertation.
Pöchtrager, Markus A. 2006. *The Structure of Length*. University of Vienna dissertation.
Pöchtrager, Markus A. 2010. The Structure of A. Paper presented at the 33rd GLOW Colloquium, Wrocław, 13–16 April.
Pöchtrager, Markus A. 2012. Deconstructing A. Paper presented at the MFM Fringe Meeting on Segmental Architecture, University of Manchester, 23 May.
Pöchtrager, Markus A. 2013. On A. Paper presented at the Workshop on Melodic Representation, University College London, 12 March.
Pöchtrager, Markus A. 2015. Binding in Phonology. In Henk van Riemsdijk & Marc van Oostendorp (eds.), *Representing Structure in Phonology and Syntax*, 255–275. Berlin: Mouton de Gruyter.

Pöchtrager, Markus A. 2018a. Sawing off the branch you are sitting on. *Acta Linguistica Academica* 65(1). 47–68.
Pöchtrager, Markus A. 2018b. Tense? (Re)lax! A new formalisation of the tense/lax contrast. Paper presented at the 26th Manchester Phonology Meeting, University of Manchester, 24–26 May.
Pöchtrager, Markus A. 2020. Tense? (Re)lax! A new formalisation for a controversial contrast. *Acta Linguistica Academica* 67(1). 53–71.
Pöchtrager, Markus A. 2021. Towards a non-arbitrary account of affricates and affrication. *Glossa: a journal of general linguistics* 6(1): 61. 1–31. DOI: https://doi.org/10.5334/gjgl.1116.
Polgárdi, Krisztina. 2012. The distribution of vowels in English and trochaic proper government. In Bert Botma & Roland Noske (eds.), *Phonological explorations: Empirical, theoretical and diachronic issues*, 111–134. Berlin & New York: Mouton de Gruyter.
Rositzke, Harry. 1939. Vowel-Length in General American Speech. *Language* 15(2). 99–109.
Scheer, Tobias. 1996. Une théorie de l'interaction directe entre consonnes. Contribution au modèle syllabique CVCV, alternances e-Ø dans les préfixes tchèques, structure interne des consonnes et la théorie X-barre en phonologie. Paris: Université Paris 7 dissertation.
Scheer, Tobias. 2003. Von kölnischer Gutturalisierung, virtuellen Geminaten und ambisilbischen Konsonanten. Ms, University of Nice.
Ségéral, Philippe & Tobias Scheer. 2001. Abstractness in phonology: the case of virtual geminates. In Katarzyna Dziubalska-Kołaczyk (ed.), *Constraints and Preferences*, 311–337. Berlin & New York: Mouton de Gruyter.
Szigetvári, Péter. 2016. No diphthong, no problem. In Jolanta Szpyra-Kozłowska & Eugeniusz Cyran (eds.), *Phonology, its Faces and Interfaces*, 123–141. Frankfurt: Peter Lang.
Szigetvári, Péter. 2017. English stress is binary and lexical. In Geoff Lindsey & Andrew Nevins (eds.), *Sonic Signatures. Studies dedicated to John Harris*, 264–275. Amsterdam/Philadelphia: Benjamins.
Szigetvári, Péter. 2020. Posttonic stress in English. In Krzysztof Jaskuła (ed.), *Phonological and Phonetic Explorations*, 163–189. Lublin: Wydawnictwo KUL.
Trubetzkoy, Nikolai S. 1938. Die phonologischen Grundlagen der sogenannten 'Quantität' in den verschiedenen Sprachen. In *Scritti in onore di Alfredo Trombetti*, 155–174. Milan: Ulrico Hoepli Editore.
Umeda, Noriko. 1975. Vowel duration in American English. *Journal of the Acoustical Society of America* 58(2). 434–445.
van der Hulst, Harry. 1984. *Syllable structure and stress in Dutch*. Dordrecht: Foris.
van der Hulst, Harry. 1985. Ambisyllabicity in Dutch. In Hans Bennis & Frits Beukema (eds.), *Linguistics in the Netherlands 1985*. 57–67. Dordrecht: Foris.
van der Hulst, Harry. 2020. *Principles of Radical CV Phonology: A Theory of Segmental and Syllabic Structure*. Edinburgh: Edinburgh University Press.
Walker, Douglas C. 1984. *The Pronunciation of Canadian French*. Ottawa: University of Ottawa Press.
Wells, John C. 1982. *Accents of English 1. An Introduction*. Cambridge et al.: Cambridge University Press.
Živanovič, Sašo & Markus A. Pöchtrager. 2010. GP 2.0 and Putonghua, too. *Acta Linguistica Hungarica* 57(4). 357–380.

Kuniya Nasukawa & Nancy C. Kula
Reanalysing 'epenthetic' consonants in nasal-consonant sequences: A lexical specification approach

Abstract: A nasal prefix that occurs before vowel-initial stems in Bantu languages results in epenthetic consonants whose shape varies depending on the following vowel. It is argued that [g] is the default epenthetic consonant that results from the lexical representation of the nasal prefix containing velarity in its lexical representation. Under palatalization this epenthetic consonant changes to [ʤ]. Epenthesis is effected by so-called overlapping concatenation that can be either asymmetric or symmetric. This difference captures the fact that epenthesis only applies at the juncture between a prefix and a stem involving asymmetric overlapping concatenation, while it fails to apply in a prefix-prefix context that involves symmetric overlapping concatenation. The processes involved require element sharing, agreement and enhancement to fully capture the epenthesis process as well as the attested variation.

Keywords: nasal-consonant sequences; overlapping concatenation; epenthesis; prefixation; asymmetries.

Acknowledgements: This paper is the development of a paper presented at "Elements: State of the Art and Perspectives", held at the University of Nantes, France, on 15 June 2018. We gratefully acknowledge constructive comments from participants. We are also indebted to two anonymous reviewers whose comments have helped to sharpen and clarify the arguments presented in this paper for which we take full responsibility.

This work was supported by the following MEXT/JSPS KAKENHI grants: Grant-in-Aid for Scientific Research on Innovative Areas #4903 (Evolinguistics) Grant Number JP20H05007, Grant-in-Aid for Scientific Research (S) Grant Number JP19H05589, Grant-in-Aid for Scientific Research (A) Grant Number JP19H00532 awarded to the first named author. It was also supported by a British Academy Grant SRG20/201369 awarded to the second named author. These are gratefully acknowledged.

Kuniya Nasukawa & Nancy C. Kula, Tohoku Gakuin University; University of Essex & University of the Free State

https://doi.org/10.1515/9783110691948-007

1 Introduction

Nasal-consonant (NC) sequences have been widely investigated cross-linguistically and specifically in Bantu languages with the focus generally being on their representation as unit segments or as clusters (see e.g. Herbert 1975, 1986; Downing 1996, 2005; Kula 1999, 2002, among others). In this paper we assume NCs are represented as clusters and rather focus on specific cases involving the emergence of consonants in the creation of NCs in Lungu (Bickmore 2007) and Bemba (Kula 2002), although these phenomena are widely attested in many Bantu languages.[1] The cases we discuss involve nasal prefixes affixed to vowel-initial stems, specifically verb roots, that then result in a consonant emerging in stem-initial position. The nasal prefixes involved are of either the 1sg subject marker *N*-, the 1sg object marker *N*- or the noun class 9/10 nasal prefix *N*-. A number of other processes apply to post-nasal consonants, such as homorganicity and strengthening, which are secondary to the consonant emergence discussed here.

The surfacing consonants are contextually determined, with both the preceding nasal consonant and the following vowel influencing their shape. This means that the emergent consonants in these contexts cannot be treated as the default true epenthetic sounds used in all contexts. In other cases where epenthetic consonants may be an option, particularly in some hiatus contexts, vowel gliding is usually the option chosen. In this sense [Nasal prefix + Vowel-initial stem] sequences provide a unique context where we see consonants other than glides emerging. Both Lungu and Bemba have 5-vowel systems with the consonant emergence process dividing the vowels into the low and back vowels, on the one hand, and the front vowels, on the other.

The structure of this paper is as follows. First, in section 2, the relevant data are presented. Then in section 3, we propose the structure of the nasal-prefix in Lungu and Bemba that we assume, and present the dovetailing morphological concatenation that captures the nasal-prefix and stem interactions, and deal with cases where the stem-initial vowel is a back vowel. Section 4 presents the analysis of the cases that involve element agreement with high front vowels, and those with glide-initial stems and also discusses the specific assumptions for prefix-prefix interactions involving symmetric concatenation. We finally offer some concluding remarks in section 5.

---

[1] Lungu (also icilungu) and Bemba (also icibemba) are Bantu languages that are predominantly spoken in Northern and Central Zambia, both classified as part of zone M in Guthrie's classification (Guthrie 1967–1971). Bemba data come from the second named author, most of which are published in Kula (2002); and Lungu data are from Bickmore (2007).

2 Post-nasal consonant emergence data

We present the relevant data from Lungu (Bickmore 2007) and Bemba (Kula 2002) in (1), as well as a few other Bantu languages further in (3) and (4) below. The nasal prefix in all cases is considered to be underspecified, getting its place features from the following consonant. Thus, in (1a) we see homorganicity and also stem-initial consonant hardening when an initial lateral is involved. The examples in (1b) show the relevant cases of consonant emergence in Lungu and the same pattern in (2) for Bemba.[2]

(1) Lungu N- + C/V-initial stems
    a. N + C-initial stem
        ukuu-N-lem-a → ukuu-n-dema 'to grab me'
        NC15-1SGOM-grab-FV
        ukuu-N-peel-a → ukuu-m-peela 'to give me'
        NC15-1SGOM-give-FV
        N-ful-a → ɱ-fula 'I wash'
        9SM-wash-FV

    b. N- (=1SGOM) + V-stem + (final -e = imperative marker)
        N-imb-e → ɲ-[dʒ]-imbe 'dig me out!'
        N-elel-e → ɲ-[dʒ]-elele 'fish for me!'
        N-oc-el-e → n-[g]-ocele 'burn for me!'
        N-um-e → n-[g]-ume 'beat me!'
        N-am-e → n-[g]-ame 'call me!'

The data in (1a) show examples from Lungu where we see an *l~d* alternation in the first example and homorganic nasal agreement in all examples. But crucially for all three examples there is no consonant emergence between the *N*-prefix and the following consonant-initial stems. In the examples in (1b) and in (2) below for Bemba, on the other hand, we see a consonant appearing in vowel-initial stems.

---

2 Data are presented following general Bantu notation. For verbal forms the nasal prefix will be followed by a verb root of CVC-/VCVC- shape, followed by optional VC suffixes and ending in either the citation form final vowel *-a* or a tense-aspect vowel. The verb root can be preceded by a subject marker, object marker or tense/aspect/mood marker. Forms in a left hand column will show the morphological breakdown while corresponsing forms on the right will show output forms without boundaries apart from the relevant one involving the nasal prefix *N-* that is under discussion. Nominal forms will have the nasal prefx followed by a nominal stem. The morphological glosses used are: NC: noun class; 1SGOM: 1st singular object marker; SM1SG: 1st singular subject marker; FUT2: Future 2; FV: Final Vowel; COP: copular; and PRN: pronominal form/marker.

Two possible consonants g and ʤ occur between the nasal-prefix and following vowel-initial stems. The affricate ʤ appears between the nasal prefix and the stems when a given stem begins with the front vowels, *i* or *e*, while stems beginning with the non-front vowels *o, u, a*, get the voiced velar stop *g*.

(2) Bemba N- (1st person singular) + V-initial stems

	verb stem		N+verb stem	
a.	alul-a	'redirect'	ŋ-[g]-alula	'I redirect'
b.	olol-a	'straighten'	ŋ-[g]-olola	'I straighten'
c.	ubul-a	'peel'	ŋ-[g]-ubula	'I peel'
d.	isul-a	'open'	ɲ-[ʤ]-isula	'I open'
e.	eleel-a	'forgive'	ɲ-[ʤ]-eleela	'I forgive'

Glide initial stems are also subject to the same processes with *y* [j] initial stems having ʤ and *w* initial stems taking *g*. These cases could also alternatively be treated as sonorant hardening, depending on the status of the glides in the language in question as we will discuss further below. (3) below shows examples with glide-initial stems from Bemba, Swahili (data from Ashton 1944) and Ndali (data from Vail 1972). Examples (3c-d) are nominal forms of class 9/10.

(3)
a.	w-a	'fall'	ŋ-[g]wa	'I fall'	(Bemba)
b.	y-a	'go'	ɲ-[ʤ]ya	'I go'	(Bemba)
c.	-wati		m-bati	'hut poles'	(Swahili)
d.	-yuki		ɲ-[ʤ]uki	'bee'	(Ndali)

Similar consonant emergence/alternations can also be seen in Luganda where *y* [j] → ʤ and Ø → *g*, like in Bemba. Kwanyama (from Namibia) also has what looks like insertion or emergence of *b*, in addition to *g* and ʤ, in the formation of nouns from verbs, as the examples in (4) show. In this case the round vowel *o* patterns differently from *u* that has *g*. And also, counter to expectation, a stem with initial *e* also takes *g* and therefore fails to pattern with the high vowel *i* that as above takes ʤ as the emergent consonant. The front vowel *i* patterns with the glide *y* [j] in having ʤ as the emergent consonant. Data are taken from Tirronen (1977: 52) but with modifications from Olivia Ndapo (pc.) adding the nominal glosses.[3] Kwanyama class 9/10 nouns have an initial *o* vowel as part of the prefix.

---

3 Example (4c) has also been changed to show NC simplification in the nominal form based on data from Ndapo (pc.). This is a standard process also seen in (4a-d) that is a variant of *Meinhof's Law* (see Schadeberg's (1982) discussion of the *Kwanayama Law*), which is a process that simplies one of two voiced NCs occuring in sequence, i.e. in NCvNC contexts.

(4) Kwanyama Verb to Noun formation
    a. ol-a   'rot'   →   om-[b]-olo   'rotten wood'
    b. umb-a   'put up a fence'   →   oŋ-[g]-ubu   'fence'
    c. end-a   'walk'   →   oŋ-[g]-eda   'travel'
    d. imb-a   'sing'   →   on-[dʒ]-iba   'song'
    e. yelek-a   'measure'   →   on-[dʒ]-eleka   'measurement'

Based on forms in other Bantu languages where the verb 'rot' has an initial sonorant w or $β$ that is also reconstructed to Proto Bantu, we speculate that in (4a) the nominal form reveals a previous such segment in the verbal form on a par with, for example, the Swahili example (3c), but which has now been lost in the verbal form. The alternative would be to draw on a connection between the surfacing b and the following round vowel that could be argued to lead to the surfacing of b. This logic, however, does not work for (4b) where a following round vowel triggers g instead. Based on this form in (4a) and also g surfacing in (4c) we assume that either there are changes going on in Kwanyama that lead to these surface contrasts with patterns in other related Bantu languages or that some forms (or indeed all forms) have been lexicalized based on previous processes and must now simply be stored. What we see now would be remnants of what may have been an active process.[4]

There are some domains where consonant emergence does not apply even though the nasal prefix seen in the data above is present. This happens when the nasal-prefix is followed by other prefixes (i.e. not followed by a stem), as the Bemba examples in (5) show.

(5) *N*-prefix + Tense Aspect
    a. N-alaa-is-a   →   **n**alaaisa
        SM1SG.-FUT2-come-FV   →   *ŋgalaaisa
        'I will come' (Bemba)
    b. ni-N-ebo   →   ni**n**ebo
        COP-SM1SG.-PRN   →   *niɲdʒebo
        'It's me' (Bemba)

---

[4] The other point of note is that the other Bantu languages discussed here are all Eastern Bantu, while Kwanyama is the only Western Bantu language looked at. Although these groupings have not been reconstructed to Proto Bantu, there are a number of other processes that contrast Eastern and Western Bantu, so it is not surprising to see some contrast here as well.

In (5a) the nasal prefix is followed by another prefix that starts with a vowel and unlike in the case where a vowel-initial stem follows, we see no consonant appearing in this case as shown by the starred form. Similarly, in (5b) the nasal prefix is followed by a *pronominal* stem that starts with a vowel, but also in this case there is no emergent consonant and its inclusion would be ungrammatical.[5]

This interaction with other prefixes suggests a morphological structure where the prefixes occur in one domain and any following stem is in another domain as argued in Kula (2002). In this way, we capture the fact that only some morphological boundaries are visible to phonology and in particular in this case, only the boundary between the prefix and the stem is relevant for emergent consonants. We discuss presently how these contrasting boundaries can be phonologically distinguished.

3 An analysis of emergent consonants in Bantu languages (Lungu and Bemba)

3.1 The phonological representation of the nasal prefix /N/

Two questions arise regarding the phenomenon of emergent consonants discussed thus far. First, it is obvious that the source of ʤ which appears before the front vowels *i* and *e* is the element |I| in these vowels, whereas it is difficult to find the source of the *g* that appears before the non-front vowels *a, o, u*. Although we treat velars as represented with element-|U| for place, as also proposed in e.g. Backley & Nasukawa (2009a), Backley (2011), which is then shared between *g* and the vowels *o* and *u*, this still leaves *a* at odds with this analysis. More precisely, we assume, following Backley (2011) that velar and labiality (roundness in vowels) do not have quite identical elements in that the former is an unheaded |U| while the latter is headed |U| (headedness indicated by underlining). There is as such no common property between *g* and *a, o, u*, i.e. we cannot create a natural class that groups these segments together based on some shared property. In element terms, these vowels have no properties in common (except that they lack the privative element |I|) and thus no common element they would share with *g*.[6]

---

5 Note though that other processes like vowel fusion and consonant hardening, as also in the Lungu example in (1a), do apply between prefixes.
6 There has been a lot of discussion on the question of how velarity should be represented. For example, in Botma (2004) it is treated as the phonetic manifestation of |A| in a C position. In earlier work such as Harris (1994), a position that was quite popular, velarity has been treat-

In order to account for the lack of a local source for *g*, we will propose that the nasal prefix *N-* in Bantu languages has velarity in its *lexical* representation, as in (6) below.

(6) The lexical representation of the nasal prefix *N-*

O	N	O	N
|		|	
|ʔ|		|ʔ|	
|A|		|U|	
|L|			

   n   *g*

|ʔ|: occlusion, |U|: velarity, |L|: nasality, |A|: coronality

In this configuration, velarity is represented by the rump element |U| as noted above. The other elements |ʔ| and |L| are phonetically interpreted as occlusion and nasality, respectively. |A| represents coronal place in the nasal.[7] To explain why the emerging velar is voiced we briefly discuss the representation of voicing in the two Bantu languages we focus on here, Bemba and Lungu. Both languages have no contrastive voicing in obstruents with voicing only occurring in post-nasal position as a result of hardening of sonorants, like the *l* to *d* case seen in (1a). The voiceless obstruents in the two languages do not undergo post-nasal voicing, as also shown in (1a). In element terms we will thus treat voiceless obstruents as having the laryngeal element |H| (noise, voicelessness), while voiced obstruents will have no laryngeal element. In this way, any obstruent (indicated by the occlusion element |ʔ|), which does not have a laryngeal element, will be interpreted as voiced and as such the velar obstruent in (6) must be voiced.[8] This proposal on

---

ed as represented by emptyness (see also Kula & Marten 1998). Elsewhere it is represented by non-headed |U| (e.g. Backley & Nasukawa 2009, Backley 2011, Huber 2007), with this analysis being based on the phonological and acoustic correlations between labials and velars (cf. Kijak 2017). In this paper we have taken the latter approach of viewing velarity as the phonetic realization of non-headed |U|.

[7] As already referred to elements can appear in a more prominent form by becoming headed and thereby changing their phonetic realization (headedness is here marked by underlining), e.g. headed |U|, headed |ʔ| and headed |L| are phonetically realized as labiality, ejective release and obstruent voicing, respectively (Backley 2011, et passim). How change in headship is derived can be captured by dependency relations in element geometries that we note here but do not pursue in this paper as this is beyond the scope of the current discussion. See Liu & Kula (2020) for detailed discussion.

[8] This analysis contrasts with Kula (2002) where voicing in post-nasal position is not underspecified but treated as resulting from the spreading of |L| from the nasal to the obstruent where it

the representation of voicing in Bemba and Lungu, implies that the velar in (6) will be interpreted as voiced.

In (6), since velarity is *lexically specified*, the issues to do with how *g* is generated before *a, o, u,* do not arise. The ONON configuration follows standard assumptions in Element Theory where onsets must be licensed by a following nucleus. Here we assume that the sandwiched nucleus is licensed to be empty by onset-to-onset/C-to-C government that applies from right to left and that the empty nucleus in the prefix domain requires a licensor external to its domain since there are no final empty nuclei (FEN) in Bantu languages.[9]

One further assumption is that the mass element |A| (coronality) is lexically specified with nasality |L| in the *N*-prefix. This follows from the distribution of nasals where *ŋ* and *m* appear before velars and labials respectively, but although *n* naturally appears before coronals, it also crucially appears before vowels in prefixal contexts such as (5a-b). Given this, we assume |ʔ A L| to be lexically specified in the initial onset of the structure of the *N*-prefix.[10]

It is thus due to this lexical representation of the nasal prefix as already containing *g* that our analysis does not treat post-nasal emergent consonants as epenthesis but as part of a morpho-phonological operation. We elaborate on how the data follows from this representation of the nasal prefix below.

---

assumes head position to be interpreted as voicing. Recent work on depressor consonants which are synonymous with specified voicing in languages like Zulu (Liu & Kula 2020), suggest that the current analysis proposed here is more in keeping with depressor effects, i.e. accounting for the fact that there are no depressor effects in either Bemba or Lungu.

9 It is argued in Kula (2002) that the domain-final parameter licening FEN is not activated or is set to OFF in Bantu languages since final nuclei must always be realized. In morphological contexts though, between a prefix and a stem, a nasal prefix ending in an empty nucleus occurs in a dependent domain to the stem by which it is licensed via C-to-C government with the stem-initial consonant in the structure [NØ [Stem]]. This domain representation captures the fact that the prefix is bound and cannot occur indepedndently without a root/stem. In the remainder of the paper we will use ON representations but all aspects of the represenations and analysis are directly interpretable into strict CV phonology (Lowenstamm 1999, Scheer 2004), hence reference here to C-to-C government. Assumptions on licensing are based on Kaye, Lowenstamm & Vergnaud (1990) and Kaye (1990).

10 This proposal stands us in good stead in light of the Kwanyama data in (4) where counter to expectation initial *e*- triggers *g* as the epenthetic consonant (4c). If as suggested this is due to fossilisation and lexicalisation then the fact that the lexical representation of *N*- contains *g* would begin to explain this distribution.

3.2 The nasal prefix /N-/ plus a consonant-initial stem

We consider the concatenations involving the nasal prefix in more detail below. We assume that an overlapping asymmetric concatenation is created between the nasal prefix and the following stem, involving the final ON of the nasal prefix and the initial ON of the following stem overlapping, as illustrated in (7). Note that we assume the segment *l* in the stem contains only the mass element |A| in Bemba based on its phonological patterning and distribution.

(7) The lexical representation of *N-luk-il-a* 'I plait (for X)' (Bemba) with surface form *n-[d]-uk-il-a*

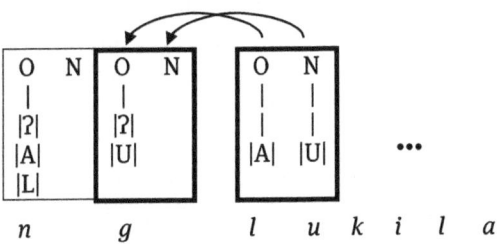

As a result of the asymmetric overlap concatenation, |A| in the stem is shared with the prefix, overriding |U| as it does so.[11] Because only the place element |A| affects the prefix we call this overlap concatenation *asymmetric*. We will see cases of *symmetric* overlap concatenation where the stem onset must impose *all and only* its melodic content on the prefix, in later discussion. The output representation derived from (7) is shown in (8).

(8) The derived representation of *N-luk-il-a* → *ndukila* 'I plait (for someone)'

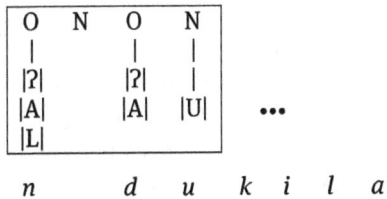

---

[11] This involves a co-occurrence restriction between place elements here. In this case, |U| and |A| fail to co-occur in a single position.

The initial *l* of the stem is hardened to an obstruent as a result of the asymmetric overlap concatenation with only |A| contributed to the prefix onset and therefore the output segment is *d*. Recall that the absence of a laryngeal element in obstruents is interpreted as voicing. This is a straightforward case where the phonetic form already shows place agreement between the prefix nasal and the following onset so no further assumptions need be made.

3.3 The nasal prefix *N*- plus a vowel-initial stem: Lexical specification

Let us now consider the cases that show emergent consonants when the nasal prefix is followed by a vowel-initial stem. We first consider cases involving *g*. The foregoing discussion on the lexical representation of the prefix *N*- captures that we consider *g* to be present in the prefix and used in stems starting with *a, u, o*, where the lexical representation of the prefix surfaces after overlap. In this case, there is no melodic content in the initial onset of the stem, contrasting with the case just discussed above in (7). The emergence of *g* in these cases is illustrated in (9) below.

(9) The lexical representation of *N-olola* → *ŋgolola* 'I straighten' (Bemba)

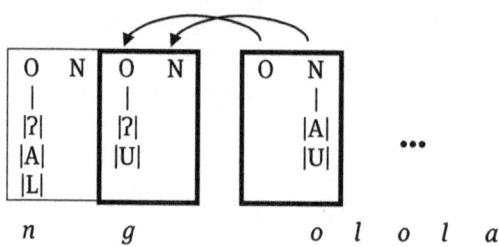

(9) shows the lexical representations of the structures that come together in the prefix-stem context. Since the stem-initial onset is empty and conversely the final nucleus of the prefix is empty, overlap concatenation involves a perfect overlap with no sharing of melodic material. The output form is then as in (10) below, giving the concatenated form *ŋgolola*.

(10) The derived representation of *N-olola* → *ŋgolola* 'I straighten' (Bemba)

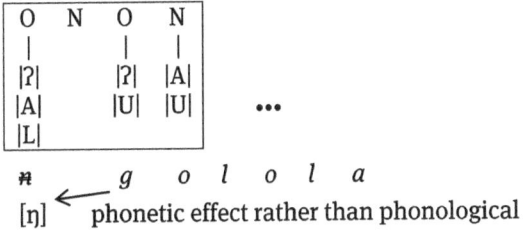

Given the phonological structure in (9), the expected realization of the sequence is *ng* without place assimilation, contra to the actual output form in (10). To account for the surface form *ŋg* we assume place (velar) assimilation as standard between the first two onsets but treat this as applying in the phonetics (rather than in the phonology), as a case of ease of articulation.[12] This implies that there is no change in the phonological representation – the phonology sends /ng/ for pronunciation and this is produced as /ŋg/. The exact same process of *g* emergence is found in cases where the nasal prefix precedes *u*-initial (e.g. 2c), and *a*-initial (e.g. 2a) stems.

Thus, for emergent *g*, it is simply the articulation of the representation of the lexical prefix in the default case, facilitated by the overlapping prefixation between the prefix and a vowel-initial stem.

4 Element agreement with emergent consonants

4.1 Consonant-vowel interaction between prefix and stem

We have already seen in the data discussion that stems beginning with front vowels show |I| agreement with the nasal prefix *N*- resulting in the emergent consonant *g* changing to ʤ. We model this as palatalization of *g* by |I|-agreement with

---

12 GP and ET have a tradition of distinguishing phonological (grammar-internal) and phonetic (grammar-external) assimilation (Harris 2003, et passim). The latter is assumed to include processes such as nasal place assimilation, which are typologically unmarked (unlike nasal place dissimilation, which is treated as being phonological because it is unnatural and marked). This type of phonetic assimilation is considered to be a natural outcome, triggered systematically and naturally by physiological requirements (cf. universal phonetics). On the other hand, structurally controlled assimilation processes such as vowel harmony are seen as phonological since they are not universally employed.

the following vowel-initial stem, i.e. as a consonant-vowel interaction of the type commonly attested cross-linguistically. We follow the representations already given above but in this case the |I| element in the vowel of the stem requires agreement with the preceding onset. The process starts out with asymmetric overlap concatenation as already described above and shown below in (11).

(11) Lexical representations and concatenation for *N-imb-e* 'dig me out' (Lungu)

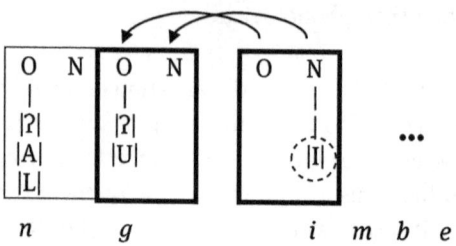

The concatenation in (11) creates adjacency between lexical *g* and the stem-initial |I| that is then a trigger for palatalization that we capture as |I|-sharing, where element |I| from the stem-initial vowel expresses itself also in the preceding onset, and in this way booting out the place element of the *g* and changing it to ʤ. This same process also holds for stems with *-e* as the initial vowel, since this also contains |I|. This is illustrated in (12).[13]

(12) The derived representation of *N-imb-e* → *ɲʤimbe* 'dig me out' (Lungu)

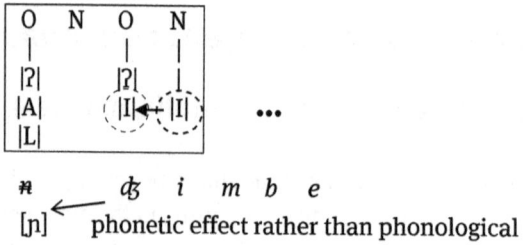

---

[13] There is an across-the-board palatalization process triggered by |I| in Bemba and Lungu and this analysis predicts that |I| will always spread to cause palatalization or Bantu spirantization, so that this interaction is not specific to this context. Furthermore, the output for Lungu in (12) prompts one to comment that the common process in Bantu languages where NC simplification applies in sequential voiced NCs (so-called *Meinhof's Law* already referred to above) does not apply in Lungu (see Kula 2006 for discussion).

In this case the emergence of ʤ is the same process as we have seen for g, namely, both cases involve the lexical representation of the nasal prefix containing g, but which in this case undergoes palatalization from a following |I| containing front vowel. Phonologically ʤ is palatal and results in place assimilation at the phonetic level, as also seen in other cases, to here produce a palatal nasal.

Recall that we had cases where initial glides triggered the same consonant emergence processes, as in the data recapped here in (13) below.

(13) a. w-a   'fall' ŋ-[g]wa   'I fall'   (Bemba)
     b. y-a   'go'   ɲ-[ʤ]ya   'I go'   (Bemba)
     c. -wati   m-[b]ati 'hut poles'   (Swahili)
     d. -yuki   n-[ʤ]uki 'bee'   (Ndali)

For these cases, let us first consider (13a-b). These are both verb forms with a short verb root consisting of only a C in contrast to the more common CVC- root shape in Bantu. The verb form w-a is a derived form created from the root and the vowel of the default citation form -a. We will assume that what appears on the surface as a C (the glide) in these forms is in fact vowel-initial, with the content of the glide represented in a nuclear position. This consists of a sequence of two ON pairs where the first represents the root and the second the citation form of the verb -a. For w-a the root nucleus contains only |U| and for y-a only |I|. In both cases the second ON pair contains the final vowel which has |A|. In Bemba, which has no phonological diphthongs, the V-V sequences in these contexts are realized as [wa] and [ja], in the same way that hiatus is resolved.

(14) a. w-a 'fall'   b. y-a 'go'

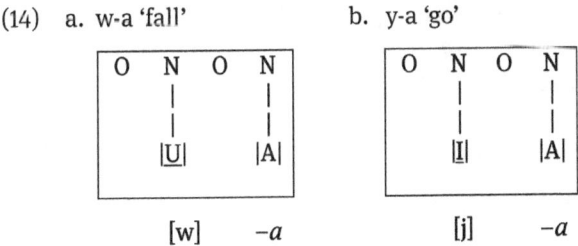

With these structures, we can now consider the overlapping concatenation process with the N-prefix. The outcome is as in (15). (15a) shows the same process as observed in previous examples, with the final ON of the prefix (N-) and the first ON of the stem (w-a) overlapping. Based on what we saw earlier in (7), (15a) shows the lexical representations of the structures that come together in the prefix-stem context. Since the stem-initial onset is empty and conversely the final nucleus of the prefix is empty, overlap concatenation involves an overlap with no sharing of melodic material. The output form is then as in (15b), giving the concatenated form *ŋgwa*.

(15) The phonological representation of N- + w-a → ŋ-[g]w-a (Bemba (13a))
   a. The lexical representation: N- + w-a

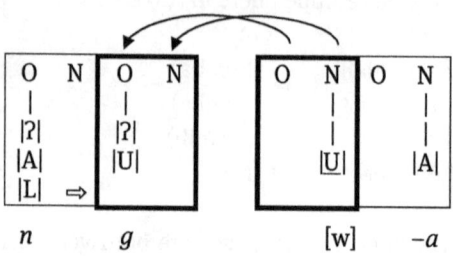

   b. The derived representation: ŋ-gw-a

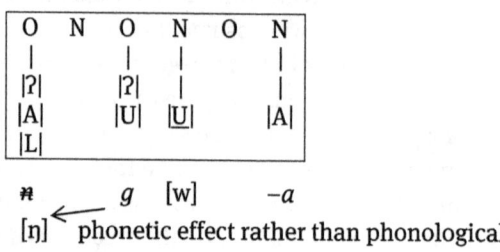

   [ŋ] ← phonetic effect rather than phonological

Notice that what we get as the phonetic manifestation is *ŋgwa* rather than *ŋgua* in the same way (generated hiatus is resolved by glide production) as discussed in (14).

Next, consider the process N- + y-a → ɲdʒa. As can be seen in (16a), the overlapping process is exactly the same as (15a).

(16) The phonological representation of N- + y-a → ɲdʒa 'I go' (Bemba (13b))
   a. Emergence of dʒ with y [j] glide

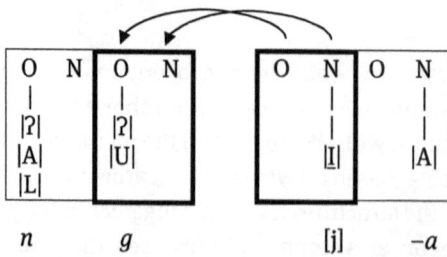

b. Output structure of ʤ from y-initial stems

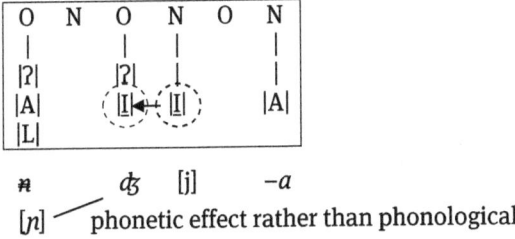

The concatenation in (16a) yields adjacency between lexical *g* and the stem-initial nuclear |I|. Then, in the same way as illustrated in (12), |I|-sharing takes place in (16b), leading to the palatalization of *g* to ʤ. The phonetic outcome is [ɲʤja]. Thus, the occurrence of emergent consonants in glide-initial stems is evidence that glides are phonologically represented in nuclear position in Bemba, as otherwise, as with other consonant-initial stems (cf. examples in 1a) we would not expect emergent consonants.

Consider next the similar but contrasting example from Swahili, where the *w* glide imposes its labial place on the *g* of the prefix, thus changing it to *b*. This patterns with cases where the stem-initial onset is filled as seen in the examples in (1a) and for which we assume the structures in (7–8). This means that the glide in Swahili, in contrast to Bemba, is represented in a C position and thus must behave in parallel fashion to cases where the place element of the nasal prefix is overridden. Thus, in this case |U| in the stem overrides |U| in *g* of the nasal prefix and the segment is as such realized as a *b*.[14] The representation for this is given in (17) below. Recall that the noise element |H| in the stem is realized as voicelessness.

---

14 The behaviour of the Swahili glide is in this sense the same as what we see with the 'voiced bilabial fricative' β in Bemba, for which there are good reasons to argue that it is in fact a sonorant – topmost of which is the fact that as a fricative β would be the only voiced sound in the language. Similar to Swahili *w*, stem-initial β hardens to *b* when the nasal prefix precedes it. Thus, *N-βula → mbula* 'I lack (something)'. β is thus in parallel fashion represented as only containing |U| in Kula & Marten (1998). There is no β in Swahili and as such *w* being in the onset as a sonorant is a perfectly viable option.

(17) The phonological representation of N- + -wati → mbati (Swahili (13c))

a. The lexical representation : N- + -wati

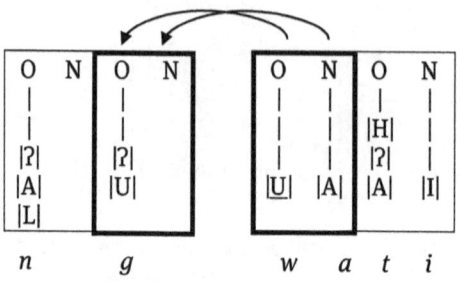

b. The derived representation: mbati

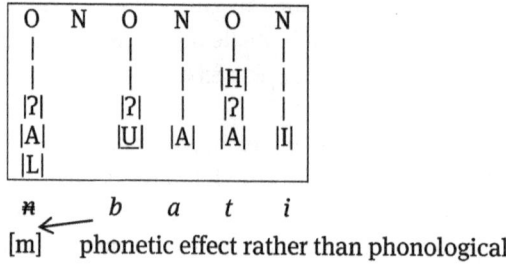

[m] phonetic effect rather than phonological

As depicted in (17a-b), |U| of the stem overrides the |U| of the suffix resulting in *nbati. This is then phonetically produced as *mbati* the final output form, showing labial place assimilation between the nasal prefix and the following onset. This is exactly the same pattern as we saw in (7–8).

4.2 Blocked consonant emergence in the prefix domain: Symmetric concatenation

A final issue to consider concerns those cases presented in the data in (5) that show no consonant insertion and which we explained as showing that post-nasal consonant emergence does not apply within the prefix domain, i.e. it applies between a prefix and a stem but not between prefixes. To recap, consider this near minimal pair where in (18a) *g* appears between the nasal prefix and a following stem that starts with *a* but where this, conversely, does not happen in the same segmental configuration in (18b), when prefixes are involved.

(18) a. N- ab-ul-a → ŋ[g]abula 'I unimmerse'
     b. N-a-ab-ul-a → naabula 'I have just unimmersed' * ŋ[g]aabula
        1ˢᵗsg-PAST1-immerse-REVERSIVE/SEPARATIVE-FV

We treat this as a contrast in the type of concatenation involved between prefixes, treating this as *symmetric* overlapping concatenation, which differs from what we have so far seen between a prefix and a stem. Since we are dealing with the same prefix, we are committed to maintaining the same lexical representation that has been proposed for the *N*-prefix and assume that among prefixes there is overlap to reflect that they belong to the same domain as shown in (19a).

(19) The representation of *N-* + *-a* of *N-a-ab-ul-a* → *naabula* (18b)

   a. Input structure

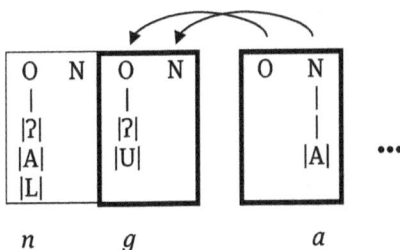

The crucial difference is that in this case *all* the properties of the overlapped part of the *N*-prefix are overridden by all properties of the following prefix. This includes cases where no melodic content is specified as in the prefix *-a* of the PAST1 prefix, which has an empty onset. This means that the *g* of the *N*-prefix is totally overridden and all its melodic content is lost or suppressed.[15] The final form will be as in (19b) below.

---

[15] This is also the case if the prefix following the nasal prefix is conosnant-initial, as would be the case with the future marker *ka-* or the habitual marker *la-*. In these cases also the *g* of the *N*-prefix is totally overridden. Thus with the verb *ya* 'to go' we get: N(g)-ka-ya → nkaya 'I will go' and N(g)-la-ya → ndaya 'I usually go', with /l/ undergoing voicing and hardening as standard in post-nasal position.

b. The derived representation of the initial *n-a-* in *n-a-abula* 'I unimmerse'

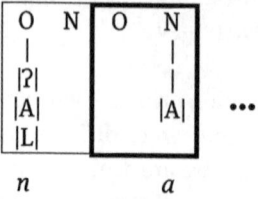

In this way we express the fact that the interaction between prefixes that are within the same phonological domain, is closer than that between a prefix and a following stem, which is in a different phonological domain. For each prefix we assume that it will adhere to the phonological constraints and language phonotactics requiring a following empty N or ON pair to show the dependency of prefixes. Thus, sequences of prefixes will be separated by empty ON pairs which then get overridden when the prefixes undergo symmetric overlap concatenation.[16]

We will end with a consideration of standard cases where no consonant emergence occurs to demonstrate that the proposed analysis works for these basic cases as well. Consider the examples in (20) from Bemba with stems with filled initial onsets, all of them voiceless as there is no lexical voicing contrast in the language (but see footnote 16).

(20) a. N-toola → ntoola 'I pick'
     b. N-seka → nseka 'I laugh'
     c. iN-kola → i[ŋ]kola 'snail' (Class 9/10)
     d. iN-fula → i[ɱ]fula 'rain' (Class9/10)

These cases would all involve asymmetric overlap concatenation where the initial ON of the stem overlaps onto the final ON of the prefix. In each case the place element of the stem onset replaces that of the prefix *g*. Note that as the obstruents in this case have a laryngeal specification for voiceless they cannot be interpreted as voiced and there is as such no observable post-nasal voicing.

---

[16] In this case an example like [ta-ba-la-[isa]] ([NEG-SUBJECT.MARKER-DISJOINT-[come]]) 'they have not yet come' will be represented as [taONbaONlaON[OisNOa]]. This, in a way, essentially does away with the hyphen diacritic representing a morphological boundary with a phonological entity – an ON or CV pair – as argued in Scheer (2012) et passim.

5 Conclusion

This paper has investigated a process that has traditionally been treated as epenthesis involving the emergence of a consonant in post-nasal contexts created by morphological concatenation. We have treated this process as essentially lexical by proposing an enriched representation of the nasal prefix *N-* of the 1st person singular (subject or object marker) or of class 9/10 in Bantu languages. The *N*-prefix is lexically contained in an ONON representation creating an NC sequence where the second onset contains melodic content that includes velarity so that the prefix can be independently interpreted as *ŋg*. We have proposed contrasting overlap concatenation where asymmetric overlapping concatenation requires only the place (and laryngeal element when present) to be interpreted in the position of *g* in the prefix. This is what leads to what appears on the surface as consonant insertion before vowel-initial stems. The *g* of the prefix can be palatalized from a following |I| containing vowel changing it to *dʒ*. Asymmetric overlapping concatenation applies between a prefix and a stem and contrasts with symmetric concatenation that applies between prefixes and which requires a preceding prefix to be totally overridden in content by a succeeding prefix. This contrast is what explains why the *g* of the nasal prefix does not surface between prefixes. Two types of assimilation emerge from the discussion – phonological element sharing in asymmetric concatenation, where a place element is shared between the stem and the prefix *g*, and phonetic place assimilation between the nasal and the following stem consonant that we assume does not entail any phonological change.

The paper contributes to the broader discussion of phonological phenomena driven by morphology and is a proposal that provides one way in which morphological information can be phonologized. We hope both the empirical facts and the specific analysis proposed here contribute to ongoing discussion in this area.

References

Ashton, Ethel O. 1944. *Swahili Grammar*. Essex: Longman.
Ashton, Ethel O. et al. 1954. *A Luganda Grammar*. London: Longmans, Green and Co.
Backley, Phillip. 2011. *An Introduction to Element Theory*. Edinburgh: Edinburgh University Press.
Backley, Phillip & Kuniya Nasukawa. 2009a. Representing labials and velars: a single 'dark' element. *Phonological Studies* 12. 3–10.
Backley, Phillip & Kuniya Nasukawa. 2009b. Headship as melodic strength. In Kuniya Nasukawa & Phillip Backley (eds.), *Strength Relations in Phonology*. 47–77. Berlin/New York: Mouton de Gruyter.

Backley, Phillip & Kuniya Nasukawa. 2010. Consonant-vowel unity in Element Theory. *Phonological Studies* 13. 21–28.

Bickmore, Lee. 2007. *Cilungu Phonology*. Stanford: CSLI Publications.

Botma, Bert. 2004. *Phonological Aspects of Nasality: An Element-Based Dependency Approach*. PhD dissertation, University of Amsterdam. Utrecht: LOT.

Downing, Laura J. 2005. On the ambiguous segmental status of nasals in homorganic NC sequences. In Marc van Oostendorp & Jeroen van de Weijer, *The Internal Organization of Phonological Segments*, 183–216. Berlin/New York: Mouton de Gruyter.

Guthrie, Malcom. 1967–1971. *Comparative Bantu*. London: Gregg Press.

Harris, John. 1994. *English Sound Structure*. Oxford: Blackwell.

Harris, John. 2003. Grammar-internal and grammar-external assimilation. *Proceedings of the 15th International Congress of Phonetic Sciences*. 281–284.

Harris, John & Geoff Lindsey. 1995. The elements of phonological representation. In Jacques Durand & Francis Katamba (eds.), *Frontiers of Phonology: Atoms, Structures, Derivations*, 34–79. Harlow, Essex: Longman.

Herbert, Robert K. 1975. Reanalyzing prenasalized consonants. *Studies in African Linguistics* 6. 105–123.

Herbert, Robert K. 1986. Language Universals, Markedness Theory, and Natural Phonetic Processes. Berlin: Mouton de Gruyter.

Huber, Dániel. 2007. *Velars and Processes: Their Treatment in Phonological Theory*. PhD dissertation, Eötvös Loránd University, Budapest.

Kaye, Jonathan D. 1990. 'Coda' licensing. *Phonology* 7. 301–330.

Kaye, Jonathan D., Jean Lowenstamm & Jean-Roger Vergnaud. 1990. Constituent structure and government in phonology. *Phonology* 7. 193–232.

Kijak Artur. 2017. Labial-velar changes in the history of English and Netherlandic. In W. Artur Kijak, Aandrzzj M. Łęcki & Jerzy Nykiel (eds.), *Current developments in English Historical Linguistics: Studies in Honour of Rafał Molencki*, 327–340. Katowice: Wydawnictwo Uniwersytetu Śląskiego.

Kula, Nancy C. 1999. On the representation of NC clusters in Bemba. In Renée van Bezooijen & René Kager, (eds.) *Linguistics in The Netherlands 1999*, 135–148. Amsterdam: John Benjamins Publishing Co.

Kula, Nancy C. 2002. *The Phonology of Verbal Derivation in Bemba*. Utrecht: Holland Academic Graphics. LOT dissertation series 65.

Kula, Nancy C. 2006. Licensing saturation: Co-occurrence restrictions in structure. *Linguistic Analysis* 32(3–4). 366–406.

Kula, Nancy C. & Lutz Marten. 1998. Aspects of nasality in Bemba. *SOAS Working Papers in Linguistics and Phonetics* 8. 191–208.

Liu, Xiaoxi & Nancy C. Kula. 2020. Recursive representations for depressor effects. In Kuniya Nasukawa (ed.) *Morpheme-internal Recursion in Phonology*, 143–180. Berlin/Boston: Mouton de Gruyter.

Nasukawa, Kuniya. 2005. *A Unified Approach to Nasality and Voicing*. Berlin/New York: Mouton de Gruyter.

Nasukawa, Kuniya. 2010. No consonant-final stems in Japanese verb morphology. *Lingua* 120. 2336–2352.

Nasukawa, Kuniya. 2017. The relative salience of consonant nasality and true obstruent voicing. In Geoff Lindsey & Andrew Nevins (eds.), *Sonic Signatures: Studies Dedicated to John Harris* (Language Faculty and Beyond 14), 146–162. Amsterdam: John Benjamins Publishing Co.

Schadeberg, Thilo C. 1982. Nasalization in UMbundu. *Journal of African Languages and Linguistics* 4. 109–132.

Scheer, Tobias. 2004. *A Lateral Theory of Phonology: What Is CVCV and Why Should It Be?* Berlin/New York: Mouton de Gruyter.

Scheer, Tobias. 2012. Direct Interface and One-Channel Translation. Vol.2 of A Lateral Theory of phonology. Berlin: Mouton de Gruyter

Tirronen, Toivo E. 1977. *OshiKwanyama shetu*. Windhoek: Inboorlingtaalburo van die department van Bantoe-onderwys.

Vail, Leroy. 1972. The noun classes of Ndali. *Journal of African Languages and Linguistics* 11.3. 21–47.

Connor Youngberg
The role of the elements in diphthong formation and hiatus resolution: Evidence from Tokyo and Owari Japanese

Abstract: This chapter examines vowel sequences and hiatus resolution processes in Tokyo and Owari Japanese. I aim to account for the peculiar behaviour of the diphthongs /ai, oi, ui/ versus vowels in hiatus such as /ae/. The former display tonal restrictions and no segmental changes, and the latter exhibit gliding, epenthesis and surfacing of hiatus with no tonal restrictions. To account for the context sensitive nature of hiatus resolution, I invoke the role of the elements, building on previous work in Element Theory (Kaye, Lowenstamm & Vergnaud 1985, Backley 2011) and Government Phonology (Kaye, Lowenstamm & Vergnaud 1990, Yoshida S. 1996, Yoshida Y. 1999). I propose an inter-segmental relation called Intervocalic Government. I utilize this novel form of government in combination with the Empty Category Principle (ECP). From the point of view put forth in this paper, hiatus resolution processes aim to satisfy the ECP either through government or the realisation of a consonantal position. The proposal rejects the role of the Complexity Condition (Harris 1990) and incorporates the role of |A| as a structural configuration (Pöchtrager 2006) in order to account for the fact that mid and low vowels cannot be the governee within a heavy diphthong.

Keywords: diphthongs; syllable structure; vowels; Japanese; hiatus.

1 Introduction

In this paper, I present a formal account of diphthong formation and hiatus resolution (HR) within Element Theory (Kaye, Lowenstamm and Vergnaud 1985, Charette and Göksel 1998, Backley 2011) and CV phonology (Lowenstamm 1996). While this article assumes some familiarity with the theories at hand, I discuss relevant concepts throughout. I focus on data from Tokyo and Owari Japanese. The first claim is that HR has a single trigger within various languages, which is the presence of an empty position and its need to be governed. The second claim is that diphthongs are formed through Intervocalic Government, which I

Connor Youngberg, LLING (UMR-6310) & Université de Nantes

https://doi.org/10.1515/9783110691948-008

propose here, and which is sensitive to the elemental structure in each vocalic position. The overall claim is that HR processes in general have one trigger with multiple repair solutions, with surface hiatus being fundamentally dispreferred and marked in phonological structures.

1.1 Hiatus, diphthongs and hiatus resolution

Diphthongs and hiatus have received a number of definitions over the years (Andersen 1972, Casali 2011), with a general understanding that both diphthongs and vowels in hiatus are adjacent heterogenous vocoids. In terms of phonological representation, vowels in hiatus are formed of two adjacent and independent nuclei, while a heavy diphthong is formed of two vocoids associated to a branching nucleus or the same syllable, exhibiting a unified metrical behaviour and patterning with long vowels (Selkirk 1982; Kaye and Lowenstamm 1984; Levin 1985; Kaye, Lowenstamm and Vergnaud 1990). Light diphthongs, or glide-vowel sequences, pattern metrically and phonotactically as short vowels and are, for example, represented as a vowel with a preceding glide attached to either the Onset or Nucleus (Kaye and Lowenstamm 1984; Kaye, Lowenstamm and Vergnaud 1990). More neutrally, I define hiatus as a bimoraic heterogenous V_1V_2 sequence where V_2 is independent for metrical purposes. I define diphthongs as bimoraic heterogenous V_1V_2 sequences where V_2 is *not* a possible site of accent, tone or stress. This papers focuses on the representation and triggering context of hiatus and heavy diphthongs with particular reference to Japanese.

Languages often contain both diphthongs and hiatus, with Tokyo Japanese permitting the site of a lexical pitch accent to be either V_1 or V_2 in hiatus, but only V_1 in words containing diphthongs (McCawley 1968; Haraguchi 1977; Yoshida Y. 1999; Kubozono 2015). I do not discuss light diphthong or CGV sequences in this paper, but they are discussed at length in the given references as well as Yoshida S. (1996) and Backley & Nasukawa (2016). In Tokyo Japanese, diphthongs are restricted only to the set {ai, oi, ui} (Kubozono 2015), while any other combination results in hiatus. The data in (1) exemplifies their contrasting behaviour, where a pitch accent is found on the antepenultimate mora in words with four or more moras in words, as in CV only words in (1a) or in hiatus sequences in (1b). In contrast, the second half of a diphthong as in (1c) is never a permitted accent site and shift is found.

(1)   Words of four or more moras (examples from Yoshida Y. 1999)
      a. [ho.to.tó.gi.su]   'lesser cuckoo'   (light syllable)
      b. [a.ó.mu.ɕi]   'green caterpillar' (vowels in hiatus)
      c. [ɕa.ká.i.ga.ku]   'sociology'   (diphthong)

Diphthong formation is the main focus in this paper, and it is one of the possible HR processes, broadly understood to consist of glide formation, vowel elision, consonant epenthesis, coalescence and diphthongization (Casali 2011). HR has been captured variously with features and linear rules (e.g. Aoki 1974), or through autosegmental operations affecting Vocalic nodes in contact (e.g. de Haas 1987), while Optimality Theory (Prince and Smolensky 1993) accounts utilize markedness constraints such as ONSET or NoHiatus (Casali 2011) to penalize input forms with vowel sequences.[1] Focusing on previous research combining Element Theory (Kaye, Lowenstamm and Vergnaud 1985, Backley 2011) and Government Phonology (Kaye, Lowenstamm and Vergnaud 1990), HR processes are captured using the contraction of governing relations and fusion or spreading of elements. The main catalyst for HR in Government Phonology work is the adjacency of nuclei with no intervening consonantal segment; this violates the Obligatory Contour Principle, argued to give rise to elision in French (Charette 1991) or coalescence in Bemba (Kula 2002). Diphthong formation in Japanese is captured by Yoshida S. (1996) and Yoshida Y. (1999) through the formation of a branching nucleus through nuclear fusion (with government holding between the two skeletal points), while hiatus results from its failure. Coalescence in Bemba is captured by Kula (2002:54–48) through bidirectional element sharing triggered by regressive internuclear government.[2] Crucially, all GP accounts contain empty onset constituents surrounded by two adjacent nuclei and invoke some form of element inequality and spread. I aim to develop these past insights below within a CV environment and a modern understanding of Element Theory (henceforth ET).

1.2 The proposal

The main proposal here is that HR is a set of syllable structure repair strategies and that diphthongs are formed through Intervocalic Government (IVG). I claim the trigger is an empty consonantal position which must be governed. Second, I propose that diphthong formation is the contraction of a governing relation between two vocalic segments in IVG. I claim that IVG enacts if 1) The governor is contentful and has higher or equal complexity to the governee and 2) the governee does not contain |A|, which is a complex structural configuration (Pöchtrager 2006, 2015).

---

[1] Casali (2011) utilizes NoHiatus as a hypothetical constraint as the exact constraint triggering hiatus is debated.
[2] See also Balogné Bérces (2006), who focuses only on elision and who takes a different view to government and licensing.

Why is a new governing relation necessary? It is clear that Proper Government (Kaye, Lowenstamm and Vergnaud 1990) is not sufficient to capture the silencing of empty positions with phonotactic restrictions. In languages such as Japanese, where vowel-zero alternations are not freely occurring and the ability of a nucleus or V position to properly govern another position is not clear, Yoshida S. (1996) and Yoshida Y. (1999) rely on Onset-to-Onset government (Gussmann and Kaye 1993) to account for the structure of NC clusters and geminates as well as high vowel devoicing. IVG can be considered the vocalic mirror of Onset-to-Onset Government (Gussmann and Kaye 1993, Gussmann 2002) or Infrasegmental Government (Scheer 2004) which rely on elemental complexities in order to silence an empty nucleus. Before presenting IVG in full, let us consider the crucial parts of ET and GP in section 2 and the data in section 3.

2 Element theory and CV phonology

The first ingredient for my analysis of HR and diphthong formation is the elements, while the second ingredient is the presence and licensing of empty positions. I present only the necessary parts of Element Theory and CV phonology used in this paper; for recent review, see Van der Hulst (2016) on various monovalent feature theories, Scheer and Kula (2017) on ET and Scheer and Cyran (2017) on GP and CV.

2.1 Element theory

In Element Theory (Kaye, Lowenstamm and Vergnaud 1985; Charette and Göksel 1998; Backley 2011), vowels and consonants are composed of one or more of unary primes, with the revised set of elements being |A|, |I|, |U|, |L|, |H|, and |ʔ|. Additional elements may be used in certain approaches (Harris and Lindsey 1995; Cyran 1997, 2010; Scheer 2004), but this is the set used most recently by Backley (2011). There are also strains of Element Theory where one or more elements are replaced with structural configurations (Jensen 1994; de Carvalho 2002; Rennison and Neubarth 2003; Pöchtrager 2006, 2015).

When associated to a vocalic position, the elements are interpreted as vowels. The element |A| is realised as an open vowel such as [a], |I| is realised as a front vowel such as [i] and |U| is realised as a vowel produced with lip compression or lip rounding, such as [u]. Elements may also be combined and create complex expressions, with the resulting expression retaining the broad qualities of each element. A vocalic expression composed of the open element |A| and the palatal element |I| would be |AI|, interpreted phonetically as [e], [ɛ] or [æ]. See the set of elements and their combinations below.

(2) Three elements for vowels, seven possible expressions
|A| [a] |I| [i] |U| [u]
|AI| [e] |AU| [o] |IU| [y]
           |AIU| [ø]

An expression is any combination of elements, with a simplex expression consisting of one element and a complex expression consisting of two or more elements. A head position is identified to differentiate between different complex expressions. A head is given more prominence compared to the other elements in a segment (Kaye, Lowenstamm and Vergnaud 1985; Harris and Lindsey 1995; Backley 2011). From a phonological point of view, heads and operators will often display different potentials with regards to phonological processes such as vowel harmony (Harris 1994b; Charette and Göksel 1996; Cobb 1997; Kula and Marten 2002; Kula 2002).[3] Heads license operators within an expression, while headless expressions are found in some languages in weak positions and in lax vowels. Headedness provides potential contrast between expressions such as |AI| with |I| as head, realised as [e], versus the expression |IA| with |A| as head, which is realised as [æ] or [ɛ]. Likewise a contrast can be made between headed |I| and headed |U|, giving |UI| and |IU| where the head element is underlined and to the right, generating [y] and [ʉ] in Norwegian, which has these contrasting high round vowels (Charette and Göksel 1998; Backley 2011).

In terms of generative capacity, six elements plus the condition on single headedness is sufficiently powerful to generate the necessary oral vowel contrasts in language, and inventories must be produced from the below possible combinations.[4]

(3) Generated vocalic expressions with single headedness
|A| |AI| |A| |AI| |IU|
|I| |AU| |I| |IA| |UI|
|U| |IU| |U| |AU| |AIU|
      |AIU| |UA| |AUI|
                           |IUA|

---

3 It can be argued that the headed or unheaded status of an expression is directly a result of licensing at metrical projections or harmonic domains. See Cobb (1997), Charette (In Press) for discussion of head licensing.
4 On generative capacity more generally, see Breit (2013) and Bafile (2017).

Assuming that there are no restrictions on the fusion of elements, 19 expressions are generated with only three elements for vowels. However, it is clear this number is not needed for the majority of languages. I turn to Licensing Constraints to further refine the vowels generated.[5]

2.1.1 Constraining element generation: Licensing constraints

To further restrict the generative capacity of ET and allow for language specific inventories, Charette and Göksel (1996, 1998) have proposed Licensing Constraints (LCs). LCs are parameters which control the licensing of complex expressions. As in the original version of Element Theory (Kaye, Lowenstamm and Vergnaud 1985), expressions contain one or more elements which may or may not have a single head element. In the revised Element Theory applied by Charette and Göksel (1998), head elements license their operators and which element may serve as a head and which may be licensed in the role of operator is restricted in the generation of possible expressions. Cobb (1997) and Ploch (1999) have further investigated the role of LCs and their ontology, while Kula and Marten (2000) extend constraints to harmonic processes and Kula (2002) to consonant generation. The final constraint set for a language is determined on the one hand by reaching the necessary vowel inventory, but also by capturing the behaviour of elements with regards to phonological processes such as vowel harmony (Charette and Göksel 1996; Cobb 1997; Kula and Marten 2000).

2.1.2 Tokyo Japanese vowel generation

I first consider the vowel inventory of Tokyo Japanese, consisting of the five vowels {a, i, u, e, o}. While the high back vowel is more accurately transcribed as [ɯᵝ] (Okada 1991), this vowel phonologically behaves as other rounded vowels as it labializes /h/, e.g. [oɸuro] 'bath'. For the remainder of this article, I transcribe this vowel as [u]. We must restrict our generated system such that we have no contrast between headed and headless expressions, as there is no tense and lax vowel contrast. We also aim to have no contrast between complex expressions, such as |AI| and |I_A| as there is no contrast between mid vowels such as [e], [æ] and [ɛ], as well

---

[5] It is worth noting that the version of Element Theory used here will differ from earlier accounts on Japanese (Yoshida S. 1996, Yoshida Y. 1999) using charm and element tiers. Charm was rejected due to incorrect markedness predictions and overgeneration (Charette and Göksel 1996, 1998).

as the expressions *|IU| or *|AIU| or *[y] and *[ø]. I propose the first of two possible constraint settings below as well as the generated vowel inventory.

(4) Tokyo Licensing Constraints, Option 1
    i. Operators must be licensed
    ii. A must be head
    iii. I and U may not combine

Generated inventory 1:
i |I| u |U|
    e |IA| o |UA|
          a |A|

In the generated expressions above, all simplex expressions are headed and in the complex expressions |IA| and |UA|, the head |A| licenses |I| or |U|. 'Operators must be licensed' prevents the generation of contrastive lax or [-ATR] vowels. Alternative mid-vowel expressions such as *|AI| are prevented through the constraint '|A| must be head'. The generation of the expressions *|IU| for [y] and *|AIU| for [ø] are prevented through the constraints the constraint 'I and U may not combine', which is used in the literature to reflect the status of these elements as being on the same tier (Kaye, Lowenstamm & Vergnaud 1985) or their status as 'natural heads' (Kaye Lowenstamm and Vergnaud 1985; Ploch 1999). Backley (2011) alternatively discusses them as being in inherent opposition. If this last constraint were not included, there would be the possibility of generating *|IUA| for Tokyo Japanese. Now let us consider an alternate set of constraints which generates the relevant five-vowel inventory of Tokyo Japanese.

(5) Tokyo Japanese LCs, Option 2
    i. Operators must be licensed
    ii. I must be head
    iii. U must be head

Generated inventory 2:
i |I| u |U|
    e |AI| o |AU|
          a |A|

As with the preceding constraint set, 'Operators must be licensed' prevents generation of unheaded expressions in the Tokyo Japanese inventory. Through the use of the constraints 'I must be head' and 'U must be head', the generation of unattested contrast between expressions such as |AI| and *|IA| is prevented, as well as *|IU| and *|AIU|. |I| and |U| may never combine as one of these elements would need to fulfil the role of operator, violating (5ii) or (5iii). Crucially, this constraint set does not need to refer to an arbitrary constraint such as '|I| and |U| must not combine'. I therefore propose that this constraint and element representation is the correct one. Yoshida Y. (2006) has proposed an alternate constraint set for Tokyo Japanese, claiming that only |A| may license operators, but this permits generation of |IUA|. On a final note, there are various claims that |U| is either unlinked in the underlying vowel inventory (Yoshida S. 1996) or that it is unheaded (Yoshida Y. 2006; Backley and Nasukawa 2016). A full review of these arguments is not possible due to limitations of space, but I briefly review two points. The representation of |U| as defective or unheaded is partially based on the unrounded nature of this vowel (Backley and Nasukawa 2016) and on the lesser occurrence of accent on this vowel compared to |I| (Yoshida Y. 2006). I do not follow these views. First, as previously stated, the vowel [ɯ] is not truly lacking a labial character as it is produced with lip compression (Okada 1991) and it is linked to the production of /h/ as a labial fricative in various strata including loanwords, such as [ɸɯᵝ] for 'who' and [ɸɯᵝre:] for 'hooray'.⁶ On the latter point, the fact that [ɯ] may be correlated with lower occurrence of pitch accent is possibly related to the occurrence of [ɯ] as an epenthetic vowel in loanwords and a suffixal vowel in verbs. The headless proposal for |U| is problematic in light of its behaviour in vowel sequences, where a defective or unheaded |U| would be predicted as a weak target for diphthong formation. This is clearly not the case, which we will see later in this paper.

2.1.3 The Owari Japanese vowel inventory

Now let us consider Owari Japanese (Terakawa 1985; Aichiken Kyōiku Iinkai 1989; Youngberg 2013, 2015; Ebata 2013; Hirako, Kubozono & Yamaguchi 2019) which has an expanded vowel inventory due to historical and synchronic vocalic coalescence of the diphthongs /ai/, /oi/ and /ui/ (Keshikawa 1971, 1983), giving rise to {a, i, u, e, o, æ, ø, y}. Tokyo words containing a diphthong such as [raineN] 'next year' are realised in this dialect as [ræ:neN], with historical length of the diphthong and vowel qualities retained. Synchronically, the vowels [æ:], [y:] and [ø:] are produced synchronically in adjectives when the stem is suffixed with Non-Past /-i/. The stem-final vowel surfaces unaffected in the past form suffixed with /-katta/. This is shown in (6) below.

---

6 These loanwords are commonly used in song titles and baseball chants respectively, so they are not uncommon.

(6) Non-Past and Past adjective formation in Standard and Owari Japanese

Standard NP	Standard Past	Owari NP	Owari Past	Gloss
[hikui]	[hikukat:a]	[hiky:]	[hikukat:a]	'low'
[hiroi]	[hirokat:a]	[hirø:]	[hirokat:a]	'wide'
[semai]	[semakat:a]	[semæ:]	[semakat:a]	'narrow'

The same products of coalescence are stable and do not alternate in nouns, nominal adjectives and adverbs, such as [æ:mæ:] 'unclear', [sy:ka] 'watermelon' and [kø:] 'carp', cf. Tokyo [aimai], [suika] and [koi]. I assume that if alternations are not evidenced, these vowels are lexical. The set of Owari LCs and the generated lexical inventory are presented below.

(7) Owari LCs
  i. All operators must be licensed
  ii. U must be head

Generated expressions:

i |I| y |IU| u |U|
  e |AI| ø |AIU| o |AU|
     æ |IA|
        a |A|

In the resultant Owari inventory, all expressions contain a head, as in Tokyo Japanese. The difference between the dialects is that in Owari, the elements |I|, |U| and |A| may all license operators, but only |U| may be head in complex expressions. The role of |I| is slightly different to that found in TJ as here, |I| may be either the head or the operator. Both |I| or |A| may be the head or a complex expression otherwise, generating a contrast between [e] and [æ]. We return to the behaviour of vowel sequences for both dialects in Section 3.

2.1.4 |A| as a structural configuration, revisited

One final proposal incorporated in this paper is Pöchtrager's (2006, 2015) proposal that |A| is represented as a structural configuration in order to capture the particular behaviour of the |A| element. |A| is the element *par excellence* for governing relations in many systems, with |A| being required in (underlyingly long) nasal vowels in Québec French (Ploch 1999), lexical long vowels in Montréal French (Charette, forthcoming) and surface long vowels in Yawelmani (Ploch 1999). Expressions containing |A| are good governors of both |I| and |U| in English diphthongs (Pöchtrager 2015), while |A| is required in the head of diphthongs in

German (Ploch 1999:240). |A| is also correlated with the special behaviour of alveolar clusters in English (Harris 1994a, Pöchtrager 2006), which may break the otherwise well-respected phonotactics of a language such as English, as in [paint] which has a super-heavy rhyme (Harris 1994a; Cyran 2010).

In the GP 2.0 framework initiated by Pöchtrager (2006, 2015), he proposes that |A| is formed of two Nuclear timing positions, where one point is in a type of relation called *control* with the other. Pöchtrager's goal is to redefine ET and GP entirely in terms of structure and to account for the odd behaviour of |A| (or coronality), first in relation to consonant clusters and later, in relation to vowel reduction, consonant lenition and diphthong formation.

(8) |A| from Pöchtrager (2006, 2015)

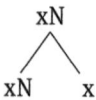

I take the proposal that |A| is structure to heart as I believe the data and arguments presented by Pöchtrager (2006, 2015) hold water, but I do not agree that an expansion of hierarchical structure and phonological tools is necessary to capture the behaviour of diphthongs. Instead, I retain only the idea that |A| is structural. This leads to it being both larger than the elements |I| and |U| and inherently different in character. However, I frame the structure of |A| within the typical structure of an elemental expression and using forces and principles already existing within the GP and ET canon.

In ET, a maximal elemental expression contains a head and one or more operator expressions and the head licenses its operator or operators (Charette and Göksel 1998). The element licensing potential of a head is received through its hosting nucleus (Harris 1992, 1997). I propose that when this relation is represented in a representational manner, a vowel such as |IU| is formed of a head element |U| which licenses an operator |I|. This is shown in (8).

(9) Sample representation of |IU| giving [y]

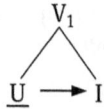

In GP 2.0, Pöchtrager (2006, 2015) proposes that a nucleus containing |A| is formed of two timing positions in a control relation (Pöchtrager 2006) or *head*

adjunction relation (Pöchtrager 2015). An example representation of [a] is given in (9). In a radical simplification of this proposal given in (10), I represent |A| as two points (the head and operator positions of an elemental expression) in a *licensing* relation. This structure is associated to a V position on the skeletal or timing tier. Note that |A| below refers not to an element, but to structure.

(10) Representation of |A| from Pöchtrager (2006, 2015)

(11) Novel representation of |A| (modified)

Throughout GP and ET, licensing is simply a force that allows one position or constituent to support another. Consider the structure of simplex |U| and complex |IU| given in (12) and (13). The representation of |A| is given in (14)

(12) Representation of simplex |U|

(13) Representation of complex |IU|

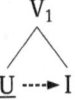

(14) Novel representation of |A| (modified)

In (12), no licensing is present as the expression is formed simply of headed |U|. In (13), the head element |U| licenses the operator |I|. Let us consider the former to be a simplex element template and the latter to be a full, complex template. In (14), licensing is present only between the positions within the full element template, but the elements |I| and |U| are absent. This structure is phonetically expressed as [a]. In a parallel to Pöchtrager's model, a schwa vowel would be a bare elemental template shown in (15), interpreted as perhaps [ə]. Finally, an entirely empty skeletal position (e.g. V_1) would be represented with no structure below the skeleton.[7]

(15)   Novel representation of [ə], drawing on Pöchtrager (2015)

The benefit of the revised representations utilised here is that there remains a division between the timing tier and melodic content, that no additional force beyond licensing is needed and no redefinition of constituency or timing tier is necessary. From this point of view, |A| is both different in character and more complex, having two 'positions', than simplex |I| or |U|. Now let us turn to the CV skeleton and briefly review the forces of government and licensing at play.

2.2 CV phonology

The second ingredient of the proposal developed here is that HR is triggered by an unlicensed empty position[8] which I frame within CV phonology (Lowenstamm 1996). Strict CV is chosen firstly because the Japanese mora is straightforwardly represented as a CV pair. In addition, it bans hierarchical structure and retains the strong predictions made regarding the existence and effects of empty categories (or more accurately, C and V positions). This builds on an earlier foundational GP work from Yoshida S. (1996) and Yoshida Y. (1999) where the syllable and mora are rejected in favour of reliance on the nucleus in accent assignment, but the major difference here is that I account for the behaviour of diphthongs without recourse to resyllabification while providing a necessary account of HR and diphthong formation with a unified trigger.

In Strict CV, syllable structure is heavily trimmed and all words are composed of alternating Consonant and Vowel positions. Hiatus is defined as two contentful

---

7 This distinction is relevant for the division of epenthesis sites and truly empty sites, as in Bendjaballah and Haiden (2008). A similar division is given by Cavirani and van Oostendorp (2019).
8 I use the term position rather than constituent as Cs and Vs are positions on a strict CV skeletal tier and not constituents containing licensing or governing relations as in Standard GP. I thank Monik Charette (P.C.) for discussion on this point.

Vs flanking an empty C. The initial structures for relevant syllable types are given below.

(16) Light syllable in [ha] 'tooth'

$$\begin{array}{cc} C_1 & V_1 \\ | & | \\ h & a \end{array}$$

(17) Geminate as in [bat:a] 'grasshopper'

$$\begin{array}{ccccc} C_1 & V_1 & C_2 & V_2 & C_3 & V_3 \\ | & | & \diagdown & \diagup & | \\ b & a & & t & & a \end{array}$$

(18) Long vowel in [ko:ri] 'ice'

$$\begin{array}{ccccc} C_1 & V_1 & C_2 & V_2 & C_3 & V_3 \\ | & \diagdown & & \diagup & | & | \\ k & o & & & r & i \end{array}$$

(19) Diphthong in [kaigi] 'meeting'

$$\begin{array}{ccccc} C_1 & V_1 & C_2 & V_2 & C_3 & V_3 \\ | & | & & | & | & | \\ k & a & & i & g & i \end{array}$$

(20) Hiatus in [kaeru] 'frog]

$$\begin{array}{ccccc} C_1 & V_1 & C_2 & V_2 & C_3 & V_3 \\ | & | & & | & | & | \\ k & a & & e & r & u \end{array}$$

In the structures above, geminates and long vowels are created by the association of a segment to two positions. Diphthongs and hiatus simply consist of two V positions flanking an empty C position, but the representations require further refinement.

Empty positions in GP and CV are further supported or silenced through the forces of licensing, which supports a position's ability realize inherent, floating, or spreading segmental content, or government, which silences them (Kaye, Lowenstamm and Vergnaud 1990, Lowenstamm 1996, Szigetvári 1999, 2013, Scheer 2004, 2012). First, I take it as fundamental that the most basic instantiation of these forces is that all nuclei (or V positions) license their preceding Onset constituent (or V position) in order to realize its segmental content (Charette 1991, Harris 1992).[9]

Next, empty positions are subject to the phonological Empty Category Principle (Kaye, Lowenstamm and Vergnaud 1990, Kaye 1995, see also Kula 2002, Scheer 2004 and Cyran 2010 for alternative formulations). These positions require government by parameter, by inter-nuclear government (or proper government), or by relations between C or V positions.

(21)   The Phonological ECP (Kaye 1995:295)
       A p-licensed (empty) category receives no phonetic interpretation.
       P-licensing:
           a. Domain-final (empty) categories are p-licensed (parameterised).
           b. Properly governed (empty) nuclei are p-licensed
           c. A nucleus within an inter-onset domain is p-licensed.

Focusing on conditions (14b) and (14c), two types of government silence empty positions. Government between nuclei, or proper government (PG) is motivated in GP and CV phonology by the existence of vowel-zero alternations in languages such as Arabic (Kaye, Lowenstamm and Vergnaud 1990; Kaye 1990; Lowenstamm 1996), French (Charette 1991), Polish (Gussmann and Kaye 1993), and Czech (Scheer 2004).

Kaye (1990) exemplifies PG in Moroccan Arabic. In short, a nucleus or V position can regressively govern and silence a preceding empty nuclear position if the governing position is filled with elemental content (lexical or epenthetic) or is itself an empty position given a phonetic interpretation. If PG succeeds, a preceding empty position remains silent and is not interpreted. Otherwise, it must receive a phonetic interpretation or be filled through assimilation or another spreading process.

Concretely, let us consider the alternation in /k_t_b/ 'write', [tan ktɨb] 'I write' [tan kɨtbu] 'we write'. The relevant representations are given in (22). In (22a) below, N_3 is empty and silent so cannot govern and silence the empty N_2. N_2 is realized phonetically as [ɨ] and being itself ungoverned, is free to govern empty N_1. However, in (22b), the suffix vowel [u] is inserted in N_3, which governs and silences empty N_2. N_2 is then unable to govern N_1, and so N_1 is realized as [ɨ].

---

[9] While Harris (1992) is the first to name Onset Licensing as a principle, Charette (1991) describes the same relation in prose. Scheer (2004) takes the CV unit as a given unit in a language without V licensing V, but I assume there is a licensing relation between these positions as the metrical status and segmental status of nuclei (filled, empty or phonetically realized empty position) has consequences on the preceding segment and syllabic structure (Charette 1991, 1992; Harris 1992, 1994, 1997; Cyran 2010).

Epenthesis and syncope in Moroccan Arabic and many other languages is thus a unified result of the conditions regarding government and its success or failure.

(22) Moroccan Arabic verbal alternations (Kaye 1990)
 a. [tan ktɨb] 'I write'

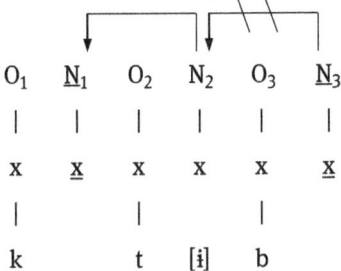

 b. [tan kɨtbu] 'We write'

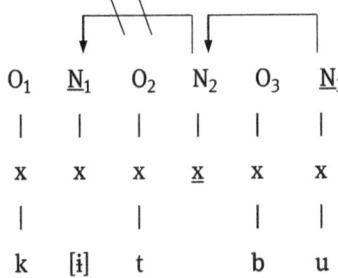

Languages may lack evidence for freely available PG and will require a further relation between Onsets or C positions; this is indeed the case for Japanese (Yoshida Y. 1999; Youngberg 2017). Onset-to-Onset government has been applied to work on Polish (Gussmann and Kaye 1993), Korean (Heo 1994), and Japanese (Yoshida S. 1996; Yoshida Y. 1999).[10] Following Yoshida Y. (1999), I presume that lateral relations between positions are necessary in order to satisfy the ECP as PG is not active in Japanese, represented below in a CV representation.

---

[10] See Charette (2003) for discussion of Onset-to-Onset government as a condition on Proper Government.

(23) Representation of a geminate as in [kap:a] 'kappa, river imp'

```
C₁   V₁   C₂   V₂   C₃   V₃
|    |         \   /        |
k    a           p          a
```

Let us now turn to licensing in long vowels. The structure of a long vowel is rather similar to that of a geminate, with a segment shared between two V positions burying and silencing an empty C position. Observations from Yoshida S. (1993), Kaye (1995), Lowenstamm (1996) and Scheer (2004) have led to the stance that the second position in a long vowel is externally licensed by a following vowel (Scheer 2004) or by virtue of being domain-final (Youngberg 2017) as in (24) and (25).

(24) Representation of [koori] 'ice'

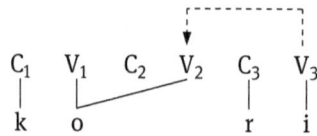

(25) Representation of [sato:] 'sugar'

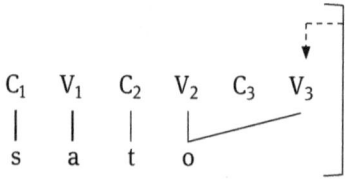

Here, I presume that the V-to-V spreading relation found above silences the empty C; an empty C does not come for free and is also targeted by the ECP.

With regards to the well-formed accent site and what type of vowels are metrically relevant, the site of a pitch accent in Japanese is defined by Yoshida Y. (1999) as a filled and unlicensed nucleus which projects, following Charette (1991). Building on this, it is claimed elsewhere (Youngberg 2017) that when translated to CV phonology, this covers governed and empty V positions in geminates as well as licensed V positions in long vowels. In simple terms, independent V positions project. If licensed or governed, Vs do not project to the level of accent assignment. Metrical status of V positions is also discussed in different terms by Scheer and Szigetvári (2005) and Faust and Ulfsbjorninn (2017). For the purposes of this article, I focus only on the CV skeleton and the first level of projection, with further cross-linguistic typology and theoretical tools discussed in the above referenced work.

With the basics established, let us now turn to the status of vowel sequences in Tokyo and Owari Japanese in Section 3 before moving on to a full analysis of HR and IVG in section 4.

3 HR in Japanese

3.1 Tokyo Japanese vowel sequences

To begin, let us examine the existing vowel sequences in Tokyo Japanese, dividing the lexicon into the Yamato (native), Sino-Japanese and Loanword strata. I rely on data drawn from normative sources (NHK 1985, Iwai and Kitahara 1995), though the accent assignment facts are in agreement with the speech of my informants and facts noted in the literature (McCawley 1968, Haraguchi 1977, Poser 1984, Kawahara 2015, Kubozono 2015). Mimetic and onomatopoeic words contain no vowel sequences, and so I do not discuss them in this paper.

3.1.1 Yamato Japanese vowel sequences in simplex words

Tables 1–3 show the attested vowel sequences found in the various lexical classes of Japanese morphemes, namely native Yamato words, Sino-Japanese morphemes and recent foreign loanwords from English, German, French and other languages. Cells marked with an asterisk are gaps not attested in mono-morphemic words, while those marked with an <H> are gaps explained by diachronic changes, discussed by Frellesvig (2010).

Table 1: Vowel sequences in Yamato morphemes.

V¹/V²	/a/	/i/	/u/	/e/	/o/
/a/		[kai]'clam'	au H	[hae] 'fly'	[ao] 'blue'
/i/	[siawase] 'happy'		iu H	[ie] 'house'	[ɕio] 'salt'
/u/	*ua	[uiro:] 'rice cake'		[ue] 'above'	[uo] 'fish'
/e/	*ea	ei H	eu H		[meoto] 'husband and wife'
/o/	*oa	[koi] 'carp'	ou H	[koe] 'voice'	

Table 2: Vowel sequences in Sino-Japanese morphemes.

V¹/V²	/a/	/i/	/u/	/e/	/o/
/a/		[ai] 'love'	*au H	*	*
/i/	*		*iu H	*	*
/u/	*	[sui] 'water'		*	*
/e/	*	*ei H	*eu H		*
/o/	*	*	*ou H	*	

Table 3: Vowel sequences in loanwords.

V¹/V²	/a/	/i/	/u/	/e/	/o/
/a/		[raibaru] 'rival'	[anaunsu] 'announce'	[baraeti] 'variety'	[kaosu] 'chaos'
/i/	[iniɕiatɕibu] 'initiative'		[kiui] 'kiwi'	[kariesu] 'caries'	[guradʑiorasu] 'gladiolus'
/u/	[njuansu] 'nuance'	[rekuiemu] 'requiem'		[rikuesuto] 'request'	[uok:a] 'vodka'
/e/	[aidea] 'idea'	[misuteiku] 'mistake'	[zeusu] 'Zeus'		[bideo] 'video'
/o/	[doa] 'door'	[hiroik:u] 'heroic'	[had:ouea] 'hardwear'	[poemu] 'poem'	

A few notes must be made regarding the above data. /Vi/ in all strata only exhibit accent on the first portion of the vowel sequence when the second half of the diphthong is in antepenultimate position, e.g. [rekúiemu] 'requiem'. Some gaps are explained historically, and native gaps may be explained through the retention of glides that were lost in other environments, with surviving glide vowel sequences being {ja, ju, jo, wa}. Finally, the sequences /ei/ and /ou/ are marginal, usually being realized as [e:] and [ou] as in <meiku> [me:ku] 'makeup'. Crucially, all vowel sequences are evidenced, with only /Vi/ sequences behaving as diphthongs.

3.1.2 Sequences in morphologically complex words

Turning to morphologically complex words, it is clear upon viewing the data that there is no restriction upon the occurrence of vowel sequences at a morpheme boundary, including identical sequences. Consider the tables below. Morphological boundaries are represented with a full stop

Table 4: Vowel sequences in complex Yamato words.

V¹/V²	/a/	/i/	/u/	/e/	/o/
/a/	[uta.awase] 'poetry contest'	[akita.inu] 'Akita (dog)'	[arabia.uma] 'Arabian horse'	[abura.e] 'oil painting'	[ama.otɕi] 'roof leak'
/i/	[ami.age] 'high laced shoes'	[ajumi.ita] 'foot/scaffold board'	[juki.usagi] 'snow rabbit'	[mi.e] 'pretension'	[hiki.otoɕi] 'debit, withdrawal'
/u/	[haru.are] 'spring storm'	[ɸuru.i] 'old-NP'	[karasu.uri] 'snake gourd'	[juku.e] 'course, direction'	[bu.otoku] 'ugly man'
/e/	[magure.atari] 'lucky shot''	[make.iro] 'signs of defeat'	[jane.ura] 'loft'	[ise.ebi] 'spiny lobster'	[kake.otɕi] 'defeat and flight'
/o/	[kumo.aɕi] 'cloud movements'	[kamo.i] 'lintel'	[ko.uri] 'retail'	[kokoro.e] 'understanding, knowledge'	[sato.oja] 'foster parent'

Table 5: Vowel sequences in Sino-Japanese complex words.

V¹/V²	/a/	/i/	/u/	/e/	/o/
/a/	[dʑa.aku] 'wicked'	[ka.i] 'effect'	[ɕa.uN] 'company fortunes'	[sa.etsu] 'examination'	[ka.oku] 'house'
/i/	[ɕi.aN] 'thought'	[tɕi.I] 'social status'	[ki.uN] 'trend'	[ki.e] 'conversion'	[ki.oku] 'memory'
/u/	[ɸu.aN] 'anxiety'	[u.iki] 'rainy area'	[ɸu.uN] 'misfortune'	[ku.eki] 'hard toil'	[hatsu.oN] 'pronunciation'
/e/	*	*ei H	*eu H	*	*
/o/	[so.aku] 'crude'	[nʲo.i] 'one's wishes'	*ou H	[o.etsu] 'weeping'	[dʑo.o:] 'queen'

The lack of systematic restrictions is due to the existence of a morpheme boundary, as in [kiuN] 'trend'. Homogenous vowel sequences such as [satooja] 'foster parent' are for some speakers phonetically identical in some realisations to long vowels found within monomorphemic words, as in Yamato [sato:] 'sugar', though a glottal stop or vowel rearticulation may also be inserted between hetero-morphemic vowels, giving [satoʔoja]. Gaps in complex Sino-Japanese words are found where HR has levelled the sequences in cells marked <H>. I assume that the gaps for *[e.a], *[e.e], and *[e.o] are accidental in Sino-Japanese words, as I find no clear cases for these sequences at a morpheme boundary. It is clear that gaps attested in complex Sino-Japanese and Yamato words are fewer in number than those in simplex words.

3.1.3 Tokyo Japanese diphthongs and hiatus

When one considers how the vowel sequences behave with regards to accent assignment, one realises that the attested sequences can be sorted into two classes. When V_2 is the vowel [i], it is a diphthong and may not receive an accent (Haraguchi 1991; Yoshida Y. 1999; Kubozono 2015). All other sequences are vowels in hiatus. Consider the data below for words of more than four moras, where the expected antepenultimate accent is pre-antepenultimate in words with diphthongs in the relevant position.

(26) Diphthong sequences with pre-antepenultimate accent (Kubozono 2015)
  a. [hok:áido:]   'Hokkaido'
  b. [masáizoku]   'Maasai Tribe'
  c. [oɕiróibana]   'Marvel-of-Peru, *Mirabilis jalapa*'
  d. [torusutóiden]   'Biography of Lev Tolstoy'
  e. [ɕinsúiɕiki]   'Ship launching ceremony'
  f. [kaisúijoku]   'Swimming in the sea'
  g. [kotozúieki]   'Bone marrow'

(27) Hiatus sequences with antepenultimate accent (Kubozono 2015)
  a. [asagaóitɕi]   'Morning glory market'
  b. [saódake]   'Bamboo pole'
  c. [kigaéɕitsu]   'changing room'
  d. [naéuri]   'seedling peddler'
  e. [bideóɕitsu]   'video room'
  f. [bideóken]   'video coupon'
  g. [aroéitɕi]   'aloe market'
  h. [donaúgawa]   'Donau river'

(28) Hiatus accent possibilities (drawn from NHK 1985, Iwai and Kitahara 1995)
  [saó] 'rod'   [áo] 'blue'
  [nué] 'chimera' [júe] 'reason'

[ié]	'home'	[hié]	'chilliness'
[shió]	'salt'	[mío]	'channel, wake'
[osaé]	'weight'	[kamáe]	'structure'

While /Va/ sequences are less common and found largely in loanwords, I note that many form hiatus sequences, such as [mademoázeru] 'mademoiselle', where the antepenultimate [a] in hiatus is accentuated, as well as [iniɕiátɕibu] 'initiative'. No similar examples exist for [ua], but gliding may break up this hiatus, giving [karu:wa] 'kahlua'. The sequence [au] is not a diphthong candidate based on the existence of accent on [u] in loanwords as in [donaúgawa] 'Donau River', though this sequence is only found in a few loanwords and at morpheme boundaries thanks to diachronic coalescence in native and SJ words with a modern reflex of [o:].

As for words that are morphologically complex, no systematic gaps are found at a morpheme boundary. As these sequences are ostensibly in separate domains, sequences are freer and may be broken up with a glottal stop or vowel re-articulation (McCawley 1968, Vance 2008). The existence of any diphthongs or long vowels is, I propose, not possible when the relevant vowels straddle a morphological boundary, as in the commonly cited example *sato-oja* 'foster parent', realised as [satoʔoja], versus *satoo-ja* 'sugar seller' [sato:ja] (cf. McCawley 1968, Labrune 2012:45).

Two processes affect vowels in hiatus in TJ, with the first being gliding and the second being epenthesis of a glottal stop or vowel rearticulation. Let us consider gliding. According to Kawahara (2003), an optional process of glide insertion is active in Japanese. Gliding gives rise only to the sequences [ja] [ju] [jo] and [wa], which are phonotactically permitted in other strata of the lexicon. (McCawley 1968; Vance 1987, 2008; Yoshida S. 1996; Yoshida Y. 1999; Frellesvig 2010). No novel sequences are introduced.

(29) Gliding in hiatus sequences (Modified slightly from Kawahara 2003:11)
    a) /ia/ => [ija]:
        i. [dai(j)a] 'diamond' (loan)
        ii. [pi(j)ano] 'piano' (loan)
        iii. [si(j)awase] 'happiness' (Yamato)
        iv. [sai(j)aku] 'worst' (Sino-Japanese)
    b) /io/ => [ijo]:
        i. [i(j)on] 'ion' (loan)
        ii. [oni(j)on] 'onion,' (loan)
        iii. [rai(j)on] 'lion' (loan)

c) /ea/ => [eja]:
    i. [he(j)a]   'hair'   (loan)
    ii. [pe(j)a]   'pair'   (loan)
    iii. [e(j)akon]   'air conditioning'   (loan)

d) /ua/ => [uwa]:
    i. [gu(w)ai]   'condition'   (Sino-Japanese)
    ii. [karuu(w)a]   'kahlua'   (loan)
    iii. [ɸu(w)an]   'worry'   (Sino-Japanese)

e) /oa/ => [owa]:
    i. [do(w)a]   'door'   (loan)
    ii. [o(w)aɕisu]   'oasis'   (loan)
    iii. [ko(w)ara]   'koala'   (loan)

Above, gliding occurs where a diphthong cannot be formed and where a glide is permitted to occur before the following vowel, such as [a] or [o].

Martin (1987:13), McCawley (1968) and Vance (1987:14–15) have noted that preceding a vowel with no onset, a glottal stop is often realised. Vance (2008:58) provides further acoustic evidence that process is also manifested as vowel re-articulation. According to McCawley, the process of glottal stop insertion is evidenced word-initially in the simplex words [ʔahiru] 'duck' and [ʔitɕi] 'one' and in the morphologically complex words /oN-iN-roN/ [ʔoNʔiNroN] 'phonology', /su-uri/ [suʔuri] 'vinegar seller' and /wara-u/ [waraʔu] 'laugh-NP' (McCawley 1968). Importantly, McCawley (1968) observes that a glottal stop never breaks up a long vowel or diphthong. The author does not explicitly discuss the case of vowels in hiatus explicitly, such as [hae] 'fly', but does note glottal insertion in certain examples within the text. Glottal stop insertion is of course not obligatory and may be absent, cf. Poser (1984). The main outcome here is that rearticulation or glottal stop insertion never occurs in diphthongs.

3.2 HR in Owari Japanese

Let us briefly review the HR facts for Owari Japanese. As noted in section 2, diphthongs are not found in this dialect but rather /ai/, /oi/ and /ui/ are realised as [æ:], [ø:] and [y:].[11] This change is lexicalized within a word, but active in affixed

---

11 There are some Tokyo words with [ae] which have cognates with Owari [æ:] as in [kaeru] and [kæ:ru] 'to go home' but this is due to reduction of /ae/ to /ai/ historically; this is irregular (Keshikawa 1971, Youngberg 2013).

adjectives, as in [samy:] 'cold-NP', Tokyo [samui]. Hiatus sequences result anywhere else, as in [sao] 'rod', [koe] 'voice' [kotaeru] 'answer' and [sakiototoɕi] '3 years ago'. Hiatus is not realised with gliding or glottal stop epenthesis, but these vowels do not undergo coalescence. Some exceptions to coalescence are found, however, in the case of noun-noun compounds. I discuss these in section 4.

(30) Owari compound noun exceptions (Ebata 2013)

    a. [koibi]   'little finger'   [ko] 'small'   + [ibi] 'finger'
    b. [nakaibi] 'middle finger' [naka] 'middle + [ibi] 'finger
    c. [yosoiki] 'going out'   [yoso] 'outside' + [iki] 'go-NOMZ'
    d. [wataire] 'cotton stuffed' [wata]'cotton'   + [ire]'stuff-NOMZ'

Having reviewed the facts, we must now consider how to divide the diphthongs {ai, oi, ui} from other vowel sequences, and how to motivate HR within CV and ET.

4 Capturing diphthongs and HR

In this section, I turn to previous proposals and the current IVG proposal. While full analyses of HR are inexistent in the GP literature, it is worth considering previous proposals for diphthong formation. Here, I focus on accounts relevant to the analysis to come, namely nuclear fusion (Yoshida S. 1996; Yoshida Y. 1999) or relations between V positions (Szigetvári 1999, 2011; Caratini 2009).

4.1 Previous proposals for diphthong formation

To capture the behaviour of long vowels and diphthongs when Japanese has no underlying branching nuclei, Yoshida S. (1991:94–96; 1996) proposes that adjacent nuclei separated by an empty onset undergo nuclear fusion (NF). NF operates '. . . If (i) N_1 and N_2 are linked to a charmed segment and simplex charmless segments respectively, or (ii) N_1 and N_2 are linked to a single segment.' (Yoshida S. 1991:94). Without delving into charm, it is enough to say that the vowels {a, i, u, e, o} are represented as |A⁺|, |I°|, |U°|, |AI°| and |AU°|. The model predicts that only |A| can govern |U| or |I| and create a diphthong, as in [ɕakáigaku] 'sociology'. Sequences such as [ao] do not meet these conditions, and so a hiatus sequence with two independent nuclei surfaces as in [aómuɕi] 'caterpillar'. In the fused nucleus, the first skeletal point governs the second under Constituent Government (KLV 1990). I exemplify this process below.

(31) Nuclear fusion in a diphthong /ai/

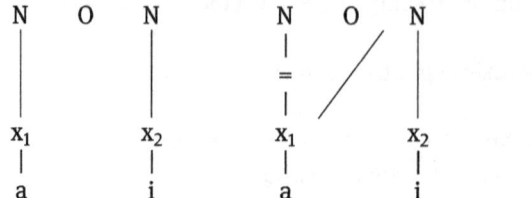

(32) Lack of nuclear fusion in hiatus e.g. [ao]

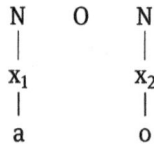

Yoshida Y. (1999) relies on NF to account for non-accentuation of diphthongs. Consider the following derivation from Yoshida Y. (1999:105). Below, skeletal point x_4 associated to N_2 re-associates to N_3, forming a branching nucleus. This skeletal point x_4 is the governor and head of a surface branching nucleus. This head is the site of interpretation for the accent assigned to this nucleus.

(33) Underlying representation of [ɕakáigaku] 'sociology'

O_1	N_1	O_2	N_2	O_3	N_3	O_4	N_4	O_5	N_5
x_1	x_2	x_3	x_4		x_5	x_6	x_7	x_8	x_9
ɕ	a	k	á		i	g	a	k	u

(34) Representation of [ɕakáigaku] 'sociology' following nuclear fusion

O_1	N_1	O_2	N_2	O_3	N_3	O_4	N_4	O_5	N_5
x_1	x_2	x_3	x_4	>>	x_5	x_6	x_7	x_8	x_9
ɕ	a	k	á		i	g	a	k	u

I argue NF in fact provides an analysis where branching nuclei are present but only on the surface, introducing branching constituents through a back door. Complexity and charm correctly exclude {ae, ue, oe, ua} and other hiatus sequences, but it is undesirable that the theory wrongly predicts the set of diphthongs to be {au, ai} and excludes {oi, ui}. The role of the elements and complexity must be considered in further detail, as charm has been discarded, and the general role of the empty onset should be revisited.

Other positions have been described for diphthongs within CV phonology. First is the idea that diphthongs are two vocalic positions in a licensing relation (Szigetvári 1999, 2013; Cyran 2010), with Szigetvári (2013) proposing that V_2 licenses V_1 in a diphthong. The word [kaigi] 'meeting' is used in the below examples.

(35) Diphthong as a licensing relation

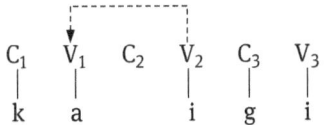

The issue here is that V_2 in a vowel sequence is unlicensed, ungoverned and has no diminished power in comparison to V_2 in hiatus, which simply lacks this licensing relation. V_2 would be capable of projecting to the metrical level where pitch accent is assigned (Yoshida Y. 1999, Youngberg 2017), which makes the incorrect prediction that V_2 would support high tone or pitch accent assignment in both hiatus and diphthongs.

Caratini (2009) proposes that diphthongs are formed in German with a spreading relation from V_1 to V_2. While this captures the fact that V_1 may influence the segmental content of V_2 as in Owari Japanese, it is unclear how V_2 is metrically restricted and what conditions affect spreading.

(36) Diphthong as a spreading relation

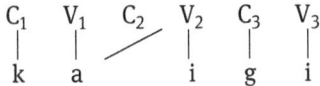

Elsewhere, Polgárdi (2015) proposes that English diphthongs are VC sequences, which is inappropriate if V_2 supports an accent or tone. Pimenta (2019) examines European Portuguese diphthongs and differentiates them from hiatus by using complex structures below the skeleton, but importing this analysis would reintroduce branching structures which I attempt to avoid in order to provide a parallel structure for all 'moras' as a CV unit. However, these analyses cannot capture the facts of Japanese under the aims of reducing skeletal structure and treating a diphthong as two vowels.

4.2 Diphthong formation as IVG

I propose a new form of government, Intervocalic Government (IVG). This aims to satisfy the ECP, with its success dependent on the elemental content of V_1 and V_2. This proposal is similar in spirit to Infrasegmental Government (Scheer 2004), where a governing relation between two segments in C positions silences the empty V position within, forming a TR cluster (i.e. branching onset). IVG forms between two segments below the CV tier. Consider the examples below, with government represented with a solid arrow.

(37) Representation of [kaigi] 'meeting'

$$\begin{array}{ccccc} C_1 & V_1 & C_2 & V_2 & C_3 & V_3 \\ | & | & & | & | & | \\ k & a & & i & g & i \\ & |A| & \longrightarrow & |I| & & \end{array}$$

(38) Representation of [kaeru] 'frog'

$$\begin{array}{ccccc} C_1 & V_1 & C_2 & V_2 & C_3 & V_3 \\ | & | & & | & | & | \\ k & a & & e & r & u \\ & |A| & & |I| & & \\ & & & |A| & & \end{array}$$

4.2.1 Elemental complexity in diphthongs and hiatus

In hiatus sequences, the first vowel is one of the set {a, i, u, o}, while the second vowel is {a, e, u, o}.[12] Represented in elements, there is a rise in elemental complexity in words where the first vowel is {a, i, u} and the second is {o, e}; that is, V_1 is a simplex expression comprising a single element, while V_2 is a compound expression containing two elements. Examples include [ie] 'house', [ue] 'above' and [amae] 'dependency' or [uo] 'fish', [ɕio] 'salt' and [ao] 'blue'. When the hiatus is [oe] as in

---

12 Further sequences may be found in loanwords but may have their hiatus broken by glide insertion, discussed by Kawahara (2003).

[koe] 'voice' or [eo] as in [meoto] 'husband and wife', the vowels are represented as |A̲U̲| and |A̲I̲| with an equal complexity profile. Hiatus is also found where the second member is |A| or |U| and equal or falling complexity profiles may be found, as in [au] in [kaunto] 'count' and [ia] in [piano] 'piano' or [doa] 'door' and [hea] 'hair'.

Diphthongs, on the other hand, always have {a, o, u} in the first V position and [i] in the second position. The elements found in the first V position of a diphthong are |A̲|, |A̲U̲| and |U̲| while the second position is always |I̲|. In a diphthong, V_1 is more complex than V_2 in the case of [oi], while V_1 is equally complex as V_2 in the case of [ai] and [ui].

The formation of IVG is dependent upon two initial conditions. First, there must be no segment separating the two V positions – the trigger for diphthong formation and HR is the empty C position, which must be governed in order to satisfy the ECP, triggering IVG. Second, the first vowel position must be more or as complex as the governee, as per the Complexity Condition (KLV 1990, Harris 1994a), reproduced below.

(39) **The Complexity Condition** (Harris 1994a:170)
Let α and β be melodic expressions occupying the positions A and B respectively.
Then, if A governs B, β is no more complex than α.

Initially, let us assume that IVG is complexity-based government between segments from left to right, forming wherever it can apply. A hiatus sequence results from failure of IVG, and two individual V positions are the outcome. This is similar to the proposal from Yoshida Y. (1991), but crucially IVG does not involve branching constituents or charm. Let us first consider the diphthong [oi] as in [oçiróibana]'Marvel of Peru (flower)'.

(40) Representation of [oçiróibana]'Marvel of Peru (flower)'

C_1 V_1 C_2 V_2 C_3 V_3 C_4 V_4 C_5 V_5 C_6 V_6
　　　|　　　|　　　|　　　|　　　|　　　|　　　|　　　|　　　|
　　o　　ç　　i　　r　　o　→　i　　b　　a　　n　　a
　　　　　　　　　　　　　　|U̲|　　|I̲|
　　　　　　　　　　　　　　|A|

Consider V_3 and V_4, which form a diphthong. |A̲U̲| is more complex than the |I̲| or [i]. The Complexity Condition is easily satisfied, as V_3 is more complex than V_4, and a governing relation contracts, represented with a solid arrow. V_4 does not project, being governed, and accent is assigned to the pre-antepenultimate V_3, the antepenultimate projectable nucleus.

Now let us consider words containing the diphthongs [ai] and [ui], such as [masáizoku] 'Masai tribe' and [kaisúijoku] 'swimming in the sea'. The representation for each is shown below.

(41)   Representation of [masáizoku] 'Masai tribe'

$$C_1 \quad V_1 \quad C_2 \quad V_2 \quad C_3 \quad V_3 \quad C_4 \quad V_4 \quad C_5 \quad V_5$$
$$|\,|\,|\,|\,|\,|\,|\,|$$
$$m \quad a \quad s \quad a \longrightarrow i \quad z \quad o \quad k \quad u$$
$$|A||I|$$

(42)   Representation of [kaisúijoku] 'Swimming in the sea'

$$C_1 \quad V_1 \quad C_2 \quad V_2 \quad C_3 \quad V_3 \quad C_4 \quad V_4 \quad C_5 \quad V_5 \quad C_6 \quad V_6$$
$$|\,|\,|\,|\,|\,|\,|\,|\,|\,|\,|$$
$$k \quad a \longrightarrow i \quad s \quad u \longrightarrow i \quad j \quad o \quad k \quad u$$
$$|A||I||U||I|$$

In words containing [ai] and [ui], the Complexity Condition is satisfied as the complexity between the segments is equal. IVG thus enacts. A diphthong can form when a V position contains |A| or |U|, and these positions govern a position containing |I|, but the reverse sequences are not possible. Note that the reverse vowel sequence [ia] is largely absent in modern Standard Japanese while, *[iu] has undergone gliding and compensatory lengthening historically e.g. <iu> 'to say' is now [ju:]. These sequences may be found in loanwords as in [radʑiumu] 'radium' or [ɕiata:] 'theatre', but these sequences show no behaviour typical of diphthongs. It is clear that equal complexity does not *automatically* convert into an IVG relation, and that we ought to consider other factors.

4.2.2 |A| as a good governor through structure

Let us consider now the governing property of |A|. Why is it possible for it to govern |I|? The answer is structure. Recall that I represent |A| as two points in a *licensing* relation associated to a V position.

(43)   Representation of |A| (modified)

Here, I show that the points composing |A| are themselves in a licensing relation, giving [a]. From this point of view, the complexity condition is satisfied as |A| is more complex in structure than |I|, which consists solely of an element associated to the V position. Let us consider why |U| is a good governor, even though it is simplex.

4.2.3 |U| as a good governor through inequality of the elements

What is more mysterious is why the sequence |U|-|I| is permitted to form a diphthong, but the sequence |I|-|U| is not. One could first argue that the rarity of /iu/ sequences is solely due to diachronic HR, with gliding occurring before diphthongization. Under this view, |I| evacuated its V position to join the preceding C position and form a palatalised glide followed by a vowel during Middle Japanese (cf. Poser 1986), while |U| did not have the same potential as labialised glides were restricted. The [ui] sequences then later formed a diphthong. These arguments say nothing about the reason why [ui] behaves as a diphthong and not [iu]. Diachronic sound change has little to do with explaining synchronic facts. The sequence [iu] *is* in fact acceptable in modern loanwords such as [radʑiumu] 'radium' or [ɕimpodʑiumu] 'symposium', and [iu] here exhibits no special accentual behaviour.

I propose that a V position dominating |U| has the potential to govern a V position dominating |I|, while the opposite governing relation is not possible, making |U| a better governor than |I| as perhaps it is the stronger element. It should be noted that other languages display a difference between the abilities afforded to |I| and |U| and expressions which contain them. One example is Turkish, which has unrestricted harmony of |I|, while |U| is restricted in its ability to spread (Charette and Göksel 1996, 1998). Pöchtrager (2015) also notes cases where |I| and |U| are unequal with respect to their distribution in Putonghua (Mandarin Chinese) rimes, English diphthongs and Japanese glide-vowel combinations. Here, |U| may govern |I| and form a diphthong through IVG, but |I| fails to govern |U| and results in hiatus.

4.2.4 |A| and |U|

I must point out that |A| cannot govern |U|, which is not predicted by the theoretical account provided here. I base this on loanword examples, with only two clear cases of [au] exhibiting hiatus-like behaviour, namely [donaúgawa] 'Donau river' and [rindaújiN] 'person from Lindau' noted by Kubozono (2015). I assume here too that |U| cannot be governed, though this is perhaps otherwise expected (c/w English having [ai] and [au] as diphthongs). It is worth noting that [au] sequences mostly occur in verbal non-past forms, such as /kana-u/ [kanau] 'come true-NP', and *[au] is otherwise absent due to sound change except in loans. This is also the case for compounded or prefixed forms with V*u*, such as /ta/ 'rice field' + /ue-/ 'to plant' giving [taue] 'rice planting' or /ko/ 'child, small' + /ume/ 'plum blossom' [koume] 'small plum blossom'.[13] It is possible that the inability of |U| to be governed is based on induction during the learning process, where /au/ and other V*u* sequences are always heteromorphemic in non-loanword strata.

4.2.5 Hiatus sequences as the result of IVG failure

Now let us consider hiatus sequences. Vowels in hiatus are composed of two V positions, but either position is accentable. Some minimal hiatus pairs are repeated below.

(44) Hiatus accent possibilities (sample)

[saó]	'rod'	[áo]	'blue'
[nué]	'chimera'	[júe]	'reason'
[ié]	'home'	[híe]	'chilliness'
[ɕió]	'salt'	[mío]	'channel, wake'
[osaé]	'weight'	[kamáe]	'structure'

The theory *must* accommodate the possibility of accent on both V_1 and V_2 in hiatus. Formally, this is captured through the projection of an unlicensed and ungoverned nuclear or V position (Yoshida Y. 1999; Youngberg 2017, 2021).[14] Recall that hiatus shows no accent shift effects, e.g. [hikaéɕitsu] 'waiting room' with antepenultimate accent and not pre-antepenultimate. Hiatus sequences can be defined as two independent V positions with no governing relation. Hiatus is formed when IVG *cannot* be enacted and fails, as the potential governor is typically less complex than the governee. Sample representations are shown in (45), with failure of government represented with a crossed solid line.

---

13 I thank a reviewer for asking about these forms. These words and many others are formed of combined bound morphemes, independent nominal morphemes and deverbal nouns or stems. They are not necessarily productive in the modern language, but they are always easily recognized as composed of independent nouns, verbs stems or components of nouns or names. While part of this recognition may be orthographic and related to the *kanji* ideographs, it is clear that the a+u or o+u boundary is recognized as the division between morphemes.

14 Following the formalism of Yoshida Y. (1999) who builds on Charette (1991), a stress or tone supporting nucleus are those which are unlicensed and ungoverned which project in order to be 'metrically' licensed at the nuclear projection. Not that no constituents such as the Foot are formally recognized in GP. See also Scheer and Szigetvári (2005)

(45) Hiatus sequences, as in [nue] 'chimera', [ɕio] 'salt' and [hae] 'fly'.

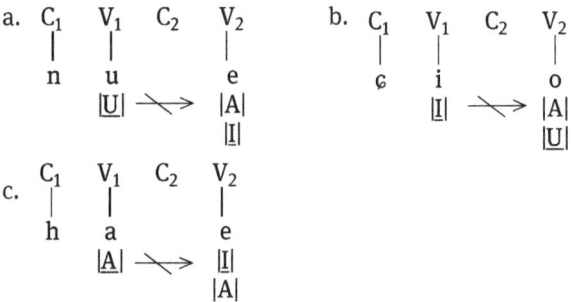

However, the current definition of IVG as being reliant on complexity cannot account for failure in the sequences with equal complexity terminating in |A| or an expression containing |A|, namely [ia], [ua], [eo] and [oe], nor those sequences where falling complexity is found in the hiatus sequences [ea] and [oa]. Let us first consider [ia] and [ua].

4.2.6 The role of |A| in hiatus formation – minimality revisited

Now, let us consider why IVG fails in a word such as [pi(j)ano] 'piano', allowing the empty C to be vulnerable to gliding. I propose that IVG fails to form a diphthong in the sequences [ia] and [ua] as |A| is a licensing domain, and this domain cannot be externally governed through IVG as this would violate the Minimality Condition (Charette 1989).

The relevance of the Minimality Condition (Chomsky 1986) to phonology is proposed by Charette (1989) to account for the observed fact that branching constituents remain resistant to phonological processes. One example of this is Korean umlaut, which affects only short vowels, never long.[15] This is seen in noun and noun-nominative alternations like [pam] 'night' [pæmi] 'night-NOM', but [pa:m] 'chestnut' [pa:mi] 'chestnut-NOM', *[pæ:mi]. Umlaut is analysed by Charette as the spread of |I| under inter-nuclear government from a following nucleus. Branching nuclei are protected from umlaut by the effects of Minimality. I repeat the portion of the Minimality Condition (Chomsky 1986:42) used by Charette (1989) below.

---

[15] I am aware that the length distinction is largely lost for younger South Korean speakers, but the length facts are historically accurate.

(46) The Minimality Condition (Narrow interpretation)
In the configuration . . .α. . .[γ. . .δ. . .β. . .], α does not govern β if γ is the immediate projection of δ excluding α.

In short, the Minimality Condition excludes alteration of a branching nucleus or onset as they are governing domains. The benefit of this condition is that geminate inalterability (Hayes 1989) and the resistance of long vowels both fall out from one condition. It is unnecessary to devote fuller discussion of this condition to the current framework; it must be reformulated as branching constituents are banned in Strict CV, and the government found within and across branching constituents and their skeletal points within Standard GP is entirely absent.

I argue that the spirit of this principle and its benefits can be reformulated as a ban on the attempted government of licensing domains, found in CV long vowels, or governing domains, found in CV as Infrasegmental Government (Scheer 2004) C-to-C domains (Cyran 2010, Szigetvári 2013) and IVG (proposed here). I put forth a proposal for Revised CV Minimality below.

(47) Revised CV Minimality
A segment α in position A cannot govern segment β in Position B if position B or segment β is in a governing or licensing relation.

The above condition would prevent the government of long vowels or geminates and IVG domains. Now recall that the licensing relation in the |A| structure is associated to a V position. As an additional effect, Minimality excludes all government of positions containing |A|, which I have characterised as a licensing domain.[16] IVG cannot enact in the sequence [ia] or [ua] as Minimality would be violated.

(48) Failure of |I| governing |A|

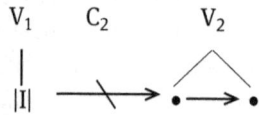

Let us now extend this line of reasoning to the sequences [ea] and [oa]. Without referring to the revised structure of |A| and Minimality, there is no reason why

---

[16] This also predicts that the complex expression cannot occur in V_2, as the structure of [y] would contain a licensing relation.

IVG should fail as the Complexity Condition is satisfied. A word such as [doa] 'door' exhibits optional gliding as in [dowa], meaning the empty C is not silenced within an IVG governing domain. I claim that the failure of IVG here too is due to Minimality. I adapt the structure of [o] from Pöchtrager (2015) which contains |U| in the complement position.

(49) Failure of |AU| governing |A|

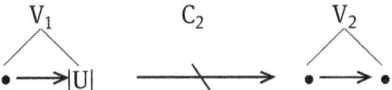

4.2.7 IVG failure and minimality extended – [oe] and [eo]

Now let us consider words with the sequence [oe] as in [koe] 'voice' or [eo] as in [meoto] 'husband and wife'. Accent may be placed on either V, as in the minimal pair [koé] 'manure' and [kóe] 'voice', or found on the antepenultimate vowel as in compound examples like [bideóɕitsu] 'video room'.[17] The vowels are equal in their complexity, but as both positions are accentable, it is clear that IVG fails and [oe] must be analysed as a hiatus. Again, IVG fails as [e] contains the |A| structure which is a licensing domain; IVG cannot enact or Minimality would be violated.

(50) Representation of [koe] 'manure'

$$
\begin{array}{cccc}
C_1 & V_1 & C_2 & V_2 \\
| & | & & | \\
k & o & & e \\
& |U| & + & |I| \\
& |A| & & |A|
\end{array}
$$

(51) Failure of |AU| governing |AI|, leading to hiatus in [oe]

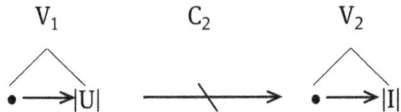

---

17 This is the only nominal pair of words exhibiting accent on either vowel. The only other simplex accented words listed in Iwai and Kitahara (1995) are [tatóe] 'even if, ADV' and [oboé] 'memory'.

4.3 Gliding and epenthesis as ECP satisfaction

Gliding and glottal stop insertion or vowel re-articulation can be found in hiatus. Gliding is easily analysed as the spreading of the elements |I| or |U| from a V position into a following empty and ungoverned C position, as in [he(j)a] 'hair'. IVG fails and gliding operates in order to satisfy the ECP. This process only operates where the elements |U| and |I| form phonotactically permitted glide-vowel sequences, i.e. no formation of *[we].[18]

(52)   Gliding in [he(j)a] 'hair'

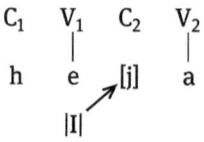

Glottal stop 'insertion', or vowel re-articulation, occurs in hiatus contexts where gliding is not possible due to aforementioned phonotactic restrictions on [j] and [w]. As IVG fails in these contexts, the ECP remains unsatisfied and the empty C position must be realized if possible. I claim that re-articulation or epenthesis are the phonetic interpretation of an ungoverned empty C.

Now let us consider empty C positions at morpheme boundaries. Here, glide insertion is blocked (Kawahara 2003). McCawley (1968) has claimed that glottal stop insertion occurs at morpheme boundaries and separates all vowel sequences, even where diphthong formation is otherwise expected. This is found in a complex word such as [kurumaʔído] 'well with a pulley', formed from the morphemes /kuruma/ 'wheel, car' and /ído/ 'well' as in (46).

(53)   Structure of [kurumaʔído] 'well with a pulley'

$$\left[\begin{array}{cccccc} C_1 & V_1 & C_2 & V_2 & C_3 & V_3 \\ | & | & | & | & | & | \\ k & u & r & u & m & a \end{array} \quad \begin{array}{ccc} C_4 & V_4 & C_5 & V_5 \\ | & | & | & | \\ [ʔ] & i & d & o \end{array} \right]$$

---

[18] This process is slightly more complicated and it seems to me, anecdotally, that some speakers indeed glide in the sequence [ue] as in [ue] 'above' or [uwe]. This requires further systematic investigation in the field. In addition, Kawahara (2003) notes that gliding does not seem to affect [iu], [eu] and [eo], but I assume for the time being that this is due to phonotactic glide restrictions.

This word is formed of two independent morphemes, which I assume at PF is formed of two analytic domains (Kaye 1995) of the shape ((noun)(noun)), giving [kuruma] and [ido] or [[kuruma][ido]]. The inner domains are scanned by phonology individually, concatenated and the entire noun is scanned again.[19] Without reference to the morphologically complex nature of this word, a diphthong is predicted to surface but this is not the case. In the processing of this word, IVG is prevented from applying not by the segmental context, but by the fact that each morpheme is assessed by the phonology individually and then concatenated for further processing. In the resultant word [kurumaʔido], the glottal stop (or vowel re-articulation) is the realisation of an empty and ungoverned C position in the cycle processing [ido]. C_4 violates the ECP in and it is realized phonetically as [ʔ], as V positions in Japanese have no power to freely govern. IVG is not enacted in the full cycle of the concatenated word as C_4 is no longer in violation of the ECP, having been interpreted.

Kawahara (2003) claims that gliding is blocked in compound noun, adjective and verbal formation, and the reason here is domain structure. This can be seen in the adjectival compound [muɕiʔatsui] 'muggy' formed from the constituent terms /muɕi/ 'humidity' and /atsui/ 'hot-NP', which I analyse as [muɕi][atsui]. The segmental conditions for gliding are met, but *[muɕijatsui] is not attested. I argue that here too gliding is blocked by domain structure and cyclicity – gliding cannot affect the empty C as it has already been interpreted and no HR is necessary as the ECP is not violated in the full domain.

4.4 Coalescence of diphthong sequences in Owari Japanese

In contrast to the Tokyo dialect, the Owari dialect has no diphthongs and any such sequences found in Tokyo Japanese are coalesced. Hiatus exists, but undergoes no other process. We have seen earlier that coalescence applied diachronically in morphologically simplex forms wherever a /Vi/ sequence is found, while synchronically it applies in adjectives. This is seen in the surface form [samy:] 'cold-NP' from underlying /samu-i/, cf. Tokyo [samui]. However, the stem is realized without alteration when affixed with consonant initial suffixes, as in /samu/ 'cold and /-kat:a/ 'PAST', as in [samukat:a] 'cold-PAST'. Consider the underlying

---

19 In depth discussion of Kaye (1995) is found in Scheer (2011). I assume simply that domains are scanned and any necessary licensing, governing or element assimilation processes in the language apply.

and surface representations of the stem and non-past suffix below in 0. IVG is shown with a solid line.

(54) UR of /samu-i/ 'cold-NP/
   a. Underlying form /samu-i/ with IVG

   C_1 V_1 C_2 V_2 C_3 V_3
   | | | | |
   s   a   m   u   →   i
                        |U| |I|

   b. Surface form [samy:] 'cold-NP'

   C_1 V_1 C_2 V_2 C_3 V_3
   | | | |
   s   a   m   y
                        |U|
                        |I|

This word has the analytic shape of ((A)B) or ((stem)suffix) and here, coalescence is a side effect of IVG, rather than a separate HR process. In the full domain, C_3 is empty and requires a governor in order to satisfy the ECP. IVG applies and the elements fuse while being shared across both positions, producing [y:].[20] Note that each element preceding coalescence is headed. Upon combination, one element *must* be demoted to the status of operator. In order to respect the lexical LCs discussed in Section 2, |I| is relegated to the status of operator. The resultant expression representing [y] is |IU|. Such an analysis also accounts for the vowels [ø] and [æ], with |I| being demoted to the role of operator as retention of elements is preferable to their non-realization.[21] Hiatus results where IVG fails, as in Tokyo Japanese, giving rise to sequences such as [sao] 'rod'. No further elaboration is necessary.

There are some limited lexical exceptions to coalescence in Owari Japanese; predictably, these words are nominal compounds. Consider the following exceptions evidenced in Ebata (2013).

---

[20] This is not dissimilar to Bemba coalescence in Kula (2002), but I do not rely on regressive inter-nuclear government. The present analysis will be extended to Bantu and Semitic diphthong formation, gliding and coalescence in further work.

[21] See Youngberg (2017) for discussion of a Tokyo dialect discussed by Kubozono (2015), where the |I| element is in fact deleted as complex expressions where |I| is not head are not licensed by the LCs of this dialect. A similar case also obtains for one speaker of Kagoshima Japanese (field notes, April 2019), but it is unclear to me how systematic coalescence is here.

(55) Owari compound noun exceptions (Ebata 2013)
   a. [koibi]   'little finger'   [ko] 'small'   + [ibi] 'finger'
   b. [nakaibi] 'middle finger'   [naka] 'middle'   + [ibi] 'finger
   c. [yosoiki] 'going out'   [yoso] 'outside'   + [iki] 'go-NOMZ'
   d. [wataire] 'cotton stuffed'   [wata] 'cotton'   + [ire] 'stuff-NOMZ'

Note that these words do not constitute exceptions to coalescence as they are composed of two analytic domains of the shape ((noun)(noun)). Consider the representation of the word [koibi] 'little finger' below, which I assume is composed of the domains [[ko][ibi]]. The surface [oi] sequence straddles the boundary between the [A] and [B] domains.

(56) Structure of [koibi] 'little finger'

$$\left[\begin{array}{cc}\begin{bmatrix}C_1 & V_1 \\ | & | \\ k & o\end{bmatrix} & \begin{bmatrix}C_2 & V_2 & C_3 & V_3 \\ | & | & | & | \\ & i & b & i\end{bmatrix}\end{array}\right]$$

While Ebata (2013) does not note glottal stop realization in these forms and I have been unable to elicit this word from speakers in person, I assume that IVG does not apply as C_2 in this form is already processed in the first cycle and that further alteration to the righthand term of the compound is banned through cyclicity.

5 Further issues

This proposal is a first step to considering a new analysis of diphthong formation and HR. The main outcome is that 1) HR is satisfaction of the ECP and 2) diphthongization is formation of an intervocalic governing relation, with the structure of the element |A| playing a crucial role in it's success or failure.

Some further areas of investigation remain. First, investigation into HR in languages without diphthongs is necessary, namely languages such as Bemba (Kula 2002). Second, the inequality of |I| and |U| remains an issue for Element Theory. I must stipulate above that |U| cannot be governed, but this does not follow from any principled explanation besides the extreme rarity of /Vu/ sequences in common words. On a further note, it is clear that the role of LCs and the Complexity Condition should be re-evaluated. The theory of LCs requires a rethink as it is not necessary to capture the intervocalic interactions modelled here, while the Complexity Condition is largely redundant if we rely on Minimality. A more streamlined view of ET and CV phonology is possible and will be pursued henceforth.

Additionally, it is necessary to consider languages where [a] or [ə] are the second portion of a true diphthong as the government of the |A| structure invoked above is predicted to be impossible. What is clear at this point is that this needs to be refined. Briefly turning to New York English, r-dropping gives rise to diphthongs terminating in [ə] such as [dɔə] 'door', derived from coda /ɪ/, represented as |A|. I tentatively propose that [ə] does not have an identical structure to |A|; while it is derived from |A|, lenition weakens the structure and associates it to the available V position and [ə] is composed only of the points below a V position. IVG in [dɔə] does not violate Minimality here as |A| without a licensing relation to produce [a] is not a licensing domain. What is more problematic for the theory is a language with true /Va/ diphthongs, with one possible candidate being Crow (Krämer and Golston 2020). My initial proposal to capture such diphthongs is the parameterization of IVG, not just from OFF to ON, but with IVG having further parameters controlling the government of |I|, |U|, and then the government of |A| or [ə] and [a] being nested parameters to reflect the markedness of a diphthong like [ea], similar to the markedness of licensing parameters discussed in Charette (1991, 1992) and element licensing in Harris (1992, 1997), developed into licensing scales by Cyran (2010). The final question is whether the structure of |A| above can give rise to a new element geometry, where |I| and |U| being associated to the positions creating |A| is sufficient, and whether the licensor and licensee positions within the |A| structure can replace the head and operator distinctions. Further consideration of these issues will be explored in future work.

Abbreviations

CV	CV phonology
ECP	Empty Category Principal
ET	Element Theory
GP	Government Phonology
IVG	Intervocalic Government
LC	Licensing Constraint
PG	Proper Government
NF	Nuclear Fusion
NOM	Nominative
NOMZ	Nominalized
NP	Non Past

References

Aichiken Kyōiku Iinkai. 1989. *Aichi-ken no hōgen. [The dialect of Aichi Prefecture]*. Nagoya: Bunkazai Tosho Kankōkai.

Andersen, Henning. 1972. Diphthongization. *Language* 48 (1). 11–50.

Aoki, Paul K. 1974. An observation of vowel contraction in Xhosa. *Studies in African Linguistics* 5. 223–241.

Backley, Phillip 2011. *An Introduction to Element Theory*. Edinburgh: Edinburgh University Press.

Backley, Phillip & Kuniya Nasukawa. 2016. The origins of Japanese h from an element-based perspective. *Papers in Historical Phonology* 1. 269–284.

Bafile, Laura. 2017. L'individuazione dei primitivi della Teoria degli Elementi: la questione dell'economia. *Rivista di Linguistica, Letterature, Cinema, Teatro, Arte* 12 (2). 4–18.

Balogné Bérces, Katalin. 2006. What's wrong with vowel-initial syllables? *SOAS Working Papers in Linguistics* 14. 15–21.

Bendjaballah, Sabrina & Martin Haiden. 2008. 'A Typology of Emptiness in Templates.' In Jutta Hartmann, Vera Hegedus & Henk C. van Riemsdijk (eds.), *Sounds of Silence: Empty Elements in Phonology and Syntax*, 21–57. Amsterdam: Elsevier.

Breit, Florian. 2013. *Formal Aspects of Element Theory*. London: University College London MRes thesis.

Carvalho, Joaquim Brandão de. 2002. *De la syllabation en termes de contours CV*. EHESS Paris habilitation thesis.

Casali, Roderic. 2011. Hiatus resolution. In Marc van Oostendorp, Colin J. Ewen, Elisabeth Hume & Keren Rice (eds.), *The Blackwell Companion to Phonology*, vol.3, 1434–1460. Malden, MA: Wiley-Blackwell.

Caratini, Emilie. 2009. *Vocalic and consonantal quantity in German: synchronic and diachronic perspectives*. Nice and Leipzig: Université de Nice-Sophia Antipolis and Universität Leipzig dissertation.

Cavirani, Edoardo & Marc van Oostendorp. (2019). Empty morphemes in Dutch dialect atlases: Reducing morphosyntactic variation by refining emptiness typology. Glossa: A Journal of General Linguistics, 4(1), 88. DOI: http://doi.org/10.5334/gjgl.689

Charette, Monik. 1989. The Minimality Condition in Phonology. *Journal of Linguistics* 15 (1). 159–187.

Charette, Monik. 1991. *Conditions on phonological government*. Cambridge: Cambridge University Press.

Charette, Monik. 1992. Mongolian and Polish meet Government Licensing. *SOAS Working Papers in Linguistics and Phonetics* 2. 275–291

Charette, Monik. 2003. Empty and pseudo-empty categories. In Stefan Ploch (ed.) *Living on the Edge: 28 Papers in Honour of Jonathan Kaye*. 465–479. Berlin: De Gruyter Mouton.

Charette, Monik. In Press. Headedness, A and head-alignment: capturing the properties of the vowels of Montreal French. To appear in *Glossa*.

Charette, Monik & Aslı Göksel. 1996. Vowel Harmony and Switching in Turkic languages. In Henryk Kardela & Bogdan Szymanek (Eds). *A Festschrift for Edmund Gussmann*, 29–56. (1996). Lublin: University Press of the Catholic University of Lublin.

Charette, Monik & Aslı Göksel. 1998. Licensing Constraints and Vowel Harmony in Turkic Languages. In Eugeniusz, Cyran (ed.), *Structure and Interpretation: Studies in Phonology*, 65–89. Lublin: Folium.
Chomsky, Noam. 1986. *Barriers*. Cambridge MA: MIT Press.
Cobb, Margaret. 1997. *Conditions on nuclear expressions in phonology*. London: University of London dissertation.
Cyran, Eugeniusz. 1997. *Resonance Elements in Phonology: A Study in Munster Irish*. Lublin: Folium.
Cyran, Eugeniusz. 2010. *Complexity Scales and Licensing in Phonology*. Berlin: Mouton de Gruyter.
Ebata, Yoshio (ed.). 2013. *Aichiken no kotoba* [The dialect of Aichi Prefecture]. Tōkyō: Meiji Shoin.
Faust, Noam & Shanti Ulfsbjorninn. 2018. Arabic stress in strict CV, with no moras, no syllables, no feet and no extrametricality. *The Linguistics Review* 35 (4). 561–600.
Frellesvig, Bjarke. 2010. *A history of the Japanese language*. Cambridge: Cambridge University Press.
Gussmann, Edmund. 2002. *Phonology: Analysis and Theory*. Cambridge: Cambridge University Press.
Gussmann, Edmund & Jonathan D. Kaye. 1993. Polish notes from a Dubrovnik Café: I. The yers. *SOAS Working Papers in Linguistics and Phonetics* 3. 427–462.
Haas, Wim G. de. 1988. *A formal theory of vowel coalescence: A case study of ancient Greek*. Dordrecht: Foris.
Haraguchi, Shosuke. 1977. *The tone pattern of Japanese: An autosegmental theory of tonology*. Tōkyō: Kaitakusha.
Haraguchi, Shosuke. 1991. *A theory of stress and accent*. Dordrecht: Foris.
Harris, J. 1990. Segmental complexity and phonological government. *Phonology* 7. 255–300.
Harris, John. 1992. Licensing Inheritance. *UCL Working Papers in Linguistics* 4. 359–405.
Harris, John. 1994a. *English sound structure*. Oxford: Blackwell.
Harris, John. 1994b. Monovalency and Opacity: Chichewa height harmony. *UCL Working Papers in Linguistics* 6. 509–547.
Harris, John. 1997. Licensing Inheritance: an integrated theory of neutralisation. *Phonology* 14. 315–370.
Harris, John & Geoff Lindsey. 1995. The elements of phonological representation. In Jacques Durand & Francis Katamba (eds.), *Frontiers of Phonology*, 34–79. Harlow: Longman.
Heo, Yong. 1994. *Empty Categories and Korean Phonology*. London: University of London dissertation.
Hirako, Tatsuya, Ai Kubozono & Kyōji Yamaguchi. 2019. *Kisogawa hōgen bunpō gaisetsu*. [Grammatical Sketch of the Kisogawa Dialect]. In Aoi Hayato & Kibe Nobuko (eds.), *Aichi ken Kisogawa hōgen chōsa hōkoku-sho [Research report on the Kisogawa dialect of Aichi prefecture]*, 7–70. Tokyo: NINJAL. https://kikigengo.ninjal.ac.jp/reports/2019- 03_kisogawa_new.pdf. Last Accessed: July 11th 2020.
Hulst, Harry van der. 2016. Monovalent 'features' in phonology. *Language and Linguistics Compass* 10 (2). 83–102.
Iwai, Yasuo & Mafuyu Kitahara. 1995. *Accented Romanised E-Dictionary*.
Jensen, Sean. 1994. Is ʔ an Element? Towards a Non-segmental Phonology. *SOAS Working Papers in Linguistics and Phonetics* 4. 71–78.

Kawahara, Shigeto. 2003. On a certain kind of hiatus resolution in Japanese. *On'in Kenkyuu* [Phonological Studies] 6. 11–20.

Kawahara, Shigeto. 2015. The phonology of Japanese accent. In Haruo Kubozono (ed.), *The Handbook of Japanese Language and Linguistics: Phonetics and Phonology*. 445–492. Berlin: De Gruyter Mouton.

Kaye, Jonathan D. 1990. Government in Phonology: the case of Moroccan Arabic. *The Linguistic Review* 6. 131–159.

Kaye, Jonathan D. 1995. Derivations and Interfaces. In Jacques Durand & Francis Katamba (eds.), *Frontiers of Phonology*, 289–332. London and New York: Longman.

Kaye, Jonathan D. & Jean Lowenstamm. 1984. De la syllabicité. In François Dell, Daniel Hirst & Jean-Roger Vergnaud (eds.), *Forme Sonore du Langage*, 123–159. Paris: Hermann.

Kaye, Jonathan D., Jean Lowenstamm & Jean-Roger Vergnaud. 1985. The Internal Structure of Phonological Elements: A Theory of Charm and Government. *Phonology Yearbook 2*. 305–328.

Kaye, Jonathan D., Jean Lowenstamm & Jean-Roger Vergnaud. 1990. Constituent Structure and Government in Phonology. *Phonology 7*. 193–231.

Keshikawa, Ritsuji. 1971. *Nagoya hōgen no kenkyū [Research on the Nagoya dialect]*. Nagoya: Taibundō.

Keshikawa, Ritsuji. 1983. *Aichi-ken no hōgen [The dialect of Aichi Prefecture]* In Kiichi Itoyo, Sukezumi Hino & Ryoichi Satō (eds.), *Kōza Hōgengaku*, Vol. 6, 207–241. Tōkyō: Kokusho Kankōkai.

Krämer, Martin & Chris Golston. 2020. Diphthongs are micro-feet: Prominence and sonority in the nucleus. *Proceedings of AMP 2019*. DOI: https://doi.org/10.3765/amp.v8i0.4675.

Kubozono, Haruo. 2015. Diphthongs and Vowel coalescence. In Haruo Kubozono (ed.), *The Handbook of Japanese Phonetics and Phonology*. 215–250. Boston: De Gruyter Mouton.

Kula, Nancy C. 2002. *The phonology of verbal derivation in Bemba*. Leiden: Universiteit Leiden dissertation. LOT dissertation series 65.

Kula, Nancy C. & Lutz Marten. 2000. Constraints and processes: evidence from Bemba, Herero and Swahili. *SOAS Working Papers in Phonetics and Linguistics* 10. 91–102.

Labrune, Laurence. 2012. *The phonology of Japanese*. Oxford: Oxford University Press.

Levin, Juliette. 1985. *A Metrical Theory of Syllabicity*. Cambridge, MA: MIT dissertation.

Lowenstamm, Jean. 1996. CV as the Only Syllable Type. In Jacques Durand & Bernard Laks (eds.) *Current Trends in Phonology Models and Methods*, 419–442. Salford: European Studies Research Institute, University of Salford.

Martin, Simon E. (1987). *The Japanese language through time*. New Haven, CT: Yale University Press.

McCawley, James D. 1968. *The Phonological component of a grammar of Japanese*. The Hague: Mouton.

NHK. 1985. *Nihongo hatsuon jiten. [Japanese Pronunciation Dictionary.]* Tōkyō: Nihon Hōsō Shuppan Kyōkai.

Okada, Hideo. 1991. Japanese. *Journal of the International Phonetic Association*, 21 (2). 94–96.

Pimenta, Heglyn. 2019. *Nasalité et syllabe: Une étude synchronique, diachronique et dialectologique du portugais européen*. Paris: Université Paris 8 dissertation.

Ploch, Stefan. 1999. *Nasals on my mind: the phonetic and the cognitive approach to the phonology of nasality*. London: University of London dissertation.

Polgárdi, Krisztina. 2015. Vowels, glides, off-glides and on-glides in English: A Loose CV analysis. *Lingua* 158. 9–34.
Poser, William J. 1984. *The Phonetics and Phonology of Tone in Japanese*. Cambridge, MA: MIT dissertation.
Poser, William J. 1986. Japanese Evidence Bearing on the Compensatory Lengthening Controversy. In Engin Sezer & Leo Wetzels (eds.), *Studies in Compensatory Lengthening*, 167–87. Dordrecht: Foris.
Pöchtrager, Markus. 2006. *The Structure of Length*. Vienna: University of Vienna dissertation.
Pöchtrager, Markus. 2015. Binding in Phonology'. In Marc van Oostendorp and Henk van Riemsdijk (eds.), *Representing Structure in Phonology and Syntax*, 255–275. Berlin: Mouton de Gruyter.
Prince, Alan & Paul Smolensky. 1993. *Optimality Theory: Constraint Interaction in Generative Grammar*. Technical Report, Rutgers University Center for Cognitive Science and Computer Science Department University of Colorado at Boulder.
Rennison, John R. & Friedrich Neubarth. 2003. An x-bar theory of Government Phonology. In Stefan Ploch (ed.), *Living on the Edge: 28 papers in honour of Jonathan Kaye*, 95–130. Berlin: Mouton de Gruyter.
Scheer, Tobias. 2004. *A lateral theory of phonology. Vol 1: What is CVCV, and why should it be?* Berlin: Mouton de Gruyter.
Scheer, Tobias. 2011. *A Guide to Morphosyntax-Phonology Interface Theories. How Extra-Phonological Information is Treated in Phonology since Trubetzkoy's Grenzsignale*. Berlin: Mouton de Gruyter.
Scheer, Tobias. 2012. *Direct Interface and One-Channel Translation. Vol. 2 of A Lateral Theory of phonology*. Berlin: Mouton de Gruyter.
Scheer, Tobias & Nancy C. Kula. 2017. Government Phonology: Element theory, conceptual issues and introduction. In Stephen J. Hannahs & Anna R. K. Bosch (eds), *The Routledge Handbook of Phonological Theory*, 226–261. Oxford: Routledge.
Scheer, Tobias & Eugeniusz Cyran. 2017. Syllable Structure in Government Phonology. Stephen J. Hannahs & Anna R. K. Bosch (eds), *The Routledge Handbook of Phonological Theory*, 262–292. Oxford: Routledge.
Scheer, Tobias & Péter Szigetvári. 2005. Unified representations for the syllable and stress. *Phonology* 22. 37–75.
Selkirk, Elizabeth. 1982. The syllable. In Harry Van der Hulst & Norval Smith (eds.), *The structure of phonological representations: Part 2*, 337–384. Dordrecht: Foris
Szigetvári, Péter. 1999. *VC Phonology: a theory of consonant lenition and phonotactics*. Budapest: Eötvös Loránd University dissertation.
Szigetvári, Péter. 2013. The Syllable. In Bert Botma, Nancy C. Kula & Kuniya Nasukawa (eds.), *Bloomsbury Companion to Phonology*, 65–94. London: Bloomsbury.
Terakawa, Michiko. 1985. Nishikasugai-gun Shikatsu-chō Ōaza Takadaji no hōgen. [The dialect of Nishikasugai-gun Shikatsu-chō Ōaza Takadaji]. In Aichiken Kyōiku Iinkai (eds.) *Aichi no kotoba: Aichi-ken hōgen kinkyū chōsa hōkokusho [Aichi dialects: Collection of endangered Aichi Pref. dialects]*. Nagoya: Aichiken Kyōiku Iinkai.
Vance, Timothy. 1987. *An Introduction to Japanese Phonology*. Albany NY: SUNY Press.
Vance, Timothy. 2008. *The Sounds of Japanese*. Cambridge: Cambridge University Press.
Yoshida, Shohei. 1991. *Some aspects of governing relations in Japanese phonology*. London: University of London dissertation.

Yoshida, Shohei. 1993. Licensing of empty nuclei: The case of Palestinian vowel harmony. *The Linguistics Review* 10 (2). 127–159.

Yoshida, Shohei. 1996. *Phonological government in Japanese*. Canberra: Australian National University.

Yoshida, Yuko. 1999. *On pitch accent phenomena in Standard Japanese*. The Hague: Holland Academic Graphics.

Youngberg, Connor. 2013. Vocalic coalescence in Owari Japanese. *SOAS Working Papers in Linguistics* 16.

Youngberg, Connor. 2015. Coalescence in Japanese dialects is diachronic. *SOAS Working Papers in Linguistics* 17.

Youngberg, Connor. 2017. *Vocalic representation in Tokyo and Owari Japanese: Towards a syllable-free analysis*. London: SOAS University of London dissertation.

Youngberg, Connor. 2021. Representing the moraic nasal in Japanese: evidence from Tōkyō, Ōsaka and Kagoshima. *Glossa: A Journal of General Linguistics*, 6 (1). 63. DOI: http://doi.org/10.5334/gjgl.1099.

Henk van Riemsdijk
Elements of syntax. Repulsion and attraction

> It is [the] disposition of attractive force in all bodies, whatever their form or composition, to run together, coalesce, centralize, and become accumulative into a single volume to any extent or degree. [...] These facts lie at the basis of Newton's universal law. Immediately opposed to this force appears another of equal magnitude and importance, which has heretofore been ignored by physicists, but which as certainly exists, and plays as important a rôle in nature as gravitation itself. This is repulsion.
> (Winslow 1869: 75)

Abstract: In a famous article from 1989 Sylvain Bromberger and Morris Halle called "Why phonology is different" (Linguistic Inquiry 20, 51–70), the title says it all. And indeed there are few linguists who have argued that, at certain levels of abstraction, there are substantial similarities between phonology and syntax. In the present article I challenge the Bromberger-Halle doctrine. The background is that the null-hypothesis ought to be that there are close affinities between phonology and syntax. If we adhere to the idea that the main principles of universal grammar should be similar, perhaps even identical, then the Bromberger-Halle doctrine must be wrong. Of course, the principles of universal grammar are still in many ways unknown and too idiosyncratic to provide strong evidence that many (if not all) principles of universal grammar are shared by phonology and syntax. Still, there are some quite plausible general principles that seem to be common to phonology and syntax such as the OCP (the Obligatory Contour Principle). The present article explores some ways in which phonology and syntax may well be more similar than is generally assumed. In particular, it speculates to what extent we could arrange the structures of phonological and syntactic objects in such a way that we might say that both types of structure are actually identical.

Keywords: CIT (Categorial Identity Thesis; Mono-valued features; NVR (No Value Reversal Condition), OCP (Obligatory Contour Principle), Privative features.

Henk van Riemsdijk, Tilburg University

https://doi.org/10.1515/9783110691948-009

1 Early sources of inspiration

As a first year student interested in linguistics in Paris in 1967, I had read André Martinet's Éléments de linguistique (Martinet 1960).[1] That was what made me decide to attend Martinet's classes on diachronic phonology. One of the central concepts that he discussed was the idea that sound changes are often chain reactions. A vowel, say [ɑ], may shift to become [e]. But if the system already has an [e] in it, that [e] is likely to shift further up in the phonetic triangle and become [i] to create room for the original [ɑ]. This type of chain he called a 'push chain'. In another scenario, however, some slot in the triangle, e.g. that of [i] might be unused in some language. In that case [e] might shift upward to become [i], leaving a void in the [e] position. As a result [ɑ] might then raise to become [e]. This is what Martinet called a 'drag chain'. See Samuels (2009) for insightful discussion of Martinet's views.

Martinet's push chains and drag chains principle was thought to apply both to syntax and to phonology. It was a source of inspiration to me since 1967 (see for example Van Riemsdijk 1997, 1998). More generally, it has always been my conviction that if there are some very general principles of design that co-determine the structure and functioning of syntax, it would be very strange to find that such principles are completely absent in phonology and vice versa. The fundamental formal similarity between phonology and syntax was one of the core insights of the late Jean-Roger Vergnaud's work which has inspired me since the mid seventies.[2]

My purpose in this article is to sketch a bit more of the background of these abstract ideas and to illustrate how they manifested themselves in a number of interesting and inspiring proposals over the years. This is the goal of Section 2.

---

[1] The two other works I had read at that time were Louis Hjelmslev's *Omkring sprogteoriens grundlaeggelse* (Hjelmslev 1943; Hjelmslev 1953) and Pike's *Language in relation to a unified theory of the structure of human behavior* (Pike 1967). I still had to discover the existence of generative grammar.

[2] For more recent inspiration and feedback I wish to thank audiences at the following occasions where I presented various aspects and versions of the present work: Josef Bayer's Birthday Workshop, Konstanz November 2010; the Parallel Domains Conference in Honor of Jean-Roger Vergnaud, USC, Los Angeles, May 2011; the conference on New Perspectives on Language Creativity at UQAM, Montreal, September 2011, the City University of Hong Kong, October 2011; the Joint Symposium on the Interfaces of Grammar, Chinese Academy of Science, October 2011; and the Faculty of Foreign Languages and Literatures of the University of Bucharest, May 2013. I dedicate this article to the memory of Jean-Roger Vergnaud. Thanks are due to Laurence Voeltzel for excellent help with the formatting of this article.

In Section 3. I draw from these ideas some major guidelines for a theory of syntactic categories and representations. Finally, in Section 4. I will sketch some very immature and programmatic ideas as to how a theory of the type outlined in Section 3. might be implemented.

2 A bit of "early" history

In the late seventies, Longobardi, following up on Ross' inspirational work on the exclusion of sequences of two verbs carrying the ing- suffix in English (1972b), discovered that sequences of two bare infinitives in Italian are excluded unless they have undergone restructuring (making them in a sense a single complex verb), see Longobardi (1980). Generalizing, this amounted to a principle that excludes two independent verbs in close proximity. On the one hand, infinitive markers suffice to separate the two verbs sufficiently to make them survive the restriction. On the other hand, restructuring makes them so close that the restriction does not apply either. Using our metaphor, we may say that the configuration VV is unstable and cannot survive unless either repulsion (such as by the intervening infinitive marker) or attraction (such as in restructuring) saves the configuration. In addition the relative morphological identity (-ing-form, infinitive form) plays an important role. We may summarize these results as

(1) $*V_{Fi}V_{Fi}$ (where Fi stands for some inflectional feature(s))

Van Riemsdijk (1984) showed that the same principle is at work in the distribution of infinitives in German.

Around the same time, comparable considerations were found to apply in the domain of nouns. In a letter commenting on Chomsky and Lasnik's 'Filters and Control' (Chomsky and Lasnik 1977), Jean-Roger Vergnaud proposed the Case Filter (1977; Vergnaud 2008). This filter stated, among other applications, that noun phrases that fail to be assigned (abstract) case cannot survive in a derivation. This was effectively the birth of Case Theory. One of the core instances where this filter was supposed to apply is the absence of noun phrase complements to nouns, due to the absence of structural case assigned to such complements (*of* or some other preposition) makes up for the absence of structural case. This idea can be summarized as (2):

(2) *N-NP

Clearly, (1) and (2) have more in common than a superficial glance suggests. Indeed, in (1) one of the infinitives is part of a verbal projection. Hence, another way of stating the two principles would be this:

(3) *V – V^{max} and *N – N^{max}

Put this way, the two principles cry out for a generalization. In a GLOW talk in the early 80s, Kayne indeed made a proposal along these lines (Kayne 1982). Kayne's proposal, which was based on the idea of syntactic structure being fundamentally a continuous alternation of predicates (verbal elements) and arguments (nominal elements), was never written up beyond the GLOW abstract.

Two years later, however, Hoekstra did follow up, abandoning the predicate-argument alternation and extending instead the observations about N and V to the two remaining categories A and P (cf. Hoekstra 1984). In effect, Hoekstra proposed what he called the Unlike Category Constraint (UCC).[3]

(4) The Unlike Category Constraint (UCC): *VV, *NN, *AA, *PP

While such a generalization seems tantalizingly interesting, it fails on a number of points. As I argued in Van Riemsdijk (1988), the UCC is both too strong and too weak. Before presenting a rough overview of the relevant evidence, it must be noted that we are, at least for the present, limiting ourselves to cases of the (in-) compatibility between a head and a phrasal complement to that head. Furthermore, the question arises as to how we treat functional projections from this perspective. Anticipating the discussion further below, I will assume, following Emonds (1985), that CP has essentially the same categorial status as PP. I will also assume that functional projections above the lexical heads N, V, A are categorially identical (modulo a feature that distinguishes lexical from functional heads, see Grimshaw (1991, 2005), Van Riemsdijk (1990, 1998)).

With this in mind, let us briefly consider the predictions of the UCC.[4] In addition to *VV and *NN, which we have already mentioned above, what about *A-AP and *P-PP? *A-AP seems perfectly correct in the sense that adjectives do not appear to select AP-complements. On the other hand, it is far from clear that *P-PP is warranted. While most recent work on the structure of PPs assumes that there are functional head positions for both Place and Path, there are other cases

---

3 In the formulation of (4) the projection level is, again, ignored.
4 For more discussion, see Van Riemsdijk (1988).

that do not fit into such a structure. To cite just one example, take a Dutch sentence like (5).

(5) a. *Voor bij het dessert serveren we een Château d'Yquem*
for with the dessert serve we a Château d'Yquem
'We will serve a Château d'Yquem to accompany dessert'

b. *Tips voor naar de trimsalon*[5]
tips for to the pet-grooming-salon
'Advice for [going to] the pet salon'

These examples suggest that the preposition 'voor' selects complete PPs as complements. Therefore the UCC is too strong in that it should not exclude *P-PP.

On the other hand, the UCC is too weak in that it fails to exclude a fair number of combinations. In particular, it does not prevent V and N from taking a (bare) AP complement. While V can take a small clause with an AP predicate, it is not particularly plausible to assume that the small clause is an AP. N cannot even take such a small clause.

These considerations led me to suggest a different way of looking at the overall situation. Hoekstra's proposal takes syntactic categories to be atomic. But since Chomsky (1970) there has been a simple way of decomposing syntactic categories in terms of the features $[\pm N]$ and $[\pm V]$.[6] These features determine the four major categories as follows.

(6) N = [+N, –V]; V = [–N,+V]; A = [+N,+V]; P = [–N,–V]

One way of summarizing the discussion of the UCC above is to say that AP is the most restricted category in that it basically hardly ever occurs as a complement to a lexical head.[7] On the other hand, PP seems to be the most versatile category in that it can be a complement to all of the four major categories and in turn can select a maximal projection of each of the four major categories. What this suggests is that it is not the atomic categories but the plus values of Chomsky's cat-

---

5 Found on: http://www.debbystrimhut.nl/pages/sub/54311/Tips_voor_naar_de_trimsalon.html
6 For some discussion of these features, see Jackendoff (1977), Van Riemsdijk (1978) and Muysken and Van Riemsdijk (1986).
7 For reasons that will become clear below I will assume that P does take AP complements in cases like *The weather changed from pleasant to foggy*.

egorial features that are relevant. Accordingly, in my 1988 paper (see Van Riemsdijk 1988) I proposed to replace the UCC by the Unlike Feature Constraint (UFC).[8]

(7) The Unlike Feature Constraint (UFC): $*[+F_i]° - [+F_i]^{max}$
where F_i = N or V

This formulation permits a fairly close approximation of what I believe we want to say. Systematically:[9]

(8) a. Excluded by $*[+V]°-[+V]^{max}$: $V° - V^{max}$ and $V° - A^{max}$
$A° - V^{max}$ and $A° - A^{max}$
b. Excluded by $*[+N]°-[+N]^{max}$: $N° - N^{max}$ and $N° - A^{max}$
$A° - N^{max}$ and $A° - A^{max}$
c. Versatility of P: $\sqrt{P}° - N^{max}$; $\sqrt{P}° - A^{max}$; $\sqrt{P}° - V^{max}$;
$\sqrt{P}° - P^{max}$
$\sqrt{N}° - P^{max}$; $\sqrt{A}° - P^{max}$, $\sqrt{V}° - P^{max}$;
$\sqrt{P}° - P^{max}$
d. Also permitted: $\sqrt{V}° - N^{max}$; $\sqrt{N}° - V^{max}$

The fact that it is the positive values of the categorial features and not the negative ones suggests immediately that the features should be (re-)interpreted in a privative, monovalued way. This is indeed what I concluded in the 1988 paper. And I was inspired by work in autosegmental phonology and more particularly by Jean-Roger Vergnaud's work.

In seminal work in the late seventies, Vergnaud proposed to treat the 'categorial features of phonological structure,' that is, features such as consonantal and vocalic as autosegments (see Vergnaud 1976, 1980). The idea was, put very simply, to have exactly those elements represented on a separate tier that play a crucial role in certain phonological processes. Vowel harmony, as the name suggests, is a process that affects vowels and disregards consonants. This way of thinking about phonological structure presupposes that phonological features are interpreted as mono-valued, privative, in other words not as binary, equipollent features as conceived in early generative phonology.[10]

---

[8] In the formulation of the UFC, as in the (sub-)principles and – generalizations above no strict ordering is implied.
[9] The systematic way of representing the predictions in (8) implies some redundancies that are not, of course, present in (7).
[10] This way of thinking about phonological categories has become a cornerstone of so-called government phonology (see Kaye, Lowenstamm & Vergnaud 1985, 1990). An attempt to apply similar reasoning to syntax was presented in Van Riemsdijk (1982).

Having switched our attention briefly to phonology, note that there is an important principle in phonology called the Obligatory Contour Principle (OCP, see McCarthy (1986) and references cited there). The OCP does in phonology what the principles discussed above try to do for syntax, viz. regulate attraction and repulsion. Indeed, the essence of the OCP is often rendered as the constraint *X X, where X stands for some phonological feature or feature bundle. To exemplify, two adjacent short vowels that are identical, say [e e], cannot survive by the OCP. They either fuse to the single long vowel [ē], or one of the two short vowels is deleted, yielding [e], or dissimilation applies, yielding, for example, [i e], or epenthesis inserts some element between the two identical vowels: [e?e].

The fact that there is such a clear conceptual similarity between the OCP in phonology and a principle such as the UFC in syntax reinforces the idea that we should pursue the possibilities of (largely) identifying the formal apparatus used to express them in syntax and phonology. Thus the inspirational influence of Martinet's push chains and drag chains, married to Vergnaud's formal work on models that encompass phonological and syntactic structure continued to guide my work.[11]

The highly simplified representation of vowels and consonants that I based my suggestions in Van Riemsdijk (1988) on amounted to saying that there is a vowel tier and a consonant tier, and that vowels are segments that are linked to the V-tier while consonants are segments (x) linked to the C-tier, as illustrated in Figure 1:

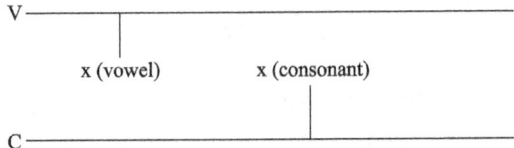

Figure 1: Representation of vowels and consonants, see Van Riemdijk (1988).

This way of representing phonological segments permits a very simple way of stating the OCP: two adjacent segments that are linked to the same tier, as shown in Figure 2.

This seemed to me to be a promising direction to take for a theory of syntactic categories, and in the 1988 paper I made some very preliminary suggestions as to how one might proceed from here. Then, however I temporarily dropped this line of research in favor of other research topics. And it took me ten years

---

11 For an important more recent study along these lines, see Vergnaud (2003).

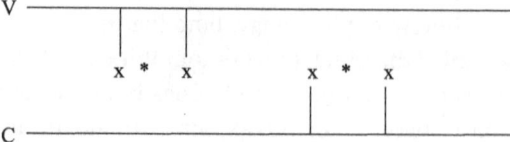

Figure 2: The Obligatory Contour Principle, see again Van Riemdijk (1988).

to return to the problem of finding a good representational system for syntactic categories. The results, which I turn to in the next section, are published in Van Riemsdijk (1998).

3 Some ideas about categories, projections, the internal cohesion of projections, and the contexts in which they occur

Let us be a bit more specific as to what fundamental insights we want a theory of syntactic categories to express. What we have looked at so far is the relationship between heads and the complements that they select. And our conclusion was that this relationship is characterized by the UFC, a type of OCP that forces the positive values of the syntactic features to be different – a case of repulsion. If we think of the complements as (extended) maximal projections, then one way to look at this is to say that in a complex syntactic tree, full of nodes with categorially labelled nodes it is hard to know where one maximal projection ends and where another starts. In other words, how are phrases recognizable and delimitable within larger syntactic configurations. The UFC provides at least a partial answer to this question.

This reasoning rests on one crucial assumption, viz. that the spine of an (extended) maximal projection does not contain any categorial transitions that could be (mis-)interpreted as the start of a new extended maximal projection. This is an idea that has come to be known as the Categorial Identity Thesis (CIT), proposed independently in work by Grimshaw (1991, 2005) and Van Riemsdijk (1990, 1998). Since the introduction of functional shells around the projection of lexical heads, a core question that needed to be answered was how the notion of endocentricity, once central to X-bar theory, should be interpreted. If every functional projection is a head sui generis with its own maximal projection, then what we originally wanted to express is not longer expressed. The idea that a noun phrase is headed by a noun, while still encoded in the structure, has become almost meaningless in that there are potentially so many functional heads above it (NumP, ClassP, QP, DP etc.) that endocentricity becomes a virtually empty notion. Instead, we want to make a much stronger statement: a noun phrase with all its functional projections around (or on top of) it always has a lexical N in it. Similarly for V, A, and P. That is, there is a one-to-one relationship between N and DP (assuming that DP is the outermost functional shell of the noun phrase; and there is a one-to-one relationship between a C and its outermost functional shell, say, the IP; and so on and so forth. What this amounts to is that there can be more than one head in a single extended projection, but that the privileged one-to-one relationship still holds between the lexical head N, V, A, P and its respective maximally extended projection.

If this is the right way of looking at things, then we will want to avoid stipulating which functional heads/projections belong with which lexical head. Yet it seems clear that these are privileged relationships as well. Verbs have tense, aspect, mood, modality and presumably quite a few other functional shells around them, while nouns have determiners, quantifiers etc. In many cases functional heads cannot be easily associated to some categorial notion. Negation, for example English not, is not in any obvious way a verb or a noun. But in many cases, such an attribution is possible. Articles (determiners), for example, are very often simliar, or even identical, to (clitic) pronouns. Similarly, modality, when expressed as part of the verbal projection, shows up as modal verbs, not as modal nouns in, again, English and many other Indo-European languages.

This, then, is the core of the Categorial Identity Thesis (CIT): the spine of a maximally extended projection is characterized by the fact that all functional heads of some lexical head L and their functional projections all the way up to the top share the same categorial specification in terms of the values for [N] and [V].[12] We thereby have a counterpart of the UFC idea: the internal cohesion of a maximal projection is formally expressed in terms of the CIT. And for cohesion, we can substitute the notion of 'attraction' in line with the major metaphor guiding this line of thinking.[13]

---

[12] An interesting question that arises from this is whether intermediate functional heads truly need their own maximal projection nodes. To the extent that they do not seem to act as privileged nodes (they generally cannot move inside or out of their maximally extended projection), it would seem that we do not need them, thereby further strengthening the endocentricity of maximal phrase: one lexical head, one maximal phrase node. This is the line that I defended in Van Riemsdijk (1998). I will not pursue this issue here.

[13] Note that my 1998 article was entitled 'Categorial Feature Magnetism' – another attempt at finding an expressive metaphor from the physical world for the fundamental forces determining the categorial configurations in complex syntactic objects.

The idea of categorial identity as one of the core organizational principles determining the internal structure of (maximal) phrase needs to be translated into the framework built on categorial features. In other words, is it plausible to abandon the notion of binary features in favor of monovalued, privative features in the case of the CIT as well? It would seem that the answer is yes. The main prediction of such a monovalued system will be, again, that P/PP is the most versatile category in that P does not affect the CIT when interspersed with the features N or V. Take the fact that infinitive markers are often morphologically identical with prepositions. Nevertheless, these infinitive markers do not turn an infinitival complement into PPs. Or take nominal projections. As I argued in Van Riemsdijk (1998), container expressions such as *a glass of wine* are really mono-projectional in that it is the lexical head wine that is selected by a governing verb, as in *John drank a glass of wine*. Lexical prepositions on the other hand do block selection of the lower head as in **John drank a glass with/for wine*. Indeed closely related languages such as German omit the preposition, and furthermore, the lower head (and its modifiers) express the case required by the governing head. The preposition *mit* ('with') requires the dative case, hence we get *mit einem$_{DAT}$ Glas rotem$_{DAT}$ Wein* ('with a glass of red wine').[14]

The CIT can be formulated as follows.[15]

(9) The Categorial Identity Thesis (CIT): In a structure like the one in Figure 3, all nodes H/h must be identically specified for the values of the features N and V.

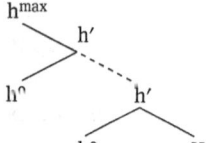

Figure 3: The Categorial Identity Thesis.

The two major principles, UFC and CIT, taken as grammatical reflections of repulsion and attraction, are principles that cry out for unification. But before addressing that problem, three more important aspects of categorial representation must be addressed: the distribution of lexical, semi-lexical and functional categories

---

[14] See Van Riemsdijk (1998) for more extensive discussion. In particular, the question arises as to what status we should assign to the first (container) noun in such expressions. I proposed to introduce the notion of semi-lexical category for such cases. See also Corver and Van Riemsdijk (2001) for discussion.

[15] In Figure 3 I employ a convention I proposed in Van Riemsdijk (1990) in that I use upper case letters for lexical heads and lower case letters for functional (and semi-lexical) heads.

within a maximal projection, the status of CP and PP, and the problem of mixed categories.

Starting with the latter, gerunds are a typical example of a mixed category. They are nominal on the outside and verbal on the inside. Clearly, this state of affairs is in flagrant contradiction with the CIT unless we say that gerunds consist of two maximal projections, which appears to be wrong.

Turning now to the second problem, the distribution of lexical, semi-lexical and functional categories within a maximal projection, the generalization appears to be that the lexical head is at the bottom, the functional categories are at the top, and the semi-lexical categories are in between. There does not seem to be any alternative to adding this as a separate stipulation to the theory.

Consider finally the status of CP and PP. It has been argued that CP is really categorially identical to PP (cf. Emonds 1985). The idea could be that CP is the outermost functional shell of the V-projection, while at least a subset of PPs, prepositional objects, are really N-projections within a PP shell. This would be compatible with the formulation of the CIT, as P (or p) is not categorially specified for either N or V. However, nothing predicts that the PP must be the outer shell.

With these problems in mind, let us now turn to my next attempt to come to grips with what I consider to be the fundamentals of categorial structure in syntax, the article called 'Categorial Feature Magnetism' (Van Riemsdijk 1998).

4 A monumental mistake

When, in the second half of the nineties, I returned to the issue of finding a system of representation that would incompass the main properties of syntactic categories as I saw them, I made a serious mistake. In fact I abandoned the idea of monovalued categorial features (or perhaps I just forgot about it) and attempted to develop a theory in terms of binary features. Nevertheless the article contained some useful empirical underpinnings of the notions that guide the search for a good system of categorial representation, which is what it is mostly cited for. On the theoretical side it was ambitious and misguided. I use this opportunity, however, to give a brief explanation for what I tried to achieve and why I did it with binary features.

The core idea was to take two of the problems mentioned at the end of Section 3, viz. the problem of PP/CP shells and the problem of lexical heads being innermost, semi-lexical heads intermediate, and functional categories outermost, and to combine them with the UFC and the CIT into one system. The way this was done was to add two additional types of features to the two categorial features [±N] and [±V]. First, the distinction between lexical, semi-lexical and functional categories was expressed by means of the two features [±F(unctional)] and [±G(rammatical)]. Call these the functionality features.[16] Second, the levels in a projection could be distinguished by means of the two level features that Muysken (1983) had proposed earlier, [±PROJ(ection)] and [±MAX(imal)]. These features yield the following distinctions:

(10) L-features:
[+PROJ, +MAX] = maximal projection node (Hmax)
[+PROJ, −MAX] = intermediate node (H')
[−PROJ, −MAX] = head (H°)
([−PROJ, +MAX] = unprojected particles ([H°]H max))

(11) F-features:
[+F, +G] = functional category
[+F,−G] or [−F, +G] = semi-lexical category[17]
[−F, −G] = lexical category

Take the level features first. One way guaranteeing that only structures like the one given in Figure 3 are allowed is to say that in a projection the minus value of one of the features may never dominate the plus value of that feature. In the normal case (forgetting about unprojected particles), the lexical head will be [−PROJ, −MAX], all intermediate nodes are [+PROJ, −MAX], the maximal projection node is [+PROJ, +MAX].

Similarly, to express that lexical is at the bottom, semi-lexical is above lexical, and functional is at the top, we can say that the minus value of one of the features ([±F] and [±G]) may never dominate the plus value of that feature. The two principles can then be subsumed under what I called the No Value Reversal Condition.

(12) No Value Reversal 1 (NVR1):
Within a single projection, the following holds:
*[−F_i]   where F_i ranges over PROJ, MAX, F, G
 |
[+F_i]

---

[16] Grimshaw (2005) uses an F-feature as well, but in a somewhat different way. It is a ternary feature that distinguishes lexical from functional (these are the F-values F0 and F1). F3 is used to designate the PP-shell above N/D and the CP-shell above V/I.

[17] Whether there is any grounds for choosing between [+F, −G] and [−F, +G], or whether there is a distinction that might be traced to these two options (as in the case of [−PROJ, +MAX]) remains an open question.

Let us turn now to the issue of PP being, at least in the cases of prepositional objects, a functional shell above N/D, while CP could be interpreted as a functional shell above V/I.[18] Looking again at the categorial features as binary features, we may say that full identity of these feature specifications in a projection is not required, but that, going from the bottom to the top an N-projection may turn into a P-projection, and a V-projection may also turn into a P-projection. This would imply an inverse version of the No Value Reversal Condition:

(13) No Value Reversal 2 (NVR2):
Within a single projection, the following holds:
*$[+F_i]$ where Fi ranges over N,V
|
$[-F_i]$

It is easy to see that the two principles in (12) and (13) could be collapsed if we were to change some features. For example, we might replace Muysken's level features by [±HEAD] and [±MIN(imal)], and the functionality features by [±LEX(ical)] and [±OPEN (class)].[19] This would reverse the feature specifications.

However, even this relatively simple case should teach us one thing: it is too easy to change the names of the features, and thereby manipulate what is a plus value and what is a minus value. And the same criticism applies to my attempt at 'unifying' the CIT and the UFC. To cut a long and arduous story short, this is the result of my labors, grandiosely called the Law of Categorial Feature Magnetism.

(14) Law of Categorial Feature Magnetism (cf. Van Riemsdijk 1998: 46)
A configuration
$[αN, βV]_{c \cup} Li$ (where α, β, γ, δ range over + and –,
| $[+PROJ] \subset Li$, and $[±PROJ, ±MAX] \subseteq Lj$)
$[γN, δV]_{c \cup} Lj$

is illicit (*) unless: (i)   at most one of α, β, γ, δ is '+'
             or   (ii) $[-MAX] \subset Lj$ and α=γ and β=δ
             or   (iii) $[+MAX] \subset Lj$ and α≠γ and β≠δ

---

18 See also Grimshaw (2005), Haider (1988), and Van Riemsdijk (1990).
19 Lexical heads = [+LEX, +OPEN], semi-lexical categories = [+LEX, –OPEN], functional categories = [–LEX, –OPEN]; Lexical heads = [+HEAD, +MIN], intermediate projections = [–HEAD, +MIN], maximal projections = [–HEAD, –MIN]. The No Value Reversal Condition Revised (NVR3) would be like NVR2, with Fi ranging over N, V, LEX, OPEN, HEAD, MIN.

At this point I am, quite frankly, unsure whether this formulation ever expressed what I wanted it to express. But what is more important, it never was a unification as it contains several disjunctions. Furthermore, as noted above, the use that is made of plus and minus values of C-, F-, and L-features is quite artificial and stipulative.

My conclusion from this adventure is that it is now, 25 years after the appearance of Van Riemsdijk (1988), high time to return to the idea that the issue of developing a valid theory of categorial representation should be rethought in terms of monovalued features and the OCP. In the next and last section I will suggest some very preliminary ideas as to how one might go about such a research program.

5 First ideas about a new approach

In what follows I will present a very tentative sketch of how we might put a little bit of flesh on the bare bone that was presented in Van Riemsdijk (1988). Much of it will be wrong or misguided or redundant. My goal is modest: to explore some of the directions that a theory of categorial representation might go.

There are, now, several phonological theories that work with mono-valued, privative features. The main ones are Dependency Phonology (Anderson & Ewen 1987), Particle Phonology (Schane 1984), and Element Theory, which is one of the core components of Government Phonology (Kaye et al. 1985, 1990; Harris 1994; Harris & Lindsey 1995). I have chosen to adopt the term element theory, mainly because Particle Phonology appears to me to be conceptually inferior and because Element Theory seems closer to the ideas developed in my (1988) paper and offers an easy way of representing things. My borrowing from Element Theory is, in any case, quite minimal, leaving aside (for now) notions such as headedness and government.

As a starting point, let us assume that there is a Categorial Tier, on which the values N and V are displayed in the form of a template: N V N V N V. A template like this is very much like the standard template C V C V C V in phonology, i.e. it incorporates ideally the avoidance of identity (*X X) as the core idea of the OCP (Yip 1998; Van Riemsdijk 2008; Richards 2010). This will be the cornerstone for an account of the UFC.

Similarly, we will use a second tier to represent the Level features. Deviating somewhat from Muysken's (1983) level features [±PROJ, ±MAX], the three major levels: head, intermediate and maximal will be represented by means of the features H(ead) and M(aximal). These features will also be displayed on the Level Tier in the form of a template: H M H M H M.

There are slots that I will represent as 'x' that can be linked both to the Categorial Tier and to the Level Tier. These slots we may call the complete syntactic units. These correspond to the notion of syntactic phrase. The resulting graphs represent at least some of the core insights summarized in Section 2. In addition, in order not to stray too far from the notion syntactic tree, I will represent heads as separate (dotted) slots that are on the one hand linked to the Level Tier and on the other hand to what I call the Merge Tier which is, in essence, the spine of the (dendromorphic) projection as we know it (see Figure 4).

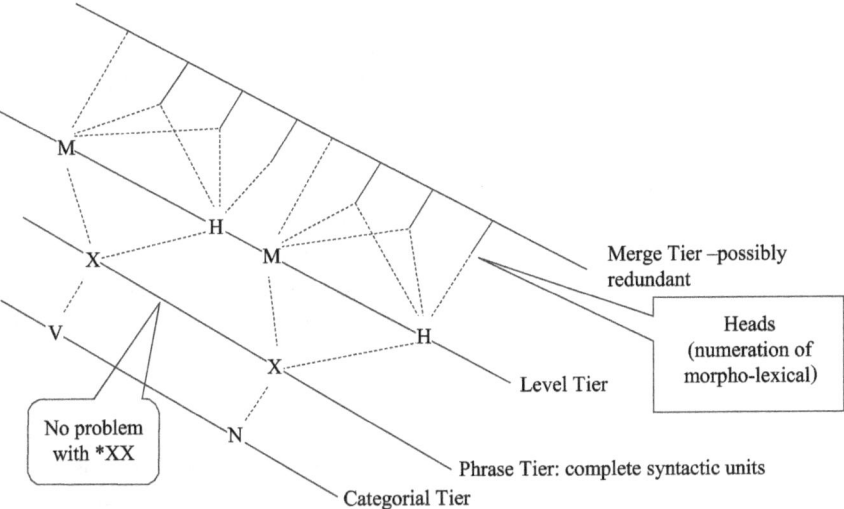

Figure 4: The representation of N and V, expanding the ideas in Van Riemsdijk (1988).

The intermediate head nodes in the syntactic tree are variably linked with M and or H. This at least partly solves the problem of [±F,±G], necessitated by the introduction of semi-lexical heads, which implied that the [±F] feature was insufficient. A node uniquely dominated by H is the lexical head, a node uniquely dominated by M is the maximal (extended) projection node. Intermediate nodes are all dominated by H, hence are heads. Those that are in addition dominated by M are functional heads or semi-lexical heads. However, the functional – semi-lexical gradient is only contextually defined: those intermediate heads that are close to the lexical head are semi-lexical, those that are close to the maximal projection node are functional heads. I leave a more principled solution for future research. One promising possibility would be to make use of the notion of headedness that phonological element theory (cf. Harris & Lindsey 1995, and references cited there) employs: |M|•|H| for functional heads, |M|•|H| for semilexical heads. The underlined Label, the head, is in a sense dominant, while the other is recessive. This yields the desired distinction. But proximity to M and H respectively might work well too, as the distinction between lexical and functional is, to a certain extent, gradual, squishy (cf. Ross 1972a, 1973).

No problem arises with *X X from the point of view of the categorial features for N and V. Note however that *X X is blind to the fact that the two slots are also both dominated by M and H. This may be a matter of hierarchy, but it requires further thought.

A/AP is defined as a slot dominated both by N and V. By *X X it cannot be structurally adjacent to either N or V. This is desirable to the extent that APs can never be categorially selected by either N or V, nor can A take any N^{max}-complements (obliquely case marked DPs are PPs, see below) or "bare" V^{max} complements. Hence APs can only occur as predicates or attributively. For predicates, see below, for attributive APs I will assume that they are always grafted, i.e. are on a different tier altogether.[20] This may also extend to adverbial phrases in the verbal projection (originating perhaps in Keyser 1968). See Figure 5.

Muysken's (1983) insight about heads that function by themselves as phrases (such as adpositional particles or 'short' adjective-based adverbs), which he expressed as [−PROJ, +MAX], by linking an x-slot simultaneously to H and M. can be straightforwardly represented in this system, as shown in Figure 6.

An interesting question arises as to the status of 'dummy' adpositions as found in direct partitive constructions such as English *a glass of wine*, which is arguably (cf. Van Riemsdijk 1998) a single (extended maximal) projection. One way of expressing this type of dummy preposition would be as in Figure 7. It is adpositional by not being linked to either N or V, furthermore, while as a word it will fill a dotted slot, but it will have no level features. Other approaches may be possible, but I will not pursue this issue here.

More generally, the question arises as to how the versatility of P/PP should be incorporated into this system. In the old system this was done by allowing both [+N, −V] and [−N, +V] to be dominated by [−N, −V], at the expense of making arbitrary use of the +/− values of the features. Here I propose to introduce a third category feature: R (for Relator), cf. Den Dikken (2006). See Figure 8. Once we have introduced the category label R, this label might also be used for the representation of predicative APs and DPs. Details remain to be worked out, but the two types of PP that we have distinguished above, viz. adpositional objects interpreted as a PP-shell on top of a DP and CPs interpreted as an adpositional shell on top of IP/ TP could be represented as in Figures 8 and 9 respectively.

---

[20] For the notion of 'graft', see Van Riemsdijk (2001, 2006).

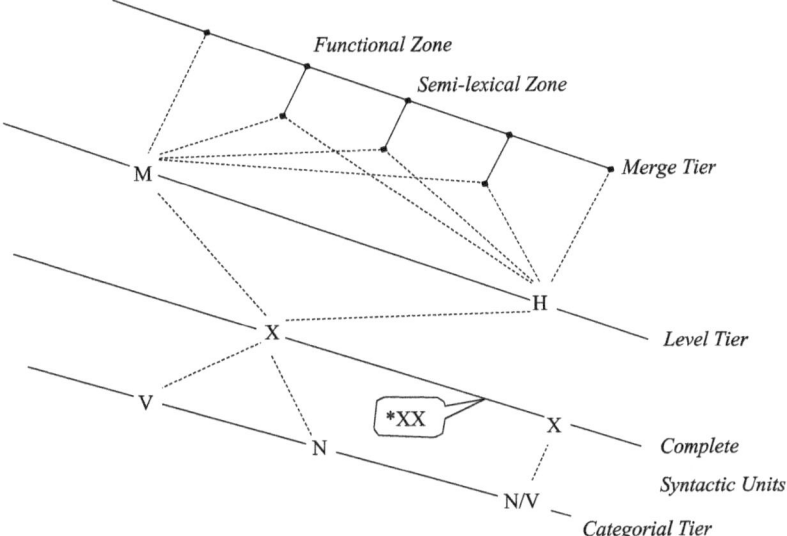

Figure 5: AP.

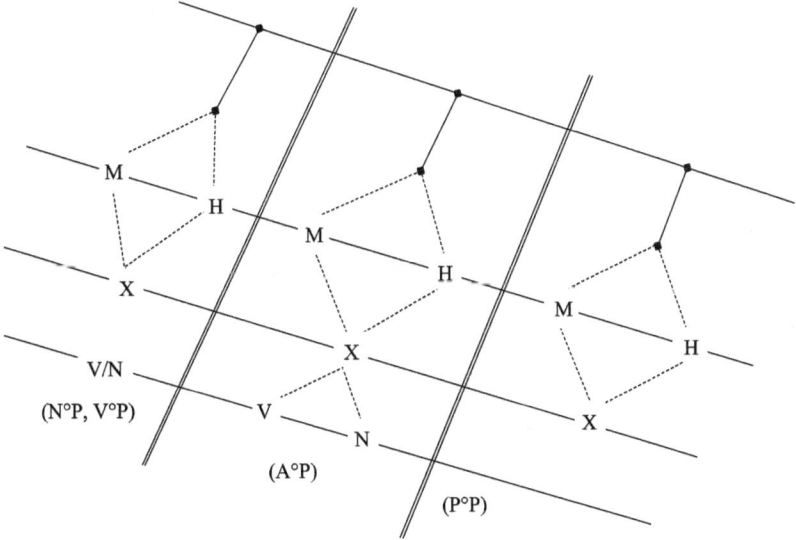

Figure 6: Muysken's 4th case.

A distinct advantage of the present approach to categorial features is that hybrid categories such as nominalizations and gerunds can be straightforwardly represented by using multiple slots as in Figures 8 and 9. This is illustrated in Figure 10.

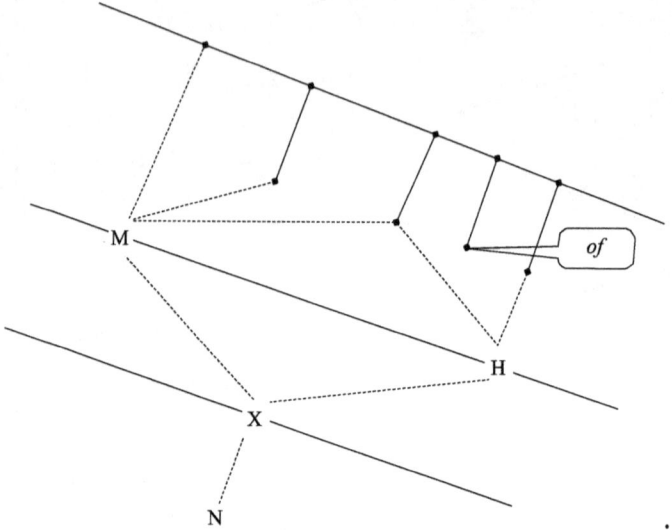

Figure 7: 'Dummy' prepositions inside projections, e.g. Direct Partitives, as in *a glass of water*.

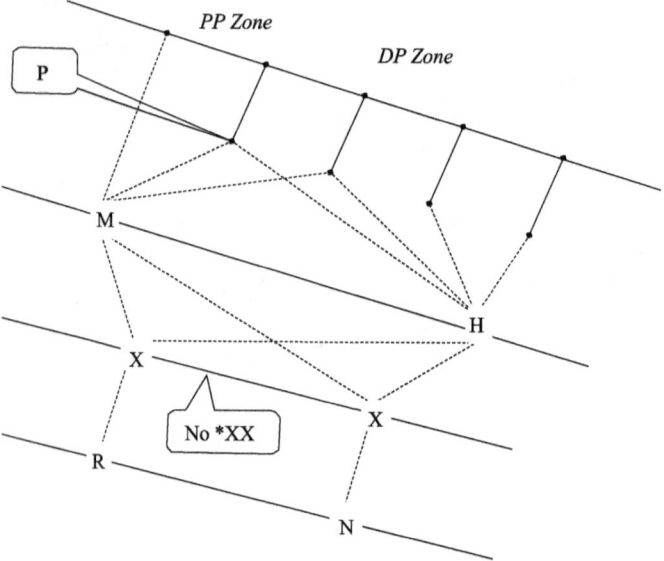

Figure 8: PP (object of Adposition).

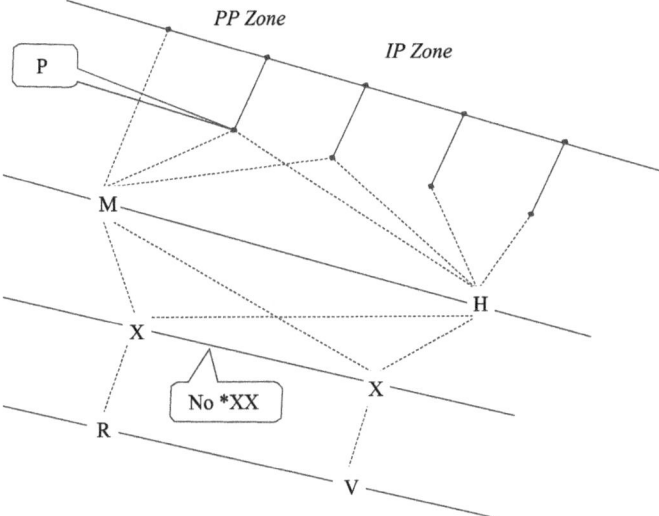

Figure 9: CP (adpositional shell containing IP).

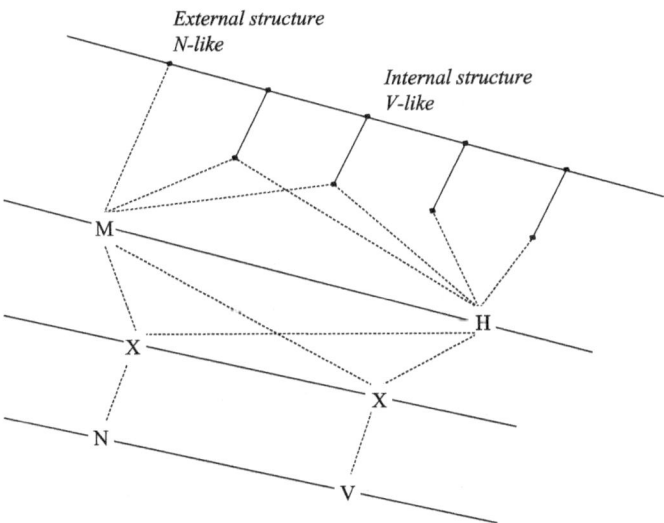

Figure 10: The structure of PP as a model for hybrid categories.

It is a well-known fact that phonological structure is hierarchically organized, as is evident, for example, from the structure of the syllable which is generally taken to consist of an onset and a rhyme, where the rhyme in turn is made up of a nucleus and a coda. Nevertheless, phonological structure is often taken to be flat in the sense that phonological units are concatenated. In this sense, then, phonology would be fundamentally different from syntax in that it would lack recursion. Given the representational model I have presented a sketch of here, we must ask whether simple concatenation, as in phonology, would be sufficient. The answer has to be no: we need to incorporate the notion of merge into the system. How this is to be done is another difficult question. If we want to express the notion that a head combines with a phrase to create a new phrase, then merge needs to be incorporated. My preliminary idea is to interpret MERGE as a special connector between a head and a complete syntactic unit, as in Figure 11. This at least would be the core case. This is very impressionistic (as is most of the above) and ways of formalizing these notions have to be studied. A solution may be found along the lines of Vergnaud's clock-style concatenations (Vergnaud 2003). See also Liao (2011). Take a simple example (from Dutch).[21]

(15) 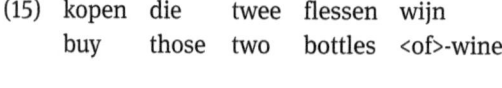 kopen   die   twee   flessen   wijn
     buy   those   two   bottles   <of>-wine

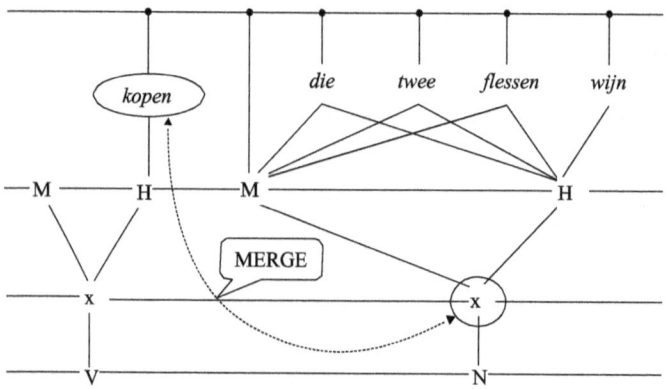

Figure 11: Representation of "kopen die twee flessen wijn", expanding again the ideas in Van Riemsdijk (1988).

MERGE can be seen as a concatenation operator on a par, say, with the one that concatenates syllables, where, depending on how much structure there is, the core relation can be taken to be the one between the nucleus of one syllable and the complete following syllable, schematically:

(16) [$_\sigma$ Onset [$_{Rhyme}$ Nucleus Coda] σ

---

[21] The example abstracts away from the fact that Dutch is SOV.

6 Conclusion

Much remains open. For example, if the representations I have proposed are on the right track, it is not clear that the notions of X-bar theory, bare phrase structure and tree structures are not an epiphenomenon. That is, it is possible that the 'merge tier' in Figure 5 above can be eliminated altogether. It is equally unclear whether there is any real sense (beyond habitude and convenience) in which these structures can or should be translatable into tree representations. I do, however, feel that the notions (lexical) head and maximal phrasal unit must be primitives in some way in order to properly express the magnetic forces at work in intra- and extra-phrasal structure. The rather informal, impressionistic considerations presented in the present contribution do not pretend to be more than an idea for a potential research program.

References

Anderson, John. & Ewen, Colin. 1987. *Principles of dependency phonology*. Cambridge: Cambridge University Press. https://doi.org/10.1017/CBO9780511753442

Chomsky, Noam. 1970. Remarks on Nominalization. In Roderick A. Jacobs & Peter S. Rosenbaum (eds.), *Readings in English Transformational Grammar*, 184–221. Waltham MA, Toronto, London: Ginn and Company.

Chomsky, Noam & Lasnik, Howard. 1977. Filters and control. Linguistic Inquiry 8. Reprinted in Norbert Corver & Henk C. van Riemsdijk, (eds.). 2001. *Semi-Lexical Categories. The Content of Function Words and the Function of Content Words*, 425–504. Berlin: Mouton de Gruyter. https://doi.org/10.1515/9783110874006

Dikken, Marcel den. 2006. Relators and Linkers: The syntax of predication, Predicate Inversion, and copulas. Cambridge, MA: MIT Press.

Emonds, Joseph. 1985. *A unified theory of syntactic categories*. Dordrecht: Foris. https://doi.org/10.1515/9783110808513

Grimshaw, Jane. 1991. "Extended projection". Ms., Brandeis University.

Grimshaw, Jane. 2005. Extended Projection. In Jane Grimshaw, *Words and Structure*, 1–69. Stanford: CSLI Publications.

Haider, Hubert. 1988. Matching Projections. In Anna Cardinaletti, Guglielmo Cinque & Giuliana Giusti (eds.), *Constituent Structure: Papers from the 1987 Glow Conference*, 101–121. Dordrecht: Foris Publications.

Harris, John. 1994. *English Sound Structure*. Cambridge, MA., Oxford: Blackwell.

Harris, John & Lindsey, Geoff. 1995. The elements of phonological representation. In Jacques Durand & Francis Katamba (eds.), *Frontiers in Phonology*, 34–79. London and New York: Longman.

Hjelmslev, Louis. 1943. *Omkring sprogteoriens grundlæggelse*. København: B. Lunos bogtrykkeri a/s.

Hjelmslev, Louis. 1953. *Prolegomena to a theory of language*. (Indiana University publications in anthropology and linguistics, memoir 7.) Baltimore: Waverly Press.
Hoekstra, Teun. 1984. *Transitivity*. Dordrecht: Foris.
Jackendoff, Ray. 1977. *X-bar syntax: a study of phrase structure*. Cambridge, MA: MIT Press.
Kaye, Jonathan, Lowenstamm, Jean & Vergnaud, Jean-Roger. 1985. The Internal Structure of Phonological Elements: A Theory of Charm and Government. *Phonology Yearbook* 2. 305–328. https://doi.org/10.1017/S0952675700000476
Kaye, Jonathan, Lowenstamm, Jean & Vergnaud, Jean-Roger. 1990. Constituent Structure and Government in Phonology. *Phonology* 7. 305–328. https://doi.org/10.1017/S0952675700001184
Keyser, Samuel Jay. 1968. Review of Sven Jacobson 'Adverbial Positions in English' (Stockholm: Studentbok AB, 1964). *Language* 44. 357–375. https://doi.org/10.2307/411633
Liao, Roger Wei-wen. 2011. *The symmetry of syntactic relations*. Ph.D. Dissertation, Department of Linguistics Los Angeles: USC, Los Angeles.
Longobardi, Giuseppe. 1980. Remarks on infinitives: a case for a filter. *Journal of Italian Linguistics* 5. 101–155.
Martinet, André. 1960. *Eléments de linguistique générale*. Paris: A. Colin.
McCarthy, John. 1986. OCP effects: gemination and anti-gemination. *Linguistic Inquiry* 17. 207–263.
Muysken, Pieter. 1983. Parametrizing the notion head. *The Journal of Linguistic Research* 2. 57–76.
Muysken, Pieter & Henk C. van, Riemsdijk 1986. *Features and projections*. (Studies in generative grammar, 25.) Dordrecht, Holland; Riverton, N.J.: Foris Publications. https://doi.org/10.1515/9783110871661
Pike, Kenneth Lee. 1967. *Language in relation to a unified theory of the structure of human behavior*. (Janua linguarum Series maior, 24.) The Hague: Mouton. https://doi.org/10.1515/9783111657158
Richards, Norvin. 2010. *Uttering Trees*. Cambridge, MA: MIT Press. https://doi.org/10.7551/mitpress/9780262013765.001.0001
Riemsdijk, Henk C. van. 1978. *A case study in syntactic markedness: the binding nature of prepositional phrases*. Lisse: The Peter de Ridder Press, later published by Foris Publications Dordrecht and currently by Mouton de Gruyter, Berlin.
Riemsdijk, Henk C. van. 1982. Locality principles in syntax and phonology. In The Linguistic Society of Korea (ed.), *Linguistics in the Morning Calm*, 693–708. Seoul: Hanshin.
Riemsdijk, Henk C. van. 1984. On pied-piped infinitives in German relative clauses. In Jindrich Toman (ed.), *Studies in German Grammar*, 165–192. Dordrecht: Foris.
Riemsdijk, Henk C. van. 1988. The representation of syntactic categories. *Proceedings of the Conference on the Basque language, 2nd Basque World Congress*, 104–116. Vitoria-Gasteiz: Central Publication Service of the Basque Government.
Riemsdijk, Henk C. van. 1990. Functional prepositions. In Harm Pinkster & Inge Genée (eds.), *Unity in Diversity: papers presented to Simon C. Dik on his 50th birthday*, 229–241. Dordrecht: Foris Publications. https://doi.org/10.1515/9783110847420.229
Riemsdijk, Henk C. van. 1997. Push chains and drag chains: complex predicate split in Dutch. In Shigeo Tonoike (ed.), *Scrambling*, 7–33. Tokyo: Kurosio Publishers.
Riemsdijk, Henk C. van. 1998. Categorial feature magnetism: The endocentricity and distribution of projections. *The journal of comparative Germanic linguistics* 2. 1–48. https://doi.org/10.1023/A:1009763305416

Riemsdijk, Henk C. van. 2001. A far from simple matter. Syntactic reflexes of syntax-pragmatics misalignments. In István Kenesei & Robert M. Harnish (eds.), *Perspectives on semantics, pragmatics, and discourse*, 21–41. Amsterdam: John Benjamins. https://doi.org/10.1075/pbns.90.06rie

Riemsdijk, Henk C. van. 2006. Grafts follow from Merge. In Mara Frascarelli (ed.), *Phases of Interpretation*, 17–44. Berlin: Mouton de Gruyter. https://doi.org/10.1515/9783110197723.2.17

Riemsdijk, Henk C. van. 2008. Identity Avoidance: OCP-effects in Swiss Relatives. In Robert Freidin, Carlos P. Otero & Maria Luisa Zubizarreta (eds.), *Foundational Issues in Linguistic Theory. Essays in Honor of Jean-Roger Vergnaud*, 227–250. Cambridge, MA: MIT Press. https://doi.org/10.7551/mitpress/9780262062787.003.0010

Ross, John Robert. 1972a. The category squish: Endstation Hauptwort. In Paul M. Peranteau, Judith N. Levi & Gloria C. Phares (eds.), *Proceedings of the Eighth Regional Meeting of the Chicago Linguistic Society*, 316–338. Chicago: The University of Chicago.

Ross, John Robert. 1972b. Double-ing. *Linguistic Inquiry* 3. 61–86.

Ross, John Robert. 1973. Nouniness. In Osamu Fujimura (ed.), *Three Dimensions of Linguistic Research*. Tokyo: TEC Company Ltd.

Samuels, Bridget. 2009. *The structure of phonological theory*. Ph.D. Dissertation. Department of Linguistics, Harvard University.

Schane, Sanford A. 1984. The fundamentals of particle phonology. *Phonology* 1. 129–155. https://doi.org/10.1017/S0952675700000324

Vergnaud, Jean-Roger. 1976. Formal properties of phonological rules. In Robert E. Butts & Jaakko Hintikka (eds.), *Basic Problems in Methodology and Linguistics*, 299–318. Dordrecht: Reidel.

Vergnaud, Jean-Roger. 1980. A formal theory of vowel harmony. In Robert Vago (ed.), *Vowel Harmony*, 49–62. Amsterdam: John Benjamins. https://doi.org/10.1075/slcs.6.03ver

Vergnaud, Jean-Roger. 2003. On a certain notion of "occurrence": the source of metrical structure, and of much more. In Stefan Ploch (ed.), *Living on the Edge. 28 Papers in Honour of Jonathan Kaye*, 599–632. Berlin: Mouton de Gruyter. https://doi.org/10.1515/9783110890563.599

Vergnaud, Jean-Roger. 2008. Letter to Noam Chomsky and Howard Lasnik on "Filters and Control", April 17 1977. In Robert Freidin, Carlos P. Otero & Maria Luisa Zubizarreta (eds.), *Foundational Issues in Linguistic Theory: Essays in Honor of Jean-Roger Vergnaud*, 3–15. Cambridge, MA: MIT Press. https://doi.org/10.7551/mitpress/9780262062787.003.0002

Winslow, Charles Frederick. 1869. *Force and Nature. Attraction and Repulsion: The Radical Principles of Energy, Discussed in their Relations to Physical and Morphological Developments*. Philadelphia: J.B. Lippincott & Co (Facsimile edition by the University of Michigan Library)

Yip, Moira. 1998. Identity avoidance in phonology and morphology. In Stephen G. Lapointe, Diane K. Brentari & Patrick M. Farrell (eds.), *Morphology and its relation to phonology and syntax*, 216–246. Stanford, CA: CSLI.

General Index

A *as structure* 160, 167, 168, 171
Adjunction 132, 216
Affricates 17, 27, 78, 79, 120, 188
Agreement 21, 186
Aperiodic noise 16, 25, 26, 27
Aspiration 12, 26, 27, 87, 93, 95, 99
Asymmetry 9, 18, 24, 94, 123, 139, 171
ATR 112, 126, 127, 131, 141, 142, 143, 144, 146, 148, 149, 150
Attraction 253, 257, 259, 260, 253, 257, 259, 260
Autonomous interpretation 17

Baseline resonance 18
Bipartite structure 160, 168, 177, 178, 179
Branching trees 35, 36, 40, 52

Casali's Correlation 142, 143, 148, 150
Categorial Identity Thesis (CIT) 258, 259, 260, 261, 263, 258, 259, 260, 261, 263
Class nodes 141
Coalescence 209, 214, 215, 227, 229, 241, 242, 243
Cold vowel 136, 140
Contrastive hierarchy 37, 41, 44, 45, 46, 48, 53, 69
Contrastive Hierarchy Theory (CHT) 33, 34, 36, 37, 38, 41, 42, 46, 47, 49, 53, 56, 57, 58, 112
Contrastivist Hypothesis 37, 41, 50, 51
Co-occurrence restriction 56, 193

Dependency 112, 117, 118, 119, 120, 123, 127, 128, 132, 136, 139, 140, 191, 202
Dependency Phonology 10, 66, 115, 116, 119, 127, 137, 139, 140, 264, 264
Diphthongs 159, 166, 167, 168, 169, 170, 172, 173, 174, 175, 197, 207, 208, 209, 210, 214, 215, 216, 218, 219, 224, 226, 227, 228, 229, 230, 231, 232, 233, 234, 235, 241, 243, 244
– diphthongization 11, 209, 235, 243
– formation 209, 214, 216, 218, 228, 229, 233, 234, 235, 237, 240, 243

Element sharing 198, 199, 203, 209
Element Theory (ET) 9, 10, 15, 25, 26, 33, 34, 41, 43, 46, 47, 49, 51, 56, 57, 58, 65, 66, 95, 103, 104, 111, 138, 185, 195, 207, 209, 210, 212, 216, 244
Embedding 19, 20, 24
Emergent consonant 186, 188, 190, 199
Empty
– categories 218
– nucleus 12, 13, 17, 18, 23, 24, 48, 49, 51, 70, 122, 171, 174, 192, 202, 210, 220, 221, 222
– onset 164, 165, 197, 209, 219, 222, 229, 231, 237, 239, 240, 241, 242
– position 13, 21, 168, 171, 174, 207, 209, 210, 218, 219, 220, 222, 233, 240
– structure 12, 160, 202
Empty Category Principle (ECP) 164, 174, 220, 221, 222, 232, 233, 240, 241, 242, 243
Endocentricity 258, 259, 258, 259
Enhancement 36, 38, 39, 54, 74, 75, 85, 86, 87, 89, 93, 94, 99, 102, 114, 150, 185
Epenthesis 185, 203, 209, 218, 220, 227, 229, 240, 257
Epenthetic
– consonant 24, 185, 186, 192
– vowel 214, 221

Feature Economy 40
Feature Geometry 68, 71, 83, 92, 116
Features
– binary features 33, 34, 40, 42, 52, 53, 56, 57, 65, 66, 67, 73, 75, 89, 90, 94, 124, 127, 131, 256, 260, 261, 263, 256, 260, 261, 263
– distinctive features 9, 10, 51, 66, 68, 71, 101, 102, 104, 124, 131
– emergent features 33
– innate features 33, 39, 41, 101, 102, 113
– privative features 36, 42, 50, 56, 65, 66, 67, 68, 69, 70, 71, 73, 75, 76, 89, 91, 93, 94, 103, 104, 256, 260, 264, 256, 260, 264
F-Features (Functionality Features) 262, 263, 262, 263

General Index

Geometry 116, 162, 244
Gliding 186, 227, 228, 229, 234, 235, 237, 239, 240, 241
Government 192, 207, 209, 210, 218, 219, 220, 221, 230, 232, 233, 236, 237, 238, 242, 244, 264
Government Phonology 2.0 (GP2.0) 12, 17, 43, 46, 112, 113, 116, 117, 119, 129, 137, 138, 139, 140, 141, 143, 157, 158, 159, 160, 162, 164, 167, 171, 195, 209, 210, 216, 217, 218, 219, 220, 229, 236, 238, 256, 264

Head-dependency 9, 20, 21, 23, 117, 119, 122, 139
Head-dependent 15, 18, 23, 24, 118
Hiatus 159, 163, 164, 165, 174, 186, 197, 198, 207, 208, 209, 218, 219, 226, 227, 228, 229, 231, 232, 233, 235, 236, 237, 239, 240, 241, 242
Hierarchical Structure 9, 14, 17, 20, 21, 22, 25, 28, 216, 218
Hoekstra, Teun 254, 255, 254, 255

Interface 14, 74, 80, 84, 85, 99, 100, 115

Jakobson, Roman O. 33, 34, 35

Kayne, Richard S. 254, 254

Laryngeal 65, 66, 75, 78, 79, 80, 82, 84, 85, 88, 89, 90, 91, 92, 95, 96, 98, 99, 117, 122, 123, 129, 131, 132, 141
– Elements 16, 24, 25, 96, 117, 123, 124, 126, 127, 202, 203
– features 56, 57, 78, 87, 89, 90, 94, 119
– Realism 66, 78, 79, 80, 92, 100
– Relativism 97, 98, 99, 100
Length 158, 159, 162, 214
– lexical length 158, 159, 162, 163, 164, 165, 175, 178
– phonological length 158, 161, 162, 163, 164, 165
Lexical Representation 21, 103, 114, 185, 191, 197
L-Features (Lexical Features) 264, 264
Longobardi, Giuseppe 253, 253

Mackenzie, Sara 56, 57
Manner 117, 119, 120, 122, 123, 124, 126, 127, 129, 131, 133, 134, 135, 136, 137, 140, 141, 143, 144, 147, 148, 149, 150, 151, 152
Markedness 33, 37, 42, 43, 44, 46, 67, 94, 101, 209, 212, 244
– marked 13, 16, 17, 18, 37, 39, 42, 43, 44, 49, 50, 67, 73, 75, 80, 82, 84, 95, 96, 98, 99, 104, 123, 124, 195, 208
– unmarked 13, 17, 37, 42, 44, 45, 48, 49, 50, 51, 66, 67, 70, 71, 73, 75, 84, 85, 91, 95, 96, 134, 139, 195
Martinet, André 252, 257, 252, 257
Melodic Function of Elements 19, 22, 24
Melody-prosody integration 12, 13
Minimal Contrast Principle/Sisterhood Merger Hypothesis 38, 48
Modified Contrastive Specification (MCS) 36, 65, 68, 69, 71, 73, 101, 102
Modularity 65, 73, 103, 104, 115
Monophthongs 11, 69, 159, 168, 170, 171, 176
Muysken, Pieter 262, 263, 264, 266, 262, 263, 264, 266

Nasal-Consonant Sequences (NC) 186, 188, 196, 203
Neutralization 38, 43, 44, 45, 52, 86, 96, 114, 134
No Value Reversal Condition (NVR) 262, 263, 262, 263
Nuclear Head 19, 21, 22, 160, 161, 163, 164, 165, 166, 168, 169, 170, 171, 172, 174, 177

Obligatory Contour Principle (OCP) 251, 257, 258, 264, 251, 257, 258, 264
Overlapping Concatenation 185, 197, 198, 203

Palatalization 49, 50, 185, 196, 197, 199
Palatalized 52, 203, 235
Parameter 18, 212, 220, 244
Particle Phonology (PP) 10, 66, 264, 264
Phonetic
– determinism 33, 58, 90, 95
– interpretation 43, 45, 29, 80, 97, 98, 124, 125, 126, 129, 143, 144, 175, 220, 240
– realization 44, 51, 191

General Index — 277

Phonological Acquisition 34, 35, 39, 113, 137
– Child language 35
Phonological Activity 36, 38, 39, 42, 51, 53, 58, 66, 67, 68, 73, 74, 76, 78, 94, 99
Place 16, 17, 26, 86, 95, 117, 119, 122, 123, 126, 127, 129, 131, 132, 133, 134, 136, 137, 147, 151, 160, 187, 190, 193, 195, 197, 199, 200, 202, 203
Precedence (Linear order) 27, 28, 116, 128
Precedence-free Phonology (PfP) 9, 10, 12, 13, 14, 15, 17, 18, 19, 20, 21, 22, 23, 24, 25, 26, 27, 28, 29, 159
Prefixation 195
Primes
– phonological 33, 34, 36, 41, 42, 57, 58, 124, 125
– Unary 40, 46, 47, 48, 57, 114, 118, 124, 125, 210
Projection 23, 160, 161, 166, 168, 169, 170, 171, 173, 178, 179, 211, 222, 236, 238, 254, 255, 258, 259, 260, 261, 262, 263, 265, 266, 254, 255, 258, 259, 260, 261, 262, 263, 265, 266
Prominence 9, 20, 25, 133, 211
Prosodic Constituent 13, 14, 28
Prosodic Function of Elements 14, 17, 19, 22, 23, 24, 28
Push Chain/Drag Chain 252, 257, 252, 257

Radical CV Phonology (RCVP) 47, 111, 112, 115, 116, 117, 119, 121, 122, 123, 124, 125, 126, 127, 128, 131, 137, 138, 139, 140, 141, 149, 151, 159
Ranking 69, 72, 73, 93, 133, 134, 136, 137
Recursion 29, 128, 270, 270
Repulsion 253, 257, 258, 260, 253, 257, 258, 260
Resonance Elements 14, 16, 17, 18, 24, 26, 28
RTR 44, 45, 112, 141, 142, 143, 144, 148, 149, 150, 151

Segmental structure 12, 111, 112, 118, 120, 122, 131, 137, 140, 141
Semi-Lexical 260, 261, 262, 263, 265, 260, 261, 262, 263, 265

Specification 36, 39, 54, 56, 57, 66, 67, 68, 71, 73, 74, 78, 80, 87, 88, 90, 92, 96, 101, 112, 114, 117, 121, 123, 124, 131, 132, 133, 134
– minimal specification 114
– overspecification 94, 95, 98, 102
– overspecified 66, 69, 75, 86, 93, 94, 95, 99
– specified 38, 56, 93, 94, 95, 96, 123, 134, 135, 192
– underspecification 95, 114
– underspecified 12, 67, 69, 71, 74, 75, 86, 94, 98, 99, 101, 102, 114, 122, 187, 191
– unspecified 17, 18, 47, 56, 57, 66, 67, 68, 73, 75, 78, 82, 88, 91, 96, 97, 98, 124, 135, 136, 140
Stress 143, 151, 160, 161, 175, 176, 177, 180, 208, 236
– main 23, 175
– pre-stress 44, 45, 175
– primary/secondary 177, 179
– stressed 43, 44, 157, 161, 170, 172, 173, 176, 178, 179, 180
– stressed/unstressed dichotomy 176
– unstressed 43, 44, 45, 53, 134, 172, 173, 175, 176, 180
Strict CV Phonology 14, 21, 26, 192, 207, 210, 218, 220, 222, 231, 244
Structural Analogy Assumption (SAA) 115, 127, 128
Subjunction 132
Substance
– substance Impoverished Phonology 65, 100
– substance-based phonology 42, 113, 114, 124
– substance-free phonology 33, 34, 42, 46, 58, 114, 124
Successive Division Algorithm (SDA) 69, 70, 101, 102, 133, 134, 136
Successive Division Algorithm (SDA) 33, 36, 47, 50, 51
Superordinate 71
– category 71, 72, 73, 74, 75, 82, 85, 86, 104
– marking 65, 66, 73, 75, 80, 84, 89, 91, 92, 98, 104

Syllable structure 21, 111, 115, 116, 119, 124, 128, 129, 132, 209, 218, 220

Tense(ness)/ Lax(ness) 157, 159, 160, 163, 167, 169, 170, 174
− L-type 159, 163, 164, 165, 166, 169, 174, 179
− T-type 163, 165, 166, 169, 170, 171, 172, 174, 178, 179
The Opponent Principle 113, 120, 121
Tier 80, 81, 82, 83, 212, 213, 217, 218, 232, 256, 257, 264, 266, 256, 257, 264, 266
− Categorial- 264, 265, 264, 265
− Level- 264, 265, 264, 265
− Merge 265, 271
− Merge- 271
Tone 15, 39, 104, 117, 123, 124, 125, 126, 132, 141, 160, 208, 231, 236
Trubetzkoy, Nicolai S. 35, 44, 45, 51, 52, 53, 103, 163

Umlaut
− i-umlaut 53, 54
− Korean 237

Unlike Category Constraint (UCC) 254, 255, 256, 254, 255, 256
Unlike Feature Constraint (UFC) 256, 257, 258, 259, 260, 261, 263, 264, 256, 257, 258, 259, 260, 261, 263, 264

Velarity 185, 191, 203
Vergnaud, Jean-Roger 42, 252, 257, 252, 257
Voice assimilation 78, 79, 82, 88, 89, 90, 91
Voicelessness 78
Vowel
− harmony 112, 142, 144, 149, 150, 151, 195, 211, 212
− openness 20, 158, 167, 169, 171, 177, 179, 180
− quality 18, 157, 160, 175, 177
− reduction 43, 44, 46, 180, 216
− Strong/Weak 49, 176, 177, 178, 179, 180
− system 34, 35, 42, 47, 48, 51, 52, 53, 54, 58, 186, 68, 70, 71, 72, 73, 102, 134, 135, 137, 143, 144, 148, 151, 157, 179

X-Bar 117, 119, 159, 160, 258, 271, 258, 271

Language Index

Adyghe 122
Algonquian 38
Arawakan 47
– Amuesha 47, 51
– Wapishana 47, 48
Archi 52
Austrian German 165

Bantu
– Bantu Languages 142, 185, 186, 187, 189, 191, 192, 196, 203
– Proto Bantu 189
Bemba 186, 187, 188, 189, 192, 196, 197, 199, 202, 209, 242, 243
Berber 47
– Tamazight 47, 51
Brazilian Portuguese 35, 43, 44, 180
Bulgarian 53

Caucasian 52, 122
Chadic 56, 57
– Hausa 57
– Ngizim 56

Dutch 35, 255, 270, 255, 270

Eastern Catalan 180
English 12, 18, 24, 25, 26, 47, 48, 80, 84, 85, 86, 87, 89, 114, 134, 157, 158, 163, 166, 167, 168, 169, 170, 171, 172, 173, 175, 180, 215, 216, 223, 231, 235, 253, 259, 266, 253, 259, 266
– American 80, 94
– British 168, 175, 177
– Early Modern 11
– New York 170, 244
– Old 34, 56
Estonian 158, 162, 163, 164, 166

Finnish 133, 168
French 24, 209, 220, 223
– Quebec French 169, 171, 215

Gaam 144
German 168, 215, 223, 231, 260, 260
Germanic 12, 26
– early 53
– Proto 54
– West 34, 54, 56, 58

Inuit-Yupik 48, 50, 58
– Barrow Inupiaq 49
– North Baffin 49
– Proto-Eskimo 48, 49

Japanese 18, 52, 87, 208, 209, 210, 212, 221, 222, 227, 229, 232, 234, 235, 241
– Owari 207, 214, 223, 228, 231, 242
– Sino 223, 226
– Tokyo 207, 208, 212, 213, 214, 215, 223, 241, 242

Kabardian 122, 134
Kikuyu 146
Kru languages 142
Kwanyama 188, 189, 192

Latin 51, 52, 53
Lugbara 148
Lungu 186, 187, 190, 196

Mongolic languages 142, 146, 150

Ndali 188
Nez Perce 144, 148, 149

Polish 51, 65, 66, 75, 76, 78, 80, 82, 83, 84, 85, 86, 87, 88, 89, 90, 94, 95, 100, 220, 221
– Cracow 51, 78, 79, 83, 88, 89, 96, 97, 98, 99, 100
– Warsaw 51, 78, 83, 88, 89, 95, 96, 97, 98, 99, 100

Rennellese 24
Romance 46

Scandinavian 47
Swahili 188, 189, 199
Swedish 12, 93, 94, 99

Tungusic languages 142, 150
Turkish 235

Wiyot 24

Yurok 24, 147

www.ingramcontent.com/pod-product-compliance
Lightning Source LLC
Chambersburg PA
CBHW031423150426
43191CB00006B/376